BERNARD-LAZARE

Bernard-Lazare
(Photo. Gerschel; reproduction, Roger-Viollet)
Frontispiece

BERNARD-LAZARE

Antisemitism and the problem of Jewish identity
in late nineteenth-century France

NELLY WILSON

Lecturer in French, University of Bristol

CAMBRIDGE UNIVERSITY PRESS

Cambridge

London · New York · Melbourne

Published by the Syndics of the Cambridge University Press
The Pitt Building, Trumpington Street, Cambridge CB2 1RP
Bentley House, 200 Euston Road, London NW1 2DB
32 East 57th Street, New York, NY 10022, USA
296 Beaconsfield Parade, Middle Park, Melbourne 3206, Australia

© Cambridge University Press 1978

First published 1978

Printed in Great Britain by
Western Printing Services Ltd, Bristol

Library of Congress Cataloguing in Publication Data
Wilson, Nelly.
Bernard-Lazare: antisemitism and the problem of
Jewish identity in late nineteenth-century France.

Bibliography: p.
Includes index.
1. Lazare, Bernard, 1865–1903. 2. Jews in France –
Biography. 3. Journalists – France – Biography.
4. Antisemitism – France. 5. Dreyfus, Alfred, 1859–1935.
6. France – Biography.
DS135.F9L398   301.45′19′24044 [B]   77–82524

ISBN 0 521 21802 0

CONTENTS

PREFACE

When Charles Andler, the historian, learnt of Bernard-Lazare's death in 1903, he wrote to a friend:

> Je crois que nous avons un devoir envers Lazare. Je crois que nous devons écrire sa biographie. Nous devons présenter son œuvre entière, politique, philosophique, sociologique, journalistique...Lazare est sûrement une victime de l'Affaire. Et il est maintenant la principale. Picquart lui-même n'a compromis que sa situation. Scheurer et Zola n'avaient pas une jeunesse et un avenir à donner. Il y a là quelque chose de simple et de grand...Nous devons le dire très haut...

Regrettably the life was never written. Nor was 'the history of a conscience' which Péguy began in 1903 and never completed. He has left us, however, a magnificent portrait of his friend in *Notre Jeunesse* (1910). Since reading it, many years ago, I have tried to discover more about Bernard-Lazare's life and work, at first for my own satisfaction and later with a view to making good an unmerited oblivion. The more I came to know him the more I agreed with Andler and Péguy that the history of such an exemplary figure must not go unrecorded; not only because he devoted his life to defending the freedom of others, though this entitles him to be remembered; but because he understood so well why and what liberties needed to be defended in the era which began with the French Revolution and ended with the Armenian massacres and the Dreyfus Affair – liberties which still need to be defended in our own age.

A later biographer can never equal the personal account which close friends might have given. My task was all the more difficult because Bernard-Lazare wrote little about himself, and many of the personal records such as correspondence have been lost.

Those of his personal papers and unpublished works which are deposited at the Alliance Israelite Universelle have been an invaluable source. In addition, and with the generous help of many people, I have been able to trace letters and diverse records which have also been most useful. I have learnt much from twenty or so obituaries, and even more from the police dossiers (though of course police informers are not the most reliable witnesses) and the Dreyfus Affair records at the Archives Nationales in Paris. As for Bernard-Lazare's published books, the literary and historical works are available in several National Libraries. I have managed to collect together over 300 of his widely scattered articles and studies in French as well as foreign periodicals and newspapers and some of them will be discussed in the following pages.

A detailed (though by no means exhaustive) bibliography of his works and works on him will be found at the end of the book.

My research has taken me to several countries and numerous libraries and archives, both public and private. I met with kindness and encouragement everywhere, and I would like to record my thanks to some of the many people and institutions which have helped me:

> The director and staff of the Bibliothèque de l'Alliance Israelite Universelle in Paris and of the Central Zionist Archives in Jerusalem.

> The director of the Archives du Gard, M. Sablou, and the librarian of the Bibliothèque Séguier at Nîmes and their staffs, who were most helpful. In Nîmes, I also interviewed several people and I would like to thank them for receiving me.

> Rudolf de Jong and the librarian at the International Institute of Social History, Amsterdam. M. Léon Danse, conservateur at the Bibliothèque Royale Albert Ier of Brussels and Mme Despy of the Université Libre de Bruxelles.

> M. Xavier Durand let me read his thesis on the *Entretiens Politiques et Littéraires* and drew my attention to Bernard-Lazare's letters to Jean Grave which I was able to consult, among other useful material, at the Institut Français

d'Histoire Sociale (Paris). Mr Michael Janes found some
interesting material for me at the Jewish National Library,
Hebrew University (Jerusalem) and the prompt service of
the University's Bibliographic section was greatly appreciated. Mme Fropo of the Institut Pédagogique National
(Paris) gave me much of her valuable time and sent me
some precious documents. The conservateur-en-chef of the
Préfecture de Police Archives (Paris) was most kind and
helpful.

I am grateful to the following libraries and their staff: the
British Museum, the Wiener Library, the London Library,
the Jewish National Library, the Bibliothèque Nationale,
the Archives Nationales, and the Centre Charles Péguy.
My fellow Péguyste Jacques Viard put me in touch with
Mme Ardouin, Emile Meyerson's great-niece, who received
me warmly and generously allowed me to consult Emile
Meyerson's papers.

My special thanks go to Rabi, for long interested in Bernard-
Lazare, who has not only been very hospitable but who has
allowed me to make use of his documentation, which was
particularly instructive in connection with the projected
Bernard-Lazare commemoration ceremony in 1933 of
which he had been one of the organisers.

I also wish to thank Rabi for lending me a copy of the
brochure from which the jacket illustration is reproduced.
After I had finished my work and when the typescript was
already completed M. Jacques Cherchevsky (whose father
was married to one of Bernard-Lazare's nieces) sent me an
unpublished study of his, devoted to Bernard-Lazare. I read
it with the greatest interest and I am grateful to him for the
opportunity it afforded me to fill certain gaps in my knowledge of Bernard-Lazare's personal life, notably his happy
marriage. However, since details of this intimate nature do
not affect the main issues discussed in this book, I have not
incorporated them into the body of the work but reference
is made to M. Cherchevsky's material in the notes where
relevant; I thank Madeleine Bernard for confirming certain
details concerning the fate of the Bernard family during the
last war.

I am grateful to the British Academy for a grant towards

my research expenses, and to the Sir Ernest Cassel Education Trust and to the University of Bristol for additional aid. Last but not least I must thank my long suffering husband without whose help and encouragement I might not have persevered.

Bristol, 1977   Nelly Wilson

PART I: BEFORE THE DREYFUS AFFAIR

I

ROOTS, MILIEU AND SYMBOLISM

The Nîmes Years

The whole drama of Bernard-Lazare's life consisted of a search
for his own roots, or a rebellion against them. There is a point in
saying as much as can reasonably be inferred from the scant
evidence available[1] about his origins, family background, upbringing and education – all those important formative influences
of what Taine called 'race, milieu et moment' against which the
young Bernard-Lazare rebelled, fashioning a philosophy and
style of life for himself which few people would have predicted.

He was born Lazare Marcus Manassé Bernard on 14th June
1865 in Nîmes, the eldest of four sons of Douce Noémi Rouget,
whose family came from Toulouse, and of Jonas Bernard, a small
but fairly prosperous *marchand-tailleur*, born and bred in Nîmes.
As the eldest son, he was named after his paternal grandfather
(Lazare) and great-grandfather (Marcus). In later adopting
Lazare as his family name (with the publication of his first literary
work in 1888) he may have gone back to still more ancient roots,
for Marcus's father, that is to say Bernard-Lazare's paternal
great-great-grandfather, was Abraham Lazare, Lazare being the
original family name.

Two vague claims are usually made about Bernard-Lazare's
ancestry. First, that on his mother's side he came 'd'une de ses
familles juives du midi, peut-être venues avant les Francs, même
avant les Romains. . .'[2] Second, that his father's family originated
in Alsace and emigrated to the South, like many other Jews, at
the time of Napoleon. One can only say of the first claim that an
ancestry stretching back to the Romans, the Franks or even the
Popes of Avignon (it was part of the family legend that one of his
mother's ancestors was an 'argentier du pape à Avignon') is
difficult to substantiate. In his initial reaction to antisemitism,

Bernard-Lazare was in the habit of making proud affirmations about his roots: 'people forget that we have lived in France for two thousand years'. In a general historical sense this is undoubtedly true, particularly in the case of Languedoc Jewry, whose earliest settlements in this very ancient part of France are said to go back to Graeco-Roman times. Without taking it too literally, it can reasonably be assumed that Douce Noémi Rouget was indeed of 'vieille souche méridionale'.

As for his father's family, at least as far as the main Bernard line goes, the assumption of Alsatian origin appears to be erroneous, according to the Archives in Nîmes. On the other hand, the family's connection with that city is of longer standing than has hitherto been assumed, going back at least to the eighteenth century, and making Bernard-Lazare a third or fourth generation Nîmois. For Jews of the mid-nineteenth century these were respectably ancient roots, even if the great-great-grand-parents, Abraham Lazare and his wife Bella Marcus, appear to have been of German origin. Their son Marcus, the first to take the family name Bernard, was a native of Creglingen in the province of Brandenburg. In 1793, at the age of 28, he came to Nîmes and there the recently arrived 'marchand-colporteur' married a young Nîmoise with the charming name of Sage Israel Suisse. To them was born, on 29 Germinal in the sixth year of 'La République Française une et indivisible', Lazare Bernard (Bernard-Lazare's grandfather), child of the Revolution, the first member of the family to be a free man and equal citizen from birth.

The French Revolution, as Bernard-Lazare often observed, did not greatly change, at least not immediately, the way of life and way of thought of Jewry. His grandfather (Lazare Bernard) became a small trader like his father before him, married into a Jewish family (Miriam Milhaud, also from Nîmes, was his second wife) similarly engaged in commerce, and went on living in the ancient ghetto district of Nîmes. There Jonas was born in 1837. Again, whatever secular education Bernard-Lazare's father may have received, his ultimate ambition did not go beyond carrying on the family business of buying and selling clothes. He continued to be an observing Jew within a generally practising and tightly knit Jewish community which looked after its synagogues and its businesses. True, Jonas Bernard moved his home and business away from the narrow back streets into a spacious

property at the corner of the rue Thoumayne and boulevard
Victor Hugo, one of the main boulevards of the city. He also
extended the business to an additional small shop at Sète. The
Bernards moved in wider and no longer specifically Jewish circles.
According to one account,[3] even the local aristocratic family, the
Bernis, were sometimes to be seen at the Bernards – as clients
presumably, rather than on social visits. A small but telling
example of increased intermingling can be seen in the witnesses
present at the civil registration of Bernard-Lazare's birth. Hitherto
the signatories at marriages and births had always been members
of the family or Jews, invariably described as 'négociants'; not
long before some of these traders had signed their names in
Yiddish and in Hebrew letters. In 1865 the signatories were a
teacher, Léon Boissier, and a watchmaker called Nicolas. Assimilation had undoubtedly made progress, but it did not reach
its height until the next generation, when it was accompanied,
inevitably perhaps, by a break in family tradition and a severing
of roots. Jonas's four sons all received a full-time lycée education;
three of them proceeded to higher education; all entered the
so-called liberal professions; Fernand became an Army officer,
eventually rose to the rank of colonel; Edmond became an art
publisher and Armand a doctor. Lazare aspired to be a writer.
All moved to Paris, as did many other young Jews of the area.

To walk today through the large, neglected, and deserted
Jewish cemetery of Nîmes is a lugubrious experience. The dates
on the tombstones and family vaults provide a sad record of
dispersion and uprooting of what was once a numerous and
flourishing community. And there are here and there the more
recent memorials to the remnants who died in Auschwitz or
Buchenwald. One is reminded of Bernard-Lazare's account of his
visits to the Jewish cemeteries in Eastern Europe at the beginning
of this century. The keepers always began their explanations with
the same words: in those days there was a persecution of the Jews.
By that time Bernard-Lazare had learnt a great deal about the
fragility of roots, even two thousand years old; but not even he
could have imagined the memorials of fifty years later in the
cemetery of his native Nîmes.

Nothing definite is known about Bernard-Lazare's primary
education. He probably went to an ordinary State primary school
where the teaching, if it ran true to pattern, would have been
secular, ardently patriotic and Republican, strongly civic, and

respectably middle-class in the social and moral values it proposed. Jewish children with a religious home background, possibly strengthened by some formal religious instruction, did not experience the same tensions as their Catholic contemporaries for whose minds Church and State, anti-Republican priest and anticlerical teacher, and not infrequently home and school, vied with each other. Jewry and the Synagogue, being ardently Republican, confirmed the teaching of the classroom. Generally speaking, the sort of religion practised in assimilated Jewish milieux did not conflict with the secular morality taught at school. It was not of sufficient spiritual fervour, intensity or depth to challenge the positive spirit of State education. This is the sort of religion Bernard-Lazare had probably known at home, a family ritual accompanied by festive meals, a twice or three-times yearly visit to the 'temple', occasions for remembering the past and the dead, organising charity for the living, and thanking God for the French Revolution. For the parent generation these were still powerful ties but not so for the young who quietly drifted into humanism, agnosticism or atheism, without this causing any anguish either to themselves or their parents, provided the young non-believers continued to participate in the ritual, as part of family life and tradition. As far as we know this is what Bernard-Lazare and his brothers did. They played their parts for the parents' sake. But in Bernard-Lazare's case this went hand in hand with a search for some other faith than the rationalised, self-satisfied, uninspiring and middle-class Judaism of his upbringing and republicanism of his education. Home and school, secular and religious education went well together and Bernard-Lazare was to rebel against both.

Paul Bourget once described the *lycée* education of those days as a system of training conceived against nature which turns the youth into an automaton or a rebel. The young Bernard-Lazare resolutely resisted being turned into an automaton. This was not too difficult, for he had an instinctively rebellious nature, an anarchist temperament.

> J'ai toujours eu l'horreur du maître, tout ce qui m'était ordonné m'était odieux...J'ai été durant de longues années de collège le modèle des indisciplinés, non le mauvais gars qui guette les tours à faire, mais le rebelle que ne veut pas obéir.[4]

At the same time, the rebel against authority and imposed discipline was capable of the greatest self-discipline and respected the authority of knowledge and true learning.

Positivist in spirit and formal in its teaching methods, the *lycée* was decidedly not designed to appeal to a highly individualist and intellectually precocious youth whom a boyhood friend described as an 'esprit réfléchi et pondéré', 'âme adolescente grave et contenue'[5] with a passion for philosophy and literature, a taste for the erudite and the esoteric, and a certain haughtiness and ironic disdain for the common. It was in Mallarmé's *salon* that the young Bernard-Lazare found the sort of leisurely education of the mind which remained his ideal and which he later wished to extend to all.

> Il a repris la tradition des philosophes et des sages de jadis, de ceux qui entretenaient leurs disciples dans les jardins ou sous les portiques, à l'orée des bois ou sur les bords des fleuves.
>
> Si M. Mallarmé avait vécu à Alexandrie ou à Antioche, il aurait publiquement enseigné, traînant après lui, par les voies de la ville, des élèves que sa parole eut inquiétés, charmés et retenus. De telles déambulations ne sont, hélas! plus de mode: la foule et la police même verraient d'un mauvais œil le passant qui, dans les Tuileries ou le Luxembourg, réunirait autour de lui des éphèbes enthousiastes. La vie publique ne sait plus faire place aux doux péripatéticiens, et l'enseignement que veulent donner les rares métaphysiciens ou moralistes qui subsistent encore doit être privé, mieux même: mystérieux.[6]

Nothing could have been further from this ideal than the examination-orientated instruction he received at the *lycée*. To make matters worse, this studious young man with a love of classical literature and an aristocratic disdain for the utilitarian was made to follow the practically orientated *enseignement secondaire spécial*.[7] First instituted in 1865 as a shorter and less academic alternative to the traditional *enseignement classique*, these studies were intended for future managers and businessmen: 'esprits impatients d'action, portés vers les choses positives, esprits rebelles aux raffinements de la culture classique'.[8] The distinguishing features of the course were the reduced place of classics, an emphasis on the sciences and mathematics, and the introduction of such practical subjects as accountancy and commercial law.[9] Did Jonas Bernard think that such an education was sound preparation for his eldest son, who would be expected to carry on the family business? It seems likely and it was a grave miscalculation. Fortunately for the son, who had altogether different aspirations and who largely educated himself, the worst feature of the non-academic, shortened studies was remedied by the fact that schools were invited to provide classical studies for the abler pupils wishing ultimately to take the traditional bac-calauréat-ès-sciences. This is what Bernard-Lazare seems to have done, for in 1882 he passed his baccalauréat-ès-sciences with the 'mention *passable*'.[10] He immediately turned to literature, for he wanted to become a writer.

Bernard-Lazare's subsequent severe criticism of the educational system was obviously influenced by unhappy personal experiences, by a tendency to beat an ugly present with the stick of an idealised past. He loved contrasting the ancient 'mystagogues' and 'hiérophantes' who *educated* in idyllic surroundings with the modern 'pédants', 'sorbonnagres', 'barbacoles', 'manuels', who *instructed* in dreary classrooms. These exaggerations do not detract from the pertinence and relevance of his main objections. He deplored the centralised system which cast everyone in the same mould. The teachers were paid by the State to prepare the young for State examinations and in the process fashioned the minds of the young until no originality was left. The taught, ambitious 'fils à papa soucieux de ne point s'écarter de la voie des honneurs et privilèges conférés par l'Etat',[11] *repeated* what was written in the 'manuels'. The 'manuels' and what he called the 'tranche' method, thanks to which great men and great works were cut into neatly labelled slices, were ideally suited to the superficially wide but shallow education which for Bernard-Lazare was the hallmark of bourgeois culture: rapidly acquired, with an impressive surface brilliance but no depth.

More significant for our understanding of Bernard-Lazare's later development are his objections to the philosophy behind the method and the system. He once observed of the *Normaliens*, the intellectual *élite* trained at the high-powered *Ecole Normale Supérieure*, that they were conservatives and traditionalists who never departed from what they had learned at school. One could say of him that he never ceased to rebel against what he had been taught at school. He began by reacting against the simplistic,

positivist rationalism[12] which explained, classified, solved and
settled everything. It had all the disadvantages of religious dogma
without any of its poetry and mystery. Revolt against this spirit
led him to take flight in symbolism and to flirt with all sorts of
mysticisms. Though the rationalist educators were ultimately
instrumental in checking these early flights, they were given little
credit for it. By then, Bernard-Lazare was deeply committed to
anarchism; he looked back through Proudhon's eyes at his lessons
on the French Revolution, or lessons in civic duties which extolled
respect for property, law and the magistrature, and defined the
reciprocal duties between masters and servants. This retrospective
assessment of the social and moral content of his teaching led to
some angry outbursts.

'Vos premiers ennemis ce sont les éducateurs bourgeois', he
told an audience of young left-wing intellectuals:

> ils déforment vos cervelles, ils vous inculquent des principes
> qui paralysent votre volonté, qui dénaturent votre énergie.
> Notre premier devoir à nous autres révolutionnaires est donc
> de combattre ces éducateurs et de nous substituer à eux.[13]

The paralysing principle uppermost in his mind was the historical determinism by which the right to rule of the bourgeoisie was
proved and its moral values justified. Equally paralysing was the
determinism behind Taine's 'race, milieu and moment', which
denied the individual the freedom to rise above his own nature
and nurture by individual effort, will-power, or the cultivation of
inner energies. The idea that the individual could not step outside
or rise above his milieu was totally unacceptable to the young
Bernard-Lazare. He found in Carlyle's conception of the hero
arms to be used against Taine. 'Ce jeune homme goûtait avec
une ivresse silencieuse cette philosophie de Carlyle formulée dans
le *Sartor Resartus*', a friend recalls.[14] Carlyle's fierce anti-positivism, his mixture of mordant irony and high seriousness appealed
to Bernard-Lazare, and made him a favourite author in his
youth. Carlyle's friend and correspondent Emerson, was another
maître to be opposed to Taine's fatalism which takes no account
of 'l'individu et sa réaction constante sur son milieu et sur son
temps'.[15]

Much in Bernard-Lazare's life could be seen as such a reaction
to his milieu and times. One can speculate whether he was
developing the innate qualities which made him different, or

whether it was in some measure a deliberate attempt to emancipate himself, to assert his individuality. The fact remains that he played roles and chose a style of life for which little in his environment and upbringing had prepared him. He did not become a trader in clothes or engage in commerce of any sort; neither did he proceed to formal higher education (for which he was qualified). He did not choose a safe career with good economic prospects and a pension at the end of it. Immediately upon completing his baccalauréat-ès-sciences he turned to literature and the arts. Later, in Paris, he did continue to educate himself, but as he understood the process and in disciplines of his own choice. It is difficult to imagine studies less vocationally orientated than the courses in Christian, Indian, Semitic and Far Eastern Religions for which he enrolled at the *Ecole Pratique de Hautes Etudes* (part of the Sorbonne specialising in religious studies) upon his arrival in the capital. He came from a comfortable, well-to-do, middle-class home, yet as anarchist he was to be for ever fulminating against the comfort and the wealth of the middle classes. As a Jew, too, he was an odd man out: antisemitic first and Zionist later; first chiding French Jewry for not being sufficiently assimilated to forget the ossified religion of their ancestors, and bitterly reproaching them later for being merely synagogue Jews, for not being sufficiently assimilated to insist on every man's right to choose his cultural *patrie*. Bernard-Lazare once remarked of his differences with some anarchist friends: 'Je ne suis orthodoxe en rien.' It could serve as his motto, and it began at school where he had been 'le modèle des indisciplinés'.

Although he had some harsh things to say later about the dreariness and deadliness of provincial life which kills individuality,[16] the four years or so that he spent in Nîmes after completing his secondary education do not seem to have been altogether unpleasant. He read a great deal, began writing, and was in his element, one imagines, in the activities of the recently created *Société Littéraire et Artistique de Nîmes*. The society had been founded in June 1881 and rapidly became an active cultural *foyer*, organising public lectures, musical and literary *soirées*, competitions and a library. There were also more intimate gatherings at which members read and played their own works. Almost the whole of Bernard-Lazare's family seems to have been active in the Society in one way or another, probably enrolled by him. He and his friends took an active part in the administration of the Society's review, *Le Bulletin de la Société Littéraire et Artistique de Nîmes* the first issue of which appeared in June 1882. Its aim was to reach all those 'qui se plaisent à l'étude de la littérature et des arts et au développement de l'intelligence'. In 1883 Phoebus Jouve became one of the vice-presidents, Georges Milhaud and Leopold Cabanis 'sécrétaires-archivistes' and Bernard-Lazare, then eighteen years old, 'sécrétaire-correspondant'. It was his first experience with reviews.

Of his youthful writings, which included at least two novels and a critical piece on Zola (the writer who personified everything he most detested), only echoes remain in the delightful correspondence by Bernard-Lazare's cousin, Ephraïm Mikhaël (Georges Michel), himself an aspiring poet of great talent. The gentle Mikhaël was a severe critic who believed, like Bernard-Lazare, in absolute sincerity, a virtue to which we probably owe the disappearance of at least one of Bernard-Lazare's novels. After bluntly demolishing it, Mikhaël added: 'entre nous, nous n'avons pas à nous écrire des phrases. Je te dis ce que je pense.'[17] Sincerity was a moral imperative to these young men who bruised each other's sensibilities rather than tell an artistic lie. Mikhaël's other mission was to keep his provincial cousin informed of what was happening in the literary world of Paris where young writers were fighting their battles against the 'monstres sacrés'. They had their own 'maîtres sacrés': Mallarmé, whose *l'Après-Midi d'un Faune* the provincial cousin was advised to buy in the *plaquette* with Manet's illustrations, and Villiers de l'Isle Adam, described as one of the most astonishing and impressive men of the times. In the summer of 1886 Mikhaël wrote again that Paris was the only place for the aspiring writer, and this time the call proved irresistible. Bernard-Lazare had apparently been putting off the departure from the provincial 'ogre', perhaps because he remained, for all his intellectual revolts and independence, emotionally attached to home and family, particularly to his parents, whom in later busy years he would rush to see whenever he could. In October 1886 he broke free, and complete with 'monocle de guerre et lunettes de l'archiviste' the twenty-one-year-old Nîmois arrived in Paris, with dreams of making a name for himself in the world of letters and ready to join his contemporaries in the battle for symbolism.

Symbolism, a door to spiritual freedom

Nothing is easier than to ridicule the excesses and puerilities of the group of arrogant young poets or would-be poets who gathered adoringly round Mallarmé and Villiers de l'Isle Adam like some secret freemasonry with its own mystical rules and symbols comprehensible only to the initiated. The group flourished in Paris for an eventful decade or so between 1885 and 1900, issuing numerous manifestoes, attacking the vulnerable figures of the literary and intellectual establishment – the successful writers, the academic critics, Zola's meaningless realism, Anatole France's superficial clarity, the banalities of Parnassian poetry, the rhetoric of the romantic rearguard, the bourgeois' love of creature comforts, in short anybody or any group which was not part of or sympathetic to the higher ideals of the fraternity. Bernard-Lazare himself, having been a member of the fraternity for a little while, later had harsh things to say about the mumbo-jumbo of the mystico-symbolist adolescents and their mystique of failure, their cult of the obscure and the hermetic, and their escape from life and reality into shallow mysticisms.

There is of course a more serious side to symbolism. In essence there was nothing new about the search for the spiritual behind the material and the representation of the spiritual by the material. It had been a long-standing practice in religion and in art to use symbols as instruments connecting visible reality with the invisible reality behind it. The symbol is the key which opens the gates to paradise. It is assumed here of course that there is such a connection, that what lies beyond is deeper, more permanent or more perfect than what we can see, and that we can grasp it, or at least catch a glimpse of it, provided we choose suitable means of approach.

In all these assumptions, nineteenth-century symbolism went against the prevailing positivist spirit which was content to observe and determine relationships between observable phenomena. What, if anything, lay behind these phenomena was of no concern to positivism. At its simplest, symbolism represents a swing of the pendulum away from rationalism in the same way as earlier in the century romanticism had swung away from eighteenth-century materialism. What is original about the symbolist reaction, and I am speaking here of the mainstream and not of its mystical and transcendental extensions, is that its critique of rationalism is humanist and secular in nature. It is really a quarrel between two kinds of rationalisms. On the one hand, the positivist who limits enquiry to what can be observed, rationally deduced or logically inferred; and on the other hand, the symbolist who starts from the premise that there are unconscious and irrational forces at work behind the rational and conscious processes and that together they make up the complex whole. Exploring the unconscious or trying to understand the irrational is not an escape into mysticism or a rejection of reality but a widening of it, an attempt to gain a deeper and more *complete* understanding of ourselves and the world around us. 'Mysticisme scientifique' is the awkward but nonetheless meaningful term used by Bernard-Lazare to describe this sort of open rationality which derives its sense of mystery essentially from a sense of the complexity of things, but which is ready to explore this complexity, forging for itself means sufficiently subtle for the purpose.

The paradise we are offered is not necessarily a more perfect world but a more subtle and complete one. It is an attainable paradise, through art or poetry, for example; or through knowledge and the heightened awareness which can come through knowledge. Instead of restricting knowledge to the observable, as did the positivists, the symbolists sought knowledge to extend the thinkable and ultimately to liberate the spirit. Our generation, André Fontainas recalled, thirsted for knowledge and we went to the richest and the most diverse sources to quench our thirst. 'Nous voulions savoir, pour nous sentir libres et nous conquérir sur les autres et sur nous.'[18] It is in psycho-analysis, anthropology, linguistics – new 'sciences' at the time – that the symbolist approach has been most fruitful by shifting the emphasis from externals to internals, from the biological to the psychological, from the historical to the philosophical, from the evolutionist to the essentialist, from logical analysis to intuitive synthesis.

The symbolists were great synthesisers; in the arts, for example, traditionally separate forms of expression – poetry, music, drama, ballet – were drawn together in a synthesis considered to correspond more closely to the multiple and subtle harmonies within wider reality. The appeal was to several senses simultaneously, to a fusion – 'correspondance', Baudelaire said – between sensation and emotion which heightened awareness by engaging the complete being. In the widespread interest shown in ancient religions

and their symbolics we can see a cultural and spiritual synthe-
sising. From the positivist point of view, this was tantamount to
putting the clock back, a retreat to primitive times.

Undoubtedly the eulogy of primitivism and decadence was at
times a retreat, an escape from an ugly present. Villiers de l'Isle
Adam was a genuine reactionary, fulminating against everything
modern. Some of his disciples, including Bernard-Lazare for a
little while, followed in his footsteps. But at its best the interest
in the past was no more an escape from present realities than the
sense of mystery was an escape from rationality.

In Bernard-Lazare's life, symbolism represents in some ways a
period of confusion and groping, but it was also a period of
exuberance and intoxicating intellectual freedom where everything was permitted, everything was food for thought. His post
as *répétiteur* ('crammer') in a *pensionnat* paid little but gave him
time to follow his varied intellectual interests. There were, to
begin with, the intimate evenings of discussion and reading among
members of the *bande* (Camille Bloch, Marcel Collière, Ephraïm
Mikhaël, Pierre Quillard, Hérold, André Fontainas and Bernard-
Lazare). Occasionally they collaborated in their writings. Mikhaël
and Bernard-Lazare wrote *La Fiancée de Corinthe* (1888). Five
of them composed a satire against the handsome General Boulanger whom popular support almost swept to power in 1889.[19]
Bernard-Lazare loved '*la vie en bande*', life lived in the company
of a few close friends. It is interesting to note that several members
of the group were students at the *Ecole de Chartes*, a milieu which
Bernard-Lazare came to know well through them, and where he
later made distinguished converts to the dreyfusard cause. He
remained attached to nearly all of his early friends, notably to
Pierre Quillard, poet and soon to become French spokesman for
the oppressed Armenians, and André Fontainas, also a poet and
great admirer of Bernard-Lazare. Much to the grief of the group
and especially of Bernard-Lazare, the talented Mikhaël died in
1890, at the age of twenty-four. The friends raised a fund to
publish his beautiful, melancholy poetry (*Oeuvres*, Paris, Lemerre,
1890).

Important in their lives were the *salon* gatherings at the homes
of the '*maîtres*': Mallarmé, Heredia, Henri de Régnier. Mallarmé's evenings in particular were to Bernard-Lazare like
ceremonies of initiation into the most polished form of symbolist
art, the art of unlocking mental doors with a gentle tap and

gradually releasing, by a series of decipherings, the most profound mental states. Bernard-Lazare used to listen spell-bound to the master though he later came to wonder whether those who had not been privileged to hear him illuminate the intricacies and hidden meanings of his poetry would ever be able to decipher them. For some time he savoured the pleasure of being among the select initiated, and he has left us a charming, solemn picture of the magic of the *soirées* spent in the temple of the rue de Rome.[20]

Magic of a more transcendental kind was the speciality of Edmond Bailly's *Librairie de l'Art Indépendant*, in the rue de la Chaussée d'Antin. Bailly, who brought out the short-lived *Revue de la Haute Science*, 'revue documentaire de la tradition eso-térique et du symbolisme religieux', was immensely interested in mystical religious writings. Quillard, Hérold and Bernard-Lazare, uncommonly erudite for their age, helped him with translation, editing, and research. It was there that Bernard-Lazare published *La Télépathie et le Néo-spiritualisme* (1893), a fascinating document on the current state of research into telepathy, hypnosis, hysteria and other psychical phenomena and extra-sensory perception. Bernard-Lazare's own attitude is interesting, revealing his effort to find his own level of mysticism. Reason and rational understanding are not banished, but suspended when encountering mysterious phenomena, i.e. things which are at present unknown without necessarily being unknowable at some future date. What is deadly and irrational to his mind is the attitude of 'les orthodoxes de la science' and 'les orthodoxes de l'Eglise' who reject extra-sensory perception out of hand and in so doing limit the limitless power of nature; 'mysticisme scientifique' has all his sympathy.

It was probably in a similar spirit that he approached the studies in comparative religion assiduously pursued for two, possibly three, years at the *Ecole Pratique des Hautes Etudes*. Among his teachers, who included Sylvain Lévy (Indian Re-ligions) and Louis Massebieau (Christian Literature), he most admired the irreverent, scholarly and critical abbé (later Mon-seigneur) Duchesne, 'le moins crédule des croyants'.[21]

The crowning experience of the early symbolist years came with the *Entretiens Politiques et Littéraires*. Francis Vielé-Griffin, Paul Adam and Henri de Régnier had founded this review in March 1890; it started as a pamphlet, by way of reply to some insulting comments made in the *Figaro* about the ivory tower and symbolism. In April 1890 followed the first proper issue of the new and in many ways pioneering 'revue de combat' with its blood-red covers. Bernard-Lazare started contributing in July of that year and before long became one of its leading lights, editor (from February 1891), *gérant* (from August 1891), literary critic (from January 1892). He also wrote the *revue des revues* and was the author of at least some of the anonymous and delightfully ironic *notes et notules*. Among his major contributions were his early antisemitic studies, the virulent anti-parnassian pamphlet 'Les Quatre Faces', articles on literary criticism and his first anarchist writings. All in all, it was a busy three years of writing, controversy, administration and editing, making the review one of the liveliest forums.

In a newspaper interview[22] Bernard-Lazare explained the delicate principle of unity within diversity which grouped together 'de si distinctes individualités dans un effort harmonieux'. Freedom of expression, respect for differences of opinion, the free development of individual aptitudes and aspirations unhindered by dogma or doctrines – these were fairly common symbolist articles of faith honoured and practised at the *Entretiens*. But, as he also pointed out, a certain communion of ideas was necessary, especially in a *revue de combat:* 'Nous ne pouvions faire de la revue une halle qui aurait retenti de cris discordants. Nous exigions une certaine homogénéité.'

This homogeneity proved ultimately difficult to achieve. It was easy enough to be united in common hatred of one's enemies, naturalism and the Parnasse; to demonstrate a common dislike of the 'chers maîtres' of the literary and intellectual Establishment whose only claim to respect was age, position or success. Bernard-Lazare was as outspoken in his dislike of respected elders whose fixed ideas and power made life difficult for the struggling young artists as he was generous in his praise of the latter. Encouraging the young, rescuing the 'maudits', was for Bernard-Lazare, himself a young man, part of the symbolist battle. The *Entretiens* opened their doors wide to a diversity of young and then unknown talents. Gide, Valéry, Pierre Louÿs, Henri Bordeaux, Claudel, Jules Laforgue were among them. Even Proust's first efforts were noticed, though they did not arouse great enthusiasm.

Negative lucidities and common enemies can be powerful unifying elements, but they cannot create a lasting, fighting unity,

especially if, as in the case of the *Entretiens*, political convictions
entailing divergent conceptions of the positive purpose of art come
to divide and separate.

The revolutionary aim of the founding fathers had been to
bring symbolism down from the Ivory Tower and to have political
as well as literary 'entretiens'. But it was one thing to talk about
politics and attack the bourgeoisie, long the artist's *bête noire*, and
quite another thing to commit art and the artist to political ideals.
For some time Bernard-Lazare managed to be a keen and
committed observer of what was going on in the market place,
and at the same time to sing the praise of Mallarmé as a 'pure'
artist, indifferent to what went on around him, living in his own
world of dreams above the vulgar, noisy crowd. He recommended
that the statue of Baudelaire be erected in a solitary, sad allée of
the Cemetery at Montparnasse, where 'no crowd would pollute it
with its presence'. An even more direct defence of the poet's
splendid solitude, which must not be tarnished by contact with
the vulgar crowd, is to be found in 'Les Quatre Faces'.[23] It almost
seems as if he considered solitude and alienation part of the poetic
condition. And since poetry was the highest creative process, the
poet must be left undisturbed in his tower: this was his privilege
as supreme interpreter of the mysteries of Creation.

In the end, however, as Bernard-Lazare moved closer to anarchism, he found it difficult to accommodate within his conception of
social art the poet-high-priest interpreting from above. The
poet-prophet as Carlyle had envisaged him, yes; provided that,
like the ancient prophets, he spoke to humanity in a language
that ordinary men could understand, and provided that he lived
among men. It is in the *Entretiens* that Bernard-Lazare began to
fight his first battles for 'l'art social' (not to be confused with
socialist art).[24] But his friends and collaborators, though attracted
by some aspects of this argument, did not wish to sacrifice their
artistic freedom. The campaign for 'social art' led to disputes,
notably with his old friend Pierre Quillard. The dispute occurred
in the issue of 25 May 1893, the last issue to which Bernard-
Lazare contributed. Two months later, in July, he gave up the
administration of the *Entretiens*. The review folded at the end of
the year. It had been an exciting and stimulating collaboration.
As such things went, three years of existence with never a number
missed or late was a long time and no mean achievement.

The critic and writer

Bernard-Lazare's conception of literary criticism – or any other criticism – was as a perpetual *combat*, a struggle to defend and affirm one's ideas against those judged to be pernicious. In 'De la Nécessité de l'Intolérance' he asserts that 'La tolérance est la caractéristique des âges sans croyances, elle est la vertu des esprits sans foi. L'intolérance est le levain des idées grandes, elle est la vertu des âmes vigoureuses et hautes.' Elsewhere he wrote in praise of hatred as a positive virtue, engendering and sustaining love. In 'Des critiques et de la critique' he divides critics into three main groups: the subjective critic who paraphrases the work; the historical critic who seeks to explain it by reference to time and circumstances; and finally the dogmatist who judges according to his own ideas and doctrines. If this dogmatic critic is not at the same time a practising artist, then he is likely to be, like Brunetière, 'un incompréhensif'. The ideal is to be a critic-artist who, living by ideas, like all writers, will always be ready to defend them because they are part of his existence and not merely 'matière littéraire'.[25]

This intolerant and subjective approach, a reaction against the objectivity and the historical method then prevailing, sounds most unpromising. It produced one savage piece, 'Les Quatre Faces', with which the young symbolist made an unforgettable début as critic in the *Entretiens*. But apart from this, his extensive critical writings, in the *Entretiens* and in the national press, are of greater value than the theory would lead one to believe. Moreover, it is remarkable how close he sometimes came to the hated historical method simply because his mind saw things in synthesis. He rarely discussed any single work or idea without reference to something wider into which it fitted. In this emphasis on the whole rather than the part we have a beginning of the historical method. The crucial question will be whether the whole *determines* the part. For the moment any 'product theory' is firmly rejected, except in the case of bad writers and weak characters. Good writers and strong characters, he claims, rise above milieu and time – and therefore are often rejected by their age.

A satirical illustration of this idea was given in the series of literary portraits which Bernard-Lazare wrote for the Literary Supplement of the *Figaro*, beginning in February 1894, and which soon became known as the 'éreintements bilatéraux du

Figaro'. Indignation mounted as these sarcastic double portraits, drawn with 'un coup de crayon qui égratigne jusqu'au sang', went on week after week. But the editor, Antoine Périvier, stood firm and Bernard-Lazare completed his twenty-five dyptichs entitled *Figures Contemporaines, ceux d'aujourd'hui, ceux de demain*. They were published in book form the following year (Perrin, 1895), with an introduction setting out his ideas on critics and criticism. It provoked lively reviews with plenty of quotations from the 'feu crépitant d'épigrammes' by the 'merveilleux maître ès-coups d'épingles'.

The bold idea behind the dyptich needs to be explained, for it greatly added to the irritation, for those who saw the point. Each dyptich contrasted an 'author of today' who will be succeeded in the public's favour by an 'author of tomorrow' in the same genre. The prediction was not based on Bernard-Lazare's personal preference for the 'author of tomorrow' but on what he thought would be the development of public taste. Thus there was an implicit criticism of the spirit of the times. Some critics were baffled: why, for example, should Brunetière be dethroned by Lemaître? The answer was not to do with greater scholarship or perception, but that Brunetière was an honest retrograde and Lemaître a *rusé* one. Similarly, Desjardins is an 'author of to-morrow' because 'il nous fait prévoir l'insipide, plate, vaniteuse et égoïste génération future, dont il aura été un des béats précurseurs'. Here is a selection, from the mordant to the more gently ironic.

BRUNETIÈRE

   C'est le modèle des hommes myopes et têtus que M. Brunetière, et il a parfois le courage du bœuf qui fond sur une loque rouge, mais sa myopie n'est pas sournoise et son entêtement est sans fourberie. M. Brunetière est un critique loyalement rétrograde, et je l'aime mieux ainsi que tant d'autres qui sont faussement intransigeants (pp. 52–3).

LEMAÎTRE

   M. Lemaître est le courtisan du succès, l'avocat des causes gagnées, l'enfonceur des portes ouvertes, et il sait avoir le courage de ses opinions, quand ses opinions ne sont plus courageuses (p. 62).

A. FRANCE

   . . .c'est un homme paisible qui met, je crois, sa tranquillité

au-dessus de ses convictions, un de ces hommes qu'une
croyance aurait gêné et que la crainte a rendu tolérant. . .
Il ne sait jamais quels principes passagers lui donneront le
plus de quiétude (p. 128).

ZOLA

Il est. . .le générateur de cette lignée de chiffoniers sans
lanterne qui ramassent les débris au petit bonheur du croc et
vident leur hotte à date fixe pour faire un livre (p. 2).

HUYSMANS

Il a le génie de la pourriture, il sait les sanies les plus
rebutantes, les pus les plus abjects, mais aussi la splendeur
des gemmes auxquelles il sait donner des splendeurs insoup-
çonnées, des puissances inconnues. Ses phrases ont la
résistance des brocarts abbatiaux et l'effritement des plus
basses lèpres (p. 7).

DE VOGÜÉ

Il a résolu le double et difficile problème d'être à la fois
l'amant ossianesque du passé et un des petits prophètes du
présent. . .il chante la Tour Eiffel, craignant sans doute
d'être accusé de hanter les catacombes (pp. 100–1).

A. SILVESTRE

M. Armand Silvestre est un des rares heureux de ce temps.
Il peut dire avec fierté que jamais une idée ne trouble sa
cervelle (pp. 45–6).

DAUDET

Un langage petit nègre, émaillé de parisianismes les plus
répandus (p .24).

Before very long Bernard-Lazare found himself trying to convert
to dreyfusism some of the people most cruelly portrayed – Desjardins and Zola for example. These writers did not bear him any
grudge, but others forgot and forgave less easily. As one critic
put it: 'Bernard-Lazare possède tout ce qu'il faut pour être
cordialement détesté: le mot mordant, peu de bienveillance et
beaucoup d'esprit.'[26] He was fundamentally a kind and compassionate man, but not when he wore the critic's 'monocle de
guerre'.

Not all is irony, though he is better at irony than at praise. His
admiration goes to the poets (Dierx, Heredia, de Régnier, Ver-

laine) and more particularly to Mallarmé, depicted in his temple where the faithful speak in hushed voices and hang on the master's lips. The master is, alas, a '*figure d'aujourd'hui*'; he will be dethroned by Maeterlinck, whose shallow mysticism is likely to tickle the senses and emotions of the *bourgeois raffinés*. Yet Bernard-Lazare is disturbed at the thought that the sibylline character of the master's poetry will always need commentators. Mallarmé wrote a charming letter of thanks: 'Merci d'un certain portrait, cher ami, il représente une des seules décorations qu'on puisse mettre ici-bas, celle d'un ordre glorieux et discret.'[27]

Bernard-Lazare practised symbolist art in three youthful works of uneven quality. *La Fiancée de Corinthe* (1888), written in collaboration with Ephraïm Mikhaël, is a lyrical drama based on a strange legend of mystery and magic. 'Les Initiés', an uncompleted dramatic poem in prose, might be summed up as a pantheistic, mystical version of Shakespeare's *A Midsummer Night's Dream*. It appeared in the most symbolist of symbolist reviews, *La Wallonie*. Finally there are the 'contes symbolistes' which became *Le Miroir des Légendes* (1892) and which had first appeared (1889–91) in the most serious literary reviews (*La Wallonie, La Revue Indépendante, La Jeune Belgique, Le Mercure de France, L'Ermitage* and *Les Entretiens Politiques et Littéraires*). A closer look at these works will illustrate the achievements and weaknesses of Bernard-Lazare's early symbolism, the passing fashions as well as more fundamental attitudes.

Stylistically, *La Fiancée de Corinthe*[28] is a somewhat eclectic exercise in which one recognises the influence of several admired masters. From the point of view of ideas it is much more interesting. Speaking of the work, Anatole France[29] observed that it was less inspired by Goethe and more by the strange, mystical writings of Phlegon of Tralles. If by this France meant to suggest that the emphasis is more on the mystical aspect of the original and less on the anti-Christian sentiments that the humanist Goethe had drawn from it, and which France himself had greatly developed in the *Noces Corinthiennes*, he is not altogether wrong, though he may have missed the real point. In his own work France had stressed the clash between pagan and Christian civilisations and regretted the historical victory of Christianity. Conflict and victory are personified in the story of a fanatical Christian mother who sacrifices the happiness of her unconverted, pagan daughter.

Bernard-Lazare was also fascinated by periods of cultural

transition, the moments in history when civilisations and religions meet and confront each other. But he preferred to envisage the outcome in terms of spiritual synthesis, a merging into underlying essences and harmonies, rather than the extinction of one civilisation by another. On an intellectual or doctrinal level such merging was difficult, but it could be achieved on a mystical level. In *La Fiancée de Corinthe*, he and Mikhaël, lovers of Greek antiquity but also attracted by Christian mysticism, tried to reconcile pagan antiquity and Christianity within man's natural sense of mystery and his psychological need for some sort of supernatural force. Pagan gods and prayers are juxtaposed, rather than opposed, to the Christian God and prayers. When Appollonia's Christian mother lies dying, for example, the pagan daughter implores her Gods while the Christian priest prays to his God for the same recovery. The ending taxed the authors' efforts at reconciliation. Victory ultimately lies with Christianity, symbolised by the Christian mother whose life is saved by the daughter's conversion. The converted daughter dies of grief for her pagan lover. But Christian victory is not ultimately obtained at the expense of the pagan lovers who are united, ironically enough for pagan lovers of life, in death. And yet it is a joyful death, presented as an escape from an increasingly christianised Corinth where divine joy is no longer known, and where everything proclaims that Pan is dead. The lovers, having affirmed the triumph of Eros over Christ, vanish into 'mystérieuses harmonies. . . .dans la nuit resplendissante de surnaturelles clartés' with the mother's final blessing: 'Sauveur du monde, donne à leur âme le repos éternel.'[30]

If there is an anti-Christian note in this drama it lies in the loss of joy Christianity is shown to bring to civilisation where previously the Gods themselves commanded the people to be joyful. Bernard-Lazare's mysticism was of the joyful, optimistic variety, unusual in the general symbolist gloom. Having escaped from the pessimistic philosophy of 'nature and nurture', he was unlikely to find satisfaction in what one might call, if the anachronism were allowed, philosophies of the absurd. Freedom was not an illusion for Bernard-Lazare; nor the universe an undecipherable chaos; he did not believe that life need necessarily be a story told by an idiot. Despair was not part of his temperament and neither was a sense of sin. He had a sense of mystery and of the metaphysical but it was not fundamentally an anguish. It extended and heightened reality, giving it an extra dimension.

However, it took Bernard-Lazare a little while to be sure where he stood. There is an autobiographical passage in *Le Fumier de Job* which describes the tensions and spiritual wilderness of the early years:

> Il était trop tiraillé par les exemples divers qu'il voyait autour de lui. Chacun trouvait le port à ses côtés : soit dans l'indifférence, soit dans la croyance irraisonnée, ou bien dans une foi profonde et motivée, ou encore dans un mysticisme hardi et rayonnant, d'autres dans la science et l'athéisme; lui seul ne pouvait rien.[31]

The way out seemed at first to lie in 'mysticisme hardi'. As literary critic of the *Nation* (January–November 1891) he hailed every book on mysticism, from the occult to the erudite, as a healthy reaction against rationalism and intellectualism. In 'Les Initiés' he tried his hand at a mystery, and the result is a most obscure piece of writing, symbolist in the worst sense. The fantasy, suggested perhaps by *A Midsummer Night's Dream*, is set in mythological Greece, complete with Orphic mysteries and choruses of animals, plants and spirits all singing of their essences, while the human lovers muse on the transmigration of souls and express the hope that life on earth will in future be ruled by the loving Zagreus rather than the inflexible Zeus (an allusion to Christ and Jehovah perhaps).

Bernard-Lazare never completed this mystical exercise, or rather only parts two and three were published. The unpublished first part has survived in his papers. From it one gathers that the basic idea behind it was this: Why have the Gods endowed man with the desire to penetrate the mysteries which surround him while at the same time denying him the power to do so? It is difficult to decide whether what follows is intended to unveil the mystery or to draw a veil of obscure symbols across it in order to keep things 'entre initiés'.

The *Miroir des Légendes* is a much more characteristic work, and one which has a genuine *souffle mystique*. Here Bernard-Lazare has found his style and favourite genre: a highly polished, poetic, concise and evocative style which seeks to suggest and stimulate; and the 'conte symboliste' in which past myths and legends are interpreted and re-interpreted.

Nearly all the twenty legends are in one way or another dramas of faith, dealing with religious cults and mystical rites, from the

ancient world of India and China to Greece and early Christianity. They constitute an evocation of stages in civilisation, stages
in man's explanation of mysterious phenomena. Their symbolic
significance is open to interpretation, perhaps deliberately so.
Interesting in this respect are the Jewish stories with which we
shall deal later. The most powerful drama of faith is told in
'L'Ineffable Mensonge'. It describes the anguish of one of Christ's
disciples who cannot believe. Christ explains to him that he too
does not believe. One day he had met some poor, unhappy people
and out of pity and from a desire to bring them peace he told
them: 'Aimez-vous; voici la foi nouvelle, voici la vraie loi, voici
le vrai Dieu.'[32] This is the lesson the disciple is asked to teach,
whatever his personal doubts or anguish. Christ even suggests that
personal anguish may be selfish. Christ himself is crucified without
believing in his own message. The fact that others believe is
sufficient.

Commenting on this story, Anatole France doubted the wisdom
of procuring man's happiness at the price of a lie. How can one
be sure that the illusion in which mankind will believe will turn
out to be for the good? Bernard-Lazare's prophet, he went on, is
of a rare but very dangerous kind.[33] Like other commentators,
France remarked on the underlying violence in most of the stories.
He did not care for the fervour, frenzies and sacrifices. 'Il
[Bernard-Lazare] aime à voir fumer le sang des justes sous un
ciel étouffant, au milieu des foules furieuses.' There is indeed
violence, but then Bernard-Lazare is depicting ages of faith,
sacrifices and heroism, when one died for one's ideas and beliefs.
Perhaps this is the 'message' to the non-heroic age of his own
times. On the other hand France, who was on bad terms with the
symbolists whose 'obscurities' offended his love of classical clarity,
was glad to be able to say that here was a symbolist with a
beautifully limpid and harmonious style who expressed the violence of his thought with the greatest clarity.

It is probably this vehemence together with the social message
in such stories as 'L'Ineffable Mensonge' which led some critics
to suggest that the book was one of revolt leading straight to
anarchism. This is probably a misinterpretation, helped by the
fact that the book was published in 1892 when Bernard-Lazare
began to be involved in the anarchist movement. But the legends
were actually written before that involvement, and they strike me
as reflecting more his spiritual gropings, the search for an ab-

sorbing, strong faith to which he could devote his spiritual energies without becoming a prisoner to any set of doctrines. In this sense, in the combination of search for faith and freedom, *Le Miroir des Légendes* could be called a genuine mystical work as well as an anarchist work, illustrating an idea of Spinoza's which Bernard-Lazare developed in *La Télépathie et le Néo-spiritualisme*: 'Aucune saine raison ne nous permet d'attribuer à la nature une puissance et une vertu limitée.'[34]

Later works

Les Porteurs de Torches (1897) and *La Porte d'Ivoire* (1898), both collections of short stories, belong to a later period and reflect different preoccupations, but it is appropriate to deal with them at this stage as successors to *Le Miroir des Légendes*.

If many legends of the *Miroir des Légendes* represent dramas of religious faith, those of the *Porte d'Ivoire* are in the main dramas of human love. The atmosphere is very similar in its stifling concentration, its underlying violence of passion, devotion and sacrifice, of total absorption, physical and especially psychological, to the point of self-destruction. Tenderness is as rare as are vulgarity, common adultery, eroticism or perversity. The strangeness of the stories lies not in any perversity but in the power of love, as mysterious and irrational, as fanatical and often as tragic (seen from the outside) as the power of faith for which only exceptional beings, the most heroic or the most deluded, are prepared to die. One such story of delusion, this time on a collective scale, is told in 'L'Illusion', where Moses leads the Jews towards the promised land, but this time the waters of the sea swallow them up. Yet they die blessing his name, in ecstasy, believing that they had reached the promised land.

The miracles are all of man's making in this book, and it is not always easy to decide whether the author feels exalted or revolted by them, whether he regards them as miracles of faith by which the modern, non-heroic and faith-less age ought to be inspired, or as miracles of illusions which belong to a past age. True, the narrator and the group of friends listening to him comment on some of the legends. More often than not these serene rationalists prefer hope to delusion, living in love to loving in death, truth to consolation. But they also have, like their creator, a poetic self which is stimulated by the opium of myths and symbols, by fables which become, as one of them says, 'des amies excitatrices. . . Je les charge de mes visions et de mes rêves...Je crois à tout comme poète, si je crois à peu de choses comme philosophe.'

The introduction of brief discussions between narrator and listeners is an interesting new feature which fulfils several functions. It is in the first instance a convenient unifying device, linking one legend with the next and thus giving the work as a whole a certain formal, if often artificial, unity. It also provides light relief, allowing the reader to catch his breath, as it were, before passing on to the next drama. Most important is the expository intention behind the light relief, which adds to the hitherto self-contained and subjective *conte symboliste* a critical and more objective *dialogue philosophique*. This mixture may well go against the conventional symbolist aesthetic, precisely because it intellectualises and rationalises, but it admirably suited Bernard-Lazare's temperament, satisfying both the poet's imagination and the philosopher's search for more objective truth by confronting, through several characters, different facets of the same problem, different approaches and interpretations. In these dialogues there is often also an unmistakable personal element: Bernard-Lazare is engaged in dialogue with himself, confronting the poet in him with the rationalist, the sceptic with the optimist, past aspirations with present attitudes, at times harshly criticising former ideas and temptations. This is the case in *Les Porteurs de Torches* where the main character, Marcus, clearly acts as the author's mouthpiece and where Marcus's motley companions also represent the different personae Bernard-Lazare was or had been. We shall find a similar, veiled intellectual autobiography contained in a later work, *Le Fumier de Job*.

In *Les Porteurs de Torches* the new genre of symbolic legend and philosophical dialogue is fully developed and extended to include the *drame philosophique* in Renan's sense of the word: ideas seen in action, in daily life. The three genres, parable, dialogue and drama, are fitted together in the simplest of structures: Marcus, a 'heretical' philosopher, meets Juste, a sceptical and Epicurean vagabond who has opted out of Gerontian society after having been a helpless victim of injustice. He agrees to introduce Marcus to the city of Geronta, and in the course of their wanderings and participation in the life of the city three more misfits join them: a poet who is ever ready to seek refuge in the past, a compassionate girl who believes that charity is the answer to injustice, and a rich man with a bad conscience who indulges in philanthropy. Between them they observe and discuss, with Marcus always obligingly ready to explain the *cause* of the social and moral ills with the help of an illuminating parable, where his companions only see and deplore the effects.

Paradoxically enough, this anarchist-inspired work is the least violent, at least in atmosphere. In fact, Marcus–Bernard-Lazare stresses that violence towards certain individuals or even towards certain hated groups of men, be they judges or usurers, is as ineffective as charity and philanthropy, which may help the few but can never succour all. What is needed is a change in the system. The story ends with a threat or promise of an altogether different violence, that of social revolution which the gentle Marcus, through his eminently reasonable parables, has inspired and of which the companions, turned disciples, will be the torchbearers.

At its simplest level, each of the twenty-nine stories is an obvious satirical or critical comment on some aspect of social life or pillar of society. To the question, what is an economist? the answer is: 'un citoyen patenté qui a la charge pénible mais fructueuse de prouver aux pauvres la légitimité et la douceur de leur état'.[35] A usurer is a man who is convinced that he fulfils the useful function of selling money. The lawyer believes that it is his mission to defend the client against the indifference of the impersonal judge, provided the client can pay. In all other cases the lawyer's motto is: innocence needs no defence. As for the judge, he believes that justice means knowing the law – until he is confronted with the poor he has condemned according to the law for theft. There are similar satirical sketches on such venerable institutions as marriage (a commercial arrangement), the University (professors of political economy teach students to collect facts and classify people, the whole process proving, objectively and scientifically, that the system could not be otherwise), society's conception of honour (respect for property) and order (maintenance of the *status quo*). What is being attacked here in a calm, gently satirical fashion are not so much flagrant acts of injustice but the humbug and the fictions which keep a moribund bourgeois morality alive.

The tone changes when Marcus faces his companions and the victims of the system. They see through the humbug, but have become resigned to it, opt out, or try to remedy the evil by means destined to maintain it. Christian ethical teaching – charity, abnegation, sacrifice, consolation, glorification of poverty, promise of a better life to come – bears a heavy responsibility. With Christian ethics as support and modern science as justification, an immoral society can look forward to a long and secure life.

There are a few hot-headed rebels in Geronta for whom Marcus has a special message. This is the third level of criticism, and it is the most serious, for it is addressed to fellow-travellers who act before they have sufficiently thought out their ideas, and who are too prone to shout slogans and vent their anger in futile acts of terrorism against individuals or groups. The judge may be a hateful person, but he is merely applying the law of the land. The banker and the money-lender are equally hateful but they too are part of the system. In a different context, there is a telling demonstration that shallow libertarian conceptions of free love, marriage and the liberated woman are ultimately not very different from the greatly detested bourgeois conceptions. To the Romantic middle-class woman, who has contracted a 'mariage de raison', perhaps against her will, Eros is god, having a lover is ennobling, and committing adultery is an act of liberation. What do some misguided libertarians say? '. . .le libre don de son corps était pour une femme le symbole de la liberté dont elle doit jouir, et pour ainsi dire la préface à sa libération'.[36] To which a pure libertarian objects that the only free woman is a virgin. 'Ni amante, ni mère! vierge! tenir loin de soi la meute des désirs tyranniques.'[37]

It is not surprising that anarchist reviews generally welcomed this 'petit bijou littéraire et philosophique', which so forcefully demonstrated 'la nécessité d'une éthique'.[38] *L'Ouvrier des Deux Mondes* thought the work would have been perfect if there had been among the torchbearers a Souvarine.[39] Souvarine, it will be remembered, is the anarchist in Zola's novel *Germinal* who not only understands and highlights the evil but sets about destroying it by blowing up the mine. But, one might add, the mine-owners rebuilt the mine without too much trouble and life continued as before. Perhaps that is why there is no Souvarine in *Les Porteurs de Torches*. The revolution preached there is more profound and more radical.

One of the most personal dialogues which Bernard-Lazare holds with himself concerns art and the role of the writer, the torchbearer *par excellence* if he so chooses. Illuminating the past, exploring catacombs and necropolises, judging 'à la pâle clarté

des mornes lampes antiques le rouge soleil',[40] is not enough. It is
still more futile to believe that the key which will unlock the doors
of truth lies buried in the symbols of ancient myths if only we
could decipher them. The code-crackers of the symbolist school
come in for severe criticism. Their mystifications and arbitrary
interpretations may gratify the esoteric aestheticism of the initiated, but have little to do with truth or with life and nothing
whatever with present realities from which 'les adolescents
énervés, les hystériques primitifs, les délicieux sadiques' do their
utmost to escape. If Bernard-Lazare was never any of these things,
not even in his most esoteric period, he had still been a great
admirer of Villiers de l'Isle Adam. Here he breaks free from the
spell once exercised by the master of 'le conte symboliste' who
believed that he was the chosen interpreter of universal truths
symbolised in ancient myths. With his adoration of the past, his
contempt for the present and indifference to the future, Villiers
was as unsuitable a torchbearer as the frenetic modernists who
deprive the present of its depth in their contempt for the past.
Between these two poles, Bernard-Lazare was trying to find his
roots, his time and his role as a writer. In *Les Porteurs de Torches*
he found them. Although he was to express himself in other forms
than myths and legends, and although a short life, filled with
action, left him little time to complete the many works conceived
or begun, this passage expresses the essentials of what was to
remain his personal conception of a symbolist art committed to
life in its full perspective of time.

> Nos pères, comme nos sauvages, créaient des mythes
> informes pour expliquer les phénomènes, car ils avaient cette
> divine vertu sans laquelle l'humanité ramperait encore dans
> les ténèbres et dans la boue fétide : la curiosité. Leurs mythes
> ne peuvent nous apporter qu'un témoignage : ils reflètent
> l'esprit de ceux qui les ont conçus. En se perpétuant,
> beaucoup se sont épurés, et, si la méthode des néoplatoni-
> ciens, qui consistait à leur donner un sens symbolique, est
> vaine, le poète peut cependant se servir des ces fables,
> incarner en elles des pensées nouvelles, et faire, de la légende,
> le véhicule qui portera aux esprits les idées de demain.[41]

2

THE JOURNALIST WITH A MISSION

Let us briefly recall the essential facts about the 'penny-press' revolution and the emergence of two new powers: the press and public opinion, the one forming, and largely *deforming*, as Bernard-Lazare bitterly remarked, the other. As a result of educational reforms and increased literacy, there was a demand for quick, easy reading material. The development of steam-powered rotary presses, which by 1892 could in an hour or two turn out 75,000 to 80,000 copies of a four-page newspaper, all neatly separated into bundles of a hundred, ready for delivery, satisfied the demand at a price most people could afford. By 1899, there were 60 papers, including the big Paris dailies, selling at 5 *centimes*, as compared to 23 in 1881. The low price led to immense increases in circulation as well as an increase in the number of papers. The popular *Petit Journal* headed the list with a daily circulation of over 200,000. It claimed 5 million readers. In their heyday, in the early 1890s, even such quality papers as *Le Figaro* had a daily circulation of 80,000. The *Journal* broke into the market in September 1892 with 200,000 copies sold of its first issue. The total number of newspapers and periodicals in Paris, on the increase since the liberal press law of 1881, shot up dramatically from 1,811 in 1890 to 2,401 in 1895.[1]

It was a paradise for the writers and journalists who already had a name[2] (they were used as advertisement to attract the more literary clientèle) and provided they asked no questions about the paper's finances and editorial policy. These conditions fulfilled, the writer even enjoyed a certain freedom. At no stage in the history of the press have so many writers contributed regularly to the press in one capacity or another. There is hardly a name in the world of letters which cannot also be found in the daily press, in *Le Journal, L'Echo de Paris, Le Figaro, Le Temps* in particular.

But the participation of distinguished writers and the presence of many excellent journalists did not prevent the 'crise de la presse' from developing. This crisis, unlike the 'crise du livre' which it largely provoked, was not of a commercial but of a moral nature. Sensationalism, muck-raking, scandals, smear-campaigns, bribery, corruption, extortionate offers of publicity or pressures for silence, all these things were rife. This state of affairs led the philosopher Fouillé to claim that the press was responsible for the increase in the crime rate. Investigating the charge, *La Revue Bleue* opened an enquiry into the state of the press in December 1897[3] which confirmed the immorality but firmly rejected any tampering with the freedom of expression. Such was the 'crisis' to which young men such as Péguy proposed their own solution: he started collecting money among his friends to create a 'journal vrai'. It was also Bernard-Lazare's life-long dream.

Bernard-Lazare was a born journalist in the age of the newspaper. But his lofty conception of the press as the nation's college of further education and the conscience of government cut short a promising journalistic career. At first, interestingly enough, his missionary zeal combined with a predilection for preaching to the unconverted led to intensive collaboration with, or rather use of, the bourgeois press which raised no qualms in his mind. The specialised *review*, as he then saw it, was for discussion and self-expression among the converted; it was created by a small group for a small group of like-minded people. It was the indifferent or hostile majority which had to be converted, and what better way than to use its own press? So we find him extolling poetry and mysticism in the very bourgeois *La Nation*, defending anarchism in *Le Journal* and *L'Echo de Paris*, and drawing irreverent portraits of respected literary figures in the conservative *Figaro*. Ultimately, however, this happy arrangement raised serious moral problems. Relative freedom of expression in one article, increasingly 'relative' as time went on, could not justify complicity in the paper's general immorality. The individual journalist may be incorruptible, Bernard-Lazare wrote, but if he works for a corrupt paper and is paid by it, then he bears his share of responsibility for the corruption of public opinion. At this stage collaboration became impossible.

I shall examine, as far as possible in chronological order, some of Bernard-Lazare's contributions to the major daily papers. In these scattered writings we see changes taking place in his thinking as he moves from criticism to commitment. His journalistic output was considerable before the Dreyfus Affair, reaching its maximum in 1893 and early 1894 when he was writing for several papers and reviews at the same time. There will be space here to discuss only a small sample of over 300 articles of comment on the spirit of the times. He had himself intended to publish a collection of fifty articles entitled 'Paroles Modernes', and this is the spirit which has guided my choice.

In January 1891 he took over the book review for the daily paper *La Nation*. His weekly contributions for a period of ten months amount to a total of 34 articles; with an average of two to three books discussed at a time, this means a review of some eighty books. For someone so interested in what his age was thinking, this was an excellent opportunity to become acquainted with the trends and preoccupations of the times. Indeed, he is more concerned with extracting the spirit of the age – and even more the reaction against that spirit – from the work under discussion than with its intrinsic value. The stronger the evidence of the writer's reaction against the spirit of materialism, the better the critic likes him.

A conviction that it is the function of the critic to exercise an influence by encouraging healthy trends undoubtedly determined the selection of books. Naturally, Bernard-Lazare was not entirely a free agent; his job was to review current publications for the wider audience of a daily newspaper. However, this still left him considerable freedom, and his choice of books is revealing. There is a great deal of poetry, and it is always enthusiastically received. There is hardly a poet, from Mallarmé to now forgotten minor Symbolist poets whose praise he does not sing. The novel, on the other hand, a very popular genre, gets little attention. Zola's *L'Argent* and Huysman's *Là-bas*, it is true, each occupy the entire six columns of the review-space,[4] but they serve as a springboard for an attack on realism. The attack on Zola, who is portrayed as at best an uneducated observer of banalities and as more usually a clumsy compiler of ugly facts, is ferocious. Apart from the *Jardin de Bérénice*, by the egotistically inclined Barrès, and the more remarkable *Cahiers d'André Walter* by the promising young writer André Gide, the only other prose-works discussed are almost all historical, philosophical and above all of a mystical character or about mysticism.

In short, the main feature of the *Nation* articles is a concentration on poetry and mysticism. Both are regarded as a spiritual reaction, one to be encouraged, against the materialism of the age.

From the *Nation* Bernard-Lazare progressed to *L'Evénement*, a bigger, more influential daily paper, where his column first called 'Mouvement Littéraire' soon became, significantly enough, 'Chronique d'Aujourd'hui'. The *Evénement* contributions (more or less weekly from May 1892 to September 1893) show some important developments.

On the literary side, poets and poetry continue to arouse his enthusiasm. He gauges the health of contemporary literature by the state of poetry, and since it is alive and flourishing, all is well: witness the daily appearance of poetry reviews filled with excellent work by promising young poets – a certain Paul Valéry for example 'dont les volumes sont attendus' (28 July 1892).

But the fifty-nine articles for *L'Evénement* clearly show Bernard-Lazare's increasing preoccupation with social problems. Hand in hand with this goes a vehement criticism of Republican democracy and institutions. The symbolist had moved to anarchism. Election manoeuvres, the joyless celebration of the Fourteenth of July, the suppression of freedom of speech, conditions in prison, the courts and administration of justice, the military mystique and military justice, elections to the Academy, uninspiring education, student activities and organisations, these are the major topics of discussion in the 'Chroniques d'Aujourd'hui'. We also have the first 'conte du présent', a social fable, an attempt to present contemporary social issues in literary form, and to reconcile within himself writer and social commentator. This particular fable is entitled 'Le Vagabond' (24 August 1893) and is an attack on the property-dominated capitalist system defended in the story by a Republican economist. Within a relatively short time Bernard-Lazare had moved from criticism of the spiritual malady of the age, its mental materialism, to an attack on specific social and political institutions in the capitalist Republic. The new political forces are also presented, 'Les Socialistes' (14 November 1892) to whom he evidently prefers 'Les Révolutionnaires' (4 May 1893), that is to say Anarchist Socialists. Bernard-Lazare speaks relatively freely about anarchism, a subject which was sensitive at the time. However, this freedom was not to last.

There is one trend of the times which still greatly preoccupied him: mysticism. Here too we can see an important development. Nothing is more instructive in this respect than to compare the *Nation* articles of 1891 with those of the *Evénement*. In 1891 his exaltation of mysticism had shown a strong streak of anti-rationalism, anti-positivism and even hostility towards science. Bernard-Lazare is now evidently alarmed by the growing anti-intellectual movement, with its rejection of the pursuit of knowledge, science and civilisation, and its exaltation of the simple in mind and pure in heart, preferably living in the country near a lonely church. The idea that 'the secret of happiness is not to think', is totally unacceptable to him. Even at the height of his flirtation with mysticism he was never against rational thought. In three articles he takes to task Téodor de Wyzewa, a symbolist and now Christian mystic, who represents this dangerous trend, a form of intellectual egotism. The trouble with Valbert, he declares, (Valbert is the hero of de Wyzewa's *Récit d'un jeune homme*) is not that he thinks too much but that he thinks too much about himself.[5] In the face of the gathering crusade to 'think less and pray more', Bernard-Lazare rushes to the defence of intellect and science.

Another and not unrelated trend which worries him is the 'think less and do more' cult of superior individuals and spectacular actions. These heroes are no longer regarded as symbols of what is best in humanity, as with Emerson or Carlyle, but as forces above and outside humanity. The revival of Stendhal and 'beylisme' ('Stendhal et les Stendhaliens', 2 July, 1892) and the new cult of Napoleon ('Le Retour de l'Empereur', 1 July 1893) were ominous signs. Equally disturbing was the influence exercised by Maurice Barrès, egotist, 'anarchist', brilliant writer, former admirer of General Boulanger and sympathetic towards Boulangism, a new political force born out of Boulanger's failure to seize power, and whose real hero was Napoleon.

Unlike other anarchists, Bernard-Lazare was never deluded by Barrès' novels, *Un homme libre* and *L'Ennemi des Lois*. Egotism, alienation and aristocratic individualism have nothing to do with anarchism, he commented severely. The Barrèsian hero can afford to withdraw from society and devote himself to a life of self-contemplation because he is rich (2 December 1892). Nothing is more dangerous than the egotist turned man of action, especially when he looks to Napoleon for lessons in energy and brandishes ideas found in a misunderstood Goethe – the idea, for example, that injustice is preferable to disorder. This 'appel au sabre', as he called it in 'Napoléonisme et Goethisme' (*Revue Parisienne*, 25 February 1894) frightened Bernard-Lazare.

The flamboyant Fernand Xau, one of the most successful newspaper magnates of the times, launched *Le Journal* in September 1892 in grand style with American-type publicity: giant posters in a continuous band with the words 'le Journal' stretching along the pavements from the Grands Boulevards to the Place de la République. Xau engaged the biggest names, to whom he offered, to the despair of other newspaper proprietors, the highest rates of pay, with the added security of the then unusual system of firm contracts. *Le Journal* became, as Xau had intended, a writers' paper, bringing literature to a wide readership. Zola, Coppée, Mirbeau, Séverine, Maupassant, Becque, Barrès, Bourget are among the many writers who at one stage or another wrote for *Le Journal* and won for it a special clientèle. Bernard-Lazare was in illustrious company and the fact that he joined the paper almost as soon as it came out and stayed for over two years (September 1892 to December 1894) speaks well for his reputation as journalist and writer.

His contributions are predominantly literary, social fables of the present (which in 1897 went to make up *Les Porteurs des Torches*) and the beginning of the 'stories of the past' which he continued in the *Echo de Paris* and which ultimately became *La Porte d'Ivoire* (1898). These didactic, largely anarchist-inspired stories, which set out to disturb and to instruct, are perfectly consistent with his conception of the educative role of the writer, journalist and critic, who must practice positively in creative writing what he preaches theoretically, and at times negatively, in criticism. If these anarchist tales were read by a mainly bourgeois public, that was all to the good. Bernard-Lazare liked preaching to the unconverted. And the public did not object, it seems – at least, not to anarchism in a highly pleasing literary style with just sufficient remoteness from turbulent realities. More surprising, the political and polemical *Journal* articles[6] reflect little of the events of outstanding importance which were then taking place and in which Bernard-Lazare was deeply involved. Nobody would gather that this was the time (1892–4) of a veritable epidemic of 'anarchist' terrorism. The 'Chroniques d'Aujourd'hui' of the *Evénement* are in this respect a more interesting *témoignage*. It seems as if Fernand Xau, independent-minded

though he was, exercised a restraining influence over the propagandists by word on his staff. In an atmosphere of fear and panic,
when some newspapers called for anarchist heads to roll, and
notably those of writers and journalists who spread the gospel, it
was difficult to defend such people in the press. Bernard-Lazare
tried to do so on two occasions in the *Journal*, once *à propos* Jean
Grave (5 March 1894) and again in defence of Félix Fénéon (27
April 1894). This last article appeared with a cautious editorial
note stating that the views expressed were those of the author and
not of the paper. Shortly after, Bernard-Lazare left the *Journal*
and joined its rival, the *Echo de Paris*.

Editorial censorship within an allegedly free press, probably
the first clear example he personally came across, was an important journalistic experience. So was the veritable panic which
the press helped to spread through the country in the daily and
sensational reports about the anarchist peril. It was a staggering
example, soon to be repeated in another context, of denunciation
and trial by the press.

The writing he contributed to the *Echo de Paris* over a period
of two years (November 1894 to August 1896) is considerable
and varied: some twenty short stories, some social and political
observations, some polemics, notably those directed against Barrès
and like-minded 'revolutionary reactionaries' who in their search
for ancestors distorted the revolutionary Proudhon ('Fédéralistes
et Fédéralisme', 17 November 1895; 'Le Fédéralisme Révolutionnaire', 12 December 1895). It was also from the *Echo de Paris* that
Bernard-Lazare launched his first real attack on antisemitism.

His most interesting contributions to the *Echo de Paris* are the
series of *reportages* and the 'enquête' on science. Reporting was
something entirely new in Bernard-Lazare's journalistic career
and behind it lies a profound change in attitude towards history
and the value of the documentary. The symbolist had loved the
past, but it was the distant, fabulous past of myths and legends
to which his search for essences, the archetypal and the absolute
had taken him. There are some interesting though indirect *mea
culpa*, as for example in *La Jeunesse* (16 February 1896) in which
the 'mystico-idealist' young generation lost in contemplation of
the dead is scorned, and a quasi-apology is extended to Zola, now
seen as representing life. A more direct expression of regret is
found in the charming story ('Le Passé', 4 November 1895) of the
young poet remorse-stricken at his wasted youth which he spent

trying to live the past; he is saved from the cold embrace of yester-year by love, but exhorted by a wise master not to go to the other extreme of living exclusively in the present. Bernard-Lazare has found the right sort of continuity. He now wants to understand not relive the past, to draw lessons from history for living in the present and building the future.

With this new sense of history came a growing awareness of the importance of fact, of carefully controlled and verified documentation. In the *Nation* articles of 1891 he had been severe about the naturalistic trend in contemporary historical writing, the concentration on the factual, the documentary, the detail. For this reason Jules Huret's famous 'enquête' of 1891 on the current state of literature had aroused no great enthusiasm in him. This kind of investigation, which poses certain questions and then records the answers, had been to him just another unexciting piece of contemporary documentation of uncertain critical value. But he now speaks approvingly of the reporter, the chronicler, the documentary novelist, all intent to 'faire vrai', and whose work will later be of immense historical and human value. Even Taine and the once detested 'historical method' are promoted to precursors of the 'socialist method' in history and literature.

It must be said that as far as Bernard-Lazare was concerned the reporting of facts without comment and interpretation went against the grain. He was too committed, too much of a polemicist. His reporting is a mixture of fact and comment designed more perhaps to influence present developments and attitudes than to provide simple evidence for future historians; or rather, what he offers the historian is the voice of an articulate and critical participant in events.

The opening of the Kiel Canal by the Kaiser, an event which Europe was invited to celebrate as a great civic achievement and a contribution to trade and peace, was Bernard-Lazare's first assignment abroad as special correspondent. Once there, he also acted as representative of the Paris press. The first two articles ('A Kiel', 21 and 23 June 1895) are factual and descriptive: the boats, the banquets, the people, the festive international atmosphere; the Kaiser's speech 'For Peace' is given without comment. The comment comes in 'Lendemain de la Fête' (29 June) and in the following three articles. A few more peaceful celebrations of that sort and war is bound to break out, such were his reflections. He regards the whole affair as a charade in which Germany speaks of friendship and thinks of war, celebrates before her assembled enemies a work destined to serve her warlike interests. Like many of his countrymen, though without the Germanophobia of some, Bernard-Lazare was suspicious of Germany and even more so of the Kaiser, the 'mystical warrior', of whom he drew an unflattering portrait. In order to understand fully his bitter comments on the French Republic we must remember that France's official policy of friendship with Germany, which on this occasion was expressed by sending a squadron of ships, was to some extent forced on her by the alliance with Czarist Russia, an alliance which Bernard-Lazare condemned as the most un-Republican act in foreign policy, surpassed only by France's non-intervention in the massacre of the Armenian community by the Turks – a silence also in part dictated by the alliance with Russia. If we had a real Republic in France, he wrote, we should have refused to go to Kiel and that would have been a real gesture of peace.

From this international 'charade' he went to a strike of glass-workers at Carmaux which he reported and commented on with feverish interest (11–20 August 1895). Again, we have first the presentation of the facts, very brief in this case, followed by comment and his own analysis of the situation, with a portrait of the 'patron' concluding the series of articles. If the portrait of Kaiser Wilhelm is unflattering, the portrait of Rességuier is fierce. He seems to personify all the power, deviousness and cruelty of capitalism determined to break the growing strength of organised labour and of any politician, in this case Jaurès, sympathetic to workers' syndicates. These were the early days of syndicalist organisation, and in common with other socialists and syndicalists, Bernard-Lazare regarded the strike at Carmaux, called over a union issue by the workers and prolonged by the management in order to break the workers, as a test case.

In July 1896 he went to London to report on the International Socialist Congress. Readers of the *Echo de Paris* (25 July to 4 August) and also of *Le Paris* (5 and 21 August) were given long and biting accounts of the 'cacophonous congress' bogged down in lengthy, futile, procedural discussions, thanks to Marxist politics and 'the Holy Family' (so called because of the pre-eminence of members of Marx's family in the Socialist leadership) whose aim was to dominate and regiment, excommunicate anyone who disagreed. We shall come back later to this notorious congress and Bernard-Lazare's account of it.

Like Péguy, and indeed like many anarchists who made a virtue of public self-criticism and of criticism of those closest to them, it was a point of honour with Bernard-Lazare not to spare friends or kindred spirits, and to thrash out differences in public. Those who fell short of the ideal were more important than those who never shared it. For that reason, Jaurès was of greater concern to him than the Marxist Guesde, an honour Jaurès may not have appreciated. From a political point of view these attacks on fellow-socialists in the bourgeois press may have been unwise. But Bernard-Lazare did not possess that sort of political wisdom. Frankness, often brutal frankness, was a necessary condition for dialogue.

Borrowing his title from Brunetière's famous essay, Bernard-Lazare began in January 1895 an *enquête* on 'la Banqueroute de la Science'. It took the form of a ten-point questionnaire which eminent scientists and scholars in various fields were invited to answer. Some ten replies were received[7] and published over a period of several weeks (until the beginning of April). Few people answered all the questions: there were too many and they were too complex.[8] Most were quite happy to commit themselves on the first and last questions with a more or less straightforward 'No' and 'Yes' respectively. Has Science ever promised to unveil mystery and explain the unknowable? No. Has M. Brunetière not exaggerated the intensity of the reaction against Science and the strength of the religious revival? Yes. But between this simple opening and conclusion there lay a metaphysical mine-field into which few scholars were prepared to rush. One sympathises with Gaston Paris from the Collège de France who wanted to reflect a little more before committing himself on such complex issues as the relation between Science and Religion, the role of science in modern life, whether the unknowable in science is merely that which is not yet known, the nature of historical laws, whether it is possible to have morality without religion and to build a society on ethics other than those derived from Christianity.

The two most interesting replies came from Gabriel Tarde, the sociologist, and Berthelot, the chemist. Tarde went straight to the heart of the matter by suggesting that the debate was not really between Science and Religion, for no one in his right mind would claim that mathematics and physics have 'failed'. The debate was between *certain* sciences and religion: it is the young sciences of Psychology, Sociology and Anthropology which offended Brunetière's religious sensibilities. It was a very pertinent observation, but did little to satisfy Bernard-Lazare's aim. The intention behind the whole enquiry was to prove Brunetière wrong. Bernard-Lazare felt that Brunetière's challenge to science had to be answered and who could do it better than scientists? The scientist who went all the way with him was Berthelot, first in a brief reply to all the ten points and later in a much longer article published in the *Revue de Paris* (1 February 1895) on which Bernard-Lazare commented with great enthusiasm. The whole debate, which had many repercussions, including a cautiously worded pro-science article by the Archbishop of Paris, ended in a banquet offered to Berthelot. Some seven hundred guests were invited to celebrate the progress of Science and its victory. On the invitation cards were printed the following words: Homage to Science, the source of the liberation of the spirit.[9]

This curious enquiry on science was not a documentary like Jules Huret's enquiry on literature, but it constitutes a fascinating little chapter in the great debate of the late nineteenth century. In Bernard-Lazare's intellectual development it represents a milestone. His flirtation with mysticism is well and truly over. On the other hand he will always regard as *unscientific* the attitude of mind which dogmatically rejects in the name of science new fields of research or knowledge, however strange they may appear at the initial, obscure stage. A reactionary or conservative scientist was a great contradiction. This is the point so forcibly made in *La Télépathie et le Néo-spiritualisme* (1893), which is not a defence of telepathy but a plea addressed to scientists not to reject new phenomena out of hand before investigation, thus leaving the door wide open to mystifiers. Nor will he ever indiscriminately transfer to other domains theories or methods applicable in science. Accurate documentation in historical research for example was important, but a biological interpretation of the history of civilisations was a very different matter. One of his great criticisms of certain social thinkers will be that they look at social organisation in terms of biological organisation. The result might be tyranny: a head- or brain-dominated society.

1896 marks a date in Bernard-Lazare's journalistic career for two very different reasons. At the beginning of the year he fulfilled one of his most ardent dreams: he created his own weekly paper.

Alas, *L'Action Sociale*, born on 1 February 1896, died four weeks later, after only five issues. By the end of the year, the well-known and brilliant journalist whose career was then at its height and who had just added two more papers, *Le Paris* and *Le Voltaire*, to his long list of connections, found his career brought to a sudden close. No one wanted his signature; many of his former colleagues did not wish to know him or insulted him. The Dreyfus Affair had begun, and Bernard-Lazare was its prophet and – as far as the press was concerned – a pariah.

The first major article of *L'Action* (it became *L'Action Sociale* with the second issue, after it had been pointed out that there was a financial paper called *L'Action*), is devoted to the press: 'La Grève des Journalistes'. Faced with the increasing commercialisation of the press, with a new class of newspaper proprietors who, determined to get rich quickly, use writers like advertisements to attract clients, and who flatter their clients, particularly those who help to finance the paper – faced with such an immoral commercial enterprise, journalists and writers should go on strike. Half a dozen resolute men would suffice to 'refaire de la Presse du négoce, du chantage et de la corruption de nouveau la Presse des idées' (1 February). The following week he returned to the attack, adding that among the journalists' demands must be complete independence and the right to know how the paper is financed. Buying the silence of the press was not uncommon. Bernard-Lazare lashed out against named papers, which he accused of having been paid to keep silent over the Armenian question and over Panama. With the exception of the Dreyfus Case, all major issues would be aired in *L'Action Sociale*.

He returned again to the subject of the crisis of the press in the last issue, explaining how difficult it was for an opposition paper to survive. By opposition he meant opposition to the formidable combination of government and capitalism which constituted the official press and which held all the trump cards: the journalist was paid to mould public opinion according to the wishes and interests of his employer.

Bernard-Lazare obviously felt restricted in his freedom of speech, especially on the three subjects which most preoccupied him in 1896 and on which editorial censorship operated: anarchism, antisemitism and Dreyfus' innocence. This probably explains why in the summer of 1896 he campaigned against Drumont from the relatively less well-known radical paper *Le*

Voltaire,[10] whose Jewish editor (Klotz) approved, instead of from the *Echo de Paris* which had an infinitely larger circulation. Similarly, he turned to *Le Paris* to express himself freely on political matters. When Bernard-Lazare joined *Le Paris* (originally founded as a daily by Ranc) in March 1896, it had become a Republican evening paper and it was stressed that it was 'absolutely independent' and open to all shades of Republicans who were to be able 'to express their personal ideas freely'. Bernard-Lazare made full use of this freedom in fifteen biting and brilliant 'Tribunes Politiques'. The main targets were the dying Radical Party without ideals and ideas, and the Socialist Party, 'celui qui banquette à Saint-Mandé'. The latter split into two factions: the radical-socialists who flirted with the socialist-radicals and the 'marxistes-opportunistes' who made up for intellectual poverty and narrowness of soul with a wealth of formulae trotted out on every occasion. There were also progressives: 'Nous avons maintenant en France deux sortes de progressistes: ceux qui veulent rester en place et ceux qui veulent aller en arrière.'[11]

The last of the *Paris* articles is dated 2 October (1896). A month later the once 'distinguished contributor' was accused by his colleagues of apologising for treason (i.e. Dreyfus). Commenting on the abrupt end to what might have been a promising journalistic career, Charles Andler wrote: 'Le vrai journaliste c'est-à-dire le journaliste du vrai, dont la presse ne veut pas à cause qu'il apporte le vrai. . .voilà Lazare.'[12]

3

ANARCHISM

Introduction

Anarchism is still a misunderstood term likely to conjure up strange and horrific images. The anarchists with whom I am concerned are not terrorists, egotists, undisciplined misfits, lovers of chaos, advocates of free love, vegetarians, children of nature or any of the things which characterise the fringe groups which anarchism attracted and with which it was confused.

Most persistent has been the confusion between anarchism and terrorism. In French political history the image of the anarchist as a criminal terrorist, bent on destroying all forms of order and authority (two concepts which are rarely distinguished) by violent means, goes back to the French Revolution. It became widespread in the early 1890s which saw a wave of bombing and destruction all over France. Bombs, violence and terror became facts of life, all the more frightening because they could strike anywhere at any time, in public buildings and private houses. Most newspapers carried a column entitled 'la dynamite' which apart from listing all the attacks, told lurid stories and elaborated the myth of a world-wide underground anarchist organisation intent on destroying the very fabric of civilised society. The authorities reacted by meeting terror with terror. The police made indiscriminate searches and arrests on a large scale; the courts dealt severely not only with the guilty but also with the innocent. This in turn led to more violent acts of revenge on the part of the terrorists who called themselves anarchists and went to prison or the scaffold shouting 'long live anarchy'.

The story of the most notorious 'dynamiters' well illustrates the spiral of terror and violence which dominated public fears and debate for three years. It began with Ravachol who, in March 1892, placed bombs at the houses of two magistrates involved in a previous trial of two anarchist militants. Ravachol was caught by the police at Véry's, a restaurant. It was promptly bombed, even before his trial. Condemned to life imprisonment for the bomb outrages and, a little later, to death for a murder previously committed (he had a criminal record), the courage with which he faced death and the impertinent articulateness with which he had defended anarchist theories before the court made Ravachol into a revolutionary hero and a martyr, 'a sort of violent Christ [Ravachol was thirty-three when he was guillotined] whose legal death would usher in a new era'.[1] One of several songs composed in his honour, *La Ravachole* (inspired by the well-known Revolutionary song *La Carmagnole* of 1793), celebrated the bomb as the modern revolutionary weapon, taking the place of the traditional barricade, and promised death to the 'magistrats vendus. . . financiers ventrus. . .sénateurs gâteux. . .députés véreux'. All these were to be precise targets.

In November 1892 a young, well-educated student, Emile Henry, an admirer of Ravachol, decided to deal with the financiers in the shape of the offices of the Carmaux Mining Company (whose miners were on strike). The bomb was discovered before it exploded and was taken to the nearby police station where it went off, killing and injuring several people. For Henry, who had envisaged such a possibility, it was a stroke of good luck that the Company's offices and the police station were just the right distance apart. Very different from this cold-blooded killer (who got away) was Auguste Vaillant, a self-taught man who had lived all his life in grinding poverty. He did not intend to kill, only to injure. Hence he filled his bomb with nails. The target this time was Parliament (December 1893). In fact, Vaillant's bomb only slightly injured one or two people but he was nonetheless executed, an act which aroused wide-spread disapproval, including that of Emile Henry who decided to avenge Vaillant as well as the numerous anarchists who were arrested or harassed as a result of Vaillant's bomb. Outraged by this principle of collective guilt, Henry planted his bomb at the Café Terminus, near Gare Saint-Lazare (February 1894), at a time when the place was crowded with its usual clientèle of petits bourgeois. His intention, as he serenely explained to the jury at his trial, was to kill as many bourgeois as possible. 'Vous frappez en bloc, nous aussi, nous frappons en bloc.'[2] He went to the guillotine, shouting 'vive l'anarchie', as others had done before him.

The next and last act of revenge was not aimed at society *en bloc* but at the head of that society, Sadi Carnot, President of the Republic, because he had refused to pardon Vaillant. Jeronimo Caserio, a young, gentle, half-literate Italian assassinated the President (June 1894). Though less articulate than his predecessors, and having to use an interpreter, he too tried to read the judge and jury a lesson on the injustices, immoralities and murders committed every day by the capitalist State. Like the others, he died without regrets for what he had done, convinced that propaganda by word had to be realised in propaganda by deed.

What these misguided activists protested about had an authentic anarchist ring. Moreover, they were evidently familiar with anarchist literature and possibly influenced by it. But their methods were entirely alien to the philosophers and writers whose ideas were used, or rather misused, to justify criminal deeds. Kropotkin and Elisée Reclus were uncommonly gentle men, scholars of international repute, who never threw a bomb in their lives. The same applies to the well-known militants, Jean Grave, Charles Malato, Emile Pouget, Pelloutier and many others who did not envisage their action in terms of assassination, injury or terror; nor did they approve of those who did. Bernard-Lazare was a happily married man, he liked good food, elegant clothes and precious books, and he hated physical violence. Though outspoken, caustic and at times vehement in polemic, he even regretted the verbal violence which was a more common feature of anarchist literature, as indeed of most polemical literature of the time.

Anarchism was a Socialist movement whose essential doctrine could negatively be summarised as a liberal critique of authoritarian socialism and a socialist critique of capitalism. Proudhon, now as then a controversial figure, was generally recognised to be the modern 'maître', not so much for any specific doctrine, but because of his general vision of a society in which economic organisation based on the principles of justice, equality and liberty for one and all would take the place of political government as hitherto exercised by the State. He was the first political thinker to adopt, in 1840 (*Qu'est-ce que la propriété*), the term 'anarchie', signifying 'without a ruler', with the positive meaning of an organic social structure without need for conventional forms of rule artificially imposed from the top and usually benefiting only the ruling élite or class.

But Proudhon was an isolated anarchist thinker and critic of the capitalist democratic State and – even then – of Marx's political and pontifical socialism. It was not until the end of the century, after Bakunin's struggle against the Marxist domination of the First Socialist International and his eventual expulsion from it in 1872, that anarchism developed into an international movement with its own congresses, literature, national groups and federations. Throughout its life the movement was plagued by police infiltrators and *provocateurs*, held responsible for all terrorist outrages, and its members subjected to searches, deportations and arrests, all of which encouraged an unusual solidarity among men who spent many years of their lives in exile or dodging the authorities.

In spite of this constant struggle, or perhaps because of it, the movement attracted a considerable following in the 1890s, especially among writers and artists. The police were flabbergasted when, in 1894, they seized the subscription list of Grave's *La Révolte* and found that the country's leading intellectuals and writers subscribed to the 'subversive' journal. They had a similar shock when seizing the donors' list of Rousset's 'soupes-conférences', another 'subversive' enterprise which provided the hungry with a bowl of hot soup and food for thought, anarchist thought admittedly. The enterprise was supported by Zola, Anatole France and other respected figures. Mallarmé accompanied his contribution of 10 francs with the words: 'Voulez-vous accepter le don d'un homme qui n'est pas riche. De coeur avec votre oeuvre.' Sarah Bernhardt donated the princely sum of 100 francs as well as five seats for the theatre of *La Renaissance*.

It is not difficult to understand the attraction of libertarian socialism to young litterati who felt a vague, sentimental sympathy for the poor (outcasts from bourgeois society like themselves) and who saw in anarchism a parallel to or an extension of their own individualist aesthetics. Vielé-Griffin declared that all art was *anarchist* in essence, that is to say 'spontanément harmonieux et librement hiérarchique'. To Camille Mauclair 'l'anarchie est, primordialement, la réforme de l'éthique selon le principe de l'individualisme'. Barrès, the Barrès of 1893, favoured anarchism because he felt restricted 'dans un ordre social imposé par les morts'.[3] With most writers, this sympathy did not last long or go very deep. There were some exceptions however, and among them was Bernard-Lazare.

Under his direction the Symbolist review *Les Entretiens Poli-tiques et Littéraires* (see pp. 15–17) became an important vehicle for the expression of anarchist ideas, carrying extracts from Proudhon's *La Justice* (May 1892), Stirner's writings ('Apologie du mensonge', November 1892), a hitherto unpublished manu-script by Bakunin on *La Commune de Paris* (August and October 1892), a discussion of Kropotkin's *La Conquête du Pain* (April 1892) and of Jean Grave's *La Société mourante et l'anarchie* (July 1893), a work which did much to popularise anarchist ideas and which was prosecuted in 1894. Grave himself explained to the *compagnons* of the *Entretiens* 'L'idée anarchique et ses développements' (March 1893) and Elisée Reclus welcomed them (July 1892) to the social revolution. Not all of those who wrote fiery articles stayed to join the battle but among them were some genuine fighters. The politically unstable Paul Adam was one of the least reliable and most violent of the *Entretiens* anarchists, singing the praise of Ravachol: 'son sang sera l'exemple où s'abreuveront de nouveaux courages et de nouveaux martyrs' (July 1892). Interestingly enough, a fair number of 'literary' anarchists expressed sympathy for Ravachol and Emile Henry. Few of the 'real' anarchists did so. Bernard-Lazare remained strangely silent on the subject, neither condemning nor condoning the 'propagandists by deed' as if he did not have the heart to condemn publicly criminal acts of which he must have disap-proved but which had an insane sort of heroism in a non-heroic age.

Critics do Bernard-Lazare an injustice when they speak of his 'literary' anarchism or 'flirtations' with anarchism. It was probably fortunate for him that the police, who started keeping a fairly regular watch on his activities in April 1893, also inclined towards thinking that he was merely following the fashion of other young 'bourgeois chics' (though at times they evidently had second thoughts). The fact that Bernard-Lazare continued to dress with meticulous care and even, according to one report, 'ondule sa chevelure', confirmed their view. Having a wife did not correspond to the police image of the anarchist either. Mme Bernard-Lazare is sometimes referred to as his mistress.[4] In the hostile bourgeois press his fashionable ties and the cut of his suit gave rise to comments about anarchist dilettantes. Elegantly dressed he may have been, but there was nothing sham about his anarchism, which was no passing mood or opinion but an outlook on life, a way of thought, an aspiration towards freedom and social justice which he embraced with passion and to which he remained faithful.

Anxious to correct the public image of the anarchist and to set the record straight for future historians, Augustin Hamon, himself a libertarian journalist who later became a disciple of George Bernard Shaw, asked leading figures to explain how and why they became 'socialist anarchists'. In reply to this enquiry, Bernard-Lazare explained how an instinctive rebellion against anything that he was *ordered* to do led to a youthful period of fierce individualism. As the years passed, he came to see his own chains in the wider perspective of everybody's chains.

> De mes propres sentiments, j'ai induit les sentiments de ceux qui, plus ou moins perpétuellement, sont esclaves et ce qui m'était apparu comme odieux à moi-même m'a paru odieux pour tous.[5]

At this stage the libertarian philosopher made the crucial discovery of poverty, the greatest enslavement of all because it paralyses the spirit. Economic misery makes slaves of men in all respects. 'La question du ventre', 'la conquête du pain' had to be settled first. He turned to socialism and before long, some time in 1891, to anarchism.

> J'ai vécu, j'ai vu autour de moi souffrir des misérables; j'ai connu la lutte atroce du capital et du prolétariat, j'ai touché du doigt les mille injustices sociales... Pendant quelque temps j'ai cru que les panacées du socialisme suffiraient... Bientôt la façon dont elles étaient présentées par les marchands d'orviétan qui les vendent, m'en dégoûta, et d'ailleurs j'en compris la vanité... Jusqu'à présent les révolutions n'ont été faites que pour changer le mode du gouvernement... Les socialistes ne feraient ni plus ni moins; ils créeraient un état nouveau, une contrainte, une puissance... Ce sont ces convictions lentement et abstraitement élaborées qui m'ont rendu anarchiste.[6]

We have here expressed the two essential sources, the two negative poles of Bernard-Lazare's anarchism: anger at social injustice and fear of State socialism. The question of social injustice was closely linked with Republican democracy, with the capitalist State into which the ideal of the French Revolution had degener-

ated. It is under these two general headings, Republican democracy and State socialism, that we shall examine Bernard-Lazare's
fundamental anarchist ideas. The discussion is based on a great
number of articles and studies, the most important of which are
listed below.[7]

Republican democracy: liberty, equality, fraternity?

The Republic was an early disappointment to this child of the
Republic. He had been taught to love and respect it; he had
grown up with a certain vision of its ideal and he found that the
reality fell far short of it. 'La Troisième République, après un
règne de vingt ans sans grandeur et sans gloire, a laissé les coeurs
vides, les esprits inquiets. . .'[8] This had already been the reaction
of the young symbolist who had tried to escape from the soulless
present by turning to a more heroic and poetic past. Anarchism
brought him back to the present at which he now looked in a
more specifically social and political context. It also led him to
question the Republican ideal itself: to wonder whether, from a
social point of view, there ever had been much of an ideal. After
a great deal of critical reading on the French Revolution, and
this was of course the time of reappraisal of the great myth by
socialist and anarchist thinkers alike, he became acutely conscious
of the shortcomings in the individualist philosophy of the Republic's founding fathers. He now saw his past education, notably
the quarrel with his history teachers, in a new light. Their enthusiasm for the Republic, which he had found so conspicuously
lacking in grandeur, no longer appeared as a generation-gap but
as a class-gap. They wore the blinkers of their class, proclaiming
that all was well with progress and humanity because the bourgeoisie was making undoubted progress. The existence of the
greatest poverty side by side with the greatest wealth in the
'République des républicains' was a scandal, but it was an inevitable scandal, given the peculiar revolutionary traditions of the
governing liberal bourgeoisie, traditions which accorded perfectly
with the philosophy of capitalism and the ideal of capitalist
democracy.

Equality before the law, for example, was held to be a sacred
principle. But, exclaims Bernard-Lazare, this abstract, legal notion
of equality is a fiction, devoid of any social reality. How can
poor and rich be equal before the law? In a wider human context
too the principle was absurd and unjust, since men are patently

not born equal. This reproach will also be addressed to socialism which aspired to make men equal by law.

What about the other sacred principle, liberty? To Bernard-Lazare's mind real liberty without social justice was very limited; freedom from want was an essential condition of liberty. 'Les prophètes se croyaient envoyés pour travailler à l'avènement de la justice, ce qui les frappait le plus était évidemment l'inégalité des conditions; tant qu'il y aurait des pauvres et des riches, on ne pouvait espérer le règne de l'équité.'[9] The revolutionary bourgeoisie understands liberty in a very different sense: everybody has the right to vote and everybody is free to make a fortune on the Stock Exchange. The individual freedom of citizens to *compete* against each other must not be interfered with. The result was a paradise for capitalists who were free to exploit others.

Fraternity was a principle inscribed on every public building. It was part of the Republican Trinity. Properly understood, fraternity could indeed be a revolutionary principle for it comprises justice and humanity, it replaces competition by cooperation. It appeals to a spirit of solidarity instead of rivalry. Fraternity in Republican democracy has become a bureaucratically organised State charity, and a highly inadequate charity at that.

It must be said that these are not mere destructive criticisms *in abstracto* encouraged by the reading of Proudhon and Bakunin, the two great masters with whose ideas Bernard-Lazare was very familiar. The social situation largely justified the criticism. Jacques Chastenet, the well-known historian of the Third Republic is no anarchist and he has written of the totally inadequate social legislation in *La République des républicains:* 'Les démocrates français, encore imbus de la tradition individualiste de la Révolution, hésitent à s'engager, même timidement, sur la route de réformes.'[10] In 1890, at a time of great social unrest, with 313 strikes and legions of unemployed and destitute, Parliament decided to devote one session a week to the discussion of 'social questions'. After much discussion of working hours, the law of November 1892 reduced the maximum of 12 hours a day to 11 hours. As a special humanitarian bonus, the law provided for one obligatory rest-day a week for women and adolescents. 'Ce sera le premier accroc sérieux apporté par la République des républicains au principe de non-intervention en matière sociale', Chastenet comments. Subsequent long and heated debates on the *possibility* of a tax on income and revenue were not designed to enhance Bernard-Lazare's opinion of the social conscience of *La République des républicains*. 'They are teasing', was his sarcastic comment.[11]

The tragic Hayem affair of July 1890, briefly evoked in an article, was a shattering illustration of several things. First of all, there was the despair of stark poverty: desperate and destitute, a family of eight committed suicide on 14 July, while Paris was celebrating the fall of tyrannies. Then there was the reaction of a conscience-stricken society which covered the coffins of the children with flowers. When the feeling of guilt had worn off, society looked for scapegoats on which to discharge its responsibility. An immorality to be expected when religion is not taught at school, some exclaimed. Others scrutinised the father's past life for murderous instincts. In general there was an outcry against the *Assistance Publique* which was not doing its job. The Socialist review *La Bataille*[12] took the opportunity to publish some eloquent figures: the Paris Assistance Publique spent a third of its inadequate budget on administrative costs. The money allocated to 14,574 social assistance boards (bureaux de bienfaisance) throughout the country worked out finally at four and a half centimes per day per destitute person! Bernard-Lazare proposed a more drastic solution in *Le Justicier*. This is the story of the founder of a National Institute of Pickpockets whose prophetic mission it is to take from the rich and give to the poor. Whether social theft is justified was much discussed in anarchist circles. Bernard-Lazare's story is less a justification for social theft than a warning addressed to the capitalist Republic.

Although Bernard-Lazare's objections to Republican democracy were primarily of a social and economic nature, directed against the capitalist system and its cruel philosophy of 'libre concurrence' which made slaves of the majority, grievances against 'la nouvelle monarchie' were not lacking. They became more frequent and angry as government and police, in reaction to the terrorist outbreaks of 1892 to 1894, engaged in a veritable witch-hunt, in which freedom of expression and association was seriously endangered. 'Nouvelle Monarchie' was his favourite term for the democratic State, potentially as tyrannical as any other State. Whether power rested in the hands of one man or several hundred deputies was a question of number not of freedom, and the fact that an ill-educated people, easily beguiled by oratory or demagogy, participated every four or five years in

the comedy of elections, did not alter that fact. Once elected, the
sacred reign of the parliamentary majority began. The people
at large, having expressed its will and sovereignty by delegating
power to representatives over whom it had no control for the next
four or five years, irrespective of what might happen, had no
longer any real say and was no longer consulted. The principle
of 'the sovereignty of the people' and 'the general will', as
practised in the democratic State, was another fiction which the
enfants terribles of democracy tried to explode. Bernard-Lazare
believed that Bastilles would fall without the ballot-box and that
new ones might be created with it. He preferred discussion to
voting, common consent to majority tyranny, contracts freely
concluded by all in the interests of all and always open to renewal,
to laws passed by parliamentary majorities.

It was perhaps the strong Proudhonian anti-democratic element
in anarchist thought which shocked his contemporaries, Republicans and Socialists alike. It may still offend liberal sensibilities
today. And yet it must be said that anarchism recognised some
hundred years ago what liberal opinion now more readily admits
to be weaknesses in the democratic system. Direct democracy,
community politics, public participation, decentralisation, devolu-
tion in favour of regional administration, government by smaller
councils and communities directly responsible to the electorate,
the questioning of government by political parties, all these terms
and notions, so familiar to us today, were part and parcel of the
anarchist city-philosophy. But in the 1890s proud democrats
thought it incorrigibly reactionary to look back, as Kropotkin
did for example, to the Greek city, Athenian democracy, medieval
guilds and communes, to city societies organised on social lines in
which men enjoyed a greater measure of economic security and
personal freedom than in the increasingly bureaucratic modern
State. Anarchism was prophetic but not 'progressive' in the
Republican or Socialist sense. Its adherents were neither afraid
of history nor enamoured of everything modern. They most
certainly did not subscribe to the view that 1789 and the very
bourgeois Declaration of the Rights of Man and the Citizen
constituted the beginning of a golden age. Bernard-Lazare, for
example, tried to draw up a more meaningful charter of justice
and liberty based on the prophetic writings.[18] He was convinced
that there was more real socialism in the Gospels than in Jules
Guesde.

Of all the strange reputations that anarchism acquired, that of being anti-social is perhaps the strangest. There can hardly be a more society – and community – centred doctrine, with its almost fanatical belief in solidarity, in man being naturally 'solidaire'. There is no anarchist who has not repeated in his own way Bakunin's idea that 'la loi de solidarité sociale est la première loi humaine; la liberté est la seconde loi'. The second depends on the first, for the individual can only be free, and human, within society. The crucial distinction of course is between State and society. The former always has an authoritarian basis; without this basis, the State could not function. The democratic State, claiming as it does that it represents the general will, can be more authoritarian than most, for in the name of the general will it weighs on the liberty of one and all. Society, on the other hand, is something natural and organic, with its own dynamic, its own order, its own harmonies, its own unwritten laws of intercourse. It was anarchism's optimistic, perhaps naively optimistic, belief that a free and just society could function on the basis of this inner, organic order, without any need for more artificial orders to be imposed from the top. The anarchist never doubted that a free and just society was possible in theory, because he believed that justice (solidarity) and freedom were two fundamental human aspirations. The raw material, then, was there – human nature. The question was how to get rid of the forces which had perverted, demoralised and desocialised man.

The French democratic State combined two major perversions which Bernard-Lazare traced back to the French Revolution. The State was individualist in social matters and centralising in everything else; capitalist in economics and collectivist in intellectual spheres; it tried hard to unite politically and intellectually into a 'République une et indivisible' a socially and economically divided community. Anarchism preferred it the other way round: economic communism (not to be understood as State monopoly but community ownership of wealth and distribution according to individual needs) but strict decentralisation and diversity in everything else. Bernard-Lazare wrote an enthusiastic review of Kropotkin's *La Conquête du Pain*[14] because it embodied these two principles, communism and freedom.

State socialism

If the bourgeois capitalist was the enemy, the Socialist was the 'frère-ennemi' and, as is often the case, the fratricidal war was even more bitter and mutually wounding.

United by a more or less common ideal of social justice, at least in the broadest sense of the word, the two Socialist brothers were utterly divided over the means of achieving it. To the anarchist the seizure of political power, the creation of a Socialist State, was anathema. Economic equality would perhaps be achieved, but at what price? Nor did anarchists believe the promise that State socialism would merely be a temporary means until the middle classes had been brought to heel and the proletariat was capable of governing. They rather feared that the new governing élite, once in power, would mistake the means for the end and continue to rule over an economically liberated but spiritually enslaved people with the iron hand of a red Bismarck.

Bernard-Lazare had a nightmare vision of what a Socialist State ruling by decree, without tolerating any opposition or discussion, might be like. One needs to remember that in 1892 there was no such State in existence and it needed imaginative understanding to foresee what authoritarian communism might lead to. True, the conduct of affairs at Socialist congresses provided a foretaste and gave the libertarian imagination something to feed on.

> Loi sur le travail, sur sa réglementation, sur sa durée, loi sur la propriété collective, loi sur la répartition des biens, loi sur l'intruction, loi sur l'hospitalité, loi sur les secours aux faibles, loi sur les invalides du travail. Et ainsi on en arrive au nom de la liberté à la plus étrange, à la plus folle des conceptions, à celle d'après laquelle les moindres actes des hommes seront prévus, ordonnés, réglementés d'après des lois. . . Hors des syndicats et des corporations futures, nul homme ne pourra prétendre à l'existence. . .quand l'Etat oppressif aura annihilé toute initiative, détruit toute individualité, réprimé toute aspiration; quand les actions de la vie seront soumises aux règles strictes d'une rigoureuse législation; quand les hommes seront ployés sous le plus effroyable despotisme qui jamais ait asservi la terre, alors ils comprendront le sens du mot liberté et ardemment ils le voudront conquérir.[15]

In another article, sarcastically entitled *Nécessité du Socialisme*,

he develops the paradox that the collectivist State is a necessary tyranny before both justice and freedom can be achieved. Present capitalist society, the argument runs, cannot hold out much longer; it is destroying itself. To the masses of workers brain-washed rather than educated by Socialist propaganda, to some generous but short-sighted minds, even to the liberal bourgeoisie which is frightened out of its wits by its own *misconceptions* about anarchist disorder, terror and lawlessness, State socialism may seem the only viable alternative to the dying bourgeois society. It will take the accession to power of the new 'aristocratie du travail', more oppressive than the aristocracy of birth and the aristocracy of money because it has no respect for the individual and the human person, to teach the world the value of liberty and convert it to 'l'Anarchie libératrice'.

It is not surprising, after such enthusiastic expressions of pure anarchism, that Bernard-Lazare came to be on the police black-list, in the bad books of the Socialists and greatly esteemed by such anarchist purists as Jean Grave, who reprinted in the Literary Supplement of *La Révolte* some fifteen of Bernard-Lazare's articles (between 1891 and 1894).[16]

The paradox of State socialism as an inevitable, catastrophic stage on the way to ultimate salvation is not representative of Bernard-Lazare's more usual hope – and striving – that the transformation of the capitalist State into anarchist society could be effected without the intermediate Marxist despotism. But in common with other anarchists he did believe that capitalism was a dying force, that it was burning itself out in a last flaming sunset, and that Marxism was the threatening new dawn which had to be stopped while there was still time. In his own camp, he pleaded with the *compagnons* not to erect walls of doctrine among themselves, and between themselves and other libertarian or non-Marxist groups such as the Dutch workers' party, the independent German socialists and William Morris' Socialist League. Free expression of ideas was essential but, in order to provide an effective counter-force to organised Marxism, a certain *entente* was essential.[17] Such calls for unity had little effect. The lack of cohesion among the small, scattered and diverse groups, each fiercely independent, was anarchism's great weakness.

With the aim of establishing communication, he acted as self-appointed liaison officer, collected and passed on information, organised help for needy 'compagnons' in transit in France, sometimes putting up in his own flat 'des individus d'allures équivoques'.[18] According to the same police report he received newspapers from the four corners of the earth, travelled a great deal, and had a voluminous correspondence. Of the latter little has survived, unfortunately, but what remains – letters to Max Nettlau, Jean Grave, the odd letters in the police records, various other *témoignages*, all testify to Bernard-Lazare's wide contacts with the movement, in Belgium, Italy, Germany, Rumania, even in Australia, and in England, where the Whitechapel Jewish anarchist groups and their paper *The Worker's Friend* aroused his special interest.

In common with many others, he thought it was important to maintain an effective anarchist presence and opposition at International Socialist Congresses. The moment was crucial and the international forum was the ideal place for breaking the Marxist and German domination of the socialist world and returning to the libertarian socialism which had its traditions in France. What angered him was that French Socialists, notably people such as Jaurès, instead of acting as a liberalising influence, let themselves be regimented by the German Socialist Party. Instead of rescuing Marx from the Marxists, French socialism was contaminated by them. Bernard-Lazare's quarrel was not with Marx, at least not with the master's materialist conception of history which was original and useful. 'C'était une philosophie, une vue profonde des nations et des peuples.' The Marxist party was a very different matter:

> Je connais peu de groupes d'hommes dont la médiocrité moyenne et individuelle soit aussi grande. Elle n'a d'égale que leur sectarisme... La tête est uniquement meublée de formules dont ils n'ont jamais essayé de peser la valeur, ces pauvres hères, dont l'indigence d'esprit est incroyable... Ils ont une âme étroite, une cervelle étriquée de barbacole, ou plutôt de cuistre, en même temps qu'une vanité dérisoire et pitoyable de pédant de collège.[19]

The struggle between authoritarian socialism and libertarian socialism waged at the International Congresses from 1889 to 1896 was bound to end in failure, as it had done for Bakunin twenty years earlier; for the Socialist assembly ruled by majority, and the majority excommunicated its troublesome minority in the famous London congress of 1896. In his caustic account of that extraordinary meeting which he attended 'officially' as reporter for the *Echo de Paris* and *Paris*, Bernard-Lazare wanted to persuade his readers, and perhaps himself, that the congress would go down in history as a failure for authoritarian socialism because anarchist expulsion could only be procured by the basest political manoeuvring. That may be so, but the congress marked a decided victory for Marxism.

At home, Bernard-Lazare fiercely opposed participation by Socialists in bourgeois Parliaments (at least until 1897, and even then he retained doubts about 'parlementarisme') as a matter of principle and also because he thought it useless and, possibly, dangerous.[20] The Socialist Millerand had sat in Parliament since 1885. What did he achieve? Over forty Socialists entered in 1893. What were they likely to achieve? In order to make any impact, parliamentary Socialists would be obliged to employ the usual parliamentary strategies of alliances, lobbying and bargaining. What Bernard-Lazare most feared in these opportunist 'combinaisons de couloir' and 'manoeuvres diplomatiques' was a dubious alliance between the Socialist Party and the dying Radical Party. Once again, as throughout the history of nineteenth-century French revolutions, the worker would be used to fight the battle for the bourgeoisie, this time for the lower middle-classes who needed an ally in their fight against big capitalism. And what was the purpose of such an alliance? To impose social reforms acceptable to the Radicals, on to a reluctant Parliament and hostile *patronat*. It was the whole system which needed changing. An eight-hour working day would not transform it nor would strikes for higher wages. Besides, even supposing parliamentary Socialists succeed in getting through some modest social legislation, what guarantees were there that they would be observed by hostile employers or even insisted on by helpless workers anxious to keep their jobs? In *L'Action Sociale*, Pelloutier, one of Bernard-Lazare's closest collaborators, listed examples of the law of 1892 on working hours being contravened four years after it had come into force. To be effectively enforced, a legion of government inspectors would be needed. And even then, as Pelloutier pointed out, an unscrupulous employer had a hundred ways of keeping to the letter of the law and ignoring its spirit.

So far we have considered anarchism mainly in its negative – and as such very useful – role as a 'socialist critique of capitalism and a liberal critique of socialism'. Implicit in this is an ideal, that of a just and free society in which each receives according to his needs and gives according to his ability, a society in which respect for the freedom of others is the limitation put on personal freedom. It remains for us to consider how anarchism thought the ideal might be achieved.

The moralisation of society: propaganda by word
Education was the anarchist's answer. Education was their great passion, the supreme tactic of the 'propagandistes par la parole' who were optimistic enough to believe that all men could be re-educated into solidarity. Socialism was ultimately a question of morality and in the *long term* only education could achieve 'la moralisation de la société tout entière'. It was a touching faith in education which Bernard-Lazare fully shared.

In a manifesto-article in yet another new libertarian review, *Le Courrier Social Illustré* (1 November 1894), he distinguished between political, vote-catching Socialist propaganda and the aim of anarchist propaganda.

> Les politiciens socialistes parlent à un peuple et ils ne font pas le moindre effort pour éduquer ce peuple; ils emploient toutes leurs heures à des statistiques qui leur permettent d'escompter le nombre futur des bulletins de vote. . .Ce que tous ces politiciens ne font pas, c'est à nous, les indépendants, de le faire. Toutes les écoles sont entre les mains de la bourgeoisie et du gouvernement qui possèdent ainsi le plus sûr moyen de diriger les cervelles. Groupons-nous et fondons des écoles privées. . . Groupons-nous encore, pénétrons dans les syndicats, créons y des cours et des conférences. . .
> Organisons de libres universités ou viendront aussi tous les fils des bourgeois qui renient leur caste et qui abandonnent leurs privilèges. Quant à ceux qui n'entrent pas dans les écoles, qui s'éloignent des syndicats, qui ne vont pas dans les universités, éduquons-les quand même. Créons une littérature pour eux, naïve comme leur coeur, profonde et simple comme leur âme, racontons-leur des contes qu'ils puissent comprendre, libérons-les des infâmes littératures qu'ils subissent, accoutumons-les au commerce des idées, faisons-leur connaître le beau. Intruisons-les par le théâtre,

intruisons-les par le roman. Fondons des bibliothèques, des
publications; mettons à leur portée, dans des brochures peu
coûteuses, les oeuvres des romanciers, des poètes, les
semences des philosophes qui ont travaillé au cours des
siècles à la libération de l'esprit humain. En un mot,
essayons de changer ce troupeau aveugle et captif en un
peuple d'hommes libres.

Let us stress a few points in this vast programme which by this
time, in 1894, had in part already been realised.[21]

The aim is a revolution in ideas and attitudes through a wide,
humanist education of worker and bourgeois. Education of the
uneducated workers first, so that they can direct their own affairs
as soon as possible. Anarchism viewed with horror the emergence
of an élite of working-class leaders who would think and speak
for the people. The necessity for temporary intellectual leadership,
preferably entrusted to writers and artists, was conceded but the
aim was to hand over direction, not to keep it. It is in the masses,
anarchism believed, that the dynamic of any movement or revolution ultimately lies. Education also includes the bourgeois. Bernard-Lazare firmly believed that preaching to the unconverted,
however hardened, was an essential task. One police report describes him as preparing to spread the anarchist gospel, through
lectures, in the wealthier Parisian districts. Education of the
capitalist was his reply to the Socialist class struggle and faith in
legislation. The ultimate aim was a classless – and governmentless
– society of workers and producers, not a struggle to the death
between classes and the creation of 'an aristocracy of labour'
imposing justice and happiness by a multiplicity of laws. In a
dialogue with a Socialist comrade he admits that this is perhaps
too idealistic but he rejects the Socialist illusion.

Se borner à éveiller dans les intelligences frustes, et dans les
coeurs égoistes, les notions de justice et de liberté qui doivent
être les bases intellectuelles et morales de la société future
serait insuffisant pour amener l'avènement de cette société;
mais imaginer que ce monde serait rebâti par des syndicats
ou par des législateurs, voilà une illusion plus singulière
encore.[22]

Practising what he preached, he threw himself body and soul
into 'la propagande par la parole'. There is hardly a review of

anarchist or generally libertarian tendency to which Bernard-Lazare did not contribute, from the *Entretiens Politiques et Littéraires* (1891) to *L'Action Sociale* (1896). Among his most anarchist-inspired articles are some which appeared in the 'bourgeois' press (*L'Evénement, Le Journal, Paris, L'Echo de Paris*) which speaks very well for the remarkable freedom of expression enjoyed by libertarian writers until 1894. He did a great deal of public lecturing to various groups with characteristic names, 'Les Égaux du XVII', 'l'Idée Nouvelle', 'Le Nouveau-Monde', 'Les Etudiants socialistes révolutionnaires internationalistes (ESRI)'. Thanks to publication in reviews, the text of some of these lectures has survived and together with some fifty articles and studies they make up a considerable, lively and wide-ranging corpus of libertarian writings which still makes fascinating reading today.

As in other spheres of activity, there are several unfulfilled projects. Bernard-Lazare never had enough time to write all the works which he planned and not infrequently announced as 'appearing shortly'. Essays on Proudhon were announced in this way, as well as a work on *Le parti des Enragés pendant la Révolution*. It is evident from his correspondence with Max Nettlau,[23] who was engaged in a similar task, that he was collecting material for a history of anarchism with special emphasis on figures and groups from the French Revolution to the Commune (1871), who were forgotten or treated with contempt in 'official' histories of nineteenth-century revolutions (Baboeuf and his followers, the Enragés, Jacques Roux and Jean Varlet – whose petitions to the National Convention he traced to the British Museum collection of French Revolution pamphlets – Bellegarrigue, the communist groups of 1848, and so on). One can catch a glimpse of the spirit of the projected history, a view from the Left of a hundred years of revolutionary aspirations, in a lecture on *l'Histoire des doctrines révolutionnaires.*[24] It represents, among other things, an attempt to rehabilitate 'the mob' and its spokesmen, maligned or belittled by the Republic's middle-class historians and history teachers. It also contains a warning: having toppled the Monarch and declared the Heavens empty, the Voltairian bourgeoisie is ever ready to use the forces of law and order to protect its property and ensure that it can practice in peace, unhindered by subversive syndicalist organisations, the commandment of its new gods: 'enrichissez-vous'.

Bakunin was another, more contemporary figure who had to be rescued from 'absurd legends', this time largely created by Marxists. Bernard-Lazare encouraged Max Nettlau to prepare for publication in France a volume of Bakunin's writings, and he acted as intermediary between Nettlau and Stock who published the first of several volumes in 1895. He also helped Nettlau with the introduction and himself wrote a much-appreciated study of Bakunin in the *Revue Blanche*.[25] What he admired least in the great Russian anarchist was the often violent expression of ideas. The ideas themselves he appreciated, though he preferred Kropotkin's calmer, more studious approach. Bakunin's uniqueness lay in his qualities as propagandist and apostle. He used to sleep, we are told, without taking off his clothes and boots, so as to be ready at a moment's notice to be on his way, spreading the gospel of justice and freedom. He was a magnificent organiser and a powerful leader but without ever seeking to rule or dominate. This is perhaps the kind of apostle Bernard-Lazare aspired to be.

Among the unfulfilled projects must also be included teaching at the *Université Nouvelle de Bruxelles*, the anarchist University founded by Elisée Reclus in 1894. For four years, from the opening session to 1898, Bernard-Lazare was listed as proposing to give a course of lectures (on the economic history of the Jews, a subject which became dear to his heart) but this too remained, alas, an intention, at least as far as we can see from available records.[26] Lack of time (the Dreyfus Affair was soon to preoccupy him) and also perhaps, initially, of resources (staff were not generally paid) prevented him from participating in the work of 'une école de la liberté' whose praise he sang.

> On a appelé cette université l'Université anarchiste. Si on a voulu dire par là qu'elle serait une université dans laquelle chaque professeur et chaque élève ne serait justiciable que de lui-même, une université où toute opinion aurait le droit de se manifester, où il n'aurait pas de hiérarchie de science, où chacque individu serait laissé à son indépendance et en même temps aidé par le savoir de tous, on a eu raison de dire que cette université serait anarchiste, car elle n'est pas constituée comme un Etat, soumise à des chefs, à des credos, à des codes et à des lois.[27]

The history of this admirable institute (killed by the First World War, though its *Institut des Hautes Etudes* survived for many years) has never been written.[28] This is obviously not the place to do so. It must suffice to say that it was one of the most successful and durable educational ventures of the libertarian movement. Given the importance of education as the means which would ultimately bring about the desired social and moral revolution, it was natural that anarchist thinkers should be concerned with the art of educating and should try and put into practice their pedagogical theories, theories which seem of the utmost modernity today. The *Université Nouvelle*, obliged to function in an imperfect context, on the slenderest of budgets and with little support from the public at large, fell considerably short of the anarchist ideal of higher education. Nonetheless the University embodied some advanced principles which justify Bernard-Lazare's enthusiasm. Teaching, for example, was considered to be a matter of communication and discussion between teachers and taught. Thus, lecturers provided synopses of their lectures before delivering them, so that much of the lecture-time could be devoted to discussion. As far as possible, teaching was entrusted not to teachers of subjects (anarchists distrusted the 'classe de professeurs') but to people who actually practised them (chemists taught chemistry, lawyers law, writers taught literature, and so on). A similar concrete approach guided the manner in which subjects were taught: science in laboratories, botany in nature, the history of art in museums. Apart from conventional degree subjects, the Institut des Hautes Etudes, the real pride of the establishment, provided non-examined adult courses in a variety of subjects, including what were then relatively new subjects: sociology, criminology, drama, Flemish, statistics, economic and social history. The financial arrangement, dictated by idealism (teachers were generally unpaid) and necessity (students paid fees, though with assistance if required) was a major drawback, unhappily restricting the university to those who could financially afford to teach and learn. Needless to say there was student representation on all decision-making bodies. When Bernard-Lazare said that all opinions would enjoy freedom of expression he was not exaggerating. Had he lectured there, on the economic history of the Jews, he would have been Edmond Picard's colleague, and Picard, lawyer, writer and historian, expounded his antisemitic and racial theories in all freedom.

L'année terrible

1894 is 'l'année terrible' in the history of anarchist *terror*, which had nothing to do with anarchism, and government counter-terror which made no distinction between assassins and anarchists. The government's panic-striken reaction to the series of explosions which followed Vaillant's bomb in Parliament (9 December 1893) and ended in Caserio's assassination of the President of the Republic (24 June 1894) was to strike hard, quickly and indiscriminately at anyone remotely connected or under suspicion of having connections with the anarchist movement. Massive searches, seizures, arrests were the order of the day. Some very rough justice was dealt out, especially in the daily trials before the courts of the *police correctionnelle* which did not have the limelight of the big trials at the *cour d'assises*. 'Pour garder sous les verrous des individus', Henri Varennes wrote in his account of these savage little trials, 'on tourmenta des textes, on modifia des jurisprudences, on prononça des condamnations...préventives et des peines absolument exagérées. La magistrature crut devoir seconder le gouvernement dans sa lutte contre l'anarchie; son prestige n'y gagna point.'[29] As he rightly remarks, this was hardly designed to enhance the *compagnons'* respect for law and the judiciary. It explains why so many of Bernard-Lazare's writings, especially at and after this period, were to be concerned with judges, courts and the administration of justice. He was all prepared for the Dreyfus Affair. Not least instructive in this respect was the counter-terror campaign in which the press engaged, with its daily lurid stories, insinuations and calls for anarchist heads to roll.

Anarchist writers and intellectuals, whether actually militants or merely sympathisers, became a favourite target of attack. They were considered to be the head, the inspiration, behind the terrorists' murderous arms. To a certain extent this is undoubtedly true. Emile Henry, Vaillant, even the uneducated Caserio, a baker's assistant, justified their 'propagande par le fait' on the basis of the 'propagande par la parole' of well-known anarchist writers. But they also saw themselves as heirs to Diderot, Voltaire, Hugo, Darwin, Spencer, Zola and how many others! Bernard-Lazare who did not escape attack from fellow journalists for his openly expressed sympathies with anarchism, was shocked by the atmosphere of 'down with writers and burn the books'. Wherever he could he defended anarchist intellectuals in the bourgeois press, notably the art critic Fénéon and Jean Grave. At Grave's trial in February 1894, for incitement to violence in his book *La Société mourante et l'anarchie*, he appeared as witness, in company with Mirbeau and Elisée Reclus. After Grave's condemnation, he organised a petition in the press for his liberation and he went to see him in prison – which was brave because such things were noted.

He was indeed afraid of being arrested himself,[30] a distinct possibility in view of the famous or infamous 'lois scélérates' of 1893 and 1894. The first of these laws (rushed through the Chamber on 11 December 1893, two days after Vaillant's bomb) was already dangerous to anyone defending in the press acts considered to be criminal. The second law (voted on 15 December 1893) virtually made it illegal to belong or even to have connections with associations considered to be 'des associations de malfaiteurs'. The third law (introduced 9 July 1894, two weeks after President Carnot's assassination) struck at all those who 'font par un moyen quelconque acte de propagande anarchique'. After stormy debates the law was passed 26 July 1894. For the first and only time in his life, Bernard-Lazare fled.

On 28 July 1894 he sought refuge in Belgium, not in Brussels this time but at Knocke, a quiet little place nearby, where he wisely stayed in a bourgeois hotel without seeing any 'compagnons'. But his reputation had gone before him and the Brussels police urgently requested information (1 August). After a further telegram (12 August) repeating the request, the Paris Sûreté finally replied (18 August), pointing out that 'Bernard-Lazare fait partie de cette école de jeunes littérateurs qui par dilettantisme ou conviction philosophique se sont fait les théoriciens de la doctrine anarchiste. Bernard-Lazare n'est pas noté aux sommiers judiciaires.' By this time, Bernard-Lazare was already back in Paris, urging other exiles to return, for the 'lois scélérates' had to be fought. The most encouraging sign in this dangerous period for the freedom of expression was the jury's verdict at the *Procès des Trente*, also called the 'Procès des Intellectuels' (6 August 1894) because half of the accused were anarchist writers and militants or sympathisers (Grave, Faure, Fénéon, Paul Reclus, Chatel, Pouget, Matha and others) and the other half known thieves and crooks. Together they were charged with belonging to the same 'association de malfaiteurs'. In spite of press terror, government pressure and the eloquence of the public prosecutor trying to persuade the jury that terrorists, thieves, crooks and intellectuals were all members of the same subversive organisation, the jury acquitted the intellectuals and found the criminals guilty. A wind of sanity blew through France. Not for long, alas, for a few months later the arrest of Captain Dreyfus was announced. This Affair too was to have its 'association de malfaiteurs', called the 'syndicate', and its own 'Procès des Intellectuels'.

Bernard-Lazare was to play a leading role in the Dreyfus Affair and in the battle against antisemitism which was part of it and in which he had already become engaged. Although both these events added their own complexity to his anarchist ideas, it could be said that his thoughts and actions were guided by what is fundamental in anarchist ideology.[31]

4

'LE JUDAISME VOILÀ L'ENNEMI'

Background

In the year in which Bernard-Lazare arrived in Paris an epoch-making book was published in France. It was to change his whole life, though at first it does not seem to have made much immediate impact on him. Had Drumont's *La France Juive* (1886) remained an isolated success, breathtaking though that success was, it would probably not have worried this aspiring writer with his passion for literature and esoteric philosophies. His thoughts were else-where; he did not feel particularly Jewish, was not concerned with Jewry, Judaism or the Jewish question, and most certainly did not recognise himself in the portrait drawn of the Jew in this fantastic book which enjoyed, thanks to a lively press debate, an immense *succès de scandale*. It soon became clear that *La France Juive* was very much more than a *succès de scandale*. The original edition was followed by an illustrated edition and by a cheap popular edition (1887). *Le Petit Journal*, the paper with the widest circulation, published the book in instalments, and a little later, in 1892, distributed free copies of an abridged version. The book was reviewed in all the leading dailies, from *Le Figaro* and *Le Temps* downwards, was seriously examined in serious reviews of all persuasions, from the academic and Catholic *Revue des deux mondes* to the Socialist and anticlerical *Revue socialiste*. Three further works flowed from Drumont's pen in rapid succession, all successful: *La France Juive devant l'opinion* (1886), *La Fin d'un monde* (1888), *La Dernière Bataille* (1890).[1]

By 1889 and 1890 antisemitism, barely four years old as a movement of ideas with any impact in France, was already aspiring to be an independent political party. Willette, a much-appreciated artist, presented himself as antisemitic candidate at the 1889 legislative elections and for that purpose designed his

own memorable election poster. Compared to some of the illustrations found in the illustrated edition of *La France Juive*, Willette's
drawing is relatively non-violent: it is only the Talmud that lies
broken at the feet of a united group of what looks like worker,
intellectual and high-ranking military, all armed with a variety
of tools and weapons and led by a lusty, viking-looking hero with
a double axe. The words accompanying the drawing, presumably
constituting the party programme, read as follows: 'Les Juifs ne
sont grands, que parce que nous sommes à genoux! . . .
LEVONS-NOUS! Ils sont cinquante mille à bénéficier seuls du
travail acharné et sans espérance de trente millions de Français
devenus leurs esclaves tremblants. Il n'est pas question de religion.
Le Juif est d'une race différente et ennemie de la nôtre. Le
JUDAÏSME voilà l'ennemi! En me présentant, je vous donne
l'occasion de protester avec moi contre la tyrannie Juive.'

Jacques de Biez, one of Drumont's earliest disciples and elected
vice-president of the National Antisemitic League, founded in
January 1890, explained the aspirations of the League: 'We are
National Socialists, because we attack international finance so
that we may have France for the French.'[2] With this national-
social programme, Drumont and another one of his lieutenants,
the Marquis de Morès, presented themselves at the Paris municipal elections in April 1890. Neither won a seat but it was surely
a measure of success and not failure that Morès and Drumont,
with no programme other than variations on the theme of 'France
for the French' and 'Jews out', collected 950 and 613 votes in the
Socialist Saint-Ouen and the conservative Gros-Caillou districts
respectively.

If the antisemitic party had not as yet managed to enter
Parliament, it could rely on the sympathy of certain Boulangist
deputies. François Laur, for example, proposed the expulsion of
certain Jews (1891). Paul de Cassagnac, staunchly anti-Republican and Catholic, commenting in *L'Autorité* on the failure of
the motion, had this to say: 'Evidemment, M. Laur est allé un
peu loin lorsqu'il a parlé d'expulser les Juifs de France, comme
les Russes les expulsent de Russie. C'est peut-être un peu pré-
maturé. Mais vous verrez, si cela continue, que la question sera
posée un jour ou l'autre et qu'on ne pourra échapper à ce
dilemme: ou les chrétiens ou les juifs devront sortir de France.'[3]
Among the Boulangist supporters of the Laur motion must have
been Barrès, one imagines. He loved *La France Juive*. 'Je vous

aime surtout parce que je suis né nationaliste', he told Drumont. 'Votre "à bas les Juifs" ne me choque pas. Nous allions le Vendredi Saint les tuer.'[4] Such was apparently the custom in the church of his native Charmes on Good Friday. In 1898 Barrès presented himself as 'socialist-nationalist' candidate with an overtly anti-Jewish programme. But, as he reminded the electorate of Nancy on that occasion, his ideas were the same as 'les idées nationalistes et sociales que nous avons fait triompher ensemble une première fois, en 1889'.[5]

La France Juive released a veritable flood of antisemitic literature. The works of the two main predecessors, previously unnoticed, were reprinted and enjoyed their first success. These were Toussenel's *Les Juifs rois de l'époque*, first published in 1845 and reprinted in 1886; and Gougenot des Mousseaux's *Le Juif, le judaïsme et la judaïsation des peuples chrétiens*, first published in 1869 and also reprinted in 1886. The titles themselves are indicative of the line of thought: the Catholic and conservative des Mousseaux was worried by the judaisation of Christian society and civilisation; the socialist Toussenel, disciple of Fourier, protested against the judaisation of secular society. Two immediate left-wing predecessors also benefited from the favourable climate: Tridon (*Du Molochisme Juif*, 1884) and Chirac (*Les Rois de la République*, 1885).

Another important result was the discussion and translation of German works hitherto relatively unknown in France. Most notable of these was the vicious *Der Talmudjude* (1873) by Father Rohling. It secured no fewer than three French translations in 1889.

The original French works that followed in the wake of Drumont's success are numerous and diverse. 'La préoccupation sémitique est à la mode', exclaimed Henri Mazel, the poet and editor of *L'Ermitage* (May 1890).'Nul ne se doutait naguère de la productivité de ce filon dont on n'avait encore tiré que de problématiques chaires pour quelques calvities philologiques du Collège de France, et qui maintenant fournit, coup sur coup, des livres tirés à cent mille, des journaux, des horions dans les conférences publiques, des étiquettes pour les candidats au Conseil municipal... Pour exploiter cette mine d'or, cent usines ont surgi aussi fantastiquement qu'au Nouveau Monde.'

The field in which antisemitism found its most important expression, and through which its influence spread most widely, was literature, properly speaking, and an increasing periodical literature. On the latter, Pierre Sorlin's research[6] has recently shed some interesting though necessarily incomplete light, since a number of reviews were antisemitic in tendency without it being possible to classify them as outright antisemitic. The *Revue Socialiste* in its early years as well as the *Entretiens*, for example, would fall into this category. It is nonetheless interesting that Sorlin lists for the period roughly from 1880 to 1900 some 27 specifically or largely antisemitic reviews and journals. Ten of these, including the most popular Catholic daily, *La Croix* (established in 1883), were owned by the religious order of the Assumptionists who formed a most successful publishing company, *La Maison de la Bonne Presse*. *La Croix*, the first paper to review *La France Juive*, became increasingly and violently antisemitic, as is well known. Together with its various provincial *Croix* and other periodical literature it was probably one of the most influential organs of antisemitism at the time. (Its only subsequent rival was Drumont's own paper, *La Libre Parole*, which first appeared on 20 April 1892). Bontoux's publication in 1888 of his version of the famous or infamous Krach de l'Union Générale (1882), added more fuel to the already brightly burning antisemitic fire. Eugène Bontoux, a staunch Catholic and ambitious speculator, left the employ of the Rothschilds in 1878, to create a rival Catholic Bank, the *Union Générale*. Enjoying wide support especially in Monarchist circles which welcomed the enterprise for spiritual as well as political reasons, the new Bank did rather well at first. Then suddenly, early in 1882, it collapsed. The crash was in no small measure due to Bontoux's mismanagement and wild speculation, but this is not what he told his distraught clients and supporters who for their part were quite ready to believe that a brave Catholic enterprise had been killed by Jewish financial omnipotence. It was a brilliant illustration of the thesis argued by Drumont in *La France Juive*. Bontoux's story not only became a general topic of conversation but the subject of novels and plays. Georges Ohnet's novel *Nemrod et Cie* (1892) is based on it and so are Zola's *L'Argent* (1891) and Léon Hennique's play *L'Argent d'autrui*, performed at the Odéon in 1893. The Jewish usurer is of course nothing new in European literature. His ancestry goes back to Shylock and he found his first modern expression in the novels of Balzac. But what more particularly characterises the late nineteenth century is the depiction of the financier, often a baron with a German name, as the cause of Christian or national decline engendered by Jewish conquest and domination. Novels illustrate or dramatise the titles and ideas of theoretical works: *Juifs rois de l'époque, Juifs nos maîtres*, etc. etc... Another notable feature is the absence of such vicariously redeeming features as beautiful and virtuous Jessica-like daughters who become duly converted at the end. This old literary convention had no place at a time when religion was viewed in a racial context and the Semitic race was considered to be a pernicious influence. Shylock, too, has lost all nobility. Even when he is given an admirable sense of family, as Gundermann is in Zola's *l'Argent*, this is part and parcel of ensuring the continuity of his empire. In Paul Adam's novels and articles the Jew conquers, corrupts, causes decline and war. In the very first issue of the *Entretiens politiques et littéraires* Adam relates a dream he had of a courageous politician at the tribune of the Chamber dealing with the danger posed by these unproductive and parasitic 'Princes du trafic'.[7]

The obsession with decline and decadence was strongly felt in the arts and in philosophy, indeed in the whole sphere of intellectual life. And just as in the social sphere the development of capitalism and the growing power of the bourgeoisie were identified with the liberation of Jewry from the ghetto, because historically they occurred at the same time, so in the arts, whatever was felt to be a decline, from innovation and modernisation to commercialisation, was almost automatically attributed to the liberated children of the ghetto now freely engaging in the arts and imparting to spiritual things the materialism and positivism of Judaism. Wagner's ranting against the pernicious Jewish influence on music is well known. The young Valéry confided to a friend: 'Je n'aime pas les Juifs car ils n'ont pas *d'art*. Ils ont tout pillé en fait d'architecture, etc., aux races voisines.'[8] He referred to Bernard-Lazare as 'Hébreux et pasticheur.'[9] Here is Octave Mirbeau speaking of 'le théâtre juif': 'ils [les juifs] ont remplacé la beauté des vers de Corneille et de Racine par des spectacles purement plastiques, et le rire amer de Molière et de Beaumarchais, par l'hystérie de la blague dont la gaieté sinistre hurle comme un blasphème'.[10] A list of Jewish dramatists is supplied. This was essential. Drumont never failed to list Jewish bankers, journalists, officers, civil servants, and so on. Similarly, when the *Revue Blanche* was created by the brothers Natanson, its 'ethnic composition' was calculated and this latest manifestation of 'semitic monopoly' caused alarm in the review world. A large part of this was undoubtedly professional jealousy, but the point was the insulting language, the religious perspective, the fear of Judaisation. Even the *Entretiens* did not escape censure[11] when they became the property of Kolb though they only had one regular Jewish contributor and manager, Bernard-Lazare, and he had written some fiercely antisemitic articles. Counting Jews was a favourite pastime. The Jews did it because they were proud of their contributions to French public life, and antisemitism was busy counting and multiplying them to prove the danger to public life. In the process Jewry found itself increasing by leaps and bounds.

Mirbeau's article on 'Le théâtre juif', as indeed the whole review from which it comes, *Les Grimaces*, provides a telling example of aesthetic and ethical anti-Judaism even in the days before *La France Juive*. In its short life, from the 20 July 1883 to the 12 January 1884, *Grimaces* voiced just about every antisemitic grievance that Drumont was to voice, and with a similar verve and violence. Mirbeau was looking for an explanation of what today we would call the consumer society, and which in those days was called the materialist and bourgeois society, a society in which the artist seemingly had no place. It may seem a long jump from a widespread feeling of artistic isolation and alienation to antisemitism; and yet, given the basic prejudices, religious and historical in nature, things almost follow logically. Roughly, Mirbeau's argument runs as follows. The Jew is incapable, by nature, of aspiring to higher values because Judaism lacks mystery and metaphysics. It is a positive religion concerned with the here and now, with happiness and pleasure on earth. A sense of mystery and hence of beauty and art cannot be acquired through assimilation, but a sense of shame can. The liberated child of the ghetto rushes towards the noble and hopefully ennobling liberal professions and especially the arts in order to escape from the stigma attached to the commerce practised by his parents. He abandons the stock exchange and the bank, and makes for the theatre and the press. 'Je ne suis pas un juif', he makes an imaginary character say, 'Je suis un auteur dramatique.' The Jew comes to the arts with a racial incapacity for beauty but an ability of long standing for making money. Mirbeau then looks at theatre, light opera, cabaret and so on, sees them all

as vastly commercialised, and pronounces that the Jew has commercialised drama, music, journalism and literature. 'En voyant
les Juifs essayer de sortir de leur métier traditionnel, et de s'élever
des boutiques d'usurier jusque dans les régions sereines de l'art
et de la pensée, instinctivement on serait porté à applaudir à
cette aspiration inespérée. Malheureusement ce ne sont pas les
Juifs qui ce sont haussés jusqu'à la littérature: c'est elle qu'ils ont
abaissée jusqu'au niveau de leurs comptoirs.'[12] Poetry is happily
quite safe from Judaisation. Incapable of the higher arts, and with
no prospect of making money out of it, 'les Juifs trouvent que la
poésie n'est bonne que pour les chrétiens qui se nourrissent des
rêves, et non de belles pièces d'or'.[13] The French countryside, on
the other hand, is not safe. In an article called *La Chasse*,[14] the
Rothschild's hunting-park at Vaux-de-Cernay is compared with
that next door at the castle of Dampierre, property of the
Duchesse de Luynes. Rothschild's park has become a desert; cows,
meadows and happiness have disappeared. The Jew is only
interested in hunting pheasants. At Dampierre, by contrast, there
is 'la bonne chasse'. Fields, meadows and peasants have remained.
At the end, Rothschild is promoted president of 'la Faisanderie
Française'. Comically as this article may read today, it has a
serious note, expressing extremely well the nostalgia for an old
style of life, a countryside unspoilt by industrialisation, a happy
rural feudalism. The Jew – urban, symbol of industrial capital as
opposed to landed property, the big city tycoon with no roots and
no attachment to the soil – seemed to be destroying the very
quality of life.

Like Drumont, who intended to follow *La France Juive* with
L'Europe Juive, Mirbeau proclaimed antisemitism to be a European movement of revolt, and published congratulatory letters
from correspondents in Hungary, Austria and Russia, all watching
the new movement in France with great interest. From the first
issue, *Grimaces* published an antisemitic bibliography and asked
readers able to furnish documents against the Jews to send them
in. Again like Drumont, no solution is actually put forward but
there is a great deal of violent sabre-rattling. When Arthur Meyer
wrote in to express regret at the revival of old hatreds and the
preaching of an antisemitic crusade, Mirbeau simply replied that
the hatreds of old were fierce but salutary.[15]

The artist applauded antisemitism and thought of purification,
spiritualisation, a return to the past or at least to a pre-industrial,

less financially orientated society. In the same way, the socialist said antisemitism and meant anticapitalism. But the danger lay in the identification of materialism with Judaism, in seeing the elimination of the latter as leading to the desirable disappearance of the former. Judaism meant people. By agreeing and regretting with Drumont that 'le monde est en train de devenir juif', Brunetière, without being an antisemite, was posing the Jewish question in Drumont's terms: What to do with the Jews?

Antisemitism at the turn of the century, *before* the Dreyfus Affair, was an air that one breathed, and Bernard-Lazare was exposed to a strong whiff of it in the literary, symbolist and left-wing circles in which he moved. He was stunned, shocked, hurt and confused by it all. What were the causes of this sudden revival of Jew-hatred and what was his own position in all this? Was he, a perfectly assimilated young Frenchman with deep roots in France, a Jew? He had broken with his Jewish upbringing, such as it was. Moreover, breaking with the supposedly determining influences of 'race, milieu et moment' had to some extent been a deliberate action, proof of the superiority of character over circumstances, a triumph of the will and of man's freedom. Was he, by the mere fact that he could not remain indifferent to antisemitism, letting himself be pushed into an absurd racial determinism? And why could he not remain indifferent? Was it because he loved his parents? But what did he and they have in common with the 'hordes' of immigrants pouring into France in the wake of the Russian pogroms of the 1880s?

In the *Fumier de Job*, composed in later and more serene mood, he recalls with honesty this period of doubt, confusion and anger, a tormented search for his identity. We can follow the search *sur le vif*, as it were, through his writings at the time. He turned to history in order to understand the underlying causes of antisemitism, a phenomenon which has flourished at all times. The result of five years of reading and research was the controversial opus magnum *Antisemitism, its history and causes*, published in the spring of 1894. In the meantime he reacted to events as they occurred, as unafraid of speaking his mind as he was of re-examining his attitudes in the light of new experiences and better understanding. Bernard-Lazare was constantly engaged in dialogue with himself and nowhere more so than in the painful journey from Israelite to Jew. In this chapter we shall follow him on the first two stages of that journey.

The anti-Jewish Israelite of France

Jewish antisemitism is not an unknown phenomenon. Indeed it is very possible that disparaging comments made by Spinoza, Heine and especially Marx helped to reinforce Bernard-Lazare's early antijudaism. This last is probably the result of a combination of forces: assimilationist upbringing, and with it there usually went a pronounced French patriotism; attraction to mysticism; increasing socialist commitment; ignorance of Jewish culture. What complicated life for Bernard-Lazare were his own personality and temperament. He could no more feign indifference or keep silent, even the silence of disdain recommended by Théodore Reinach, than deny his origins. This would have been cowardly.

In the event, Christian antisemitic literature, with which he became very familiar in the course of preparing his history of antisemitism, came to his rescue. In the works of Gougenot des Mousseaux and others he found a distinction between 'mosaïsme' and 'talmudisme', between Bible and Talmud, which he enthusiastically adopted and developed in all sorts of directions. The first time we hear him elaborating on 'Juifs et Israelites' is in a public lecture in April 1890. Substantially the ideas seem to be the same as those expressed in the article by the same name published a little later in the *Entretiens* (September 1890). The argument is this: the ancient Jewish nation was already divided into two very distinct groups; the monotheistic Jahweists (patriarchs, judges, prophets and nabis) who produced the Bible, and the detestable race of worshippers of Baal and the golden calf whose book became the Talmud. To that ancient division conveniently corresponds that between Sephardim, of 'hébraïco-latin' origin, and Ashkenazim, of 'hébraïco-hunnique' origin. It goes without saying that the former are noble and that the descendants of the Huns are ignoble. In modern and more secular terms the distinction corresponds to Israelite and Jew.

This specious distinction allowed him to admit an ancestry, a mere general indication of descent lost in the mists of history, and to join Drumont in hatred of the Jew. Moreover, he interprets Drumont's works to fit this distinction, believing or pretending to believe that their antisemitism is not directed against the Israelites of France at all but only against Jews. The only quarrel he, an Israelite of France, has with the antisemitic leader is a matter of terminology: 'Il sièrait que les anti-sémites, justes enfin, deviennent plutôt anti-juifs, ils seraient certains, ce jour-là, d'avoir avec eux beaucoup d'Israëlites.'

On the surface the distinction is a simple ethical one: honest workers, small shopkeepers, doctors, soldiers, artists, magistrates, men who work and live decently side by side with their fellow-countrymen are Israelites. The rest, the dishonest, the mean, the rich, are Jews. His hatred for the Jew thus defined equals that of Drumont, who could well have signed the cruel portraits Bernard-Lazare draws of the unscrupulous Jewish journalist, banker, politician, author, and so on. Their very Jewishness gives them a cunning and slyness which the rest of unscrupulous humanity does not possess.

There is also an implied social distinction, though here Bernard-Lazare was in difficulty. Ideally, the honest Israelite should also be poor. But he could not in all honesty speak of the Israelites of France, the people uppermost in his mind, as poor. Thus he describes them as 'médiocrement riches' and distinguishes them carefully from the 'monarques nouveaux', the barons of finance who are Jews. Against them, antisemitism's anti-capitalist campaign is justly directed and Bernard-Lazare the socialist welcomes it. The only thing he would ask of Drumont is another clarification of terms, for the crowd will not distinguish between the Rothschilds and the ordinary Israelite and thus 'l'équivoque. . .simplement fâcheuse pour l'instant peut devenir un jour très dangereuse'. One thing Bernard-Lazare has clearly understood: antisemitism's monolithic view of Jewry. He evidently seems to believe at this stage that it is all a matter of careless terminology. Actually, the combination of Israelite of France and Socialist was difficult to sustain. Hence the emphasis on the *respectable* professions *honestly* practised by a largely middle-class French Jewry.

If poverty was the sign of the Israelite, then the penniless immigrants from Eastern Europe should have been the most Israelite of Israelites and the saintliest of saints. Not so. For they were foreigners, strangers to whose plight he claimed to be indifferent. Just how indifferent he proved in a truly savage piece ('La solidarité juive', *Entretiens*, October 1890) in which Jewish solidarity is condemned with an assimilationist logic carried to its cruel conclusion. Who would recognise Bernard-Lazare in this, he who was to become such a fine example of what is best in Jewish solidarity?

Drumont had been greatly disturbed by Jewish solidarity and always cherished the hope of creating 'une alliance antisémite universelle' in reply to L'Alliance Israëlite Universelle. Bernard-Lazare showers insults on the latter's founder, Crémieux, and pours scorn on the aims of the organisation, to aid and protect oppressed Jews. But who, he asks, are the Algerian Jews emancipated by Crémieux? 'sordides usuriers dignes de mépris et non de pitié'. With breathtaking arrogance the Israelite of France looks down on persecuted Jewry of central and Eastern Europe, categorically refusing them the status of Israelite and opposing their entry into France.

> Que m'importent à moi, Israëlite de France, des usuriers russes, des cabaretiers galiciens prêteurs sur gages, des marchands de chevaux polonais, des revendeurs de Prague et des changeurs de Francfort? En vertu de quelle prétendue fraternité, irai-je me préoccuper des mesures prises par le Czar envers des sujets qui lui paraissent accomplir une oeuvre nuisible? ... Qu'ai-je de commun avec ces descendants des Huns? ... A quoi voit-on du reste aboutir une semblable association? A accueillir chez nous des gens méprisables, à favoriser, à les implanter sur un sol qui n'est pas le leur et qui ne les doit pas nourrir, à leur en faciliter la conquête.

As if to prove the *danger of conquest* he has recourse to a great authority and one that Drumont sometimes liked to quote. Renan said of the Talmud-formed Jews that they were – let us note the terms – 'insociables, étrangers partout, sans patrie, sans autre intérêt que celui de leur secte, fléaux pour le pays où le sort les a portés'.[16] Bernard-Lazare's fear of conquest is very personal; he is terrified of being deprived of his French roots by the 'hordes' who bring with them their ghettos, their distrust of the 'goy', their prejudices and selfishness, their tears and suffering. He is afraid of becoming a 'déraciné', and in his fear he strikes at the hordes instead of the real enemy. 'Grace à ces hordes avec lesquelles on nous confond, on oublie que depuis bientôt deux mille ans nous habitons la France.' In a final warning to his fellow-Israelites of France he bids them abandon the absurd and dangerous Alliance Israëlite Universelle. Jewish solidarity has no raison d'être, there is only human solidarity, if the persecuted are worthy of sympathy. 'Il serait plus normal de la part des Israëlites français d'arrêter. . .la perpétuelle immigration de ces Tartars prédateurs, grossiers et sales.'

In his widely and favourably reviewed 'L'Antisémitisme et ses causes générales' (*Entretiens*, September 1892), Bernard-Lazare developed the theme of Jewish exclusiveness and unsociability, which was the result of Talmudic teaching and the permanent cause of antisemitism. We shall come back to it when examining *Antisemitism, its history and causes* of which it became the un-happy first chapter, an antisemitic delight for years to come. The important point is the conclusion. If, as he claims, Talmudic teaching is the cause of this unsociability and exclusiveness, and if, as is also claimed, the pernicious Talmud has become obsolete in France, then how was it that antisemitism was enjoying such a widespread revival? Immigration is part of the answer, but there is, too, the collision of two nationalisms.[17] On the one hand, a revival of French nationalism, and on the other hand an illogical survival of Jewish nationalism through the equally illogical sur-vival of the Jewish religion. The Israelite, though happily no longer subject to a Jewish education, still clings in some way to the religion of his fathers. A mysterious fidelity has survived assimilation. But Bernard-Lazare is confident that this will not last. The Jews are destined to disappear totally. The Jewish critic of the *Archives Israëlites* frowned in disapproval at this prediction and the Catholic critic of *La Croix* in puzzlement.[18]

Judaism and the Jewish religion come in for heavy criticism. They represent everything the symbolist tempted by the beauty of Catholicism detests: a narrow rationalism, formal and ritual-istic, with no poetry:

> La religion hébraïque est depuis longtemps tombée dans un rationalisme bête, elle paraît emprunter ses dogmes à la déclaration des droits de l'homme, elle oublie, comme le protestantisme, cette chose essentielle: qu'une religion sans mystère est semblable à la paille de blé dont on a vanné le grain.[19]

In the explicit identification of Judaism, that is, the eternally triumphant Talmudic Judaism with positivism, arid rationalism, materialism and capitalism, Bernard-Lazare voices a fashionable brand of antisemitism in which religious, aesthetic and socialist objections merge. Symbolism and socialism combined to make him into Drumont's ally.

In the grim picture he draws of the Jewish religion simple ignorance obviously plays its part. But it should not be exaggerated. He may have been ignorant of many Jewish things at the time. To begin with, he had little or no contact with Jews and Jewish life outside his family, but he was not ignorant of Jewish literature, history and religious writings, including mystical writings which inspired some of the stories in the *Miroir des Légendes*. Indeed, he is so conscious of this alternative tradition to Talmudic rationalism that he has recourse to another dualism to accommodate it. 'L'âme du juif est double: elle est mystique et elle est positive.' But, and perhaps this is the point, 'l'âme mystique' is rare; it pertains to heretics like Spinoza; it has no place in the chilling Synagogue Judaism, the 'déisme cérémonial' of the modern French Jew, a religion married to business and the French Revolution. One may well wonder whether the kind of religion in which he was brought up, and against which he reacted, was as decisive a factor in the estrangement from Judaism on the part of a young man looking for mysticism and poetry as assimilation. If, as I believe, the story of the philosopher told in the *Fumier de Job* is Bernard-Lazare's own story of search, then the following reflections on Catholicism and the temptation it exercised are eloquent. We may add that Catholicism exercised a similar aesthetic attraction for Ehpraïm Mikhaël, his Jewish cousin. Let us also note in the following passage the spiritual dilemma of a man who remained a Jew and a rationalist *malgré lui*; the moral dilemma, too, of a man of conscience trying to understand the truth but afraid of being labelled a renegade by the outside world.

> Bien que la loi de ses pères en lui fût morte, bien qu'il en comprît l'insuffisance, bien que ceux de sa race lui fussent devenus odieux, il leur était attaché encore par trop de liens pour leur être indifférent. Le mouvement antisémite le préoccupait; il lut beaucoup pour pouvoir se faire une opinion sincère; il se trouvait placé entre sa conscience qui lui ordonnait la recherche de la vérité et la crainte du monde prêt à le traiter de rénégat... Le catholicisme le saisissait; il y voyait un accomplissement du Judaïsme; une sorte de colère le prenait contre son peuple qui proclamait perpétuellement le Messie pour le repousser quand il était venu à lui. Cette conception matérielle d'un âge d'or; cette inaptitude à comprendre un 'salvement' spirituel, l'emplis-

sait de fureur. . . D'un autre côté, tout en aimant profondé-
ment les dogmes catholiques, tout en reconnaissant combien
supérieurs ils étaient, et combien plus cette religion était une
religion endormeuse d'âme, il ne pouvait pas venir à elle ;
il n'avait pas la foi ; son admiration était peut-être celle d'un
artiste et d'un penseur, et le penseur, chez lui, n'était pas
assez robuste. Il était trop enserré dans l'éducation reçue, si
rationnelle et positive.[20]

A little later, speaking of his complete alienation from the Jewish
people for whom he occasionally felt real hatred, the Israelite of
France is led to some strange speculations about his origins: 'il
pensait qu'il n'était pas de cette nation, et que des aïeules infidèles
avait commis de multiples fautes avec des chrétiens'.[21] Ideally,
at this stage of his thought, the Israelite is not only completely
assimilated in a national sense, and this requires abandoning his
own religio-national faith, he is also open to spiritualisation
through Christianity.

Unlike Brunetière and like-minded idealists who had sadly
agreed with Drumont that society was indeed becoming Jewish
because it was becoming increasingly demystified and materialis-
tic, Bernard-Lazare was optimistic (a Jewish characteristic,
Brunetière thought); he believed that there was every sign that a
spiritual and social revolution was in progress and that anti-
Judaism was one facet of that revolution.

The four earliest symbolist stories, composed and published
between July 1890 and March 1891, that is to say in his most
antisemitic period, are poetic treatments of the Jewish question
seen in a religious and mystical perspective. At the same time,
however, a very curious process is already at work. Severe as
Bernard-Lazare is on the worshippers of the golden calf forever
casting out their messiahs, because these appear in forms inconceivable and unrecognisable to the souls of merchants, he is also
gently trying to absolve Jewry from guilt in a variety of ways.

'L'Eternal Fugitif' retells the story of the golden calf – an image
by which Bernard-Lazare was obsessed – with Moses prophesying
the coming of Christ, Israel's denial and punishment: it will be
abandoned by God, scattered over the earth like grains of wheat
unable to take root in any soil; a dead nation, the world for ever
lost to it. While Moses weeps over the future misfortunes of his
people they cast furtive glances, full of regret, at the departing

Samiri. Samiri is a strange invention, an alien Cain who infiltrated the Israelites and who in Moses' absence persuaded them to erect the golden calf. On his part this had been an act of personal vengeance, for he had been cast out by God. Cast out again by Moses, Samiri, the evil spirit, joyfully departs, feeling that his action has been a total success for all time: the soul of Israel has been turned towards gold and there it will stick. 'La Rédemption d'Ahasuérus' is a simple conversion story: the wandering Jew returns to the scene of his crime, Jerusalem, in the hope of a liberating death. This is promised to him by an evil tempter on condition that he insults Christ once more. An anguished Christ on the cross appears in the sky and Ahasuérus, instead of offering insults, the price of his own liberation, recognises the suffering God and resumes his wandering, only this time not as a vagabond but as a penitent. That night, however, everything shone with splendour as Ahasuérus, redeemed, ascended to heaven. There are some interesting touches in this simple tale of conversion, a theme subsequently treated with fascinating variations.[22] I did not know, Ahasuérus explains, that I was striking God; he looked like a vagabond. It is only after he himself had become a vagabond, suffering, insulted and spat upon, that he recognised the Messiah. There is also pity for Ahasuérus weighed down by the opprobrium of centuries. Pity for the outcast and the 'underdog' was to be an important emotional factor in Bernard-Lazare's conversion to Judaism. There is above all a Bloy-like vision, a whole two years before Bloy's *Le Salut par les Juifs*, of the world's salvation depending on the hideous and abject figure of the Jew. Ahasuérus himself, before the final conversion, derives strength from the knowledge that, despised and cursed though he is, he is also the supreme instrument of mankind's salvation. This knowledge had helped to calm his wrath and made him bear with greater equanimity the oppressor's wrong.

Conversion is also the theme of the intriguing 'Les Incarnations', which in certain parts reminds one even more of Bloy, with this capital difference that the ultimate conversion of the Jews is not seen to bring salvation because Christians, secret admirers of the Jews' practical gifts, will find an honourable pretext for converting themselves to something else. This is the ironic twist to a story whose main theme is Israel's perennial denial of the Messiah. It is treated with a delightful mixture of seriousness and irony. The discussion is between an Israelite of

the West, with a guilt-complex about Christ's death, and a
Celestial Jew of China whose ancestors came to China before the
birth of Christ. To be a guiltless Jew! Bernard-Lazare speculates
on what this would be like. But irony cuts short the meditation. A
Jew is a Jew. What is the accident of emigration in the face of racial
inevitability? The 'celestial Jew' of China is even marked by the
same nose as his guilty brothers. Western sceptic and Eastern sage
are severe on the worshippers of the golden calf and their meta-
physically inadequate religion. The sage much prefers the teaching of Confucius. They agree that materialism and rationalism
are responsible for Israel's inability to recognise its own Messiahs.
Man, the argument runs, conceives God in glorified images. God,
on the other hand, in his immense pity for the humble and the
most abject of sinners, takes on their form when he comes to save
humanity. How could opulent merchants and hardened Pharisees
whose image of God was that of a splendid monarch recognise
the Messiah in 'le Nazaréen pitoyable, qui marchait suivi d'un
cortège de publicains, de pécheresses et de lépreux soulagés'?[23]
At this stage the Chinese sage remembers the vision of a mystic
Kabbalist. In that vision, described in erudite detail, Israel is
absolved when the rich man at last recognises the Lord in his
third incarnation: in 'le petit juif hideux, aux cheveux jaunes et
sales, aux yeux chassieux, à la bouche tordue, à la barbe hirsute
. . .le petit juif, . . .serviteur des débauchés, patron des mérétrices,
instigateur des larrons'.[24] Do you believe in this vision, asks the
Western sceptic of the Eastern sage? Has Israel at last recognised
the Messiah? The ironic answer is: the day Israel does so, Christians will be converted to something else.

'La gloire de Judas' is one of the boldest attempts at rehabilita-
tion. Judas is rehabilitated and glorified as the apostle who fulfilled the prophesies and accomplished the supreme sacrifice, that
of bearing eternal shame and hate so that the world could be
liberated from Jehovah. Christ, returned to earth to enlighten
the anguished disciple about the glorious role he was chosen to
play and must play to the end, explains: 'Sois fier, Judas; de tous
temps, je t'avais élu. Va, ceux de mon église croient que Jean
fut l'apôtre cher, non: l'apôtre aimé ce fut toi, et si j'ai chargé
ton nom d'opprobre parmi les hommes, il sera sanctifié parmi les
bienheureux. Quelques-uns seulement de ceux qui vivront sous
ma loi sauront ta glorieuse destinée. Il faut, pour mon triomphe,
que persiste ton ignominie.'[25] As Bernard-Lazare imagines it, the

truth about Judas was revealed to Paul who had written it down so that men could come to know the truth; and in the story this has already come to pass; for a congregation of Christians, led by a prophetess from Judea, blesses Saint Judas and offers thanks to Saint Paul for his revelation.

Poor Bernard-Lazare! What a rude awakening the Dreyfus Affair was to be after such mystical dreams and efforts to reinterpret myths and symbols. Elsewhere he says of the Gnostics: 'ces extraordinaires théogonies gnostiques, multiples, si variées, si follement mystiques'. One could well say the same of these stories.

From dialogue to confrontation. From race to class

In real life events were moving in a very different direction. In March 1892 the *Journal d'Indre-et-Loire*, edited by the boulangist deputy Delahaye, carried the story of a ritual murder committed at Chatellerault. A few days later it was established that the child had been killed by its mother but the ancient legend, recently revived in all its cruelty, was about to flourish again. In May, the turbulent Marquis de Morès, believing that the time for action had come, led his 'storm troopers' (wearing sombreros and purple cowboy shirts) in an attack on the synagogue in which a Rothschild marriage was being celebrated. In the same month the 'anti-capitalist' *Libre Parole* added to its campaign against Finance and Panama, Jewish officers in the army, with lists supplied of the number of Lévys, Mayers and Meyers and so on in military establishments. The unnamed officer-writer of these articles affirmed that the vast majority of soldiers felt an instinctive revulsion against the sons of Israel.[26] The latter were invited, if they felt hurt by the insults and insinuations, to fight it out, opposing Jewish swords to French swords. Parliament declared that there were only French swords in the French army. Duels were nonetheless fought and the whole violent campaign culminated with the death of Captain Armand Mayer, killed in a duel with the Marquis de Morès. France was shocked. 'On crie ou on écrit: Mort aux Juifs! et puis un jour arrive où l'on s'arrête terrifié, désespéré, ...parce que la parole a enfanté l'acte.' Another journalist was struck by the tragic irony of an Alsatian officer being antisemitism's first victim. Yet another declared that the blood of this innocent and honourable soldier had effaced in one day all the antisemitic insults showered on the Jewish community for the past five years.[27] But in September the financial scandal of the Panama Canal Company broke and it provided *La Libre Parole* with new and excellent ammunition. Baron Jacques de Reinach and Cornélius Herz joined the Rothschilds to become symbols of Jewry, very convenient symbols since they had actually been involved in shady dealings.

Bernard-Lazare, knowing from personal experience – one of his brothers was an Army officer – that there could be no more patriotic Frenchmen than Jewish army officers, noble Israelites of France if ever there were any, was deeply shaken. The distinctions for which he had pleaded barely two years before must have seemed like an absurd fantasy. Fantasy, too, the socialist pretensions of antisemitism which he now began to see in an altogether different light. Passionate as he was, and logical and honest as he tried to be at each stage of his thought, his was also an alert mind and one, moreover, which was prepared to re-examine and reassess his ideas in the light of events, even to admit that he had been wrong or naive. This is notably the case in his dialogue with Drumont which was beginning to turn into a confrontation. In it, he also confronted his former self.

The long study 'Antisémitisme'[28] is dedicated to Drumont, 'pamphlétaire de grand talent mais inutile', and it appeared a week after the *Libre Parole*'s 'Les Juifs dans l'Armée' (23 May 1892). The former Israelite of France has not altogether disappeared. He insists for example that Provençal Jewry and that of Alsace, with French roots as old as Drumont's, must not be confused with the abject usurers of Algeria and the considerable colony of foreign Jews, 'abominables prédateurs', many of whom have come to France with the intention of making an easy living by ruse and stealth. Side by side with this mass view, he establishes a more meaningful social distinction between wealthy minority and poor majority. In the course of studying working-class conditions in Europe and America, Bernard-Lazare made the sensational discovery that there is such a thing as a Jewish proletariat, that Jewish workers suffer as much from the capitalist system as non-Jewish workers. Even in France, he writes, there are *now* thousands of Jewish workers exploited just like Christian workers. (The 'now' is interesting for it must refer to the formerly much detested immigrants.) Lest the Jewish-solidarity argument should be invoked, he cites an example of Jewish workers being oppressed by Jewish capitalists. The conclusion clearly is that the division is not between Jews and non-Jews but between poor and rich.

The distinction does of course carry its own simplifications, particularly if it is accompanied, as it often is with Bernard-Lazare, by the ethical corollary that the poor are good and the rich evil. But it had the salutary effect of making him look at the Jewish question in a much wider social context and above all of challenging Drumont on the latter's chosen ground. Antisemitism claims to be a socialist and anti-capitalist movement providing the answers to the serious social problems of the day. What, he asks, does M. Drumont intend to do with Jewish workers and Christian capitalists? After putting various answers into the mouth of the antisemitic leader and discussing them, he comes to the conclusion, greatly developed in later writings, that antisemitism is merely anti-Jewish capital and nonsensical as a socialist movement since 'les capitalistes chrétiens échapperont râflant les dépouilles de leurs concurrents juifs; quant au peuple, dont M. Drumont prend tel souci, il ne sera ni plus ni moins oppressé'. From a social point of view then, Bernard-Lazare concludes, the antisemitic movement provides no solution. What about the national solution, since it also claims to be a national movement? 'La France aux Français' is a catchy slogan but what does it actually mean? By what criteria is Frenchness to be established? If it is by roots, then a number of French Jews would qualify, which is not Drumont's intention. How far back are the roots to go? There is something to be said for the purity of 'La Gaule au Gaulois' but then how many honoured French kings and noble families would qualify, and how many Frenchmen would there be left? More serious is the socialist objection raised to the aptness of a narrow nationalism in modern times. 'Aujourd'hui, comme de tout temps, la ploutocratie est cosmopolite et internationale, c'est sans doute ce qui fait sa force: on a laissé le peuple être patriote, c'est ce qui fait sa faiblesse.' All in all, and in spite of certain naivetés, Bernard-Lazare has come a long way in a short time.

Cornélius Herz and baron Rothschild were an embarrassment. Bernard-Lazare does not in any way excuse them, but his attack shows a healthier 'class' rather than 'race' approach. Baron Rothschild positively invited his fury. Interviewed by Jules Huret of the *Figaro* (July 1892) the baron showed a breathtaking complacency and ignorance. The workers are very happy, they do not need socialism, capitalists must unite against antisemitism, this was more or less his answer to all ills. The interview caused a sensation and was excellent antisemitic ammunition. Bernard-Lazare's scathing attack on the baron in the anarchist journal *L'Endehors*,[29] promptly reproduced in Jean Grave's *La Révolte*, is understandable and from a socialist point of view perfectly justified. He cannot resist, it is true, the occasional antisemitic sideswipe, as when he likens Rothschild's optimism to that of his God who looked upon the world he created and saw that all was well; but he has realised the mistake of personifying the whole capitalist system in a few prominent Jewish bankers. The new 'class' rather than 'race' approach emerges even more clearly in the extraordinary article devoted to Cornélius Herz.[30] To begin with, the passing shots are there: the obsessive image of the golden calf, naturally; and also the love of honours and decorations. 'Il est bien le juif, amoureux de panache comme un enfant.' But both these 'Jewish' characteristics are now qualified. Historical circumstances are invoked to explain the childish love of honours, the result of centuries of humiliations. More important still, it is emphasised that Herz is representative not of a detestable race but of a detestable class; he is no better and no worse than the rest of the 'bourgeoisie agioteuse et tripotente'. Furthermore, Herz could obviously not have acted by himself, and all his associates are not Jewish. Why is the Jew singled out for attack? This greatly diminishes Bernard-Lazare's anger against the swindler. 'Le courroux est désarmé par la persécution et seul l'intérêt s'éveille, l'intérêt que provoque une belle bête de proie.' This final cruel touch may well hide a feeling of pity for the beast on which everybody is feasting so sumptuously.

The matter on which Bernard-Lazare untiringly challenged Drumont between 1893 and 1896 is the actual solution to the Jewish question. The problem is for ever raised but never solved. Bernard-Lazare took to daring the antisemitic leader on this. In the article on Herz just mentioned he had pointed out that Drumont does not dare follow out the logic of his ideas. In 'Juifs et antisémites'[31] (a more apt title would be the 'Final Solution'), Bernard-Lazare himself considers the various possibilities and solutions open to antisemitism. With what today must seem like very black humour he reviews one by one the drawbacks, illogicalities or impracticabilities of: expulsion ('je ne vois pas bien les Etats européens jouant à la raquette avec leurs juifs respectifs'); ghettos and restrictive legislation (the Jew is too clever by half for such measures); giving them their own territory (danger of the cunning Jews dominating other nations); reducing them to slavery and making them break stones as in olden days (unsatisfactory: some masters would trust their slaves, which would be dangerous; others would kill them, which would lead to a 'massacre sans franchise'); there is mass conversion ('les anti-sémites repousseraient avec horreur cette proposition si le pape venait la leur faire'); finally, we come to the only logical and foolproof solution: extermination to the last Jew. Until 1896 Bernard-Lazare was daring Drumont to say this in so many words, in the hope perhaps of shaking people into realising the logical end of the antisemitic philosophy, rationally immune from attack like all absurdities.

In October 1895 the *Libre Parole* took up the challenge and invited its readers to propose practical means of eliminating Jewish power in France, the Jewish danger being considered from a racial and not a religious point of view.[32] Drumont added that if there was a Jew who did not belong to the world of finance, and who was therefore qualified to speak on the subject, he would gladly be accorded a place on the jury. Delighted, Bernard-Lazare immediately replied: 'Le concours que vous ouvrez satis-fera, je l'espère, ma curiosité, et me fixera sans doute sur la doctrine antisémite...quoique d'avance, je trouve que la seule mesure logique serait le massacre, une nouvelle Saint-Barthé-lemy.'[33] Drumont's comment was that this solution seemed a little radical. The jury, presided over by Barrès, eventually met on 10 June (1896) to assess the merit of the 145 entries received. Bernard-Lazare was the only Jewish member of the jury. Drumont was not without admiration for the courage of this unusual Jew who came to take his seat in the midst of fifteen well-known more or less violent antisemites. However, Bernard-Lazare only had a week in which to plunge himself in his share of the manuscripts before they and his seat on the jury were withdrawn from him. The whole affair ended in a duel between him and Drumont on 18 June. The immediate cause was Bernard-Lazare's expressed intention to make public what he had learnt – with the *Libre Parole*'s permission and after the prizes had been awarded, he was careful to add. Drumont chose to ignore the proviso, calling it typical Jewish impropriety; and Bernard-Lazare, sensing the intended insult, asked for satisfaction. He hated duels, 'un duel n'est pas une réponse'. But for nothing in the world would he have given Drumont the opportunity of repeating for ever after that the Jew has no sense of honour and is a coward. The duel was held; fortunately neither combatant was hurt. Honour was satisfied, but further participation on the jury was impossible.

Some of the prize-winning entries were later published, among them the one which won the first prize, by Father M. A. J. Jacquet.[34] It could only have confirmed Bernard-Lazare's suspicions that neither mass conversion nor mass extermination recommended itself to Christian antisemitism. The ghetto solution was more acceptable.

In Bernard-Lazare's long, enthusiastic and startling review (*Evénement*, 16 October 1892) of Léon Bloy's *Salut par les Juifs*, we see a sadly ironic and yet at the same time a very positive idea to the solution of the Jewish question taking shape. The title of Bloy's work was in itself a welcome change, after so much of 'Le Judaisme voilà l'ennemi', and Bernard-Lazare made the most of it. In a general sense, it will be readily understood from what has gone before why Bernard-Lazare, unlike the vast majority of his fellow-critics, was not shocked by Bloy's vision of hallowed hideousness, and his totally different conception of God from the usual image of magnificence and omnipotence. Bloy himself, who had sent Bernard-Lazare the book for review 'parce que votre nom d'adjuteur de Dieu m'était agréable et. . .vous sachant dénué de richesses quoique circoncis',[35] was taken aback by the unusual understanding. 'This Lazare', he noted in his diary 'seems to be the only person to have understood that an adoration of the poor is the essential basis of my doctrine.'[36] More startling, and it perplexed Bloy himself, was the critic's opinion that the author of this collection of insults heaped on the Jews was 'a philosemite'.[37] How serious was Bernard-Lazare? In a curious way he *was* serious, provided that the compliment is seen against the polemical background as well as a self-projection. He uses Bloy as a means of castigating Drumont. He also projects on to Bloy his own love–hate relationship with Jewry, and the conception of Israel's mission which is beginning to form in his mind. Bloy's expressed opposition to Drumont appeals to him enormously and he makes much of it, seeing in one a modern hate inspired by jealousy and fear and in the other a prophetic wrath moved by love and a lofty conception of the people of God, its eternal mission and significance, its supreme role in the world's salvation. What are Bloy's insults, interpreted as being directed against the rich anyway, compared to such a glorification of Israel? Bloy was a genuine, old-fashioned Christian antisemite despising and loving at one and the same time. This was reassuring, for whatever the insults, if you believe that salvation depends on the Jews' conversion you are unlikely to kill them off or shut them up. Conversion and not the ghetto or massacre was the divine promise. This is *Le Salut par les Juifs* seen with the eyes of Bernard-Lazare:

> Les israélites sont inébranlables; des mondes se sont rués sur eux, des nations, peut-être, brûleront encore les confortables tentes qu'ils ont su élever, mais rien ne pourra les faire disparaître, car ils doivent persister, étant non seulement les témoins de la passion divine, mais encore ceux qui amèneront le salut.

The Christian Drumont, on the other hand, categorically rejected conversion, and maintained that Israel's mission had been magnificent but was completed: there was no reason for its religious or spiritual survival. Edmond Picard went even further and postulated that Israel had never had a mission: it is only by a terrible mistake that Christianity sees its origins and traditions in Judaism; the Nazarean Christ was an Aryan, and the story of Christ merely serves to illustrate the impossibility of aryanising the Semite; it also exemplifies the deadly and eternal conflict between the two races. How a libertarian of Picard's moral and intellectual calibre could hold such an absurdly racialist view of history and advocate a strict racial apartheid as the solution to the decline of European civilisation, baffled Bernard-Lazare. It was pointless to argue, as he later came to realise. On one matter he insisted: Jesus was Jewish; 'Jésus, c'est la fleur de la conscience sémitique, il est l'épanouissement de cet amour, de cette charité, de cette universelle pitié qui brûla l'âme des prophètes d'Israël.'[38] Compared with Picard's coldly anthropological insults and learned demonstration of the inferiority of the Semitic race, which simply could not have produced prophets or Christ, Bloy's passionate fulminations came as a relief. Bloy's Jesus, Bernard-Lazare insists, is 'le Juif excellent et parfait'. Moreover – and here Bernard-Lazare is beginning to write his own 'Salut par les Juifs' – Bloy is said to be parting company with the doctors of the Church in the emphasis he puts on the Jews being an active instrument of salvation, doing the saving rather than being saved. Israel's mission, Bernard-Lazare provocatively declares, will indeed be completed when it has delivered the world from its present state and restored to it freedom, love and joy. There is a subtle irony in the philosemitism ascribed to Bloy which the latter did not understand. What Bernard-Lazare is suggesting is that the Jews may well prove to be mankind's salvation provided they survive and remain Jews. Bloy's faith in conversion will ensure physical survival, and Jewish obstinacy, for they are as unconvertible as they have ever been, will ensure the rest. Or almost. For in order to fulfil their mission and restore freedom, love and joy (soon he will add justice) the Jews must become Jewish again.

It was *La France Juive* which made Bernard-Lazare into a Jew. But his journey was not yet completed, for he still had to learn how to live with Jews and come to grips with Judaism. *Antisemitism, its history and causes* is a step in that direction but it is also a step backwards.

5

ANTISEMITISM, ITS HISTORY AND CAUSES

'Je ne suis ni antisémite, ni philosémite',[1] wrote Bernard-Lazare in the preface to his controversial history. It would probably be fair to say that he is both. This is hardly surprising since the work was composed over a period of some five years, from 1889 to 1894, and reflects the changes in viewpoint and attitude discussed in the previous chapter.

The book indeed comprises two histories. First, a remarkable, richly documented and original study of antisemitism from Greco-Roman antiquity to the end of the nineteenth century. It is the first serious attempt by a Jew to understand the antisemitic viewpoint, the reason and reasoning behind a 3,000-year-old hatred. The fact that antisemites have regarded and still regard the work as a defence of their ideas, should not prevent its more objective recognition as, in the editorial comment of a recent English translation with no axe to grind, 'still the finest textbook on the subject'.[2] However, it is not just a straightforward 'textbook', for through this general history there also runs the poignant personal history of an 'Israelite de France' discovering his Jewish roots in the course of an impartial examination of antisemitism. Hence some of the inconsistencies in his attitude to both persecuted and persecutors.

To these two histories correspond the two distinct parts into which the work falls. An historical part (Chapters 1 to 7) which was largely completed by 1892 and reflects Bernard-Lazare's early antisemitism. The crucial introductory chapter is none other than the article on 'Les causes générales de l'antisémitisme', already published in the *Entretiens*,[3] which stressed Jewish responsibility to the exclusion, or *almost*, of everything else. The modern part (Chapters 8 to 15) and its optimistic conclusion were

conceived in a very different spirit; the final chapters indeed
show every sign of having been hastily assembled at the last hour,
with numerous bibliographical references to 1893 (the book came
out in the spring of 1894) and frantic footnotes promising more
complete studies at a future date.[4] The Preface explicitly states
that the work is incomplete in its present state. It seems as if
Bernard-Lazare was keen to get his book out, probably in the
vain hope of halting the progress of antisemitism. In the event,
the intention utterly misfired, and the unfortunate result of the
haste was that the *anti-antisemitic* second part is not as firm, as
lucid or as richly illustrated as the anti-Jewish historical part.

Looking at the past

The historical section examines the causes and development of
antisemitism from Greco-Roman antiquity to the French Revolution. Briefly summed up, he sees the causes as primarily ideological
and religious until the thirteenth century and complicated by
socio-economic factors after that. The main thesis, explained in
the introduction, is this: whatever the differences and transforma-
tions dictated by time and circumstance the one permanent and
fixed element in antisemitism is the Jew himself. This is not a
question of mere presence but of character. The Jew, as unchanging as he is ubiquitous, is at all times and in all places the product
of his religion and his law, especially of the hateful Talmud which
makes him into an unsociable, exclusive, arrogant being, fiercely
nationalistic and striving to dominate other nations. The following
lesson is put into the mouth of a Talmudist preaching to one of his
students:

> Ne cultive pas le sol étranger, tu cultiveras bientôt le tien;
> ne t'attache à aucune terre, car ainsi tu serais infidèle au
> souvenir de ta patrie; ne te soumets à aucun roi, puisque tu
> n'as de maître que le Seigneur du pays saint, Jéhovah; ne te
> disperse pas au sein des nations, tu compromettrais ton
> salut et tu ne verrais pas luire le jour de la résurrection;
> conserve-toi tel que tu sortis de ta maison, l'heure viendra
> où tu reverras les collines des aïeux, et ces collines seront
> alors le centre du monde, du monde qui te sera soumis.[5]

No wonder Maurras found this book so illuminating.
   The only precept missing from the lesson is: get rich and insist
on your pound of flesh. It is not forgotten; rather it is made into

a secondary cause, an inevitable consequence of Talmudic teaching but not inherent in the teaching itself. The spirit of the Talmud is rationalist, and rationalism is axiomatically seen as leading to usury.[6] Antisemitic admirers of the book did not make the same subtle distinction between primary and secondary causes. Nor did they appreciate the crucial qualifications contained in the following warnings (my own italics):

> C'est *en partie* l'exclusivisme, le persistant patriotisme et l'orgueil d'Israel, qui le poussa à devenir l'usurier haï du monde entier. . . Toutefois, le juif n'est *qu'un* des facteurs de l'antisémitisme.[7]

En partie and *un des facteurs* open the door to *outside* forces in which Bernard-Lazare's main interest lies. The historical part can in fact be read on two different levels, each with its own approach. There is the cruel portrait of the eternal Jew, permanent and primary cause of antisemitism. With it goes a rich collection of anti-Jewish texts and tracts used to illustrate the author's thesis of Jewish unsociability and desire for domination. At times one has the feeling that sources are being used in circular fashion, that is to say that Bernard-Lazare derived his ideas from certain sources and then uses the same sources to prove his ideas. The approach is religious, symbolist, *essentialist*. It was from Spinoza that Bernard-Lazare had learnt that 'il faut envisager chaque chose sous son aspect d'éternité'. And this is how he looks at the Jewish people and its religion, as an unchanging essence. Spinoza's comment on the Jews, 'ils se sont séparés de toutes les autres nations, à tel point qu'ils ont tourné contre eux la haine de tous les peuples'[8] perfectly coincides with Bernard-Lazare's view of Jewish essence, and the revered master may well have been an influence.

Jewish separatism is a well-known phenomenon. What is more questionable is the extent to which it generated or constituted the primary cause of antisemitism. However that may be, seeing the Jews in this one dimension – all as nationalist Shylocks and fanatical devotees of the Talmud – is bound to have distorting effects. It is interesting to consider in this respect a comment Bernard-Lazare later made on the Christian's view of Jewish history: 'la conception que les chrétiens ont du Juif est une conception mystique et non humaine'.[9] Bernard-Lazare's mystical conception is obviously not the same, but the particular view *en bloc* to which such conceptions lead is similar. Treated as a monolithic religious group, Jewish society has none of the differences and diversities, stresses and struggles, individual reactions (even to religion) of other groups. It becomes somewhat dehumanised. In much of the first part of the book Bernard-Lazare follows a 'métaphysique religioso-économique'[10] which he later criticised as the unfortunate inspiration behind Marx's *Jewish Question*. Only in Bernard-Lazare's case both *Hofjude* and streethawker are not only natural capitalists but also fiercely nationalist, dreaming of gold and power.

On the few occasions when Bernard-Lazare abandons his *idée fixe* and sees the Jew in the same social and human context as the rest of the world, the story is very different. One of the most moving and unusually emotional passages concerns solidarity, discussed for once not in terms of some Talmudic nationalistic commandment or organised domination but as the very simple result of shared suffering and need for consolation.

> Quelles fautes pouvaient mériter aussi effroyables châtiments. Combien poignante devait être l'affliction de ces êtres. En ces heures mauvaises ils se serrèrent les uns contre les autres et se sentirent frères, le lien qui les attachait se noua plus fort. A qui auraient-ils dit leurs plaintes et leurs faibles joies, sinon à eux-mêmes? De ces communes désolations, de ces sanglots naquit une intense et souffrante fraternité.[11]

A sense of solidarity with suffering Jewry past and present was to be the door through which Bernard-Lazare would eventually pass to Zionism.

Parallel to, and at times in conflict with, the religious approach to Jewish mentality is the historical and social approach to the diverse surrounding forces, political, intellectual and economic. It is this analysis (more perceptively Marxist than that undertaken by Marx in *The Jewish Question*) which gives the work its originality and significance. A few examples will illustrate the dual approach.

A sombre picture is drawn of the Jewish community in ancient Rome: masses of small traders and hawkers living in the dirtiest and most commercial part of Rome, unsociable, exclusive, separatist. 'Le Juif du ghetto est déjà là'.[12] He has voluntarily cut himself off *without* the pressure of persecution. Side by side with this portrait of the eternal Jew, there is an interesting discussion of the development of anti-Jewish feeling as we pass from ancient Greece to ancient Rome. The fusion of national and religious elements in Rome added an important new dimension to the problem of Jewish separateness. Religion having become a matter of State, part and parcel of national and political life, the Jews, by refusing to bow, made themselves into foreigners. Similarly, their proselytising activities came to be felt as a threat to the establishment.

One subject of lasting interest, and regret, to Bernard-Lazare, was the Jewish–Christian schism. On one level, the mystic blames the positivist doctors of the Synagogue for the Jewish refusal of spiritualisation through Christianity. Looking at things in a more historical context, he sees the tensions between Jews and the first Jewish Christians as being of a national and political character: the Jews, at home as it were, were engaged in a war of national liberation whereas the Jewish Christians collaborated with the occupying powers. Bernard-Lazare is not without admiration for the Jewish war of independence. Later on, in the diaspora, it was of course madness to dream of nationhood after having ceased to be a nation; naturalisation in the host country would have been the only sane solution. Yet, the assimilationist is no longer sure of all this. He shows an emotional understanding at least of how the mad dreamers, persecuted for their fidelity to Zion, came to dream ever more intensely of Zion.

> Le vieux patriotisme juif s'exalta encore. Il leur plut, à ces délaissés, maltraités dans toute l'Europe et qui marchaient la face souillée de crachats, il leur plut de sentir revivre Sion et ses collines perdues, d'évoquer, suprême et douce consolation, les bords aimés du Jourdain et les lacs de Galilée: ils y arrivèrent par une intense solidarité.[13]

The medieval Jew is portrayed as an ignoble Shylock inexorably driven by the Talmud to usury and enjoying the power gold gives him over his fellow-men. On the other hand, Bernard-Lazare not only goes through the successive legislation, both civil and ecclesiastical, which pushed the Jews towards the decried practice of usury, but he also gives a brilliant analysis of the whole strange economic system which needed the Jew to work it. On the one hand, a religious, mystical conception of the nature and function of capital imposed by the Church, and on the other hand, a socio-economic system, a primitive form of capitalism, entirely opposed to that conception. The Jew, being outside the spiritual and moral jurisdiction of the Church, was the ideal tool to make these opposing forces – spiritual aspiration and socio-economic reality – work to the satisfaction of everybody but the exploited masses of whom he was a special case. We catch here Bernard-Lazare's pity for the despised usurer:

> Ce malheureux Juif, . . .est utilisé à deux fins. On se sert de lui comme d'une sangsue, on le laisse gonfler, s'emplir d'or, puis on l'oblige à dégorger, ou, si les haines populaires sont trop exacerbées, on le livre à un supplice profitable aux capitalistes chrétiens qui paient ainsi à ceux qu'ils pressurent un tribut de sang propitiatoire.[14]

The contradiction between the two approaches is most apparent in the discussion of the Jewish situation in the Middle Ages. The picture of the masters of gold reigning supreme, 'détenteurs de l'or, ils devenaient les maîtres de leurs maîtres',[15] hardly tallies with the description of the Jew as being successively excluded from all professions, his belongings confiscated, the sums owed to him annulled by simple decree, periodically expelled and occasionally massacred. Are these the masters of masters?

The two approaches, religious and social, coincide most satisfactorily in the discussion of Jewish emancipation and the French Revolution. In opposition to most French Jews, Republican philosemites and kindred spirits, Bernard-Lazare questions the emancipatory value of a purely political revolution and the assimilation which it is supposed to have accomplished. The Synagogue survived the French Revolution and continued to foster religio-national ties. From a social point of view, similarly, very little changed. Emancipated by and into a bourgeois society, French Jewry remained by and large middle-class. There was no rush to work on the land or in the *atelier*. Rothschild could no longer be treated like Shylock; that was all. This situation was quite understandable, since no governmental decree can change habits of mind and ways of life acquired over centuries. At this stage, and it is an essential postulate for the optimism of the second part of the book, the eternal Jew becomes capable of change, presumably as a result of increased contact with the outside world since the Revolution. But political emancipation must be accompanied by intellectual and moral self-emancipation.

Assimilation, considered not as a *fait accompli* but as *à accomplir*, something still to come, must be directed not towards absorbing the mores of the non-Jewish middle-classes, who at any rate are increasingly hostile to the Jews, seeing in their one-time allies dangerous rivals; it must be directed towards the socialist society in the making which, in its general socialisation, will at last normalise the 'middle-classness' of French Jewry. What a bourgeois Revolution failed to accomplish and what Napoleon's decrees could not accomplish, socialism might bring about: it might transform a community of shopkeepers and traders into peasants and workers.

The historical section ends with what is, psychologically speaking, the most important chapter of the whole book (chapter 7). The title itself, 'La littérature antijudaïque et les préjugés' is significant. After having considered the different forms of anti-Jewish legislation devised by Church and State to combat the Jew, Bernard-Lazare turns to the myths and legends created about the Jews by theologians, philosophers, historians and poets. With this comes a significant change in emphasis: Jewish insociability and fanaticism are bad enough, but the phobias and prejudices of Christian detractors, which cannot in any way be compared with those of the ancient world, are positively hairraising. From the advent of Christianity to the Middle Ages and the Reformation, Christian apologetics have been denigrating Judaism to prove the excellence of the new religion. They have been persuading, coercing, burning the infidel and his books. But the obstinate Jew survived. This 'unnatural' survival had somehow to be explained. The door was wide open to myths.

When Bernard-Lazare set out to write his history of antisemitism, Christianity had been a temptation. When he finished it, having steeped himself in the vast body of anti-Jewish literature which haunted him for the rest of his life, he was more than a little hostile to it and all but converted to Judaism. Not that the fanatical rabbis escape his wrath. In the matter of fanaticism Synagogue and Church were matched; but in all other respects, numbers, power, freedom of action, it was a veritable battle between David and Goliath. Bernard-Lazare's pity and admiration for David was growing, even for the harassed doctors of the Synagogue whose logic and reasoning sometimes proved more than a match for the ecclesiastics who not infrequently terminated the lengthy disputations by burning the Talmud; admiration

even for the detestable Talmud, burnt for 300 years and still
surviving. This, it seemed, was Israel's special poetry and mystery:
fidelity and survival. And to have survived centuries of deaths
must pre-suppose an uncommon spiritual strength. Thus, paradoxical as it may seem, in the course of trying to understand the
antisemitic viewpoint, Bernard-Lazare discovered his Jewish roots.
Not the religion, to which he never took, but Judaism. It is no
exaggeration to speak of a conversion, especially if we compare
the beginning and the end of the book. In chapter I he regrets
that the nationalist, materialist old religion, with its eyes fixed on
the good life on earth, did not become absorbed into the new
spiritual religion. At the end, he pays Marx the following compliment. I would add that behind the judaisation of the author of
The Jewish Question, frequently quoted by left-wing antisemites,
there may well have been a polemical or satirical intention; but
there can be no doubt about Bernard-Lazare's enthusiasm for the
ideal revolutionary Jew, the combination of Talmudist and
Prophet which he himself aspires to be and which he projects
onto Marx.

> Ce descendant d'une lignée de rabbins et de docteurs hérita
> de toute la force logique de ses ancêtres; il fut un talmudiste
> lucide et clair, que n'embarrassèrent pas les minuties
> niaises de la pratique, un talmudiste qui fit de la sociologie,
> et appliqua ses qualités natives d'exégète à la critique de
> l'économie politique. Il fut animé de ce vieux matérialisme
> hébraïque qui rêva perpétuellement d'un paradis réalisé sur
> la terre et repoussa toujours la lointaine et problématique
> espérance d'un éden après la mort; mais il ne fut pas qu'un
> logicien, il fut aussi un révolté, un agitateur, un âpre
> polémiste, et il prit son don du sarcasme et de l'invective,
> là où Heine l'avait pris: aux sources juives.[16]

Looking at the present

'Conversion', 'metamorphosis', are the only words to describe the
dramatic change in attitude to Jew and antisemite as we move
from the past to the present. The unsociable Jew has become the
Socialist Jew, the conservative spirit of the Jewish religion has
given way to the revolutionary spirit of Judaism, the narrow
nationalists of the past are now seen to play their part in liberal
and libertarian movements the world over. Bernard-Lazare

enthusiastically provides a list of names to prove his point,[17] a sort
of 'Who's Who' in the 'Jewish Socialist International' which
delighted Maurras. The Talmud itself is rehabilitated, though
with certain reservations, for it lacks prophetic vision. Still, the
rabbis were the rationalist philosophers of their age, appealing to
human reason in order to understand the word of God and
teaching the faithful to love life. Jewish materialism, once so
decried, is now elevated to being the source of Messianic socialism
– seeking to establish on earth, in the here and now, the reign of
justice, freedom and equality.

Historically speaking, there is a great deal of truth in the picture
he presents of the changed Jew: a dramatic change, when one
compares the participation in revolutionary movements of young
Russian Jews with the traditional attitudes of their parents. But
logically, within the context of his own work, this dramatic
change is not adequately explained. He tries to explain it by
saying that the modern Jew has become detalmudised, and he
seems to think that a break with the Talmud signifies a return
to the Prophets, the ancient source of revolutionary traditions.
However that may be, the changeability now ascribed to the Jew
is difficult to reconcile with Bernard-Lazare's stress in the first
part of the book on the Jew's fixed and unchanging essence.

It is obvious what has happened to Bernard-Lazare personally:
in his mind and to his own satisfaction, socialism and Jewish
roots have come together, one being the secularised and univer-
salised continuation of the other. Socialism, in other words, which
already had the salutary effect of making him take a closer look
at antisemitism's anti-capitalist pretensions, has allowed him to
become proud of his Jewish roots, and we see him here celebrating
his newly-found pride and unity. Looking around him, he finds
other Jews active in the various revolutionary and Socialist movements, men forgotten today whose works it would be interesting
to rescue from oblivion one day. He sees them, and himself, as
proof that the spirit of revolutionary Judaism is alive and doing
well.[18]

One more notable change in his presentation of the Jewish
situation: whereas in the past all Jews seemed to be engaged in
commercial activity of one sort or another and thus were, according to contemporary Socialist thinking which Bernard-Lazare
shared, *unproductive* middlemen at best, and social parasites
more often than not, he now clearly distinguishes between Jewish

middlemen and capitalists, no worse and no better than any other
members of the same class, and the forgotten Jewish proletariat
of the 'sweat shops' in New York and London's East End, the
Jewish masses of Eastern Europe, wretched in their underpaid or
partial employment and more wretched still when they cannot
find work or are prevented from working by law. The existence
of a Jewish proletariat caused some surprise in France when it
impinged on consciousness, following L. Soloweitshick's work,
*Un prolétariat méconnu: la situation sociale et économique des
ouvriers juifs* (1898). Bernard-Lazare, who had been collecting
facts and figures since 1893, was one of the first to draw attention
to the wretched conditions of the Jewish working-classes.[19]

Facing the dynamic, modern, revolutionary Jew, playing his
part alongside his non-Jewish fellow socialists for the liberation
of all the working-classes, is the antisemite, a character of the
past, dreaming of the good old days, lost in vain illusions, hostile
to change and equating change with catastrophe for which the
Jew alone is blamed, taking refuge in old prejudices dressed up
as science and justified in modern terminology for the sake of
propaganda. This is, by and large, how Bernard-Lazare sees the
various forms of modern antisemitism, as variations on two basic
ancient prejudices: national (xenophobic fear of the foreigner)
and religious (essentially also a fear of the outsider). The Jew
is, as he has always been, a convenient scapegoat for every
nation's misfortunes. In this sense antisemitism is the oldest 'Weltanschauung'.

Bernard-Lazare goes through antisemitism's various forms,
ethnic, ethical, nationalist, economic, social, Christian-social in
Western Europe (where it is confined to literature) and surveys
Eastern Europe and Rumania (where persecution was legalised
as in medieval times). It must have been a lugubrious experience.
There is hardly a name, work or formative influence missing from
the discussion. The philosophical antisemitism of Schopenhauer,
that of Hegel and his left-wing disciples: Feuerbach, Ruge, Bruno
Bauer; that of the anarchist Stirner whose works Bernard-Lazare
had thought at one point of translating, that of Toussenel, a
socialist forerunner in France. Bernard-Lazare notes with regret
that there are '*traces*' in Fourier and Proudhon. Capefigue,
Stoecker, Dühring, Tridon, Regnard all receive attention. Gougenot des Mousseaux and Rohling are discussed in greater detail,
possibly because their ideas had at one stage influenced him. It is

interesting to note in this respect that he is now familiar with the reply to Rohling's misinterpretations of the Talmud. Drumont, naturally, is not forgotten, though his ideas, deliberately minimised as a collection of every possible Jew-hatred on the market, are not honoured with a special place. Tribute is paid to the lively polemicist and influential propagandist but, writes Bernard-Lazare, compared with his German fellow-antisemites, Drumont is an inferior social thinker. Drumont did not agree: 'étant Français je dois leur être bien supérieur'.[20]

A newcomer or apparent newcomer on the busy scene is racial antisemitism. Born in Germany, it is represented in the main by Germans, H. von Treitschke, A. Wagner, G. Schoenerer, E. Dühring. W. Marr[21] systematised these various theories, and his work had some success in France. Gobineau, whose *Inégalités des races* is described as remarkable in many ways, is the main representative in France nowadays, and so to a lesser extent is Renan, though he abandoned these ideas towards the end of his life. Drumont is a latecomer and has not made these obscure theories any more lucid. Neither has Edmond Picard. To Bernard-Lazare racialist theories were even less tenable than many other theories. Race is a fiction, he declares, there are only nations; they are unequal for a host of reasons, geography, climate, history, and so on, but not for any innate characteristics or specific biological constitution. All in all, he rather suspects that this newcomer is nothing more than national antisemitism dressed up in 'science', an intellectual pastime of idle brains with a mania for classifying mankind. To the very last, Bernard-Lazare refused to take racial antisemitism seriously. He liked cracking jokes about the so-called Aryan superiority when it is claimed at the same time that a few thousand Semites are capable of getting the better of several million Aryans.[22] If the Semite's power lies in corruption, then it must be concluded that the Aryans are frightfully corruptible. Today all this may seem tragically shortsighted. The truth is that Bernard-Lazare had a higher opinion of the rationality of the modern antisemite than of his more ignorant and gullible ancestor. Thus, he is constantly underestimating irrational forces. The conspiracy complex, for example, is treated rather lightly. The Dreyfus Affair was to be a rude awakening. Had Bernard-Lazare known of the *Protocols of the Elders of Zion* (the notorious Tzarist forgery which purported to present evidence of a world-wide Jewish conspiracy to seize power) he

would have thought that the world had gone mad – a madness
that is still with us. We must also add that concepts of racial
purity and hierarchy were entirely alien to his way of thinking.
What is an Aryan, he asks? And why is the white race considered
superior when there have been such magnificent past civilisations
in Africa and Asia by coloured 'races'?

The antisemitism that most preoccupied – and secretly worried
– him is that of the Left. Sadly he records that with few exceptions
Socialist thinkers of the nineteenth century all had antisemitic
tendencies or at least traces of them. Like Christians who do not
distinguish between deicides, so to the Socialist *all* Jews are
capitalists, mercantile, unproductive, parasites, the very epitome
of capitalism. Moreover, in common with reactionaries and many
Catholics, socialism also tends to see the rise of capitalism as the
consequence of the emancipation of Jewry, as if the Jew had
created the system instead of having merely been *one* of its instruments – and then only in the West, and notably in France.
Bernard-Lazare, who knew all these conceptions and misconceptions well through having largely shared them at one stage, took
great care to widen socialist horizons, to direct their eyes towards
the masses of non-French and working-class Jews. He reminds
them too that the prophets were among the first critics of Jewish
capitalists.

It is convenient at this stage to anticipate a little and say
something about the public debate which arose between Bernard-
Lazare and Drumont in 1896, concerning the place of religion in
antisemitism. One of the aspects that most appealed to Drumont
about Bernard-Lazare's book was that it refuted 'le reproche
ridicule fait à l'antisémitisme d'être une guerre de religion'.[23] To
Drumont, assured of a conservative and Catholic public but
wishing to cast his net more widely and catch radical, anticlerical
and left-wing opinion, the non-religious character of antisemitism
was of the utmost importance. In his reply, Bernard-Lazare
admitted having inadequately treated the subject in his book
with regard to *modern* antisemitism (medieval Christian antisemitism received very full treatment).

> Je récrirais aujourd'hui ce livre que j'aurais sans doute bien
> des choses à y changer, bien des choses à y ajouter, mais si
> je me fais un reproche, c'est justement de n'avoir pas précisé
> les causes religieuses de l'antisémitisme ; c'est de n'avoir pas

suffisamment montré combien elles servent les intérêts
économiques de certains capitalistes.[24]

Now, Drumont was not wrong in noticing that by 1896, after
the Dreyfus Affair, Bernard-Lazare was putting an altogether
new emphasis on religious prejudice. But he was totally mistaken
in thinking that this new emphasis was an attempt to belittle the
modern antisemitic movement. On the contrary. To Bernard-
Lazare's mind, religious prejudice and clerical politics made a
frighteningly powerful combination. Christianity's anti-Jewish
myths and symbolism remained antisemitism's lifeblood.

Actually, this idea is quite clearly stated in the book, and the
chapter on 'modern antisemitism and its literature' begins with
a full account of Christian antisemitic literature, much of it
coming from the pens of priests, following the French Revolution
(interpreted as a Jewish plot) and running right through the
nineteenth century, with a marked increase in publications in the
early 1880s, just before the appearance of *La France Juive* (1886).
Drumont, according to Bernard-Lazare, made extensive use of
his predecessors though he did not always acknowledge them.
This account, accompanied by an impressive bibliography,[25]
encourages all sorts of speculation. Contrary to common belief
Jew-hatred and religious prejudice do not seem to have been so
very dead in France before Drumont's appearance on the scene,
which may help to explain the puzzling success of *La France
Juive*. Bernard-Lazare did certainly not minimise either the
presence or the permanence of religious prejudice. But, and this is
the point, the prejudice had ultimately to be eliminated, together
with the Jewish religion which provoked it, in order to fit in with
the thesis of the book and allow an optimistic conclusion.

The future or a strange optimism
The incongruities and inconsistencies between the two parts of
the book largely reflect the author's own development and re-
appraisals. One may well ask why a writer of Bernard-Lazare's
ability and sensitiveness did not somehow manage to give the
work greater unity. It may have been a simple question of time.
It could also be that he deliberately refrained from imposing an
artificial and retrospective unity on a history which is also his
personal history.

But there is perhaps another explanation, not necessarily

exclusive of the above, for the curious juxtaposition of antisemitism and anti-antisemitism. Was Bernard-Lazare perhaps using a polemical method Bloy called 'la méthode d'épuiser l'objection'? This was apparently the reason behind the violence in *Le Salut par les Juifs*. The idea, it would seem, is to agree with the opponent, win his attention, *exhaust* his objections and, once this is done, gradually lead him on to different conclusions. Did Bernard-Lazare adopt a similar sort of method?[26] Did he let the antisemite have his way on the talmudised Jew of the past in the hope of making him realise that modern antisemitism has no *raison d'être* since the modern Jew is completely liberated from the Talmud and largely liberated from religion? Antisemitism would thus be deprived of what largely justified it in the past. Did Bernard-Lazare bury the Talmud and the past in the hope of saving modern Jewry? Whether or not he consciously used this dangerous polemical method, the strange optimistic conclusion seems to fit it.

After the presentation of a vigorous movement which had grown rapidly in Western Europe since the 1840s, and of continuing persecution and massacres in Eastern Europe, the optimistic conclusion predicting the disappearance of antisemitism reminds one a little of certain of Zola's novels with a happy ending unwarranted by the logic of the story. The optimism is inspired by three considerations: because the Jew is changing, because religious, political, social and economic conditions are changing, above all because antisemitism 'est une des manifestations persistantes et dernières du vieil esprit de réaction et d'étroit conservatisme qui essaie vainement d'arrêter l'évolution révolutionnaire'.[27]

No one will quarrel with the general validity of each of these conclusions. But it need hardly be pointed out that they did not add up to Bernard-Lazare's prediction. What strange irony to predict the imminent end of antisemitism on the eve of the Dreyfus Affair and the not too distant end of the Jewish people, as a people, on the eve of Herzl's *Jewish State*! For once Bernard-Lazare proved not to be the authentic prophet Péguy came to see in him, 'le prophète du malheur', but a false prophet seemingly blinded by his own theories, hopes and wishful thinking, predicting the future without adequate reference to the present. Actually this is not the case. In reality, in his heart of hearts, Bernard-Lazare did not believe in either of these two disappearances and

before the year was out, only a few months after the publication
of the book, he publicly said so.[28] As far as antisemitism was
concerned, he realised more than most people the extension, the
importance and the enormous popularity the movement was
enjoying. He wanted to halt the progress, challenge the opponent,
persuade and awaken misinformed or apathetic public opinion,
in particular perhaps those of his anarchist and socialist friends
who were flirting with Drumont. If he erred, it was on the side of
too much faith in the rational capacity of most men to think and
act according to the truth if the truth is put before them. One
could also say, perhaps, that his fundamental conception of the
role of the writer steered him towards optimism. He believed that
it was the writer's task not merely to expose present evil and
'malheur', important though this was, but also to point the way
to how things should be, and must be, in the future. Even in the
most hopeless hours of the Dreyfus Affair he could never bring
himself to end his works on a note other than that of hope.

As for the hopeful death-sentence pronounced on the Jewish
people, this is the greatest psychological contradiction in the book,
for Bernard-Lazare no longer really considered it possible, necessary or indeed desirable. In later years he was to refer to
Antisemitism its history and causes as already having expounded
the idea of a Jewish nation.[29] What he did not say was that in
1894 he postulated the necessity for this nation to disappear.
Perhaps only he knew that he no longer meant it, that his real
aspirations were ahead of the absorptionist logic demanded by
a thesis conceived in earlier assimilationist days. The thesis, it will
be remembered, was this: the Jew, product of a fiercely nationalist
religion, was the primary and permanent cause of antisemitism.
It follows that if antisemitism is to disappear, the Jewish religion
has to disappear. Secularised and denationalised, the Jews will be
absorbed into the host nation and cease to exist as a people. Such
was the logic of the argument, and Bernard-Lazare stuck to it.
Not without ill-concealed regret: for with the Jewish religion had
to be buried the magnificent revolutionary spirit of Judaism,
lauded in a stirring funeral oration.[30] His only consolation was
that the majority would absorb some of it and thus become a little
judaised by the minority. However, he knew that in order to
judaise one had to remain a Jew.

Reception and repercussions

Except by a few close friends, the work was generally ill understood and on occasions spectacularly misused. Official Jewish
circles were hostile. The symbolist poet Gustave Kahn was baffled.
An embarrassed Lucien Muhlfeld was flippant about this
'amusing' history. Alfred Naquet later expressed his irritation at
the suggestion of Jewish unsociability. However, he also admitted
to having borrowed extensively from this 'beau livre' in his
parliamentary speech against antisemitism. Did Théodore
Reinach have it in mind when he told the *Société des Etudes
Juives* in 1895 that while the society could not concern itself with
the present trials of Judaism however poignant they may be, it
could, from the serene level of history, contribute indirectly to
rehabilitating the Judaism of today by dissipating the errors
accumulated with regard to the Judaism of long ago? Bernard-
Lazare's method went precisely in the opposite direction.[31]

High praise indeed came from the antisemitic side. Drumont
was exceedingly complimentary about this 'livre remarquable
fort nourri de faits et dominé d'un bout à l'autre par un bel effort
d'impartialité, par la consigne donnée au cerveau de ne pas céder
aux impulsions de la race'.[32] Extracts were given to show that
Bernard-Lazare said what Drumont was saying every day, only
he said it differently. The book contained, Drumont admitted,
criticisms, but they were merely a matter of detail. More surprising was the author's insensitivity to the superiority of French
antisemitism to German antisemitism. In spite of such minor
lapses, the book was recommended reading for all students of
antisemitism. Bernard-Lazare, who had sent the book to the
Libre Parole for review, presumably with the intention of pro-
voking a debate, must have been disappointed at the praise. When
in May 1896 Drumont[33] returned to singing his praise, Bernard-
Lazare hit back with 'Contre l'antisémitisme'. This did spark off a
much commented public debate between him and Drumont, later
published in brochure-form (Bernard-Lazare's articles) under the
same title of *Contre l'antisémitisme*. From it all, Drumont drew
his own lesson about Jewish ingratitude: on the one occasion
that he had had the weakness to say something nice about a Jew,
he got no credit for it. 'Que voulez-vous? La race est comme cela.'

Edmond Picard's long and laudatory review in the libertarian
journal *La Société Nouvelle*[34] is of an altogether different standard.

He too reproduces appropriate extracts to illustrate the contention that some pages of this book are as virulent as any antisemitic pamphlet. But he also recognised that the author is 'plutôt sympathique à la nation juive'. Above all he clearly understood that Bernard-Lazare was trying to deprive antisemitism of its primary cause by killing the Talmud and the Jewish religion. He raises some pertinent objections to the logic with which this is done, but the argument *per se* is of no interest to him. What matters to him is race, not religion. He will not accept assimilability in principle, and assimilation or absorption seems to him disastrous. His ideal is a complete racial apartheid between Aryan and Semite (he is one of the few people really to mean Semite and not merely Jew) and he cannot understand why so enlightened a thinker as Bernard-Lazare dismisses racial theories as fiction. To Bernard-Lazare's assimilationist solution Picard opposes a 'Zionist' solution, albeit of a common antisemitic kind: 'Qu'ils retournent plutôt en Judée faire un essai nouveau de ce dont ils sont capables quand ils ne vivent pas en parasites sur le mouton aryen.'

More serious at the beginning of the Dreyfus Affair was the racialist exploitation of the antisemitic parts of the book, fresh in everybody's mind. While Bernard-Lazare was protesting against theories of racial inevitability which pronounced Dreyfus guilty before he was tried and made traitors of all Jews,[35] critics took pleasure in confounding Bernard-Lazare with Bernard-Lazare. This was brilliantly done by a man signing himself 'Agathon' who has all the appearance of being, not the Agathon of later fame (Henri Massis and Alfred de Tarde), but the young Charles Maurras. After stating that Bernard-Lazare could be called with equal justification an antisemite and a 'frénétique and fanatique israelite', and after leaving the Israelite to sort out his own complexes and contradictions, Agathon proceeds to illustrate with ample quotations from *Antisemitism, its history and causes* that 'les juifs sont une minorité organisée et solidaire' and that Judaism 'est encore un ethnos...il a gardé ses préjugés, son égoïsme et sa vanité de peuple'.[36] These generalisations, made by Bernard-Lazare about as yet incompletely assimilated modern Jewry, were used against Captain Dreyfus, who must have been one of the most perfect examples of completed Jewish assimilation.[37]

If, as I strongly suspect, this Agathon was Maurras, then all one can say is that *Antisemitism, its history and causes* made a deep impression.[38] Maurras never forgot to mention it whenever he spoke of Bernard-Lazare, which is not infrequently, especially at the time of the monument in October 1908. That this 'anti-semitic Jew' should have become the saviour of the traitor Dreyfus struck Maurras as characteristic of Jewish solidarity, for in times of peace 'cette nation ne s'aime pas';[39] it only draws together when its privileges are endangered. He also later recalled that this antisemitic Jew died a Zionist.[40] In 1907 the *Action Française* review brought out a weird collection of 'What is best in Anti-semitism, its history and causes'. It was introduced by Maurras as follows:

> Recueils de jugements invraisemblables mais certains, sévères mais justes et gênants, mais incontestables d'un Juif Bernard-Lazare sur le juif de tous les lieux et de tous les temps, insociable, anarchiste, cosmopolite, agent révolu-tionnaire mais conservateur vis-à-vis de lui-même.[41]

The selections took the form of a sort of text-book arranged in twenty-nine paragraphs, each with a title provided by the Action Française who also provided footnote annotations, nearly all expansions of what Bernard-Lazare had said. The only disagree-ment concerned the International which, according to Bernard-Lazare, was inspired by Marx but not founded by him alone; nor was it a secret society led by Jews. Maurras had different views, naturally. What especially delighted him, and he quotes it in full, was the list of Jewish revolutionaries, a 'Who's Who' in Inter-national Red Jewry which confirmed all his suspicions.

The syndicalist Georges Sorel, who by 1912 had evolved his own, virulent brand of socialist antisemitism, was angered by this sort of praise for the Red Jew and by the judaisation of the International. It was most inopportune at a time of dialogue (initiated by the Action Française, but its complex about the Red Peril sometimes led it astray) between the anti-democratic Left (mainly anarcho-syndicalists) and the anti-democratic Right. Sorel did his best to demolish Bernard-Lazare's contention that the Jew has been a revolutionary element throughout history, from the prophets to Marx.[42] He tried to dejudaise the socialist master though he was bound to agree with Bernard-Lazare that in 'les théories si prodigieusement nuageuses qui occupent une place considérable dans *Le Capital*',[43] Marx may well have been a Talmudist. Sorel takes up many points made by Bernard-Lazare, though curiously enough, or perhaps he is being very consistent, he never sings the praise of the antisemitic Jew. He denigrates instead the mad Jew who endowed Jewry with a civilising mission ('Il serait plus convenable de dire que les Juifs contribuèrent puissamment à maintenir l'Occident dans la barbarie')[44] and the dubious scholar who simply could not have read all the books mentioned, since this would have been a work of several years! This is a spiteful and rather stupid attack motivated by all sorts of reasons, including Sorel's wish to provoke the Jews by attacking Bernard-Lazare. It was a grave miscalculation. The last thing prominent Israelites of France were likely to do was to rush to Bernard-Lazare's defence, or their own for that matter. The most interesting thing about these denigrations is that their author personified what Bernard-Lazare had most feared and what his book and later writings were intended to prevent from developing, 'la réaction révolutionnaire'.[45] We might call it 'fascism' today.

The Librairie Française has recently republished (1969) this 'étude sérieuse très fouillée... Cette réédition s'imposait... Comment expliquer la disparition d'un document de cette valeur? Les conformistes seuls pouvaient s'en féliciter, qu'ils fussent israélites ou antisémites.' The same editorial note speaks of the author's pertinent prophecies and not so pertinent prophecies; to the first belongs hostility towards Jewish capitalism; to the second the disappearance of antisemitism. We are also told that this new edition 'vient à son heure'.[46] What is this hour? one wonders.

Bernard-Lazare never disowned his history. He repeatedly declared that certain parts needed to be modified and the work as a whole completed. Views arrived at subsequently were in patent contradiction to certain ideas expressed in this, his first serious challenge to antisemitism and the first formal proposal of a solution to the Jewish Question. However, he obstinately clung to defending his early work, perhaps because he knew its hidden intentions; perhaps because it was often used to confound and hound him. He left instructions, however, that the book should not be republished after his death without the following insertion: 'Les idées de l'auteur s'étaient modifiées sur bien des points.' After a lot of heart-searching the family agreed to have the work republished in 1934 (by Crès) but it appeared without the crucial sentence, much to Madame Bernard-Lazare's regret.[47] An old friend, André Fontainas, in a preface-study, did the next best thing by reproducing the passage from the 1896 polemic with

Drumont: 'Je récrirais aujourd'hui ce livre que j'aurais bien des choses à y changer...'[48] It is regrettable that the editor of the Librarie Française, though evidently familiar with Fontainas' preface, did not think fit even to mention the reservation.

In conclusion it should be emphasised again that a more or less justified enthusiasm displayed by antisemitic commentators for certain restricted aspects of the book should not be allowed to detract from its value as an historical work which remains unsurpassed in many ways. In a purely descriptive, fact-finding sense, it is still one of the most richly documented studies. Being among the pioneers in this field, Bernard-Lazare went to primary sources, and as a result his presentation retains even now much of its originality. From what has been said earlier it is obvious why the modern reader will not be able to accept all of Bernard-Lazare's interpretations, although his analysis of social, economic, religious and intellectual factors involved in the development of antisemitism remains as pertinent today as it was then.

The conflicts and incongruities which we have examined are not so much the result of a misreading of history as the record of a personal struggle which a sensitive French Jew was forced to wage with himself by the success of *La France Juive*.

Although *Antisemitism, its history and causes* was never rewritten in book-form, Bernard-Lazare's life was a passionate rewriting of it in action, and the first stage came with the Dreyfus Affair.

PART II: THE DREYFUS AFFAIR

6

INVOLVEMENT

Introduction: the Dreyfus case and the Dreyfus Affair

On 15 October 1894, Captain Alfred Dreyfus, an Alsatian Jewish officer with a hitherto distinguished Army career, was arrested on suspicion of having betrayed military secrets to the Germans. The incriminating piece of evidence was an unsigned, undated, handwritten letter, known as the *bordereau*, sent to an unnamed person at the German Embassy, assumed to be the German military attaché, Colonel von Schwartzkoppen. From there it was allegedly transmitted to French Intelligence through the 'usual channels', i.e. via the wastepaper basket in the Colonel's office and the French cleaner whose sideline it was to turn the scraps of paper over to the Statistical Section. This was the cover name for the special espionage and counter-espionage section of French Intelligence (le Deuxième Bureau), itself part of the War Office. The *bordereau* listed five military documents put at Schwartzkoppen's disposal. According to the official War Office version, it was decided on the basis of the nature of these documents that the spy must be an artillery officer who was or had been attached to the General Staff. Dreyfus fitted the bill. Various department chiefs at the War Office identified Dreyfus' handwriting with that of the *bordereau*. So did two groups of outside handwriting experts who were consulted, though their findings were not unanimous. Apart from this one 'clear' piece of written evidence, there was a fair amount of suspicion: Captain Dreyfus spoke German fluently; more seriously, though he had opted for French nationality, some members of his family had stayed in German-occupied Alsace. He also had a reputation for being ambitious, keen, interested in everything, hardworking to the point of working late hours. He did not mix freely with brother officers. In fact, he was generally disliked by both superiors and colleagues.

After the arrest, ordered by the then Minister of War, General Mercier, with the support of his military staff, notably the Head of the Statistical Section, Colonel Sandherr, the War Office conducted two enquiries and as a result the charge of high treason was formally brought. On 22 December 1894 Captain Dreyfus was tried by a court-martial, held in secret; he was found guilty by unanimous verdict and sentenced to life imprisonment on Devil's Island. There he remained for the next four years, in particularly cruel conditions of solitary confinement, protesting his innocence as he had done from the day of his arrest, but believed by only a handful of powerless people. Thanks to the tenacious efforts made by this small group, headed in the first instance by the victim's brother, Mathieu Dreyfus, and by Bernard-Lazare, the 1894 verdict was quashed in June 1899 and a retrial was ordered. It took place in Rennes before a second court-martial, held mostly in public this time and attended, either as witnesses or spectators, by well-known public figures as well as by distinguished visitors from abroad. The extraordinary verdict which closed an extraordinary one-month-long trial stunned France and the civilised world: guilty by a majority of five votes to two and with the baffling addition – for a crime of high treason – of unspecified 'extenuating circumstances'.

The government intervened and offered the condemned man a pardon which he accepted on condition that he would be free to prove his innocence. It was not until July 1906, twelve years after the original trial, that the Appeal Courts annulled the Rennes verdict and pronounced Dreyfus innocent without retrial. Whether this procedure was strictly legal is arguable but it was undoubtedly just since a third court-martial would almost certainly have condemned an innocent man for the third time.

This, in a nutshell, is the Dreyfus Case. The Dreyfus Affair is a very different matter. Bernard-Lazare must be given the major credit for having transformed what in 1895 seemed a closed case about which very little was known into the ever-open, endlessly interpreted and re-interpreted 'immortelle affaire', a maze of documents and subsidiary affairs, an ideological battle fought with an unusual intensity of passion and involving the whole nation. Has there ever been an occasion before or since when a country almost went to civil war over the guilt or innocence of one man? It was in a way a peculiarly nineteenth-century battle in

which the rights of the individual were of supreme importance
but were challenged by old reactionary forces (e.g. the monarchist
Maurras who regarded Republican democracy and the Revolution from which it sprang as an aberration) as well as by new
totalitarian forces (e.g. Barrès's idea that injustice to the individual
is preferable to disorder in the community).

Leaving aside for the moment both major issues and detailed
discussion of events, here is a simple guide through the labyrinth
of the Affair via the main documents and the people behind them.
As a general point concerning documents, let it be said *en passant*
that they grew to enormous proportions between the two courts-
martial, from a mere dozen or so in 1894 to over 400 in 1899.
The slender Dreyfus dossier was well and truly 'nourished', as
the Chief of Staff, General Boisdeffre, had advised. Bernard-
Lazare quoted with delight the official War Office classification
of the secret dossier – there was also a voluminous official dossier
and an ultra-secret dossier – presented to the Rennes tribunal. The
secret dossier was said to consist of papers relevant to Dreyfus,
papers irrelevant to Dreyfus, and forgeries.

From this mountain of papers, three basic documents, all used
at the first court-martial, stand out: the *bordereau* and the *acte
d'accusation*, the main evidence presented during the trial, and
the much talked of *canaille de D* note, one of four pieces which
together made up the original secret dossier. It was constituted
on General Mercier's order, or at least with his approval, because
it was felt that the *bordereau* and the *acte d'accusation* might not
secure a conviction. This dossier was communicated to the judges
after the trial, when they had retired to deliberate on the verdict.
In other words, the judges were presented with evidence which
the accused and his counsel were denied the right to contest.

This was an illegality by all standards. Whether it can be
justified on the slippery grounds of the security of the State, as
Mercier steadfastly maintained, is perhaps open to question. (It
is worth noting that the procedure adopted at Rennes, i.e. the
secret dossier was examined by the judges in closed session but in
the presence of the accused and his counsel, satisfied the require-
ments of both justice and secrecy.)

The real point about the secret dossier and its secret communication is, to put it bluntly, that it contained irrelevant papers –
and possibly one distorted piece – which would not have stood up
to cross-examination. The major irrelevancy is the *canaille de D*

note. It was an undated letter sent by the German military attaché to his Italian counterpart, Colonel Panizzardi, and intercepted by the Statistical Section. The exact date of interception is uncertain. It has been put as 1892 and 1893. At any rate it preceded the *bordereau* (September 1894) by some time. The actual text is unimportant: it concerned a common agent, designated by *canaille* (scum) *de D*, who was said to pass on useless information and with whom the foreign attachés wanted to break off relations. The three significant words were *canaille de D*. Given the circumstances in which it was presented to the military judges – on the order of the Minister of War, as a confidential document of great importance, without comment or explanation – it is understandable that the judges, questioning neither the identity of D, nor the nature of the note, nor indeed the legality of the whole procedure, were impressed. This, together with the possibly distorted Panizzardi telegram (to be discussed later), seemed more conclusive evidence than anything they had heard in court. The question is whether General Mercier knew that the 'D' referred to a minor clerk at the ministry whose relatively unimportant spying activities were by then known at the Statistical Section. Was he informed or misinformed? However that may be, a piece of evidence completely irrelevant to Dreyfus was secretly and illegally communicated to the judges.

All this was not generally known until, in September 1896, the newspaper *L'Eclair* revealed both the existence of the secret dossier and the *canaille de D* note. Only in its account, the initial D was significantly changed to Dreyfus written out in full. If such a piece exists, Bernard-Lazare replied, then it must be a forgery. Prophetic words, for at this very time Major Henry, leading light at the Statistical Section, was busy concocting a letter which bore the name 'Dreyfus' written out in full. This is the notorious *faux Henry*. Insignificant in the Dreyfus case on which it had no direct influence, Henry's suicide which followed the detection of this forgery (August 1898) remains one of the most mysterious episodes of the Dreyfus Affair.

The *acte d'accusation* is the official indictment, the charge-sheet, so to speak. Gossip-sheet, would be a more appropriate description. It was a report based on the preliminary enquiries conducted by *Commandant* d'Ormescheville, whose role as *rapporteur* to the court-martial was akin to that of an examining magistrate in civil trials, except that d'Ormescheville instead of examining whether there actually was a case set out to prove guilt. In this he followed in the footsteps of the previous War Office investigator, *Commandant* Du Paty de Clam. After having unsuccessfully tried to find evidence of guilt in Dreyfus' home and to extract a confession from the prisoner, Du Paty de Clam set about establishing motives for the crime. For this purpose he relied on unverified, often wild reports by police informers who attributed to Alfred Dreyfus all the gambling and womanising done by anyone called Dreyfus. In the archives of the Paris *Sûreté* there are several such reports as well as a note by an evidently alarmed inspector reminding his agents that there was more than one Dreyfus. D'Ormescheville suitably toned all this down but quite clearly insinuated that Dreyfus gambled and had had mistresses. He also suggested that the Captain frequently went to German-occupied Alsace, that he had relations with agents of foreign powers, and with the *Banque de France*. Much of the report, including the 'proofs' of how Dreyfus *might have* come to possess the documents listed in the *bordereau*, was made up of unfounded and unverified allegations of this nature. Where it did provide real information, as on the contradictory conclusions reached by the handwriting experts, it merely showed up the uncertainty of the case against the accused. It is said that after reading the *acte d'accusation* Edgar Demange, who had previously agreed as a professional lawyer to defend Captain Dreyfus, became convinced of his client's innocence. He wept when he heard the verdict of guilty.

The *canaille de D* note and the *acte d'accusation* were both intended to bolster up the *bordereau*, the only piece of real evidence. It could be contested on every single point, from the handwriting and the careless use of technical terminology (unlikely for an artillery officer) to the nature of the documents (were they confidential or even important?) and Dreyfus' access to them. The general tone of the missive suggested that the author had previous relations with the foreign power concerned, something the prosecution could not prove. Then there was the final sentence: 'I am about to go on manoeuvres.' This was not easily applicable to Dreyfus.

The *bordereau* was much analysed throughout the Affair. It gave rise to long and wearisome debates on technicalities, dates and handwriting, with the experts often elaborating fantastic theories (like Bertillon, the well-known criminologist who became the main prosecution expert) or indulging in dubious psycho-graphology and psycho-linguistics as did a few of the defence experts. And all these questions were debated twice over, once with Dreyfus as the alleged author and then with Esterhazy.

After Mathieu Dreyfus had publicly denounced Esterhazy as the author, in November 1897, the onus fell on him to prove that this was so. The War Office, for its part, was determined to maintain the charge against Dreyfus and went to melodramatic lengths – anonymous letters, secret meetings with a 'veiled lady' and officers in disguise – to protect and brief Esterhazy. He was twice acquitted of the charge of being the author of the *bordereau*; after an official enquiry conducted by General de Pellieux (December 1897) and at a court-martial (January 1898).

Unknown to Mathieu, no less a person than the new head of the Statistical Section, Lieutenant-Colonel Picquart, had also stumbled onto Esterhazy's trail. And for having dared to suggest to his chiefs that Esterhazy and not Dreyfus had written the *bordereau*, Picquart was dismissed from his post and sent on a mission to North Africa from where, it was hoped, he would not return. Picquart had made two disturbing discoveries. First that *Commandant* Esterhazy had been selling information to Schwartzkoppen for some time. Investigations revealed that the *Commandant* was a thoroughly disreputable character and chronically short of money. It appears that the Chiefs of Staff, Generals Boisdeffre and Gonse, were not averse to starting proceedings against Esterhazy but considered that Picquart's main evidence, an intercepted letter from Schwartzkoppen to Esterhazy (*le Petit Bleu*), was inadequate. If this is so, then the protection afforded to Esterhazy came from the Statistical Section alone, notably from its leading figure, Major Henry. The Chiefs of Staff and the Section were agreed, however, in their total opposition to re-opening the Dreyfus case, as Picquart had suggested. Picquart's argument was based on the lack of evidence against Dreyfus. With the *bordereau* removed, there only re-mained the allegedly crushing proofs contained in the so-called secret dossier. He examined the dossier and was aghast to find that it did not contain a scrap of evidence. This was the second alarm-ing discovery. The existence of the dossier was a shock in itself for on Mercier's orders it should have been dismantled. Colonel Sandherr disobeyed the instructions; together with Major Henry he tidied up the dossier, apparently removing one item and adding

Plate 1: Edouard Drumont and a typical page of his paper, *La Libre Parole* (see notes, p. 325)[1] (Photo. Roger-Viollet)

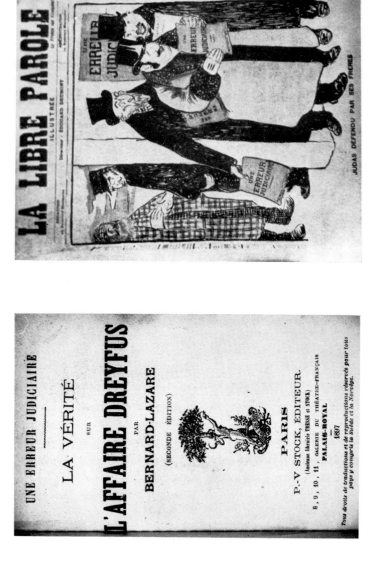

Plate 2. The title-page of *Une erreur judiciare*[2]

Plate 3: 'Judas défendu par ses frères'[3]

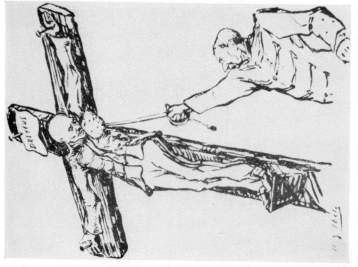

Plate 5: H. G. Ibels: 'Le coup de l'éponge'[5]

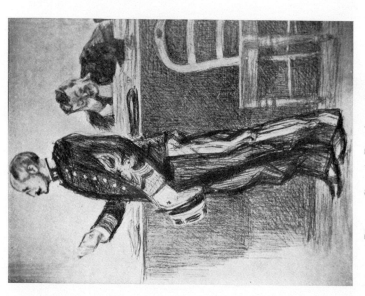

Plate 4: Captain Dreyfus at Rennes[4]

Plate 6: The Second Zionist Congress at Basle, 1898[6]

two others, and then locked it up in a safe. On leaving office, Sandherr bequeathed the secret dossier to his successor, Picquart, with the comment that it contained irrefutable proofs of Dreyfus' guilt and the less the Dreyfus case was looked into the better.

Picquart did examine it, after having concluded that the *bordereau* was not applicable to Dreyfus. He had the courage to tell his chiefs that the secret dossier did not contain any evidence either, that a mistake had probably been made in 1894, and that the Army must right the wrong. For this suggestion he had to pay dearly.

One could almost define the Dreyfus Affair, or at least one important part of it, as the implacable refusal on the part of the military leaders to re-open the Dreyfus case. In order to keep Dreyfus on Devil's Island, Picquart out of the War Office and Esterhazy – later self-confessed author of the *bordereau* – out of the courts and the public limelight, the Army went to extraordinary lengths, to the point of committing perjuries, forgeries and illegalities.

'Why?' was and remains the question. The two persons who might have been able to shed some light, Colonel Sandherr and Major Henry, both took their secrets with them to the grave. The mystery surrounding Henry is largely a matter of why he acted as he did; what he did, is fairly well established. This is not true of Sandherr about whose motives and actions we are almost completely in the dark. Having died in May 1897, before the Affair burst open, he never had to account publicly for his conduct. He is credited, however, with two disorders apt to encourage the wildest speculations. He was strongly antisemitic, according to most accounts. Given his background – Alsace, Army, fervent catholicism – this is not surprising. Secondly, he suffered from cerebral paralysis, the disease of which he died and the reason for his retirement from office two years prior to that (July 1895). It is not suggested that the whole Affair is the brainchild of a sick mind; it clearly is not. On the other hand, the possibility that the Chief of espionage, the most crucial figure in the initial drama, might not have been in full possession of his mental faculties, without this necessarily manifesting itself in an obvious way, is at least worth a thought; a thought to make the imagination boggle. One might just add that the thought had occurred to the War Office though in another connection. A note of late 1896, very probably written by General Gonse, has this to say: 'Or, le colonel

Sandherr, n'étant plus depuis du moins un an en possession de ses facultés. . .' (Archives Nationales, BB 19 94).

Leaving such speculations aside, let me complete the story of the *bordereau*. Esterhazy claimed in 1899 that he had written the *bordereau* on Sandherr's orders. Schwartzkoppen for his part not only affirmed, on his deathbed (1916), that Dreyfus was innocent but he also asserted, in personal notes posthumously published (1930), that he had *never* received the *bordereau*. One can of course choose to ignore these testimonies, coming as they do one from an inveterate liar and the other from a German diplomat. But suppose the liar told the truth for once and that for the tormented Schwartzkoppen the time for diplomatic lies or silence was over, as he claimed? If both or either of these testimonies are true then it is difficult to see the Dreyfus case as a simple miscarriage of justice, a case of mistaken identity, a tragi-comedy of errors with, ultimately, a happy ending. In fact, it has no ending, only an enforced *dénouement*.

No historian has ever done justice to the role played by Bernard-Lazare in the Dreyfus Affair. So wrote Stock in 1938.[1] Numerous histories have appeared since but the statement still holds true, with the notable exception of Professor Thalheimer (*Macht und Gerechtigkeit*, 1958).[2] The unmerited neglect on the part of modern historians is largely due to ignorance, excusable in the sense that Bernard-Lazare's action behind the scenes is largely unrecorded in traditional sources, less excusable when it comes to his published works which are readily available but which, if mentioned at all, are normally given the most perfunctory treatment. Responsibility for this neglect lies with Bernard-Lazare's contemporaries. He was, as Reinach aptly put it, 'une personnalité trop marquante'. Only those familiar with the works of Péguy can form some idea of 'le prophète de l'Affaire Dreyfus'. Even in Péguy's vibrant pages we do not see the prophet of the Affair at work. We see him dying of it, but not living it and creating it.

My interest is primarily in Bernard-Lazare the dreyfusard, his action, his approach, his interpretation of the events, and the impact they made on him personally. Though it is not my intention to write another history of the Affair, I hope that an examination of the testimony left by so crucial a witness will contribute to the understanding of a major historical event.

Involvement

The Dreyfus Affair is full of unexpected encounters and colla-borations. One of the most curious is certainly that between the anarchist writer and the wealthy, conservative, very bourgeois Dreyfus family. And yet it was, strangely enough, Bernard-Lazare's reputation as an anarchist that brought him and Mathieu together. In the course of a visit to the imprisoned Captain Dreyfus the kindly governor of the Santé Prison told the desperate and helpless Dreyfus family that he knew of only two men who could take up the cause of the unhappy Captain: Drumont and Bernard-Lazare.

Musing on how the prison governor would have heard of him, Bernard-Lazare concludes that: 'Je suppose qu'il avait eu à la Santé pendant les années précédentes des anarchistes et des révolutionnaires qui avaient parlé de moi.'[3]

Mathieu knew nothing of Bernard-Lazare. But Joseph Vala-brègue, Mathieu and Alfred's brother-in-law from Carpentras, remembered having heard the name at home. Equipped with letters of introduction from common acquaintances, Valabrègue called on Bernard-Lazare at his Paris flat. Bernard-Lazare wrote: 'Je lui exprimai aussitôt ma sympathie et la conviction que j'avais de l'erreur commise et de l'innocence du Capitaine... De tous les faits suivis au jour le jour, analysés et discutés, la certitude était née en mon esprit que l'affaire était le résultat d'une machination antisémite...'[4] The next day Valabrègue returned with Mathieu, and Bernard-Lazare immediately agreed to help. Thus began, towards the end of February 1895, the famous *syndicat*. (The term became widely used to designate an entirely imaginary organisation of powerful forces secretly working for the liberation of Dreyfus.)

The first point to be emphasised is that until that meeting Bernard-Lazare had not known the Dreyfus family (except for Valabrègue whom he had met occasionally as a child); still less had he been a friend of the family, as is so often incorrectly stated. He was to become 'l'ami de la famille Dreyfus' but in a special way, through shared anguish and suffering. Nor would he have agreed to help Mathieu on the basis of simple letters of recom-mendation. By the time of Mathieu's visit, Bernard-Lazare had already closely followed events day by day, and was already beset by the gravest of doubts. Asked by Jean-Bernard, a journalist from the *Figaro*, how he came to believe in Dreyfus' innocence, he gave the following account:

> Je me suis beaucoup occupé d'études sémitiques et j'ai eu à examiner un grand nombre de ces procès rituels qu'on a faits aux juifs dans le passé et qui, tous, plus ou moins, présentent les éléments de haines, de mensonges, de faussetés, de colères accumulées que nous retrouvons dans le procès actuel. Vous vous souvenez que les antisémites, depuis deux ans, avaient entrepris une campagne contre les juifs dans l'armée? . . . Il fallait une sanction à cette campagne brutale et on a machiné le procès Dreyfus. Dès que j'ai appris l'arrestation, en psychologue, pour mon édification personnelle, j'ai fait mon enquête; je me suis inquiété de la situation de la famille, de sa fortune, de son honorabilité et immédiatement j'ai vu que le mobile du crime manquait. . . Pas de mobile, pas de crime.[5]

By the time of Dreyfus' conviction Bernard-Lazare was certain of two things: that an innocent man had been sentenced and that a machination, and not a simple error of justice, was involved.

There are several questions one might ask at this stage. How, in the absence of any documentary evidence, could he be so certain of Dreyfus' innocence and why, in view of the importance of the matter to him, did he not get in touch with the Dreyfus family who could reasonably be expected to supply him with information? Third, on what were his convictions of foul play based?

Stock's *Mémoires* show why the anarchist was reluctant to contact the wealthy Dreyfus family. Asked by Stock, the publisher, himself an early doubter, why he, Bernard-Lazare, was not taking the Affair in hand, he replied: 'Pourquoi? Ah! si c'était un pauvre diable, je m'inquiéterais de lui aussitôt, mais Dreyfus et les siens sont très riches, dit-on, ils sauront bien se débrouiller sans moi.'[6] Dreyfus' wealth was at first an obstacle; it was to remain an embarrassment, though it did prove immensely useful when it came to 'propaganda costs'.

On the other hand it was precisely Dreyfus' wealth that allowed Bernard-Lazare to eliminate, in his own mind and to his own satisfaction, money as a possible motive for the crime. What other motives remained? Allegiance to Germany principally. That a Jew of Alsace who had opted for French nationality, had made the French army his career, and service in that army his life's ambition, should be spying for Germany for the love of Germany was inconceivable. Treason was unthinkable, not because Dreyfus was a Jew, but because of the type of Jew he was. For the same reason Bernard-Lazare felt certain that the patriotic Jewish bourgeoisie, to which Dreyfus belonged, would make it a point of honour not to speak out publicly in his defence, whatever they felt in their heart of hearts. Familiarity with Jewish mentality must have influenced to some extent his first conviction that there was no motive for the crime and hence no crime. Clearly, he could not publicly argue the case with only personal enquiries and convictions to go on. All he could do, and this he did immediately, was to protest against trial and sentence by the press of a man at first only *accused* of treason. He tried to pour scorn on theories of collective guilt, racial inevitability, semitic treachery.[7] And yet he realised only too well that a blow more powerful than any rational argument would be struck at the Judas–Dreyfus–Jewry logic if Dreyfus could be *proved* innocent. As for the machination, it was the nature of the antisemitic campaign that enlightened him. He gave an excellent account[8] of the crucial first two months of that campaign which reminded him, on the one hand, of the tactics of persecution employed at ritual murder trials in the past, and on the other hand of the very recent anarchist trials which had demonstrated the frightening power of the press to spread fear, terror and superstition through the land. Only this time the mass hysteria, whipped up by a certain sector of the press, reached an unprecedented scale. Furthermore, there was no public jury to restore sanity and few voices dared to protest.

The campaign began with the curious announcement of Drey-fus' arrest. The only paper to contain any information was the *Libre Parole*. On 1 November Drumont announced the arrest of a Jewish officer and unafraid of the consequences of the disclosure, published an anonymous note which had been communicated to him and which revealed in a series of clues the identity of the officer and the nature of his crime. Since everything connected with the arrest was then top secret, the well-briefed informant must have been someone in or close to ministry circles. Why was no enquiry undertaken into the leak? Drumont lost no time in linking this act of treason with the 'prophetic' campaign of 1892 against 'les Juifs dans l'Armée'. Bernard-Lazare needed no reminding. He was fully aware of the strange resemblances be-tween the two campaigns. However, there was one important difference. In 1892 Drumont had not been able to find or create a traitor. In 1894 there was a Jewish traitor, or rather Drumont had to make sure that the man *accused* of treason was never allowed to be anything else but a traitor. What was crucial about the anonymous note communicated to the *Libre Parole* was this one sentence: 'l'Affaire sera étouffée parce que cet officier est juif'. This was the vital phrase, 'elle frappa par avance de suspicion toute défense'.[9] Defending Dreyfus' right to be tried in court before being condemned in the press became tantamount to being in the pay of the 'syndicat'. Those papers which initially defended the accused man's right to be heard were insulted, became the object of insinuations. They fell silent or joined the mob. The liberal press was the first victim to succumb to the terror. Antisemitism had achieved one of its aims: Dreyfus became 'indéfendable' in the press.[10]

As the charges alleged against him multiplied, his treasonable activities being extended to other countries (Austria and Italy) and back-dated to 1890 (which naturally also meant that he could be held responsible for hitherto unexplained leaks of information), Dreyfus became even more 'indéfendable'. Bernard-Lazare gives examples of these extraordinary charges invented or repeated by the press from the *Figaro* and the *Echo de Paris* down to the *Intransigeant*, the *Petit Journal* and the *Libre Parole*.

> Jamais pareil acharnement, pareilles fureurs ne se manifestèrent. La presse et le public donnent. . .l'impression d'une foule sauvage dansant une danse de scalp autour du poteau où est attaché un homme. On perdait à ce point la notion, non seulement de l'équité, mais du simple bon sens, qu'on attribuait à un capitaine d'état-major la connaissance de tous les secrets de la défense du pays; il semblait qu'il eût tenu dans sa main et livré la sécurité de la nation, la vie de tous, et que sa mort seule pût délivrer chacun d'un hallucinant et terrible cauchemar.[11]

One of the most vicious allegations, guaranteed to incite public opinion, was that Dreyfus had betrayed French Intelligence officers 'en mission' who were now languishing in German prisons. The story was started in the *Petit Journal*, was immediately taken up by the *Libre Parole*, which got a military 'authority', General Riu, to confirm it and comment on this most abominable of all crimes on the part of an officer (*Libre Parole*,

2 November, 1894). Rochefort went one step further (*Intransigeant*, 8 November) and supplied the names of the officers thus betrayed. The *Gazette de la Croix*, not to be outdone, published the names of French officers imprisoned not only in Germany but also in Austria and Italy. If one considers how many people would have been incited to anger by this one – completely unfounded – allegation alone (the combined readership of *Le Petit Journal*, *La Libre Parole*, *L'Intransigeant*, *La Croix*, would be considerable) then the extraordinary hysteria displayed by the masses at the degradation ceremony does not seem quite so extraordinary. It was a measure of the success of what Bernard-Lazare called an unprecedented 'système de dénonciation et de calomnie'.

Sympathy for Dreyfus had been so effectively and speedily alienated that not only had he been sentenced by press and public opinion long before the trial had even begun, but people were speculating on the punishment to be meted out. Since the law, as it then stood, did not allow the death penalty for acts of treason committed in peace-time, these were macabre day dreams. The least cruel asked for public degradation and the firing squad. Millevoye of *La Patrie* was for lynching. A group of retired officers, 'décorés de la légion d'honneur', suggested an unspecified 'exemplary punishment' and threatened to demonstrate publicly if there was too much delay. Before the official investigation had even been completed, a reader of the *Petit Journal* (9 November) signing himself 'un vrai patriote', suggested degradation Chinese-style:

> Si j'étais son juge, eh bien! moi, qui ne ferais pas le moindre mal à un animal, je commencerais par l'enfermer dans une cage en fer, comme une bête fauve, et je le ferais passer ainsi devant le front de plusieurs régiments au Champ-de-Mars. Là, chaque officier viendrait lui cracher au visage. Ensuite, la dégradation et le feu de peloton. Je le répète, c'est encore trop doux pour les traîtres à la patrie.[12]

The *Petit Journal* added that this was one of the most moderate suggestions received.

An even worse experience than the spectacle of human cruelty on the part of the masses fanaticised by the patriotic press, was the silence of those who should have tried to stem the tide of hatred and who encouraged it by their silence or their action. Ministers, Hanotaux, Dupuy and most seriously General Mercier, also succumbed to the terror campaign. Bernard-Lazare carefully traces the mounting pressure put on Mercier. At the beginning he was accused of everything, from being in the pay of the syndicate and having imposed Dreyfus on the Intelligence Service at Reinach's bidding, to hushing up evidence and wishing to keep everything connected with the traitor secret. After some weeks of insinuations, insults and threats, General Mercier capitulated. The interview he gave to the *Journal* (17 November) announced his surrender, which was duly applauded by Drumont and Rochefort who promptly withdrew all the previous insults.

I have to disagree with Professor Thalheimer[13] on the subject of Bernard-Lazare's attitude to Mercier. Bernard-Lazare did indeed regard him as primary culprit but without attributing to him the deep-seated antisemitism suggested by Professor Thalheimer. He stated this quite clearly in 1897, at a time when he knew all about the illegality. I believe the picture he then drew of Mercier showed the way he always saw him, as a moral coward and base politician, at first not daring to oppose the antisemitic terror, then coming under its influence and eventually using it to regain popularity and recover political ground lost before the Affair. Indeed, it is because Bernard-Lazare assumes that Mercier was not antisemitic by nature or philosophy but a moral coward unable and unwilling to resist that his crime is all the baser and sadder.

Having once capitulated, Mercier's responsibility was grave indeed, for in official communiqués he freely talked about the case which was then sub-judice. In so doing, he endorsed the condemnation pronounced by press and public opinion. Most serious was the famous interview in the *Figaro* of 28 November from which Bernard-Lazare quotes a long extract. In it, the Minister of War and official head of the Army declared that Dreyfus' arrest had been ordered on the basis of 'rapports accablants' (which had been submitted to the Prime Minister and his Cabinet colleagues) and that Dreyfus' guilt was 'absolutely certain'.

It was a grave affirmation. Other men, Emile Duclaux for example,[14] later recalled their shock at this pre-trial verdict pronounced by the highest military authority before officers under his command had been called upon to sit in judgment. Yves Guyot began to have doubts after reading this interview. *L'Intransigeant*, *La Libre Parole* and other sympathisers, Guyot wrote, have made the Dreyfus Affair into the personal Affair of the Minister of

War.[15] As a result, a verdict of 'not guilty' for Dreyfus would appear to condemn the Minister of War.

To Bernard-Lazare Mercier's action was 'l'action la plus odieuse, la plus inique, la plus déloyale et la plus lâche. Il violait les principes les plus élémentaires de l'équité, il essayait d'imposer d'avance une sentence; il subornait la justice, frappait d'impuissance la défense.'[16]

Dreyfus would be 'indéfendable' to the last. Thus the threat in the *Libre Parole*'s note, 'l'affaire sera étouffée parce que l'officier est juif' had worked all the way, from inciting public opinion and silencing the liberal minority to bringing pressure to bear on the government in the person of the Minister of War, whose attitude in turn weighed on the military tribunal. It was one of the most successful terror campaigns ever staged.

Nothing infuriated public opinion more than when Bernard-Lazare later openly challenged the sacred principle that seven officers must be right. Men with diametrically opposed political and social views could all agree that Dreyfus must be guilty because seven officers said so. Nationalists and reactionaries had their own reasons. Anarchists and Socialists assumed that officers would not condemn one of their caste and class. Others believed that confirming high treason committed by an officer was so painful an experience and so damaging to the army's reputation that had there been the slightest ground for doubt, the tribunal would have clutched at the straw. At the best of times Bernard-Lazare's anarchist viewpoint did not conceive of courts and judges as infallible. He saw no reason why military tribunals should be endowed with a special infallibility. If anything, military judges had the disadvantage of being untrained in matters of law, inexperienced in the critical examination of evidence and subject to their own code, discipline, hierarchy and mystique. In the case of this particular military tribunal, given the immense pressures to which it had been exposed, including stories of bribes offered to its members to express doubt, objectivity would have been truly superhuman. But this was a most unusual attitude for the times. Together with the principle of 'la chose jugée', the idea that 'sept officiers ont jugé' proved one of the most powerful obstacles to revision.

The order that the trial be held *in camera* shattered Bernard-Lazare's last hopes. It came as the last secrecy in a series of secrecies which had encouraged the wildest speculation and the most slanderous allegations. And Dreyfus, having been cut off from the outside world, unable to defend himself and clear his name, was deprived to the last of the right to reply in public. Public opinion too was prevented to the last from learning the facts. None of these secrecies was actually illegal. No illegality had in fact been committed, as far as Bernard-Lazare could tell at the time. The letter of the law had been observed. But Bernard-Lazare could not help remarking on the helplessness and loneliness of the accused, faced as he was with the crushing weight of the machinery of law, public opinion, and reasons of State, those dangerous reasons of State which could be the death of individual liberty. And how much greater the iniquity when the *juge d'instruction* turns himself into a public prosecutor and when a frenzied press in its turn assumes the role of the prosecution.

It is in 1897 that Bernard-Lazare made the following public declaration, but who could doubt that these were his sentiments two years earlier?

> C'est parce qu'il était juif qu'on l'a arrêté, c'est parce qu'il était juif qu'on l'a jugé, c'est parce qu'il était juif qu'on l'a condamné, c'est parce qu'il est juif que l'on ne peut faire entendre en sa faveur la voix de la justice et de la vérité, et la responsabilité de la condamnation de cet innocent retombe tout entière sur ceux qui l'ont provoquée par leurs excitations indignes, par leurs mensonges et par leurs calomnies. C'est à cause de ces hommes qu'un tel procès a été possible, c'est à cause d'eux qu'on ne peut faire pénétrer la lumière dans l'esprit de tous. Il leur a fallu un traître juif propre à remplacer le Judas classique, un traître juif que l'on pût rappeler sans cesse, chaque jour, pour faire retomber son opprobre sur toute une race; un traître juif dont on pût se servir pour donner une sanction pratique à une longue campagne dont l'affaire Dreyfus a été le dernier acte.[17]

Such roughly was Bernard-Lazare's state of mind when Mathieu came to see him at the end of February in 1895. It is not surprising that he received his visitor with open arms. The information Mathieu was able to supply came as an immense relief, for it proved beyond any doubt the victim's innocence. It also tended to confirm Bernard-Lazare's suspicion that somewhere along the line a machination had taken place.

Mathieu was able to provide Bernard-Lazare with a considerable amount of information, and to begin with, copies of the two basic documents: the *bordereau* and the *acte d'accusation*. He also had another little suspected and still inadequately appreciated source of information: Captain Dreyfus' notes. Encouraged by Forzinetti (the governer of the Cherche-Midi prison whose suspicions had been aroused by the unusual haste and secrecy of the affair before he even met the prisoner) not to give way to despair but to fight and clear his name, Captain Dreyfus did the best he could in the circumstances, and this was to prove of immense value to Bernard-Lazare. In one way or another, either by talking to Forzinetti or by making notes, he left a complete account of everything that had happened to him, from the arrest to the final invitation to confess. He left notes on the evidence given by witnesses in court and on the impressions they made on him; he commented on the nature of the documents enumerated in the *bordereau* and on the *acte d'accusation*. It is even possible, though Demange (who had defended Dreyfus at the 1894 trial) and Forzinetti could equally well be responsible for it, that it was he who had copied out the full text of the *bordereau* and the *acte d'accusation*. Forzinetti himself was a valuable and intelligent witness as well as a brave ally.

The most important single piece of information of which Mathieu apprised Bernard-Lazare was the secret communication, the secret evidence communicated to the judges *after* the trial and unknown to the defence.[18] To his dying day, Bernard-Lazare believed that this *illegality* was the crux of the affair, the vital moral issue, the abscess which had to be lanced. One can well imagine the electric effect the 'communication secrète' must have had on him in 1895 when he was haunted, almost obsessed by the idea of a plot.

> . . .à notre première entrevue, Mathieu Dreyfus m'apprit
> que l'on avait communiqué des pièces secrètes au Conseil
> de guerre. C'était là cette machination qui se retrouve, sous
> une forme ou une autre, dans les procès rituels.[19]

Of the four pieces of evidence which had been secretly communicated to the judges, Mathieu only knew of one at that stage, the *canaille de D* note (described earlier) which will figure prominently in the following pages.[20]

With this information at his disposal, Bernard-Lazare set to work and by the summer of 1895 the first brochure *Une erreur judiciaire: la vérité sur l'Affaire Dreyfus* was complete. He was eager to publish, to get things out into the open, to put the facts before public opinion. In spite of everything that had happened, he saw open discussion in the press as the only means of breaking down the wall of official silence, secrecy and hostility. Unfortunately, with the exception of the bold Forzinetti, the first drey-fusards – Mathieu, Demange and soon Scheurer-Kestner – were men of an entirely different temperament. Their integrity and immense moral courage were not matched by the sort of boldness of spirit, outspokenness, readiness to *scandalise opinion* in order to change it that was to characterise the action of Zola, Clemenceau, Labori, the young Péguy and, generally speaking, the second wave of dreyfusards. Temperamentally and intellectually, Bernard-Lazare belonged to the second group but by a strange stroke of fate his very reputation as a defender of outlawed anarchists and desperate causes had brought him together with Mathieu and Demange. On this occasion, and the fact should be noted, for Mathieu is too readily credited with a predilection for secretive procedures, it was not so much Mathieu as Demange who advised postponing publication. 'Il fut décidé que j'attendrais un moment favorable pour publier cette première protestation. Je devais attendre un an. Je crois que j'aurais marché plus tôt si Mathieu n'avait pas été retenu par Me Demange dont la prudence re-doutait toute manifestation.'[21]

Demange was in an understandably difficult and delicate position. Both he and Mathieu were afraid of infringing the law on espionage. In addition, Demange was a high-principled lawyer with a respect for professional etiquette and the principle of 'la chose jugée'. He did not collaborate with Bernard-Lazare on this first brochure. In fact, the two men did not meet until after its publication in November 1896. Indirectly, however, through Mathieu, some of the information used by Bernard-Lazare must have derived from Demange. On the issue of the illegal communi-cation, the cautious lawyer and the impatient writer collided, with one refusing to believe that the communication had taken place and the other, convinced of the contrary, bent on making the illegality the major issue.[22]

While Demange was refusing to break his self-imposed silence in retirement, Mathieu was pursuing frantic researches into the identity of 'D' (of the *canaille de D* note) and even turning to a spiritualist for revelations. Bernard-Lazare was critical of the hopeless 'pistes policières suivies', of the eagerness to discover who 'D' was when what really mattered was to expose the illegality. Unlike Mathieu, he was neither disappointed nor surprised when 'D' eventually turned out to be a minor clerk at the ministry who could not possibly be the author of the *bordereau*. If anything, it confirmed the machination. Someone, he argued, must be very keen or else very desperate to find proofs against Dreyfus, for this trivial note, concerning a minor clerk suspected by his superiors, to have been attributed to an allegedly major spy.

It was a difficult time for Bernard-Lazare. The succeeding years were not to bring much joy or peace, but at least as the dreyfusard movement gathered momentum, he did not feel alone, and the frustrations he experienced were the frustrations of a man of action. Loneliness, the frustrations of inaction, the silence imposed on him, were harder to bear than the enemies' insults. It was in other respects a busy period of writing and travel, but the *one* subject that haunted him was taboo. *Une erreur judiciaire: la vérité sur l'Affaire Dreyfus* was metaphorically burning a hole in his desk drawer. 'J'ai vécu cette année-là [summer 1895 to summer 1896] dans l'attente et l'impatience, dans la fièvre d'agir. Je n'ai eu aucun confident de mes actions ni de mes désirs.'[23]

The 'favourable moment' for which Mathieu had been waiting a whole year he had ultimately to create himself in the form of the weird story that Dreyfus had escaped from Devil's Island. The circumstances are well-known today. Clifford Millage, a reporter on the London *Daily Chronicle*, had the rumour inserted in a little-known paper in the small Welsh town of Newport, the *South Wales Argus* (2nd September 1896), whence the news spread to London and before long crossed the Channel.[24] Following the fake rumour of Dreyfus' escape, some timid doubts about the 1894 trial were expressed here and there in the press. In order to silence these doubts once and for all, a daily paper close to military circles, *L'Eclair*, published what purported to be a full and correct account of what had happened at the trial. This account, entitled *Le Traître*, is known as the *Eclair* revelations (14 and 15 September 1896).

Bernard-Lazare, in Nîmes at the time, was at long last given the green light by Mathieu and he rushed back to Paris. 'La publication de ma brochure fut définitivement décidée, mais je voulus la modifier et je pris pour base au travail nouveau les articles de *l'Eclair*.'[25] The *Eclair* revelations did not actually reveal anything to Mathieu and Bernard-Lazare that they did not know already, but they were crucial for several reasons. They broke the seal of secrecy over the *bordereau* and the famous *canaille de D* piece. The illegal communication was boldly confirmed and so were a number of other factors. Finally, there were some significant distortions. The 'D' of the *canaille de D* note was changed to 'Dreyfus' written out in full[26] and the *bordereau* was amputated of the important introductory and final paragraphs, including the last sentence 'je vais partir en manoeuvres'. This sentence posed awkward problems of dating and applicability to Dreyfus. Moreover, the five documents enumerated in the *bordereau* were listed by the *Eclair* but not a single one correctly. The point about these changes is that they did not suggest to Bernard-Lazare a journalist's hasty, ill-remembered or garbled version, as many historians still assume today. To the end, he remained intrigued by the 'tripatouillement'. 'Il serait peut-être intéressant, ce qu'on n'a pas fait encore, d'étudier ce *tripatouillement* du texte. Le texte fut-il *tripatouillé* parce qu'on n'osa pas le communiquer entièrement à *l'Eclair* ou fut-il *tripatouillé* dans un sens spécial et ce *tripatouillement* avait-il un but?'[27]

However that may be, and the question is still not settled, the importance attached by the *Eclair* to the falsified *canaille de D* note was of paramount importance. It was tantamount to admitting that the *bordereau*, even in its doctored form, did not stand up as evidence. Indeed the *Eclair* referred to the *bordereau* as merely 'un élément moral dans la cause' and described the *canaille de D* note as the 'preuve irréfutable. . .qui à l'unanimité a décidé du verdict'.

The work of adaptation completed, and the Dreyfus family having approved, Bernard-Lazare set off for Brussels in October 1896 where, by way of precaution, he had decided to have the brochure printed. The 3,500 copies were despatched in sealed envelopes from Brussels, Basle and Paris, two further precautionary measures. They were addressed to deputies, senators, journalists, writers and people in the legal world.[28]

If Mathieu, naturally, saw to the bill (a quite modest amount),[29] everything else about the operation was wholly Bernard-Lazare's. Brussels was an obvious choice. Bernard-Lazare had trusted anarchist friends there. Indeed the printers of the brochure, Veuve

Monnom, are those of the libertarian Belgian Review *La Société Nouvelle*, and the address of the printers is also the address of the offices of the same review. The author's name, as well as the name and address of the printers, appeared in full on the cover page. There was, then, nothing mysterious or underhand about the publication. And yet, given the explosive nature of the subject and the general hostility, one may well question in retrospect the wisdom of the precautions taken. People were understandably suspicious of this bombshell of a brochure, containing confidential information, printed in Belgium, despatched perhaps from Switzerland, arriving one day out of the blue on important desks. One unfortunate result of all this was that it allowed commentators to speculate on such things as the significance of the foreign postmark.

While the printing presses were still turning in Brussels, and with only the proofs of the brochure in hand, Bernard-Lazare returned to Paris in order to ensure that the press would not kill it with silence. 'C'était ma seule préoccupation. Me poursuivrait-on sous différents prétextes, peu importait: au contraire j'estimais que si on me poursuivait, la cause du vrai serait ainsi mieux servie.'[30] He first approached the *Figaro*. Périvier agreed to have the brochure reviewed, but his co-director, De Rodays, was more hesitant.

Nothing illustrates more succinctly the success of the terror campaign than this hesitation on the part of an editor of so important a paper as the *Figaro*. De Rodays actually believed in Dreyfus' innocence but he was afraid to be the first to review the brochure.[31] Bernard-Lazare then decided to approach an intrepid polemicist well-known for his frankness and revolutionary past, a man who had been violently hostile to Dreyfus: Rochefort of the *Intransigeant*. Forzinetti accompanied Bernard-Lazare on this important visit. We have two entirely different accounts of what happened. Many years later, after Bernard-Lazare's death, Rochefort recalled the icy reception he gave the representative of the 'juiverie internationale et cosmopolite' who blew into his office one day, brandished the proofs of the brochure and who, when defeated by some simple observation, dramatically produced Forzinetti, who had been waiting in the wings, like some last minute deus ex machina. Rochefort, wise to all these tricks, was disgusted with the whole stage-managed affair.[32] According to Bernard-Lazare's account to Reinach and to Jean-Bernard,

Rochefort received his visitors with great cordiality and listened with interest. Unlike the editors of the *Figaro*, Rochefort was convinced of Dreyfus' guilt, writes Bernard-Lazare, but his conviction was based on rumour; he was also prepared to think the worst of the government, and he promised an 'impartial' review of the brochure. The review appeared on 9 November. Its impartiality can be gauged from the title: 'Vaine tentative de réhabilitation d'un traitre'. Mathieu was bitterly disappointed. Bernard-Lazare was surprised, even more so when a few days afterwards, at a meeting of the committee for Free Cuba of which Rochefort was president and Bernard-Lazare a member, Rochefort expressed admiration for Bernard-Lazare's courage.[33]

The first edition of *Une erreur judiciaire: la vérité sur l'Affaire Dreyfus* came out in Brussels at the end of October or the beginning of November (6 November is the date most frequently given though 28 October is also sometimes given). First reviews appeared in the French press by 9 November. Bernard-Lazare need not have feared silence. For about a fortnight the brochure was much discussed and its author greatly insulted. While the discussion was going on, Bernard-Lazare prepared a second *augmented* edition, published by Stock on 16 November. (Stock, accustomed to taking risks as a publisher of 'subversive' anarchist literature, thus made his début as publisher of dreyfusard literature.) The additions to the second edition are important. First, there is a brief *avertissement* in which Bernard-Lazare explains why the original text was published in Brussels, sent in a sealed envelope, and so on. Then, in an important ten-page introduction, he tries to answer genuine critical objections, including the reservations expressed by Demange concerning the secret communication. The main text has been expanded to take account of some new material, most importantly the facsimile of the original *bordereau* (published in the *Matin* on 10 November); certain points are amplified, notably the background to the *canaille de D* note; pertinent replies to specific points are incorporated, as are also the curious reactions of Bertillon (*Matin*, 10 November) and *Commandant* d'Ormescheville (*Le Soir*, 14 November). This second, augmented edition was *reprinted* in 1897. For reasons which will become clear presently, it is important to remember that this was merely a reprint, the augmented second edition having already been in circulation by 16 November 1896. Finally there is a third edition published by the faithful Stock in 1898.

Again, the core of the work is still the first analysis completed by the summer of 1895 and modified the following year under the influence of the *Eclair* revelations. Around this permanent basis are recorded subsequent developments. In the following discussion references will be to the 1897 reprint of the second edition.

7

THE BATTLE

'*Une erreur judiciaire: la vérité sur l'Affaire Dreyfus*'
Bernard-Lazare's immediate aim was two-fold: to rectify the
tendentious distortions given in the *Eclair* and, having set the
records straight, to establish 'par les seuls documents que je
possédais, logiquement et irréfutablement, l'innocence de Dreyfus'.[1] But he did more than that. He had in effect written the first
history of the Affair and its first *J'accuse*.

To take the history first, its importance in the context of the
time can hardly be over-estimated. From a purely documentary
point of view it was a bombshell, and appreciated as such by an
alarmed War Office: here were made public for the first time the
complete and correct version of the *bordereau*, the text of the
canaille de D note and its background, quotations from and
discussion of the official *acte d'accusation*. Unfortunately,
Mathieu (afraid of prosecution) was reluctant at this stage to
publish the full text of the *acte d'accusation* and thus Bernard-
Lazare had to tread his ground carefully, which he obviously
found irksome. Nonetheless, he quotes directly from this 'mon-
streux monument', then completely unknown to the public, and
he makes excellent use of it, extracting as much positive information as he could (dates, contradictory conclusions reached by the
first and second group of handwriting experts, the preliminary
interrogations carried out by *Commandant* Du Paty de Clam;
generally it afforded a good insight into the way in which the
proceedings had been conducted) and confronting its absurd
allegations and speculations with the diverse testimonies made by
or on behalf of the accused.

This *public* confrontation between defence and prosecution is
one of the most valuable parts of the book. It gave the accused the
opportunity to tell *his* side of the story, to defend himself before

public opinion, to challenge the *official* version, the only one then
in existence. This is brilliantly done with regard to the documents
enumerated in the *bordereau,* Captain Dreyfus' denials that he
had had them in his possession being confronted with the supposi-
tions on which the *acte d'accusation* had to fall back in order 'to
establish' how the accused 'could have gathered' sufficient information to have produced the documents. (Hence such telling
phrases as 'il nous paraît impossible que le capitaine Dreyfus n'ait
pas eu connaissance de. . .'; 'il est inadmissible que Dreyfus ait
put se désintéresser. . .'; 'les officiers ayant pu. . .s'en entretenir
entre eux et en sa présence'. . .etc. etc.) When dealing with the
bizarre dictation (under Du Paty de Clam's dictation the un-
suspecting Dreyfus was made to write a letter based on the
bordereau; his arrest immediately followed), he goes beyond
merely confronting the two versions. Thanks to careful scrutiny
of dates given in the *acte d'accusation* and to Forzinetti's valuable
testimony, he is able to demonstrate the baroque irrelevancy of
the dictation in the decision to proceed with the arrest, since not
only had the warrant for the arrest been signed the *previous* day,
not only had Forzinetti already received instructions by then to
prepare a cell for a prisoner of State; but on that day, 15 October
1894, while Dreyfus was undergoing the dictation, Lieutenant-
Colonel d'Aboville communicated secret instructions to Forzinetti
about how the prisoner was to be treated.[2] So much for the claim
made by the *Eclair* that it was the agitation shown by Dreyfus
during the dictation that had finally decided the arrest. The order
for the arrest was based on the flimsiest of evidence: the contradictory reports of two handwriting experts. The final conviction
too was essentially based on such contradictory reports, with
three experts attributing authorship of the *bordereau* to Dreyfus
and two expressing doubts. And the *bordereau* was, according to
the *acte d'accusation* itself, the only actual piece of incriminating
evidence, until the *coup de théâtre,* that is, of the 'communication
secrète'.

Historically, then, *Une erreur judiciaire* is the first connected
account of events up to that stage as seen from *outside* official
circles. It is the first history to challenge the official version on
the basis of evidence which impressed at least one lawyer then
entirely unconnected with the case, Labori, as 'logique et bien
documentée'.[3]

With the vast material accessible today, and which was of

course not open to Bernard-Lazare, the modern historian of the Affair will not find in this brochure of 1896 anything 'new'. What he will find, and this remains as valuable today as it was then, is a lucid exposition of the *Dreyfus* Affair, as opposed to all the other affairs – the Picquart affair, the Esterhazy affair, the Henry affair, the Zola affair – which have complicated beyond recognition what was in essence a simple case posing one question: was Captain Dreyfus fairly tried and justly condemned? What mattered to Bernard-Lazare was not so much *who* was the author of the *bordereau* but to prove that Captain Dreyfus was not. Similarly, the *canaille de D* piece posed a question of principle and law and not of identity.

On the other hand, since Bernard-Lazare was not merely a simple historian recording facts or defence counsel presenting evidence, but a man who questioned everything about the affair, saw it in a much wider context and offered some bold interpretations, it could be said that he himself widened and complicated the issue. *Une erreur judiciaire: la vérité sur l'Affaire Dreyfus* is also a formidable *J'accuse*. The title itself is probably ironic, for the inescapable conclusion is this: the truth about the Dreyfus Affair is that it is no simple error of justice.

The *bordereau* was submitted to the most thoroughgoing examination it had received so far, document by document, almost line by line. In the course of this scrutiny, Bernard-Lazare not only demonstrated that the *bordereau* was inapplicable to Captain Dreyfus, but he questioned the very authenticity of the document; a bold thing to have done in the first history of the Affair. Condensing his detailed argumentation, the following series of implausibilities emerges: an allegedly vital missive, which in fact was an utterly unnecessary list enumerating documents sent under separate cover, was written out in his *own hand* by an allegedly high-ranking, experienced, devilishly clever spy; it was then sent in some unspecified manner to an unnamed person at the German Embassy where – Bernard-Lazare affirmed – it was never received; from there it was transmitted to French Intelligence by the 'usual channels', i.e. the French cleaner and Schwartzkoppen's wastepaper basket. The cleaner's interest in the discarded scraps of paper had actually come to light at a trial (the Millecamps affair) held the previous year and must have been known at the Embassy; still, there she was, collecting the contents of the wastepaper basket into which Schwartzkoppen, an old hand at espionage, had carelessly thrown an important document, thereby thoughtlessly compromising a valuable agent, after having torn it into four neat pieces which the Statistical Section had no difficulty in reconstructing.

Granted that Bernard-Lazare probably had an unrealistically high opinion of the efficiency and circumspection to be found in espionage – it was a flourishing business but conducted with surprising carelessness and incompetence at times on both sides – the list of queries and implausibilities is nonetheless impressive. Moreover, few of them have been satisfactorily or indisputably explained, even to this day.

The discovery, a year later, that Esterhazy had physically written the *bordereau* did not change Bernard-Lazare's view. If anything, it confirmed his suspicion that the document was some sort of fabrication. Hence in all the subsequent editions of *Une erreur judiciaire: la vérité sur l'Affaire Dreyfus* the original analysis of the *bordereau* was left intact. Hence too, as we shall see, his reluctant collaboration in Mathieu's campaign to prove that Esterhazy was the real traitor of the crime for which his brother had been condemned. As Bernard-Lazare saw it, Esterhazy might well be a traitor and a villain, but the *bordereau* was not a genuinely treasonable document and its author was not the principal villain behind the fabrication, merely an instrument. What the purpose of the fabrication might be he did not explain here, nor was he ever very explicit about it. One gathers that he believed it to have been a cover-up operation, intended to shield or warn a highly-placed person or persons.

With all the advantages of hindsight, historians ever since have engaged in similar speculations with similar results: they make sense of the events, at least to my mind, but there is little actual evidence to support them.[4]

Accused, too, stood Du Paty de Clam whose manner and method of interrogation are discussed at length. 'Les détails de cette terrorisation racontés dans la première brochure de Bernard-Lazare sont effrayants', Paul Brulat later commented.[5] To Bernard-Lazare Du Paty was a key figure, morally and psychologically, rather than from a legal point of view. He tortured the *accused*, kept him in ignorance of the charges against him for seventeen days, treated him as guilty, gave him to understand that all was lost; he even spoke to Madame Dreyfus, distraught and terrified, of the death penalty, one day after the opening of

preliminary investigations. The behaviour of this officer was
outside any recognised ethical or military code of conduct. It
could be attributed to madness, pathological sadism or cruelty.
Bernard-Lazare did not think so. He thought of Bertillon, the
handwriting expert, as 'un maniaque dangereux' prepared to
send a man to prison to prove the excellence of his theories.[6] Du
Paty de Clam, though evidently endowed with a melodramatic
imagination and a fair share of vanity, was of a different order.
In him Bernard-Lazare saw epitomised the breakdown of normal
standards of behaviour, decency, humanity, the respect for the
human person. The purpose of the grim portrait was not so much
to arouse pity for the tormented victims as indignation at the
behaviour of the tormentor. In this, he succeeded splendidly, at
least with one person, the nationalist deputy Castelin. Alas,
Castelin was so indignant that he did not believe it.

> Comment! M. Bernard-Lazare met en doute l'équité et
> l'impartialité d'un officier français? . . . Comment admettre
> qu'un officier français ait pu se livrer à l'égard d'une femme
> à des manoeuvres de ce genre? Martyriser une femme, c'est
> l'injure la plus odieuse qui puisse être adressée à un officier
> français! Plus loin – car ce n'est malheureusement pas tout,
> . . .*c'est lui qui introduisait dans le dossier des lettres et des
> rapports de police non signés dont la fausseté fut reconnue
> plus tard*. Maintenant c'est M. du Paty de Clam qui est
> accusé de s'être rendu le complice des faussaires![7]

Before long confirmation came, and many were shocked at the
behaviour of Du Paty de Clam, notably Zola.

To Bernard-Lazare the man responsible, however, was and
remained General Mercier. He was accused of three criminal
actions. First, there was the pre-trial verdict; second, since the
acte d'accusation made no mention of the 'rapports accablants',
one must conclude that General Mercier had not been telling the
truth. Third, there was his responsibility for the secret communication of evidence to the judges. The *Eclair* had of course invoked
diplomatic complications. Apart from feeling dubious about the
principle as such, Bernard-Lazare did not for one moment believe
that there ever existed any such reasons of State; and if anything
more was needed to convince him it was the *Eclair*'s 'code' story:
that is, the *canaille de D* note, it was alleged, was written in code
which French Intelligence had managed to break. It was ob-

viously useful not to reveal this; hence the note could not be discussed in court. The code had since then been changed and so the same necessity for secrecy no longer applied. Hence its publication in the *Eclair*. But Bernard-Lazare knew that the note had not been written in code. As far as he could see, the secret communication had one reason and one reason only. 'Le Conseil de Guerre penchait vers l'acquittement. C'est alors que le général Mercier, malgré les promesses formelles faites au ministre des affaires étrangères, se décida à communiquer en secret – aux juges – la pièce qu'il avait gardée jusqu'à ce moment.'[8]

Then there was the grave matter of the *Eclair*'s falsification of the *canaille de D* note. Whoever communicated the information to the *Eclair* had changed the initial 'D' to Dreyfus written out in full. If such a document existed, then it was a forgery, said Bernard-Lazare. This was the first time that the word forgery had been pronounced in connection with the Affair.[9] Wisely, however, he concentrated on the illegality committed, and on it based the request for revision, outlining the following procedure: a commission should be set up to investigate whether an illegality had occurred; should this be found to be the case, the commission should refer the matter not to the Ministry of War but to the Ministry of Justice which alone was competent to decide whether in law a conviction based on evidence unknown to the accused and the defence was valid. And if there was no legal basis on which to deal with the matter, because 'les législateurs modernes ne pouvaient concevoir qu'il pût se produire une semblable violation des droits de la défense',[10] then such a basis needed to be created.

It was a tall order, and a drastic condemnation, suggesting, as it did, that modern jurisprudence had no legal basis on which to redress a contempt for justice reminiscent of a bygone age. Only in the last few pages did Bernard-Lazare allow himself a lyrical, passionate note, what Henri Vaugeois, founding member of the Action Française, half admiringly called 'la vieille flamme sombre des éternels prophètes juifs'.[11] It is in the final appeal too that we have the only mention of 'Jew' and allusion to antisemitism, an absence probably due to Mathieu and shortly to be rectified in the second brochure.

> Qu'il ne soit pas dit que, ayant devant soi un juif, on a
> oublié la justice. C'est au nom de cette justice que je

proteste. . . De faits nouveaux viennent d'être apportés au débat; *ils suffisent juridiquement pour faire casser le jugement*; mais au-dessus des subtilités juridiques, il y a des choses plus hautes: ce sont les droits de l'homme à sauvegarder sa liberté et à défendre son innocence si l'on accuse injustement. Resterai-je seul à parler au nom du droit? Je le ne crois pas.[12]

Eventually, it was this aspect, 'le Droit et les droits' which most troubled the liberal conscience. In 1896, however, there were few immediate converts. 'J'ai fait appel à la raison', Bernard-Lazare later recalled, 'et je me suis heurté à un dogme.'[13] *Une erreur judiciaire: la vérité sur l'Affaire Dreyfus* came too soon and was too bold; it challenged too many cherished beliefs. Wickham Steed, the *Times* Paris Correspondent, who knew Bernard-Lazare and had read the brochure, noted in his Memoirs: 'It was significant of the reactionary wind then blowing in France that Bernard-Lazare's pamphlet should have been held dangerous and impolitic even by his own relatives. . . The moment was certainly not propitious for calm consideration of a matter so controversial as the redress of an alleged injustice to a Jewish officer.'[14]

The very last words of *Une erreur judiciaire: la vérité sur l'Affaire Dreyfus* were addressed to the press. Better informed, it would not allow this iniquity to go unchallenged. Press reaction was hostile, often violent. 'Chaque fois que le nom du traître sera prononcé, s'élèvera de tous côtés l'anathème', wrote *le Jour* (10 November) and the press well illustrated this. 'Vaine tentative de réhabilitation d'un traître' (*Intransigeant*, 9 November), 'Manoeuvres savantes et ténébreuses' (*Matin*, 10 November), 'Audacieuse apologie', 'efforts imbéciles du syndicat de la trahison' (*La Patrie*, 13 November). Millevoye of *La Patrie* warned the 'sans-patrie Lazare' against the murderous fury of the masses reluctant to tolerate writers who serve treason. *Le Paris* (11 November) and *Le Journal* (9 and 13 November), on whose staff Bernard-Lazare had recently been, were full of insinuations. *Le Voltaire* was insulting. *Le Siècle* (9 November) accused him of not having had the courage to publish in France this panegyric of the degraded officer: 'like the promoters of pornographic publications he had to find a printer in Brussels'. The most vitriolic article came from Zévaès writing in the Socialist *Petite République* (10 November). The Marxist had accounts to settle with the anarchist: 'le distingué représentant du high life anarchiste, qui est en même temps l'un des plus fidèles admirateurs de sa Majesté Rothschild'. This pompous brochure did not even represent a sincere effort at rehabilitating the traitor, and was merely 'a cynical self-advertisement'. Personal insults apart, Zévaès' attitude well illustrates how the Left, using its own vocabulary and images, joined in the general outcry. As an internationalist and Marxist, Zévaès could not very well let himself be carried away by the xenophobia of the nationalist press, but he could and did join in the condemnation of 'la campagne sournoisement engagée par les journaux de la finance et de la juiverie pour faire douter l'opinion de la culpabilité du traître et de créer ensuite un mouvement de sympathie en sa faveur'. The Left itself was not known for its belief in the infallibility of military judges; but it had its own caste and class version according to which seven officers would not have condemned a brother officer unless it was absolutely necessary. This was also the attitude initially taken by Clemenceau. Zévaès added a socialist touch to the argument. What about the countless strikers, guilty only of defending their cause, maltreated and condemned by hostile, corrupt, bourgeois, civil judges? Our sympathy must go to our comrades, he wrote, and if there was any to spare it would go to Dreyfus, if and when he was proved innocent – as he certainly was not in this meaningless brochure which said nothing new and raised no doubts. With perfect bad faith but sound logic Zévaès expertly trivialised the documentary value of the brochure. Bernard-Lazare took the unusual step, unusual because he had resolved not to reply to personal insults, of protesting to Millerand, and henceforth this sort of personal attack ceased in the *Petite République*, though the Socialist paper remained hostile to the cause of a bourgeois for some time to come.[15]

The anarchist press, at first generally hostile to Dreyfus or else professing a passionate disinterest in the case of a wealthy bourgeois and army officer, remained largely silent over the brochure.[16] Jean Grave later recalled: 'La lecture de sa première brochure commença à me faire réfléchir, sans tout à fait me convaincre'.[17] Grave, whose later hesitations are not altogether typical of anarchist participation in the Affair, does perhaps voice the compagnons' initial suspicions: they admired Bernard-Lazare's courage but were not happy about the rich, middle-class company he was keeping.[18]

Bernard-Lazare felt utterly deserted and alone. A new phase had begun for him. Before, he had felt oppressed by the silence imposed on him. Now, he had spoken out, and overnight doors had closed on him, friends had deserted him, he found himself a pariah. His friends, many subsequently converted to dreyfusism by him, recalled this period of utter loneliness. He himself described it to Reinach: 'Je ne dis rien des injures et des insultes, ni des accusations. Rien de l'attitude de la presse qui me fut dès ce jour fermée. Du jour au lendemain, je fus un paria. Un long atavisme m'ayant préparé à cet état, je n'en souffris pas moralement. Je n'en souffris que matériellement. Vous savez que cela ne m'a pas découragé, ni arrêté dans l'oeuvre entreprise.'[19]

Unwittingly the hostile press helped to advance the work. The press was indeed in something of a dilemma. The idea of exposing the syndicate and its network of informers was very attractive; and some papers, led by *La Patrie*, clamoured for 'le sieur Lazare' to be prosecuted on the grounds of divulging secret information. This, however, involved recognising that the brochure did divulge such information and was not a tissue of lies or inventions. The very thought of proceedings alarmed the government, for this inevitably meant reopening the Dreyfus case. Few commentators had the intelligence to realise this. Some tried to discredit the brochure by questioning the accuracy of this or that fact or text, including the version of the *bordereau*. But this was a dangerous game. *Le Rappel* (11 November), close to government circles, warned in vain against exaggerating the importance of this 'plaidoyer' which contained no State secrets whatsoever. The 'parquet de la Seine' allegedly issued a statement to that effect (11 November) but to no avail. Speculation continued as to whether Bernard-Lazare would be prosecuted, something he devoutly wished and the government was determined to avoid. Speculation also ran high as to who communicated the documents; names were mentioned, especially those of Bertillon and d'Ormescheville; they in turn let themselves be interviewed (*Le Matin* 10 November, and *Le Soir* 14 November respectively), clearing themselves of responsibility, quarrelling with Bernard-Lazare's interpretation of their respective reports but affirming his correct knowledge of them. This was as good as an authentication.

The most impressive and important authentication, and one of far-reaching consequences, came in the shape of the facsimile of the original, hand-written *bordereau*, published in *Le Matin* (10 November) as a direct reply to Bernard-Lazare's brochure.[20]

Le Matin was obviously anxious to reinstate the *bordereau* as the one and only valid piece of evidence and so undo the harm done by *L'Eclair*. Bernard-Lazare was quick to realise the devaluation of the *canaille de D* note 'because the consequences were now appreciated'. Henceforth graphology and handwriting were to dominate the discussion and the illegality issue was somewhat pushed into the background. On the question of the *bordereau* and its handwriting, *Le Matin* had of course rendered an extremely valuable service. The facsimile put an end to all discussion about the authenticity of the version of the *bordereau* given by Bernard-Lazare. More important still, it allowed Bernard-Lazare to proceed with the one examination of the *bordereau* he had hitherto been unable to carry out: its handwriting. He was quick off the mark: 'ce bordereau je le fis clicher le lendemain – le mieux que je pus, je le soumis aux experts les plus réputés non seulement de France, mais d'Europe...'.[21] Operation 'counter-expertise' was about to begin.

At the Statistical Section, the archivist Gribelin was alarmed. How, he wondered, could the documents used by Bernard-Lazare have been stolen from the Section's safe? The deputy Chief of Staff, General Gonse, was equally alarmed. 'On ne s'explique pas comment M. Lazare connait ces faits essentiellement secrets',[22] he reported to General Billot, then Minister of War. Who was this man Lazare? A police report dated 12 November 1896 was not too reassuring. True, his anarchism was described as pure pose, the fashion among young middle-class dandies; on the other hand, his journalistic activities and his recent determination to defend the Jews (an allusion to Bernard-Lazare's public debate with Drumont) were worrying.[23] This was the 'syndicat' coming out into the open. With touching faith in the power and influence of the syndicate, a series of extraordinary collusions were assumed which generally confused matters and one of which was to have grave consequences.

While Bernard-Lazare believed – probably correctly – that the *Eclair* revelations emanated from high quarters,[24] General Gonse was equally convinced that the *Eclair* and Bernard-Lazare were working hand-in-hand, the real aim of the *apparently* nationalist and antisdreyfusard newspaper being to open the way for Bernard-Lazare's brochures under the pretext of proving Dreyfus' guilt. And since the nationalist deputy Castelin, who had attacked Bernard-Lazare for slandering Army officers, was the *eminence grise* of the *Eclair*, the plot thickened. As the War Office saw it, in return for handsome payment, the *apparently* nationalist deputy was also collaborating with Bernard-Lazare: he first opened the way for the brochure in the *Eclair* and then, under the guise of condemning it in Parliament, drew the attention of the deputies to it. A master-stroke of propaganda, in the alarmed eyes of the military. One mystery still remained: how *did* Bernard-Lazare gain access to confidential information believed to be locked away in the Ministry's safe?

In his analysis of the brochure, General Gonse was most disturbed by the details of the *canaille de D* note. 'Lazare y raconte un fait que seules trois personnes connaissaient au moment du procès Dreyfus: Le Colonel Sandherr, le Capitaine Henry et l'archiviste Gribelin. Récemment le fait avait été confié à une quatrième personne; le Lt-Cl. Picquart.'[25] An accusing finger – pointed at no less a person than the recently appointed Head of the Statistical Section, Lieutenant-Colonel Picquart.

Invited by Gonse, by way of a test, to write a report on Bernard-Lazare's brochure ('indiquant avec précision toutes les indiscrétions qu'il remarquerait')[26], Picquart produced one of the sanest appreciations of the possible and probable sources of information (*Note au sujet de la brochure de Bernard-Lazare: La Vérité sur l'Affaire Dreyfus*).[27] Admittedly, as an observer at the 1894 trial on behalf of the War Office, Picquart had an advantage over his mystified superiors. He remembered, for example, that Dreyfus' counsel, Demange, had taken notes during the trial. This could explain how Bernard-Lazare knew what certain witnesses had said in evidence. Demange is also given as a possible source for the *acte d'accusation*. Above all, Picquart, while agreeing that the brochure contained confidential information, had no illusions about how well secrets were kept. He made the reasonable – though in the event inaccurate – suggestion that the top-secret *canaille de D* note was known to several officers and that rumour might have spread. For General Gonse this was the crucial item and Picquart's suggestion was judged to be suspiciously evasive. The head of espionage had failed the test. He was dismissed from his post (14 November) and sent to North Africa.

Ironically and quite innocently, *Une erreur judiciaire: la vérité sur l'Affaire Dreyfus* precipitated the downfall of the only man

in the War Office prepared to admit Dreyfus's innocence. A
further irony of the assumed Bernard-Lazare–Picquart collusion
is that Picquart, having urged his chiefs to re-open the Dreyfus
case ever since the late summer of 1896, was himself worried by
Bernard-Lazare's brochure which confirmed his worst fears,
namely that sooner or later 'les Dreyfus' would learn the truth
and their action could be damaging to the Army's reputation.

Public reaction to *Une erreur judiciaire: la vérité sur l'Affaire
Dreyfus* culminated in the stormy and confusing parliamentary
debate of 18 November 1896 to which I have already alluded.
Castelin had announced his intention to raise the matter of the
Dreyfus Affair in Parliament *before* the publication of Bernard-
Lazare's brochure. But when the latter appeared it fitted so
perfectly into Castelin's theory of a powerful Jewish syndicate
being at work to liberate the traitor that the angriest part of the
deputy's speech was devoted to listing the confidential documents
discussed in the brochure. Amid general approval Castelin asked
the government to prosecute Bernard-Lazare. The government
had no intention of doing so. Bernard-Lazare for his part, undeterred by this refusal and using a tactic which was to prove so
successful with Zola's *J'accuse*, formally invited the Ministers of
War and Justice to take proceedings against him. The letter to
both ministers is dated 20 November (1896).

> Monsieur le Ministre,
> Dans la séance du 18 novembre M. le député André
> Castelin m'accusa, à la tribune de la Chambre, de détenir
> des pièces dérobées appartenant à 'l'enquête secrète', ouverte
> jadis contre l'ex-capitaine Dreyfus, et d'avoir injurié et
> diffamé les membres du Conseil de Guerre ayant siégé dans
> cette affaire.
> En présence de ces allégations publiques et de ces
> accusations, je demande, M. le Ministre, *à être poursuivi
> devant les tribunaux compétents.*[28]

There was great confusion all round. Castelin, the nationalist
press, and to some extent the Left, believed that in its refusal to
prosecute the government was trying to hush up a scandal. The
government, the police and the War Office suspected that Castelin
was in the pay of the Dreyfus family and determined to re-open
the case. This shows great faith in the syndicate's power, or else a
total lack of faith in the incorruptibility of a well-known

nationalist and antisemitic deputy. Moderate republican opinion – republicans haunted by the spectre of boulangism, Guyot for example – feared that Castelin was using the whole incident to bring down the government. Bernard-Lazare in turn was accused of beating a retreat now that the question of prosecution had arisen. He took the opportunity of making public his letters to the Ministers of War and Justice, adding that if anyone was afraid of prosecution it was the government.[29] This was also the view of Schwartzkoppen who noted in his diary on 22 November: 'The French government, which is doing its utmost to prevent any re-opening of the case, has taken no steps and has no intention of taking any, to call Bernard-Lazare to account although he published certain confidential communications in his pamphlet... Castelin's interpellation was not intended to break a lance for Dreyfus; its purpose was to induce the government to take action against the agitation... The government was afraid of the debate extending further than would suit it.'[30] *Le Matin* (22 November) finally spelt out the reason for the government's action, and the press as a whole came to accept that all attempts to re-open the Dreyfus case before a civil court must be resisted. *Une erreur judiciaire: la vérité sur l'Affaire Dreyfus* lost its news value and dropped out of debate, for the present at least.

There were a handful of scattered doubters on whom the brochure did make the hoped-for impact, a tiny silent minority whose troubled conscience was given public expression for the first time. The historian and scholar Gabriel Monod, beset by doubts from the beginning but reluctant, as a Protestant, to be the first to speak out, contacted Bernard-Lazare.[31] The senator Scheurer-Kestner, likewise troubled but re-assured by highly-placed friends that all was as it should be, was disturbed by the brochure, which re-kindled his doubts.[32] Zola's future defence counsel, Labori, had also had the uncomfortable feeling in 1894 that Captain Dreyfus could be innocent;[33] between them, the *Eclair* revelations and Bernard-Lazare's brochure, well documented and logically argued, re-awakened his interest: 'de pareilles allégations non démenties ne me paraissaient pas négligeables'.[34] What baffled Labori was Demange's publicly expressed refusal to believe that a violation of justice had been committed (i.e. the secret communication). Bernard-Lazare too was baffled by this and he and Demange publicly disagreed over the illegality issue.[35] In spite of this difference, a difference in faith, one might

say, in the sense of justice of political and military leaders, the
two men greatly respected each other. To Bernard-Lazare,
Demange was truly the first dreyfusard, the personification of an
independent conscience, all the more admirable in view of
Demange's army background and Catholic upbringing. His
timidity was irksome; his faith in other people misplaced, but it
was moving and indicative of great nobility. As for the timorous
lawyer, brought out of his retirement by *Une erreur judiciaire*, he
wrote to Bernard-Lazare in 1899: 'Vous avez été le premier
champion de la justice et de la vérité. L'amitié d'un homme de
votre caractère et de votre coeur est un bien dont je sens le prix.'[36]

Une Erreur Judiciaire: l'Affaire Dreyfus
Deuxième Mémoire avec des Expertises d'Ecritures

Following the publication in *Le Matin* of the facsimile of the
bordereau, Mathieu and Bernard-Lazare embarked on an
international consultation involving twelve leading handwriting
experts and graphologists from France, Switzerland, Belgium,
England, America and Germany. Together with the material on
which they had worked, their findings constitute the *Annexes* of
what is generally referred to as the second 'brochure', the 300-
page *Une Erreur Judiciaire: l'Affaire Dreyfus*, subtitled *Deuxième
Mémoire avec des Expertises d'Ecritures*. It appeared in November 1897. The 'mémoire' properly speaking is a sixty-five page
brochure which precedes the scientific work and which is by far
the most interesting part.

The reasoning behind the somewhat unfortunate entangle-
ment in the handwriting question was sound enough. Official
silence over the *canaille de D* note made it impossible to pursue
the illegality issue, at least for the time being.[37] With the
reinstatement of the *bordereau* as the only 'irrefutable evidence'
attention switched to handwriting and graphology. As Bernard-
Lazare saw it, the enemy must be challenged on his chosen
ground.[38] They were hardly in a position to object to handwriting
expertise in principle. To those sceptical of graphology in principle, the 1894 verdict, based on the positive conclusions reached
by only three out of five experts, must appear like a monstrosity.
If these sceptics fall back on the secret evidence, they find themselves in the illogical position of rejecting graphological findings
as uncertain and accepting as valid secret evidence they had never
seen. The inescapable dilemma was this: either Dreyfus was

convicted on a piece of evidence attributed to him by three out of
five experts or he was convicted on a secret and illegally communicated piece which he could not even contest. 'Ou le procédé a
été indigne, ou il a été abominable.'[39]

The reasoning was sound, but in the xenophobic atmosphere of
those days ten foreigners challenging the conclusions of three
French experts was an insanely rational act. The public prosecutor
at Zola's trial put things in a nutshell: 'Je n'ai rien à vous dire,
Messieurs, d'un groupe d'experts internationaux qui gravitent
autour de M. Bernard-Lazare. C'est l'entrepreneur de la révision.
Il y a trop d'argent et de circonstances étrangères en tout cela.'[40]

One did not have to be a fanatic or an illogical sceptic like
Anatole France[41] to question the validity or perhaps simply to
understand the competence of some of the learned experts. What
was the layman to make of near incomprehensible, pseudo-
scientific jargon, curious diagrams and tabulations, measurements
to the nearest millimetre of loops, slants, hiatus, dots, lengthy
discussions of capital 'M's and small 'b's, all based on seemingly
arbitrary methods? Bertillon's demonstrations were certainly no
better, but they had the advantage of not being known in their
entirety. If no one produced anything resembling the latter's
'citadel' drawing, described and destroyed in the brochure by
Bernard-Lazare, the dreyfusard graphology of the passionate de
Rougemont deserves Bertillon's criticism of 'de l'astrologie
judiciaire'.[42] From Dreyfus' handwriting de Rougemont deduced
not only such stirling qualities as energy, will-power, intelligence,
spontaneity ('Il a le sang chaud et parfois part comme un bouchon
de champagne'), but also unhappy past experiences and a splendid
future. As for X, the author of the *bordereau*, he is a 'fourbe',
but not of the vulgar kind; he will come to be conscience-stricken
and confess his crimes, for, however low he has fallen, his
handwriting testifies to a fundamental loyalty.[43] Anything less
likely than a conscience-stricken Esterhazy or a hot-blooded,
bubbling Dreyfus is difficult to imagine!

These reports were quickly overtaken by events, for they
appeared a few days before Mathieu's denunciation of Esterhazy
as the author of the *bordereau* (15 November 1897). The experts'
conclusion that Dreyfus was *not* the author of the *bordereau*
seemed like mere negative lucidities. On the other hand, the
theory expressed by some of them that the writing of the *bordereau* was disguised was to make things difficult for the defence,

and played into the hands of the prosecution, with the latter arguing in due course that Dreyfus had tried to *imitate* Esterhazy's writing.

In direct contrast to the learned and largely incomprehensible reports stood the outspoken, passionate and highly personal brochure. Its major theme was the antisemitic campaign of the early months, from arrest to conviction (November–December 1894), a history almost forgotten, and which Bernard-Lazare insisted on recalling, against the wishes of his rare friends. Neither Scheurer-Kestner nor Mathieu wished the Affair to be linked with antisemitism. It must not become part of 'la question juive'. As far as Bernard-Lazare was concerned, antisemitism had made the Affair into a 'question juive'; and this time he was going to draw public attention to it with his usual outspokenness. The language is terse and provocative, in the style of '*J'accuse*'.

> C'est parce qu'il était juif qu'on l'a arrêté, c'est parce qu'il était juif qu'on l'a jugé, c'est parce qu'il était juif qu'on l'a condamné, c'est parce qu'il est juif que l'on ne peut faire entendre en sa faveur la voix de la justice et de la vérité.[44]

The 'because he is Jewish' argument has the same sort of truth and weaknesses as much of Zola's *J'accuse*. It was as impossible to prove that Dreyfus was condemned because he was a Jew as it was to prove that Esterhazy had been acquitted by order. Bernard-Lazare was perhaps in a somewhat better position than Zola since the antisemitic campaign was recorded in the press, there for everyone to see, and Bernard-Lazare made it his business that people should do so. All the same, this did not amount to proof. It was an opinion, a conviction, but a conviction which had the force of truth and eventually was to carry with it many a disturbed conscience. Bernard-Lazare knew however that it would also arouse opposition, that he would be reproached for introducing antisemitism into the discussion, not least of all by those 'bons esprits' (like Scheurer-Kestner) unable to bring themselves to believe that such a thing could have happened. There were also those who thought that it was bad strategy – possibly Mathieu and Reinach. Bernard-Lazare was undeterred.

> Quand je publiai mon premier mémoire, on a regretté hypocritement que j'eusse porté la discussion sur un tel terrain. [There is only one allusion to this in the first

brochure, but it was evidently enough to cause displeasure].
Je ne l'y ai pas portée et ce n'est pas moi qui l'y ai mise.
Qui a songé à reprocher à Voltaire d'avoir dit que Calas
était protestant, que c'est comme tel qu'il fut condamné?
Voltaire n'est plus là, mais il y a un Calas encore.[45]

In a famous letter to *Le Temps* (5 November 1897) Gabriel
Monod explained that he had remained silent for three years, in
spite of grave doubts, because as a Protestant he did not think that
it was for him to play the role of Voltaire in this new Calas affair.
How much more outrageous for a Jewish Voltaire to defend a
Jewish Calas, especially in this outspoken manner, with discretion,
caution and indirect allusions all thrown to the winds.

It is a pity that this *mémoire* is tied, by circumstances of
publication, to the *Expertises d'Ecriture* which have more or less
buried it. The account of the early terror-campaign still makes
startling reading and should be required reading for all those
inclined to minimise the part played by antisemitism in influenc-
ing events, if nothing else, especially in the crucial early stages
which it became subsequently so difficult to undo. At the time, in
the autumn of 1897, the rumour, as Maurras puts it, that Dreyfus
had been condemned because he was a Jew was beginning to
disturb people, particularly the intellectual milieux. The 'moral
syndicate' was taking shape.

In the immediate circumstances the question of handwriting
continued to dominate the battle for revision. If from a practical
point of view the laboriously compiled 'International Consultation' achieved little, the simple poster operation organised at the
same time directly led to the discovery of Esterhazy. The stranger-
than-fiction coincidence is well known today: while waiting for a
bus one afternoon on the boulevard, the banker de Castro bought
a poster carrying a reproduction of the *bordereau* facsimile and
immediately recognised the writing of one of his clients, Esterhazy.
What is less well known is that this 'propaganda by poster' was
Bernard-Lazare's idea – or at least he claimed credit for it,[46]
probably justifiably. Poster and tract 'propaganda' was an
anarchist speciality, and after the *compagnons*' entry into the
battle there was a profusion of posters, no doubt financed by
Mathieu.

Bernard-Lazare's first series of posters, put on sale in the streets
of Paris, carried no learned analysis and no comments; nothing

but neatly juxtaposed specimens of the two writings in question, the *bordereau* and extracts from Dreyfus' letters. Public opinion was invited to judge and compare. That someone would actually recognise the writing of the *bordereau* probably went beyond Bernard-Lazare's and Mathieu's wildest dreams. Once this had come to pass, new posters of various sizes, shapes and layouts appeared, now also bearing specimens of Esterhazy's writing. One of the best known is 'la clef de l'Affaire Dreyfus', the key being Esterhazy's writing. Paris and France are inundated by all sorts of pamphlets and brochures, Maître Tézenas, Esterhazy's counsel, complained at the latter's court-martial. To which Mathieu replied that he would defend his brother as he saw fit and wherever possible.[47]

A new phase in dreyfusard strategy had begun. The 'wait and see', 'cause no scandal' tactic had been abandoned. Mathieu no longer relied on government intervention and promises of official enquiries. Instead, he appealed directly to public opinion. The official denunciation of Esterhazy was simultaneously communicated to the press. The full text of the *acte d'accusation* was at last published in *Le Siècle* (7 January, 1898). It made many converts and largely inspired Zola's *J'accuse*. Above all, Mathieu used the *Figaro*, opportunely converted to the cause, to make public his rapidly-constituted file on Esterhazy, thus forcing the government to take action and ensuring that the material submitted to the official investigators was not suppressed, lost, or ignored out of existence.

If police records are to be believed, Bernard-Lazare was very busy compiling the Esterhazy files and feverishly preparing all sorts of publications: 'un dossier très sévère contre Esterhazy' in November 1897; 'un livre à sensation' in March 1898; a brochure in two volumes in May 1898. None of these ever saw the light of day, at least not under his signature. It is thus impossible to say whether we are dealing with police informers' speculations, often fanciful when it comes to the 'syndicate's' activities, or else unfulfilled, perhaps abandoned projects. In the last resort, collecting Esterhazy's correspondence, publishing incriminating private letters, whether freely offered or sold, washing Esterhazy's dirty linen in public, was one way of forcing the government to act – but it was a distasteful business. Besides, it did little to elucidate the question of the illegality which remained for Bernard-Lazare *the* issue. As for Mathieu's denunciation of

Esterhazy as the author of the *bordereau*, which hopelessly tied Dreyfus' case to that of Esterhazy, this must have seemed a terrible mistake to Bernard-Lazare.

In the preface to the third brochure *Comment on condamne un innocent* (1898), published on the eve of Esterhazy's court-martial, the *Commandant* only figures briefly, and nothing at all is said about his private life. Bernard-Lazare was looking to Esterhazy's protectors for the real key to the Dreyfus Affair. The man who looms as large as ever in his mind is Du Paty de Clam, elevated from tormentor to forger and machinator. 'Il ne suffit pas de faire passer le commandant Esterhazy devant un conseil de guerre; il faut mettre la main au collet de celui qui a machiné le procès Dreyfus. . . Qu'on ouvre une enquête sérieuse sur les agissements du colonel Du Paty de Clam, ce jour-là la lumière sera faite sur le procès du capitaine Dreyfus. . .'[48]

Esterhazy's court-martial (10–11 January 1898) did nothing to elucidate the question. What it did do, in the form of *Commandant* Ravary's report, and this unwittingly and in a purely zealous effort to blacken a new accused, Picquart, was to confirm the existence of the *canaille de D* note in the secret Dreyfus dossier. Bernard-Lazare was delighted. Alas, the Picquart Affair had come to complicate matters here.

Comment on condamne un innocent

This brochure, the third, published on the eve of Esterhazy's court-martial and a few days before Zola's *J'accuse*, is Bernard-Lazare's swan-song, so to speak, before retiring from the front line of the battle.

It is an angry and defiant piece, intended to provoke prosecution. The time for allusions and discrete hints is past, he exclaims in a provocative preface of which Du Paty de Clam is the villain. He is the 'gredin', the 'infâme', the 'scélérat' who inspired the monstrous *acte d'accusation*. This document, which Bernard-Lazare had already had before him in 1896 but was prevented from discussing fully, was published in *Le Siècle* (7 January 1895) and made more converts to the dreyfusard cause than any other single text or event. In order to give more permanent form to this 'monstrueux monument' Bernard-Lazare published the full text in this third brochure accompanied by a devastating commentary.

It is difficult to imagine Mathieu and Scheurer-Kestner having given their blessing to this provocative challenge to Castelin and his friends to bring charges of defamation – this time they would have had far more justification than in 1896. Bernard-Lazare had come to breaking-point. He was exasperated by the man-oeuvres of the War Office which was so evidently protecting Esterhazy, by the insults Parliament heaped on those leading 'the odious campaign' on behalf of the 'traitor', by Méline's cynical 'il n'y a pas d'Affaire Dreyfus' (4 December 1897). He was even more exasperated by the tactics of his own side, confident that the Esterhazy trial would reveal the truth, relying on the 'voie légale', that is to say on revision based on finding the author of the *bordereau* when this last, as Bernard-Lazare saw it, was in all probability a protected fabrication. And all this time 'evidence' against Dreyfus, conveniently discovered at every turn, was piling up. 'Avec leur respect de la légalité ils n'arriveront pas à le faire sortir de son bagne.'[49] *Comment on condamne un innocent* was a last frantic attempt, before silence was imposed on him, to force the Affair out into the open by forcing the government to prose-cute him. If Zola's *J'accuse* had not appeared a few days after-wards, he might well have had his wish.

As a re-opening of the Dreyfus case, the Zola trial (February 1898) was unsuccessful. This had clearly been the government's intention in limiting the charges and the President of the Court, famous for his often repeated ruling 'the question will not be put', proved himself to be a determined and vigilant upholder of that intention. At least this was so as far as the defence was concerned. For the military witnesses managed to depart from the straight and narrow path when it suited them. In fact, one of the ways in which both the Dreyfus Affair and the Esterhazy Affair were kept out of discussion was the concentration on the Picquart Affair. At times it seemed as if Picquart and not Zola was the accused. Dreyfus was altogether forgotten. A notable example was the discussion of the *canaille de D* note. Its existence having been officially confirmed, it was back in circulation, so to speak, but the real issues, i.e. the illegal communication and irrelevancy to Dreyfus, were never debated. Instead, Henry affirmed and Picquart denied that the note had been shown by Picquart to Leblois, his friend and lawyer. A lengthy discussion followed as to whether Leblois was in Paris on that particular day and at what distance from Picquart's desk Henry could have recognised the note. All pertinent points, perhaps, given the allegation. But the result was an almost comic diversion from the serious issues posed by the note. When the defence tried to raise the real issues the President of the Court ruled that the matter was irrelevant. It must also be added that Labori, the defence lawyer in charge of the proceedings, did not have as good a grasp of the case as Demange and Bernard-Lazare had. Labori let slip several mystifications introduced by Henry on which Bernard-Lazare – the bench willing – would have grilled him.

By the time of the Zola trial, Bernard-Lazare had already agreed to withdraw from the front line of the battle 'et de laisser faire les autres'. His name, however, came up quite frequently in the course of the proceedings, mainly in connection with the 'International Consultation'. Its findings (i.e. that Dreyfus was not the author of the *bordereau*) were by now out of date; but the second group of defence experts – nearly all French and among them distinguished paleographers from the Ecole de Chartes – had based their conclusions (i.e. that Esterhazy was the author) on the two copies of the *bordereau* facsimiles reproduced in the 'Consultation'. For that reason, the 'Consultation' and Bernard-Lazare were thorns in General de Pellieux's flesh. As the man who had acquitted Esterhazy, probably in good faith, though without overstraining his critical faculties, de Pellieux could not be expected to take kindly to this challenge to his verdict. Besides, having seen or at least knowing of the 'faux Henry', the existence of which he unwittingly revealed during the Zola trial, de Pellieux was convinced of Dreyfus' guilt. He had as much contempt for Bernard-Lazare as for Picquart and Zola. He tried to morally discredit the 'entrepreneur de la révision' and thereby render suspect any handwriting samples and facsimiles emanating from him, a task in which he was ably assisted by the prosecutor and occasionally by the judge.[50] Thus, de Pellieux suggested that the two copies of the *bordereau* facsimile submitted to the experts and published in the 'International Consultation' were forgeries because they were not identical. After Labori and his high-powered team of experts had explained at length that the difference was one of quality of reproduction, the General exclaimed that *all* facsimiles of the *bordereau* were 'des faux' and only those few who had seen the original – safely locked away at the ministry – were in a position to discuss the *bordereau*.[51]

General de Pellieux also tried unsuccessfully to have a special witness called,[52] an octogenarian paleographer by the name of Victor Bouton, described in a subsequent police report as a

practised blackmailer with a grudge against Jews and baron
Rothschild in particular.[53] Bouton eventually told the *Cour de
Cassation* the following year (9 February 1899) how, in 1897,
Bernard-Lazare had offered him 100,000 francs to declare that
the *bordereau* was not in Dreyfus' handwriting.[54] Bernard-Lazare
exploded the legend in the press and nothing more was heard.[55]

8

BEHIND THE FRONT LINES

It was at Mathieu's request that Bernard-Lazare withdrew from the forefront of the battle.[1] Behind the scenes, however, he worked as indefatigably as before at a variety of tasks. Providing information and finance (Mathieu's money no doubt) for propaganda purposes was one of them. Daniel Halévy has made some disparaging comments on Bernard-Lazare holding the dreyfusard purse-strings.[2] There are also numerous police reports to the same effect. What, one wonders, would Daniel Halévy have done? The hiring of lecture-halls, printing of posters and brochures, publications of every description from cartoons to *verbatim* trial reports, all this cost money. Fortunately, Mathieu was wealthy. As for Bernard-Lazare, he threw himself body and soul into the task of informing and reforming a hostile public opinion at home and keeping up-to-date a generally pro-dreyfusard public opinion abroad. He travelled a great deal, mainly to Brussels and London where he had many press contacts: *Le Petit Bleu*, *Le Peuple*, the *Daily Chronicle*, the *Jewish World*, the *Fortnightly Review*. In the London *Graphic* he wrote an important article on the Affair.[3] He enlisted the help of friends in Austria and Germany. It was a moral syndicate on an international scale.[4] According to one police informant, apparently quoting Bernard-Lazare's own words, he even went to see Schwartzkoppen.[5] Another police report dated 20 February 1898 announced that Bernard-Lazare was preparing for publication the *verbatim* proceedings of the Zola trial, complete with the notes and the documents Labori and Clemenceau feared the judge would not allow them to read out in their summing up. The report adds: 'La brochure sera tirée à un million d'exemplaires et envoyée dans tous les coins de la France.' The 'brochure' is probably the two-volume proceedings of the Zola trial brought out by Stock (1898) which every student of the Dreyfus Affair has consulted with benefit ever since. Bernard-Lazare seems to have helped with most of the major documentary publications and indeed he constantly pressed for this.[6] Reading the evidence given by the generals was the best dreyfusard propaganda of all. Occasionally, as with General Gonse and the investigations on Picquart, he commented on it in as many newspapers, French and foreign, as possible. Keeping an eye on the press, and immediately denying legends and false rumours, was another of his tasks. As for writing, he did contribute a few articles to *L'Aurore*. One of the most bitter was on Maurras' interpretation of Henry's forgery as a 'faux patriotique' dictated by love of country. Thus a forger was made into a national hero.[7] If every age has the heroes and saints it deserves, wrote Bernard-Lazare, the elevation of Henry was a sad sign of the times. (Pierre Quillard's excellent work, *Le Monument Henry*, is a precious document in this respect.)

All in all, Bernard-Lazare was untiring in his efforts, but his role and devotion were not acknowledged, a state of affairs which continued until after his death. All those close to him protested against this silence. It led Pierre Quillard in 1906, when Captain Dreyfus was rehabilitated and no mention was made of the first dreyfusard, to call upon all friends to pay their tribute in the form of a monument, a project with an interesting history.

Bernard-Lazare did not mind the silence. On one occasion, however, he protested in a thunderous open letter to Trarieux,[8] then president of the *Ligue des Droits de l'Homme*. The occasion was the decree of the *Cour de Cassation* (June 1899) annulling the 1894 verdict on Dreyfus, a victory celebrated by the *Ligue des Droits de l'Homme* which had paid tribute to the three champions of the cause: Scheurer-Kestner, Picquart and Zola. Bernard-Lazare was revolted by this act of ingratitude towards the less high ranking and brave fighters of the beginning. Why was the heroic Forzinetti forgotten? Bernard-Lazare, who had worked closely with the courageous prison-governor, singled out the very qualities which Picquart lacked: he (Forzinetti) overcame his military prejudices, acted according to his conscience and in the interest of truth without thought for his career. Where would the latecomers be without the admirable and, one would have thought, unforgettable, tormented and steadfast Demange? *En passant* he pointed out that in June 1897 Demange's 'grand coeur' was not sufficient to convince Scheurer-Kestner. And then he comes to himself and the main reason for the protest:

> Je veux qu'on dise que le premier j'ai parlé, que le premier qui se leva pour le juif martyr fut un juif, un juif qui a souffert dans son sang et dans sa chair les souffrances que supporta l'innocent... Et si je dis cela, ce n'est pas par désir de vaine gloire, par ambition des hommages inutiles, c'est parce qu'il faut que ce soit dit aujourd'hui, parce qu'il faut que l'on sache que ce juif a trouvé parmi les siens des mains amies – comme la vôtre, mon cher Reinach – pour se tendre vers lui au jour de la lutte solitaire. Voilà pourquoi, Monsieur, Dreyfus m'a été cher, cher par ses origines et par celles qu'il incarnait; voilà pourquoi j'ai voulu parler aujourd'hui, non pour dire ce que j'ai fait, mais pour affirmer ce que je veux faire maintenant, demain, toujours, pour ceux de mes frères qui suent encore la sueur de sang qu'a suée le juif Jésus.

The letter caused a stir, as might be expected. The 'dreyfusard strategists' were embarrassed, and none more so than Reinach and Mathieu. They strove hard *not* to make it into a Jewish Affair. Bernard-Lazare was of a different frankness. The rights of man were indeed at stake; in the long-term the rights of minorities; but what was at stake immediately were the rights of a Jew. He wanted it to go down in history that a Jew had had the courage to proclaim it loud and clear.[9] One might add that Bernard-Lazare could afford to do this, having fought, and continuing to fight, for the freedom of other oppressed peoples.

Among the many preoccupations of his 'retirement', two in particular stand out: the Picquart investigations and Rennes.

Picquart

Who first thought of connecting Picquart with Bernard-Lazare is not quite clear. In the evidence he gave before the *Cour de Cassation* in December 1898, General Gonse, Deputy Chief of Staff, intimated that he suspected it from the very beginning, his suspicions being based on the fact that while Picquart was in possession of the Dreyfus dossier, from the end of August to the middle of November 1896, leakages had occurred, the most important being in Bernard-Lazare's 'second brochure' (this is the second edition, November 1896, of *Une erreur judiciaire: la vérité sur l'Affaire Dreyfus*) and it concerned the background to the *canaille de D* note. The facts given by Bernard-Lazare, claimed General Gonse, were known only to two or three officers of whom Picquart was one. 'J'en fus très ému, et je demandai au colonel Picquart de faire une note, aussi complète que possible, indiquant avec précision toutes les indiscrétions qu'il remarquerait dans la brochure Bernard-Lazare.' Picquart failed the test because he passed over in silence the 'crucial facts'. Questioned by his chief, he appeared to be embarrassed; and Gonse adds: 'Je n'approfondis pas davantage, ne voulant pas être désagréable à cet officier supérieur; mais, par la suite, quand je sus tous ses agissements, je pensais qu'il devait avoir une part dans ces indiscrétions.'[10] A handsome gesture but curious in the circumstances. A full investigation would have been more in order. The transfer to North Africa, certainly unpleasant to the 'superior officer', was hardly adequate action in the case of suspected collaboration, on the part of the Head of espionage, with the family of a convicted traitor.

The operative word is probably 'par la suite'. Whatever suspicions Gonse might have entertained in 1896,[11] it was not until the Fabre investigation of July 1898, an investigation called by the Minister of War to examine Picquart's indiscretions, that the Picquart–Bernard-Lazare collusion charge was formally made and officially thrown into the case. Interestingly enough, in his report on the Esterhazy trial *Commandant* Ravary mentioned neither Bernard-Lazare nor his brochure, but accused Picquart of having shown the *canaille de D* note to Leblois. At Zola's trial (February 1898) the same charge was made, and again there was no mention of Bernard-Lazare's brochure and collusion with Picquart.

A few months later, at the Fabre investigation, the accusation was formally made by both Gribelin and Gonse, and the collusion centred on the *canaille de D* note. Only Picquart, it was alleged, could have provided the information. It was also intimated that Picquart was the informant behind the *Eclair* and the *Matin* revelations, both intended to open the way for Bernard-Lazare.

It must be said that the whole fantasy has a logic and coherence of its own, given the 'conspiracy' and 'syndicate' complex. It all fits, and none of it is true. It never occurred to anyone to question the psychological plausibility of such a collaboration, not to speak of such simple factual considerations as to whether Bernard-Lazare and Picquart had ever met. This was a minor detail into which Judge Fabre, before whom Bernard-Lazare appeared, did not enquire. Fabre was certain, Bernard-Lazare related,[12] that he (Bernard-Lazare) would not and could not name his informant. He disappointed Fabre by naming Mathieu, who was called in turn and gave a full account, for the first time, of what information he obtained and from whom. Bernard-Lazare took care to publicise this in the press in a long article entitled 'L'Instruction contre le colonel Picquart'[13] which also carried an energetic declaration that Picquart had at no stage communicated any information to him or to Mathieu, and that the first time he, Bernard-Lazare, had met the colonel was in February 1898. This did not prevent General Gonse from repeating the collusion charge at the Enquête de la Cour de Cassation a few months later. Bernard-Lazare vigorously protested in the press, accusing General Gonse of adding 'un mensonge à ses divers faux témoignages'. Affirmations and denials went on until Rennes, when Lissajoux, a journalist and the author of the *Eclair* revelations, joined the battle. In an effort to clear himself and his still un-named source, he alleged that the 'strangely well-informed' Bernard-Lazare was the first to have revealed the secret *canaille de D* note, a claim disproved by simple verification of dates.[14]

Why did the War Office, for long silent over the *canaille de D* note, suddenly break its silence? Could it be that concentration on Picquart's alleged indiscretions in this matter was one way of diverting attention from the serious legal and moral issues raised by the secret communication of the note? After *Commandant* Ravary, in a zealous effort to multiply the indiscretions of Picquart, had confirmed the existence of the note in the Dreyfus dossier, there was no drawing back, but the damage could be minimised and, if possible, used against Picquart. At Zola's trial, Leblois denied having been shown the note by Picquart. The matter was discussed at length and nothing positive emerged. Since Leblois had put down nothing in writing, it was difficult to establish things with certainty. Bernard-Lazare's brochure was an altogether more certain and efficacious nail in Picquart's coffin; and Picquart's indiscretions, unfounded in this case but more justified in others, were an excellent means of diverting attention from the real issue. If diversion was the intention, General Gonse or the Statistical Section may well have miscalculated; for in the process of discussion he and his colleagues not only gave Bernard-Lazare's excellent first brochure new life (it was reprinted in 1898) but in their various testimonies they also authoritatively confirmed the existence of the document, its strange presence in the Dreyfus dossier and its non-applicability to Dreyfus. All these factors, grouped under the general heading of 'sur le moyen tiré de...la pièce secrète', were considered by the *Cour de Cassation* in June 1899 to warrant annulment of the 1894 conviction.

The irony of the accusation of collaboration is that when Picquart and Bernard-Lazare eventually did meet, they disliked each other. It was largely at Picquart's request that Mathieu asked Bernard-Lazare to withdraw from the official battle. 'Mathieu le premier me demanda de laisser faire les autres et de me taire. J'ai souscrit ayant plus de souci de la justice que de moi-même.'[15] In 1901 Picquart even pressed Alfred Dreyfus 'de désavouer Bernard-Lazare'.[16] A well-informed witness who knew both men summed things up by saying that Picquart's natural antipathy for Bernard-Lazare was equalled only by Bernard-Lazare's antipathy for Picquart.[17]

Beside an understandable antipathy between men so totally different in background, mentality and vision, there are other factors which aggravated the relationship. An unpublished note in Bernard-Lazare's papers helps us to understand his irritation with a man made into a hero by the aspirations and needs of others.

> Beaucoup de dreyfusards n'ont marché que lorsque Picquart est entré dans la bataille. On a eu la basse adoration de l'homme; quant à l'idée, elle importait peu... Picquart! Type du militaire qui ne sait rien accomplir en dehors de sa règle et de sa discipline. Ces hésitations, ces scrupules, cette perpétuelle balance dans le conflit des devoirs sociaux et humains et des obligations professionnelles sont les vertus d'honnête bourgeois et non une caractéristique de héros. Picquart n'a pas marché pour le droit, mais par préoccupation personnelle.[18]

One could write a whole book commenting on and justifying what may well appear at first sight a harsh judgment. Henri Guillemin, the well-known debunker of legends (and alas, at times, debunker of true courage and integrity), has a pertinent chapter on Picquart,[19] 'the model soldier', afraid of an Army scandal, personally ambitious and preoccupied with his career, given to long silences – curious indeed for a man of conscience convinced of Dreyfus' innocence. Stranger still, since he knew of this innocence and was apparently troubled by it, is Picquart's way of speaking of the efforts made by 'les Dreyfus', tenacious, dangerous, moneyed, powerful, capable of anything, to establish the innocence of one of themselves. Picquart could not exactly be expected to collaborate with 'ces gens-là' but he speaks of their efforts as if they were outrageous.

Bernard-Lazare had good reason for thinking that the colonel was at best (and it is of course a great deal) an honest bourgeois, not a hero. He may also have felt, and he was sensitive on the matter, Picquart's antisemitic tendencies. He told a reporter in 1901: 'Vous ignorez peut-être, comme beaucoup, que Picquart est énergiquement antisémite.'[20] The 'énergiquement' is perhaps an exaggeration, though by 1901 Picquart did not hide his feelings. Bernard-Lazare was saddened by the spectacle of men such as Zola, Anatole France, Clemenceau, Francis de Pressensé, Trarieux, and how many others, needing Picquart to lead them into battle. One of the most galling experiences must have been to hear the anarchist *Libertaire* proclaim that Picquart personified 'la révolte consciente', that 'Vive Picquart' signified 'Vive le Révolutionnaire' and 'à bas l'obéissance passive'.[21] All this about a man who had known of the illegality ever since the day it was committed, who had even told his chiefs (Boisdeffre and Mercier) that a conviction (at the first court-martial) was uncertain unless use was made of the secret dossier; the man who thought that it might well have been he who had transmitted Mercier's secret evidence to the president of the court-martial (wrongly, as it turns out, for the honour was Du Paty de Clam's).[22]

Picquart's evidence at Rennes, after all that had happened, is disarming in its naive, professional amorality. He calmly relates several incidents which aroused his suspicions in the course of the 1894 trial; his impression was that 'les charges n'étaient pas suffisantes'[23] and yet, or rather *therefore*, he recommended the communication of secret evidence, unknown to the accused and the defence. The only point that worried him about the procedure was the safe return to the Ministry of the secret evidence![24] (Admittedly, Picquart pleads that he did not know what was in the secret file and that he trusted his chiefs.) General Roget, evidently trying to tarnish the image of the high-principled former chief of espionage now disapproving of methods once used by himself, told of an episode which may or may not be true. The interesting point is that this involved Picquart himself using, early in 1896, the secret communication of evidence in order to secure somebody's conviction. Picquart vehemently protested: he would not have used such manoeuvres.[25] Yet in 1894 he had accepted these manoeuvres on the part of his chiefs, had even told them that conviction would not be certain without the 'pièces qu'il était convenu de montrer secrètement'.

Picquart was indeed no hero. He was made into one by infinitely more heroic men who sought in him reassurance about the integrity of the Army, people who were anxious to find proof of the conscience of a Republican soldier. He played his part well, much better than Dreyfus, who turned out to be a disappointing hero. Bernard-Lazare never had any illusions about Picquart, and before long he lost his illusions about Dreyfus.

What of Picquart's feelings towards Bernard-Lazare? In the absence of any account, one can only speculate. My guess would be that Bernard-Lazare was to Piquart what, in the sarcastic words of Péguy, Dreyfus was to the Socialist leader Jules Guesde: an inconvenient trouble-maker, upsetting plans, causing 'des ennuis'. First there were his brochures; then there was the *accusation* of collusion with 'ces gens-là'. Mathieu has an interesting passage in his *Souvenirs* which may throw light on Picquart's hostility. It concerns Demange, whom Picquart also disliked, but it may well hold for Bernard-Lazare. It was explained to Mathieu that 'le colonel Picquart ne pardonnera jamais à Maître Demange parce que celui-ci connaissait depuis longtemps la communication illégale du dossier secret aux juges de 1894 et qu'il n'en a pas fait état pour protester contre le jugement'.[26] In other words, if Demange had made his knowledge public, or if Bernard-Lazare had given in 1896 the full account of his sources of information which he gave in 1898, he, Picquart, would have been spared a great deal of unpleasantness. Mathieu's understandable reaction was that Colonel Picquart knew of it all since 1894, that he had proofs of Dreyfus' innocence in 1896 and did not come out into the open with them until 1897; and then it was done by Leblois. On a higher level one might say that Bernard-Lazare, with his obstinate cry that a violation of justice had been committed, was an awkward, embarrassing reminder of means and methods once acceptable to the brilliant officer of the Statistical Section. This vocal Jewish anarchist, lucid, fiery, unimpressed by high rank, was there to remind Picquart that he had participated in an act all dreyfusards condemned as immoral. It is very noticeable that Picquart, both at the Zola trial and at Rennes, is at pains to avoid speaking of Bernard-Lazare and his troublesome brochures.

Rennes and after

On 9 June 1899 Captain Dreyfus left Devil's Island on the way to Rennes.

Arriving in the city a few days before the opening of the trial, Bernard-Lazare took a walk along the prison walls, musing with anguish 'quel cadavre allait-on ramener? Quelle loque humaine allait-on jeter en pâture aux chiens féroces qui attendaient le morceau de chair pantelante?'[27] From early July the dreyfusard press had published accounts of the barbarous treatment to which Dreyfus had been subjected. Always quick to turn anything to its advantage, it was rumoured in the antidreyfusard press that the prisoner had inflicted suffering and illness on himself so as to make himself into 'un homme cassé' unable to stand up to strenuous interrogation. Bernard-Lazare was wondering whether Dreyfus was not in fact 'un homme cassé'. Would he be able to stand up to the ordeal? Quickly dismissing such pessimistic thoughts from his mind, he drew comfort from the sheer fact that the victim was alive, that he had hung on to life when death would surely have been a merciful solution.

> Quelle force admirable que celle de l'innocent qui veut
> vivre, qui ne veut pas que la souillure reste à son front et au
> front des siens, qui a foi en la justice de sa cause et qui puise
> dans cette volonté la puissance de résister à tout, le courage
> de garder l'espoir sur le roc des supplices où l'a enchaîné
> le destin.[28]

Dreyfus, as Bernard-Lazare imagined him, would have gained in humanity through suffering. 'Ses cinq années de souffrances n'ont fait qu'élargir son esprit et son coeur, son propre malheur a ouvert ses sens et son âme au malheur des autres. C'est un soldat qu'on avait frappé, c'est un homme qu'on vient de nous rendre.'

The next day, in the enormous *salle des fêtes* of the Rennes lycée, packed to capacity with journalists from the four corners of the earth, crowded with officers and generals, former ministers, magistrates, even a former President of the Republic, all waiting to be called as witnesses, Jean-Bernard, a journalist from the *Figaro*, observed his neighbour: 'Bernard-Lazare sourit derrière son lorgnon; il a l'air de se dire: "Et pourtant, tout cela est mon oeuvre".'[29] After Captain Dreyfus had entered the hushed hall, the incorrigible journalist in search of first impressions passed this note to his neighbour who had turned as white as a sheet: 'Quelle impression avez-vous éprouvée en voyant Dreyfus entrer; je vous regardais et vous étiez très pâle?'[30] While the *acte d'accusation* was being read out in court, that monstrous document engraved on his memory, Bernard-Lazare sent this reply:

> C'était la première fois que je voyais Dreyfus, et, dans
> l'attente de son entrée, j'ai eu une poignante impression
> d'angoisse mêlée de joie. Je me suis si souvent, depuis cinq
> ans, représenté cette minute que je savais devoir arriver un
> jour! Mon angoisse a disparu dès l'entrée, quand je l'ai vu
> tel que je n'aurais pas espéré le voir, après ces années de
> supplice, plein d'une flamme intérieure de vie, ferme et
> roide; et ça n'a plus été pour moi qu'une tranquillité d'âme
> parfaite, plus que jamais j'avais la certitude que l'innocent
> allait vaincre.[31]

If the victim inspired him with confidence, the procedure and attitude adopted by the court-martial on the first day of the proceedings (7 August) filled him with foreboding. 'Ce qui m'a surtout frappé, c'est le manque de sincérité de ces débats. Comment! Voilà des gens qui, ayant en leur possession l'aveu d'Esterhazy, questionnent Dreyfus sur le bordereau en lui demandant s'il en est l'auteur!' He had one hope, however: 'la vérité commencera à surgir avec l'audition des témoins'.[32]

At the end of the month, after numerous witnesses had given evidence, the same journalist asked him whether he was happy about the way things were going: 'Ce procès est machiné comme un vaudeville, ou plutôt comme un drame', he replied. Still, he was not discouraged: 'ayons pleine confiance. Possédant la vérité, nous devons vaincre.'[33] To the very last, while waiting for the verdict to be announced, a verdict which in his heart of hearts he knew would be unfavourable, 'Bernard-Lazare communique sa flamme et sa confiance aux découragés.'[34]

It is clear from a major, very remarkable and little known

study he wrote of the Rennes trial for the *North American Review* in November 1899, 'France at the Parting of the Ways', that in his view the whole idea of a sensational trial with new pleadings, after the *Cour de Cassation* had established Dreyfus' innocence by attributing the *bordereau* to Esterhazy, rejecting the confession legend and recognising the secret communication – that after all this a big trial was a mistake, an insult to the *Cour de Cassation*, a violation of the principles of jurisprudence, a dangerous precedent allowing lower courts to contest the acts and the judgments of higher tribunals. Annulment of the 1894 verdict without retrial by a military tribunal, the procedure eventually adopted in 1906, is what he would have preferred. In 1906, as we know, this was frowned upon by many who held that Dreyfus must be judged by his peers, an idea against which Bernard-Lazare protested in 1899.

> It was decreed, every Frenchman approving, that Dreyfus could not be cleared of the accusations hanging over him except by the judgment of his peers. Even the lawyers who defended the unfortunate man petitioned the Court of Cassation to remand him to the jurisdiction of his peers, and the court acquiesced without perceiving that by thus acknowledging the jurisdiction of his peers it denied its own. No one pointed out that this conception was only a remnant of barbarism, and that the most unsafe tribunal for a man was one composed of individuals belonging to his own class, that is to say, possessing its peculiar prejudices in addition to general prejudices, and having to uphold not only justice but also such interests of the corps as are in conflict with those of the man subject to their verdict; and not only these professional interests but also the personal interests of competitors or rivals. In reality, it was the function of the Court of Cassation to say these things, and the only effective way of saying them was to reverse the former verdict definitely, to set Dreyfus free and to absolve him by a decree which everyone would have honored.

If the *Cour de Cassation* did not do so, he argues, it is because a firm judgment of this sort would have run counter to the wishes of a cowardly government, a determined enemy and a short-sighted defence. He finds the attitude of Mathieu and his counsellors difficult to understand. Did they too want a sensational trial, with the aim of putting the Generals in the dock? This was in fact Labori's idea and caused bitter friction between him and Demange. Bernard-Lazare, as can well be imagined, had no intention of letting Mercier and company escape, but he would have wished to separate the issues. An almost necessary corollary of quashing the 1894 verdict, it seemed to him, would be to call upon Mercier to explain the violation of justice, to settle the question of the *bordereau* since it undeniably existed, and to investigate Esterhazy's declarations of authorship instead of ignoring them. Mathieu, however, was opposed to annulment, preferring a retrial, and Maître Mornard pleaded in this sense before the *Cour de Cassation*. The result was an extraordinarily vaguely phrased decree which left the Rennes court-martial free to question all over again matters the *Cour de Cassation* had already investigated. Thus, as Bernard-Lazare remarks, at Rennes 'the prosecution produced experts, notwithstanding that the handwriting of the incriminating documents had been decided not to be that of Dreyfus. The defence summoned Captain Lebrun-Renaud although the court had rejected the legend of the confession.'[35]

Mathieu was bitterly disappointed when Colonel Jouaust, president of the Rennes court-martial, asked Captain Dreyfus questions on the *bordereau* and the confession legend. 'Ses questions indiquèrent la détermination de ne tenir aucun compte, dans les nouveaux débats, des résultats de l'enquête des Chambres réunies de la Cour de Cassation, ni de l'arrêt qu'elles avaient rendu.'[36] But it must be said that the decree, as it was phrased, allowed Jouaust to do this.

Yet Mathieu was right in one way: a public retrial was likely to shed light. Bernard-Lazare quite readily admits that the Rennes trial was illuminating, especially with regard to the attitude and mentality of the other side.

> . . .The trial was planned not only in its grand outlines, but even in its smallest details. Each of the depositions of the incriminating witnesses was minutely ordered and arranged. . . The rôles had been distributed to each of the witnesses. Their testimony was given according to a sort of prescribed method. Its preparation was perfectly apparent; bearing upon the general thesis, each witness spoke with the intention of supporting the one who preceded him, and of

preparing the way for the one who followed. Never was
there a trial more radically vitiated by criminal conspiracy
among the witnesses! It was not simply an understanding
but a coalition against right and justice for the purpose of
defeating them, if necessary even by falsehood and perjury.
Never before, in any trial or before any tribunal, have
witnesses been allowed to appear without adducing a single
fact, without their having been in any way connected with
the case, but merely to make speeches for the prosecution.
This will be a unique fact in the history of jurisprudence,
that men could thus assume the rôle of prosecutors without
authority, and that a court accepted them as witnesses.[37]

In open court and before the eyes of the world, Bernard-
Lazare observes, the General Staff did its best to discredit
revisionists, by insinuation and slander. A former Minister of
War (General Mercier) even went on record as saying that
England and Germany had financed the dreyfusard movement
to the tune of thirty-five million![38] Bernard-Lazare himself did
not altogether escape insinuations though most of the time they
were directed against his brochures which were used in one way
or another *against* Dreyfus, with even General Mercier proving
himself to have been an assiduous reader.[39]

As far as Captain Dreyfus was concerned. insinuations and
moral degradation were not enough. His guilt had to be established and here the General Staff rested its case on three ancient
pillars.[40] The handwriting of the *bordereau*; the contention that
only a staff officer could have delivered the documents enumerated in it; and Dreyfus' confession. In order to maintain the
first point, refuge had to be taken in Bertillon's citadel. (Bertillon's
lengthy demonstrations provided the lighter, almost hilarious side
of the proceedings. For once Bernard-Lazare refrained from
sarcasm when speaking of Bertillon; he almost felt sorry for a
man so apt to cover himself with ridicule.) Demonstration of the
second point, entrusted mainly to Generals Mercier and Roget,
was simple: it was based upon the fact that nobody knew the
exact contents of the documents which had been delivered. With
an irony worthy of Anatole France, Bernard-Lazare comments
on how the theoretically demonstrated capital importance of
unknown documents was deemed to have established their reality,
character and delivery, *necessarily*, by a staff officer. The secret

dossiers were also conveniently used to back up the contention
that it must have been a staff officer and Dreyfus in particular.
With evident delight Bernard-Lazare quotes Captain Cuignet's
famous classification of the secret dossier into, first, papers believed
by the General Staff to refer to Dreyfus; secondly, papers which
do not concern him; thirdly, forgeries. At the last moment
ultra-secret dossiers came to the support of the secret dossier. To
substantiate the confession allegation, recourse was had to the
deposition of a dead man (Major d'Attel) because the man who
had boasted of having heard the confessions was an unreliable
witness. The defence, however, called Captain Lebrun-Renaud.

It was in the right of the defence to challenge, contradict and
confound the rehearsed actors that the positive usefulness of the
Rennes trial lay. Stage-managed though it was, some truths, and
in the event some important truths, were bound to emerge from
the confrontation. On the main points, the handwriting, the
'staff officer' contention and the confession, nothing very much
was left standing, according to Bernard-Lazare. And reading
through the extraordinary trial proceedings one cannot help but
agree with him.[41]

Most important of all, Bernard-Lazare saw the Rennes trial as
revealing that no lamentable and frightful error had been committed in 1894 but 'the most odious of crimes'. Two crimes, in
fact, for among the secret papers communicated to the judges in
1894 there figured, in addition to the *canaille de D* note, a false
text. 'La condamnation fut obtenue aux moyens de deux crimes:
la forfaiture et le faux.'[42] The 'faux' refers to the *incorrect* version
of the still much discussed Panizzardi telegram of 2 November
1894[43] which, according to the evidence given at Rennes by
Captain Freystaetter, was passed to the judges in 1894. Mercier
denied this. Bernard-Lazare accepted Captain Freystaetter's
evidence against Mercier's. On this basis, as well as on the fact
that the *correct* version of the telegram, which absolved Dreyfus
from guilt, was also known to Mercier, he argued boldly the
following theory: Mercier withheld from the judges the correct
and confirmed version of the telegram (which did not incriminate
Dreyfus) and instead communicated to them an incorrect version
which had an incriminating last sentence. Thus, Mercier did not
only withhold proof, or at least indication, of innocence, but
actually changed 'this proof of innocence into a proof of guilt'.[44]
Bernard-Lazare concluded that after the startling revelation of

the Panizzardi telegram it would be difficult for future historians to see the Dreyfus Affair as a simple error of justice. It is on these lines that he himself later intended to re-open the Affair in Péguy's periodical *Les Cahiers de la Quinzaine*. Substantially the same theory has recently been argued by Henri Guillemin[45] with a great deal more evidence at his disposal than Bernard-Lazare had in 1899. While agreeing that Mercier withheld the *correct* version of the telegram, Guillemin concludes that it is impossible to be certain whether the War Minister communicated the *incorrect* version. It is clear, on the other hand, that *an* incorrect version damaging to Dreyfus later found its way into the Dreyfus file.

Bernard-Lazare had some very harsh things to say about the clerical and military mentality of France as it revealed itself during the Affair. It is worth-while to quote a lengthy passage since it is only in an unpublished letter to Reinach that he expressed himself with quite the same degree of bitterness and candour.

> Nothing shows better the theological character so to speak, of this trial than the capital rôle which they assigned to the pretended confession of Captain Dreyfus. . . It is a clerical principle that a confession is better than a proof. All inquisitorial jurisprudence, all the ancient jurisprudence of Catholic countries, as in barbarous times, is founded upon obtaining a confession and not on finding proofs. The Church will not admit scientific demonstrations, but prefers an authoritative and hierarchical affirmation. . . When the accused is brought before it, it demands not proofs of guilt in order to confound him and condemn him, but a dogma of culpability. It is in this way that the treason of Dreyfus became a dogma for the great majority of Frenchmen, not only for those of little or no culture, but even more for those who until then belonged to the intellectual *élite*. 'Dreyfus is guilty', said M. Jules Lemaître, M. Maurice Barrès and M. François Coppée, because a courtmartial said so, because seven ministers of war proclaimed it; these assertions ought to render all examination unnecessary; they must be accepted as an act of faith, and whoever refuses to do so is a bad Frenchman, as he would be a bad Catholic who should reject the decisions of a council or the word of a Pope.[46]

As for the Army, a 'clerico-military oligarchy', here too he is at his harshest. One belief that the Affair has surely shaken is that 'the Army, as it existed in our country, was reconcilable with democracy;...unless the spirit of the Army be changed, there will be deadly conflict between that spirit and the spirit of free enquiry and research'. Rennes made clear to the French people that France had come to the parting of the ways: 'the nation must choose whom it will follow, whether the bandits who have just accomplished the most infamous of crimes, or those who, for the past few years, have been struggling every day to preserve the honour of their country'.[47] Whatever France's choice, and in spite of the Rennes verdict, it was by the example of the dreyfusards, he asked, that the world should judge France.

It is well known today that Waldeck-Rousseau, Reinach and other political 'amis de Paris' brought pressure to bear on Mathieu to try to moderate Labori's fiery eloquence and provocative tactics. They feared his outspokenness and vehemence, above all his intention of making Rennes the trial of the guilty Generals. It was the duty of Dreyfus' counsels, Cornély wrote to Labori, 'de ménager les généraux et d'exécuter dans leurs discours des variations sur ce cri: Vive l'Armée'.[48] This was a blunt, brutal statement of the strategy the Waldeck-Rousseau government, the first pro-dreyfusard government, wished the defence at Rennes to adopt. Nothing was to be done to antagonise the military judges. The debate was to be lifted out of the dilemma that 'Dreyfus versus the Army' created, a dilemma exploited by the enemy side. Dreyfus' freedom, probably his life, was at this price.

Clemenceau recommended to Labori a diametrically opposed strategy: 'Marchez sur les criminels à la barre, interrogez-les, poussez-les, ne leur permettez pas de s'esquiver. La victoire est là... Mon cher ami, il faut la bataille sans merci, sans ménagement pour qui que ce soit. J'ai même peine à comprendre qu'on délibère là-dessus à cette heure. Dreyfus n'est ici qu'un protagoniste symbolique.'[49]

Dreyfus the symbol and Dreyfus the man is at the centre of the growing division between dreyfusards. It was to reach its high point with the pardon. But there are other factors in this division which should not be overlooked. Behind the unpalatable political tactic urged by the 'amis de Paris' in order to save Dreyfus the man, there was also the concern, political concern, for the life of the government and even the Republic, both endangered by antisemitic and nationalist riots. The government felt sufficiently threatened to arrest such prominent leaders as Déroulède (12 August 1899). If the atmosphere in Rennes was tense, the situation in Paris was explosive. Indeed Reinach feared a military coup.[50] In the circumstances, it seemed wise not to anger the Generals who commanded the loyalty of the troops and the respect of the majority of the population. Seen from the other side, it all boiled down to sparing the Generals for reasons of State, the famous reasons of State which once again threatened to interfere with the course of justice, this time with bringing the criminal accusers to justice.

There was, too, the dispute between Demange and Labori. 'Les amis de Paris', soon to be sarcastically called by Labori and Picquart 'les amis de Dreyfus', were also the partisans of Demange arraigned against the partisans of Labori. The two great lawyers, totally different in every respect, had never seen eye to eye. Demange's view of his colleague's conduct of the Zola trial can be gathered from this comment made à propos the coming Rennes trial: 'Il ne s'agit pas de recommencer le procès Zola'. Labori liked great, stunning trials; he was an excellent orator, an unforgettable actor. This was not Demange's style. By the time of Rennes, the two defence lawyers were not on speaking terms or else they had actually quarrelled. The cruel attempt on Labori's life at Rennes, and his absence from the court for over a week, did not make matters any easier. In his absence the star witness whom he had intended to grill, General Mercier, had been and gone, and nobody was ever allowed to forget that he, Labori, had not cross-examined General Mercier. In the courtroom the two lawyers sat side by side, with different aims, different tactics, a whole different conception and understanding of the Affair. Demange wished to redress an *error*. Labori wanted to expose a *plot*. One concentrated on the Dreyfus case and on that alone; the other was as much concerned with Picquart and with clearing that officer's name. There were in fact two defence cases conducted at Rennes, and one might almost say there were two accused. Picquart, much blackened by prosecution witnesses, understandably took every opportunity to clear himself, being several times reprimanded by the president of the Court. At one stage Demange could no longer contain himself and agreed with the president: 'Vous avez fait une observation absolument juste

lorsque vous avez dit au colonel Picquart de se renfermer stricte-
ment dans l'affaire Dreyfus. . .Je crois qu'il serait bon en effet de
nous en tenir à l'Affaire Dreyfus et de ne pas nous occuper du
service des renseignements du colonel Picquart.'[51] Between the
two mutually hostile lawyers, each with his own supporters, there
was the unhappy Mathieu trying to keep the peace, bound in
gratitude to both, bombarded with communications from 'les
amis de Paris' urging him not to let Labori take part in the final
pleading, a rôle Labori had so much wanted to fill. Finally they
won the day.

It was ultimately to Bernard-Lazare that Mathieu entrusted the
painful and embarrassing mission of communicating to Labori the
request that he should not plead. With Jaurès and Victor Basch
as moral support, Bernard-Lazare presented himself at Labori's
house at six o'clock in the morning of 8 September, the very day
the defence's summing up was to begin. In a vivid description of
this memorable early morning visit, Labori has related how embarrassed Bernard-Lazare was, how Jaurès eventually made the
point bluntly: 'l'aquittement est certain si vous renoncez à la
parole; . . .tout est perdu si vous parlez'.[52] And so it was that in
court that day, to the surprise of all, to the regret of many
dreyfusards and the great anger of some, Labori, invited by the
president to address the court on the last day, uttered words which
no one had ever expected to come from the lips of this eloquent
orator: 'Je renonce à la parole.'

Labori was profoundly mistaken in thinking that Bernard-
Lazare, like some paid agent, was merely acting on Mathieu's
instructions. He would not have carried out this unpleasant
mission simply to save his 'employer' embarrassment, had he not
been convinced that it was in the interest of the cause. For the
first time in his life Bernard-Lazare found himself on the side of
the 'politicians' and the diplomats against the 'idealists' fighting
for the purity of the symbol. He had acted as liaison man between
'les amis de Paris' and *their* friends in Rennes. He had asked
Clemenceau, as the man most likely to have any influence on
Labori, to prevail upon him to withdraw from the final pleading.
Bernard-Lazare was an ardent Demange partisan, supporting the
prudent lawyer who was going to argue *error* in preference to the
bold and outspoken Labori, intending to expose *plot*.

Puzzling as this attitude may appear and to some extent remains, it is not entirely without explanation. We have already

seen that Bernard-Lazare thought the whole idea of a big, dazzling retrial by military court a mistake, a 'show trial desired by both sides but one unlikely to lead to the proper exercise of justice'.[53] Unlike Labori and his friends, and together with the 'politicians' in Paris, he was worried about the political situation. He had feared a coup for some time. In February 1899 he had written to his friend Emile Meyerson: 'Je crois la République fichue et un coup d'état prochain. J'ai idée que je passerai quelques années de ma vie en Belgique. Vous verrez ça. Nous allons voir un Bonaparte ou un d'Orléans remonter sur le trône de leurs pères.'[54] While the Affair had done nothing to enhance politics in his eyes, it had made him sensitive to the very real menace presented by reactionary forces. Previously, in common with other anarchists, he had underestimated these forces, his attacks having been largely directed against the tyrannies of the existing Republican *State* and the possible tyrannies of a future Socialist *State*. The Affair had shown that reactionary forces were far from dead and that the Republic was in danger. Already in 1897, in an open dispute with his friend Jean Grave, he had pleaded for anarchist participation in elections.[55] Throughout the Affair he urged that in the face of the reactionary peril anarchists should close ranks with liberals and left-wing forces.[56] By the time of Rennes, the fear of a *coup* had greatly augmented – which explains why even the appearance of General Mercier on the witness stand, a major event which his efforts had done much to bring about, was overshadowed for him by the threat of a governmental crisis in Paris. 'It is not the actual matter of Mercier's deposition which disquiets the defence', he told a journalist, 'but some underhand combination to bring about a premature convocation of Parliament and a Ministerial crisis. Such an event would be a calamity.'[57]

However, these were not the only considerations which guided his support for Demange whose cautious moderation he had found irksome and of whose intentions to soft-soap the military, if he knew of them, he must have disapproved. What endeared Demange to him was the latter's intention to concentrate on the Dreyfus Affair and to disentangle it from the infinitely more complex Picquart affair which could be used by the prosecution to complicate and obscure the Dreyfus case, to tire, baffle and confuse the military judges. Demange understood this extremely well and one only has to read the proceedings of Rennes to understand Bernard-Lazare's preference for him. Demange was a polite but firm, alert and perspicacious interrogator with an astonishingly detailed knowledge of the enormous dossier; he was quick to spot weaknesses and discrepancies in the statements made by witnesses; once they were spotted he was tenacious in his attempt to clarify them and use them to establish his client's innocence. Nor should his placating of the military be overdone; he questioned them closely, at times sternly, though never with the aim of exposing them as liars, forgers and plotters. Occasionally his readiness to admit that they were all, with the exception of Generals Mercier and Roget, honest and trustworthy men of good faith, led him into difficulties, for the honest and trustworthy colonels sometimes categorically affirmed what Captain Dreyfus categorically denied. It is mostly in his summing up that Demange went far in the direction of placating the military. He even managed to speak of Henry as 'un brave, loyal et honnête homme'[58] and of Du Paty de Clam as a man led astray by 'les ardeurs de son imagination' but who acted out of 'une conviction ferme, sûre, loyale'.[59] This all too obvious white-washing could not have been much to Bernard-Lazare's liking. But Demange's genuine sincerity and passion, albeit a contained passion, unlike the fire of a Zola or a Labori, was touching. Above all, Bernard-Lazare found in Demange a deep compassion for the victim, for the battered human being of flesh and blood whom so many expected to act as the hero they had created for themselves, to personify innocence with all the radiance, courage and emotion that they would have wished.[60] Demange, like Bernard-Lazare, was not prepared to fight for the purity of the symbol over Dreyfus' dead body. Everybody expected the most heroic virtues of Dreyfus, Bernard-Lazare told Péguy. He was innocent; that was already a great deal.

There is, however, a personal sort of symbolism which comes into play in Bernard-Lazare's attitude and which in itself separated him from the idealists fighting for *their* symbol.

Dès ces sombres matinées de novembre 1894, où la meute atroce des Judet et des Drumont se rua sur lui, Dreyfus m'est apparu comme le symbole du Juif persécuté. Il a incarné en lui, non seulement les séculaires souffrances de ce peuple de martyrs, mais les douleurs présentes. J'ai vu, à travers lui, les Juifs, parqués dans les ergastules russes

aspirant vainement à un peu de lumière et de liberté, les
Juifs roumains auxquels on refuse les droits d'homme, ceux
de Galicie, prolétaires que les trusts financiers affament, et
qu'assomment les paysans fanatisés par leurs prêtres,
malheureux se ruant sur de plus malheureux qu'eux. Il a
été pour moi la tragique image des Juifs algériens traqués
et pillés, des malheureux émigrants mourant de faim dans
les ghettos de New York ou de Londres, de tous ceux dont la
désespérance cherche un asile dans tous les coins du monde
habité, un asile où ils trouveront, enfin, cette justice que les
meilleurs d'entre eux ont tant appelée pour l'humanité
entière. . .[61]

Dreyfus, symbol of suffering and persecuted Jewry, was alive
and free, free to clear his name, and to Bernard-Lazare it was a
profoundly moving experience. He accepted the pardon sadly
and silently, without any illusions that it constituted a reversal of
the absurd Rennes verdict, was a new and higher verdict, a
proclamation of innocence, a way of saving France's honour in
the eyes of the world. All these themes were developed in the
dreyfusard press by way of consolation and justification. Bernard-
Lazare never went in for this. He was glad that Dreyfus was free
to establish his innocence in future, but the simple fact remained
that he had been condemned for a second time and the pardon,
at best an act of humanity, was a political solution which ethically
did not solve anything.

Matters were made worse by the amnesty (December 1900),
that new 'loi scélérate' which stifled all discussion and made a
mockery of the condition under which the pardon had been
accepted, namely that Dreyfus would be free to establish his
innocence. Before long this governmentally decreed silence was
broken by what Péguy aptly called 'la politique dreyfusarde'. One
might also call it 'la revanche dreyfusarde'. Against it, Bernard-
Lazare was to fight one of his last battles.

In public he refrained from all criticism either of Dreyfus'
personal conduct after his liberation or of the family's capitulation
to the politicians over the matter of the amnesty. In 1901, in an
open dispute with Labori, forever railing against the pardon
and seeing it as a prelude to the amnesty, Bernard-Lazare contented himself with saying: 'il [Labori] est furieux de ce que
Dreyfus ait accepté sa grâce et n'ait pas continué à poursuivre,

en prison, sa réhabilitation. . . A-t-il le fait nouveau? Nous l'aurons peut-être dans un an, dans vingt ans, que sais-je? Quant au gracié, il n'était pas le maître et Waldeck, bien entendu, a eu le grand tort de ne pas le consulter!'[62]

In private Bernard-Lazare would appear to have been far more critical. The Affair is dead, he is reported to have told friends, 'que voulez-vous? on ne peut pas s'apitoyer sur un héros qui est au chaud en hiver et qui mange des glaces l'été'.[63] To Péguy, too, he confided his thoughts, increasingly sad thoughts, but never bitter. He continued to love Dreyfus like a brother who must be forgiven because he has suffered.

'Quel livre', he wrote to Reinach in October 1899, 'clôra l'Affaire Dreyfus, qui dira le dernier mot, celui qui contiendra toute la vérité et qui accomplira toute la justice? Celui qui a écrit le premier mot se le demande souvent. Quand entendra-t-il la réponse?'[64]

Captain Dreyfus was rehabilitated in 1906, an event which Bernard-Lazare did not live to see. But the 'last word' on the Affair still remains to be written. Perhaps it will never be written. Siegfried Thalheimer[65] is the only modern historian to my knowledge who has gone back to the mysterious origins of the Dreyfus Affair and to Bernard-Lazare's interpretation of 1896: '. . .le capitaine Dreyfus est victime d'une machination abominable'. I am not sure whether Professor Thalheimer does not go further in his interpretation. In the note to Reinach, which is probably dated 1900, Bernard-Lazare had this to say about the antisemitic machination:

> La campagne antisémite m'avait éclairé et de tous les faits suivis au jour le jour, analysés et discutés, la certitude était née en mon esprit que l'Affaire était le résultat d'une machination antisémite (c'est encore mon opinion aujourd'-hui, tout en tenant compte des éléments que je n'avais pas à ce moment et du fait que la machination n'a pas été originelle, mais secondaire).[66]

However that may be, there can be little doubt that antisemitism played a large part in Bernard-Lazare's understanding of and commitment to the Affair. This is not to say of course that he would not have fought for justice had Dreyfus not been a Jew. But if, as Bernard-Lazare believed, Dreyfus was condemned

because he was a Jew, then it was in this context that the Affair
had to be fought, without recourse to euphemisms or screens. He
had the courage to say so, and he wanted history to record that
it was a Jew who first spoke out in defence of an unjustly
condemned Jew. This very attitude may have discomfited the
Dreyfus family and other dreyfusards and may well explain the
silence which surrounded Bernard-Lazare's name after, and even
during, the Affair. And yet it is no exaggeration to say that Dreyfus
owed his freedom to Bernard-Lazare's convictions and commitment. And not only Dreyfus but also, in a profound sense,
Republican democracy: for he created almost single-handed a
resistance movement, 'a moral syndicate', which eventually
understood and withstood an evil of which antisemitism was only
the first symptom.

9

THE MORAL SYNDICATE:
THE DREYFUSARD MOVEMENT

We have followed the events of the Dreyfus Affair but we have said little so far about *dreyfusism*. To understand its beginnings we must now go back in time.

Convinced that only the concerted efforts of all men of goodwill could break down the impregnable walls of silence and prejudice, convinced too that there were such men if only they knew what he knew, having no newspaper tribune from which to appeal and persuade, Bernard-Lazare did the propagandising in person by going from door to door, armed with such documents as he had and with his own extraordinary tenacity, unruffled by rebuffs or defeats. 'Que de démarches il a faites pour amener à la cause, et les convaincre, des savants, des journalistes, des écrivains, des hommes politiques...il apportait une ardeur inouïe pour faire des adeptes.'[1] This is how Stock has described the famous 'persuasion visits' which went on for an entire year, from 1896 to 1897, in the interval between the first two brochures. Alarmed at this activity, a reporter on the *Voltaire* disparagingly spoke of the creation of a 'moral syndicate', trying to rally public opinion.[2] Bernard-Lazare proudly accepted the term and his role as its creator.

It is interesting to follow him on the visits to some of his famous contemporaries and to learn of their first reactions as Bernard-Lazare later recounted them to Reinach and to Jean-Bernard. It is an enlightening and little-known chapter in the dreyfusard movement.

The first convert he made was Joseph Reinach; but he was a special case for it was he who had contacted Bernard-Lazare in late August 1896, not over the Dreyfus Affair but to congratulate him on *Contre l'Antisémitisme*. Much to Bernard-Lazare's

surprise, the epitome of the Jewish bourgeoisie not only approved
but encouraged him to continue the battle with greater boldness.[3]
In his reply, Bernard-Lazare did not minimise the social, economic
and philosophical ideas which separated him from Reinach. But,
he goes on, a thousand things may separate men and one may
unite them. In this particular case, the realisation that they as
Jews had to fight antisemitism was a common bond.[4] It is in a
similar spirit, of frankly appreciating the differences which divide
and of endeavouring to cooperate on the fundamental issues
which unite men, that Bernard-Lazare had always approached
team work, and the moral syndicate of liberal opinion was built
up on the same lines.

This exchange of letters was the beginning of a close relationship, if not exactly friendship, which lasted throughout the Affair
and beyond, though the two men agreed to disagree on many
issues. Reinach knew of *Une erreur judiciaire: la vérité sur
l'Affaire Dreyfus* before its publication in Brussels, and it was
Bernard-Lazare who introduced Reinach to Mathieu. In his
early, ardent and fearless dreyfusism Reinach was an exception
among his fellow French Jews, and no one appreciated this more
than Bernard-Lazare. 'Après moi, vous avez été le premier
dreyfusard et le plus ardent'.[5]

The first men on whom he actually called, and this in November 1896, immediately after the publication of his first brochure,
were Jaurès and Zola. Not a bad choice, as it turned out, though
Les Preuves and *J'accuse* were still a long way off.

Jaurès' reception was icy.

> J'avais vu, avant les attaques de la Petite République,
> Jaurès. Forzinetti voulut encore m'accompagner. Je trouvai
> Jaurès très froid, presque hostile. Ou il n'avait pas lu, ou
> il ne trouvait pas que logiquement j'avais raison, ou il
> hésistait pour des raisons politiques. J'ai eu l'occasion, cette
> année-là, de le revoir, je lui ai même écrit; je n'ai pu lui
> faire comprendre l'importance sociale de la question, ni
> même son intérêt capital pour la cause socialiste.[6]

All these elements probably entered into Jaurès' unfavourable
reaction, but the two factors which must have weighed most
heavily with Jaurès seem to have escaped Bernard-Lazare: his
own anarchism and Jaurès' initial hostility to a bourgeois cause.
The London Socialist Congress of 1896 was only a few months

old; and so were the attacks on parliamentary Socialist manoeuvres which had figured prominently in *L'Action Sociale*.
Jaurès was by no means the only public figure previously attacked
and now hopefully approached, as if yesterday's disputes were
insignificant beside the fundamental issues at stake in this injustice. Jaurès was the only Socialist Party leader whom Bernard-
Lazare tried to convert personally, and he did so with tenacity.
A thousand things separated him from Jaurès, but one, he
thought, united them: *la cause socialiste*, as opposed to *la politique
socialiste*. He expected Jaurès to see the Affair in the wider, more
revolutionary context in which the author of *Les Preuves* finally
did see it; and reading *Les Preuves* helps us to understand why
Bernard-Lazare addressed himself to Jaurès in spite of his previous
criticism of the politician. But he may well have underestimated
the strength of Jaurès' hostility towards a bourgeois affair in which
he, like other Socialist leaders, suspected that the government and
the barons of finance were involved. In December 1894 Jaurès
had asked for Dreyfus' head, accusing the government of saving
a bourgeois and an officer. 'Bravo Jaurès', Drumont had applauded. During Castelin's interpellation (November 1896)
Rouanet, animated by a sense of equality, suggested that the
Rothschilds as well as Bernard-Lazare should be prosecuted. A
year later, in another stormy parliamentary debate (4 November
1897), Marcel Sembart, making great play of Socialist impartiality, asked why *Commandant* Esterhazy, accused by Mathieu,
was the object of investigations, whereas no action was taken
against Mathieu Dreyfus, accused by the press of having
attempted to bribe Colonel Sandherr. The debate ended with
Millerand publicly insulting Reinach the dreyfusard. As so often
happened, such insults were settled by duels.

Whatever Jaurès' inner feelings may have been by then, in
public he too continued to identify dreyfusism with opportunism
('Dreyfus réhabilité, c'est l'opportunisme qui remonte', *Petite
République*, 11 December 1897). Two days after Zola's first
dreyfusard article (*Le Figaro*, 25 November 1897) Jaurès was
speculating on the gold that must have flowed for such a conservative paper as the *Figaro* to shake the only institution still
standing, the Army (*Petite République*, 27 November). Together
with other leading Socialists, Jaurès signed the manifesto of 19
January 1898 inviting the rank and file to stay above the mêlée
of 'panamisants et judaïsants'.[7] Jaurès was a great disappointment

to Bernard-Lazare; like Péguy, he was never quite sure of Jaurès' real motives when he finally entered the battle. *Les Preuves* nevertheless constitute a magnificent expression of socialism with a human face, of the socialist cause as Bernard-Lazare understood it. It contained passages which any anarchist, and especially Bernard-Lazare, would gladly have signed.

Among writers Zola was the obvious person to approach. He was a fighter. Moreover, as we have seen, the further Bernard-Lazare moved away from his former esoteric symbolism the closer he drew to Zola, especially to the more politically committed author of *Rome* (1896). In 'Le rôle social de l'écrivain' the new Zola was given a place of honour and apologies were even extended to the misunderstood chronicler of the *Rougon-Macquart* miseries.[8] There was too Zola's article 'Pour les Juifs' (*Figaro*, 16 May 1896) which had sparked off his own *Contre l'antisémitisme*. It is highly improbable that Bernard-Lazare shared Zola's view of the Jews as conditioned by history to be the world's ablest capitalists, to be imitated and not persecuted; nor would he have subscribed to the naturalist, evolutionist solution of healthy competition, survival of the fittest and intermarriage as an answer to the Jewish question as posed by contemporary antisemitism. But Zola alone among the writers of his day had had the courage to protest against the antisemitic campaign and the perceptiveness to discern that Jewry was merely the first victim of a campaign whose far-reaching aim was to make the pendulum swing back to pre-Republican and pre-Revolutionary times. And yet, in spite of everything, Bernard-Lazare was not too certain of the bourgeois novelist. He had expected Jaurès immediately to grasp the importance of the issue, but Zola's inability to do so occasioned him no surprise .

> Quand je fus le voir, je n'avais pas l'espoir de l'amener à moi; je pensais qu'il ne marcherait pas parce qu'un appareil abstrait de vérité ou de justice ne le séduirait pas, mais je cherchais à savoir l'effet produit par mon livre sur des esprits libres et susceptibles d'apporter un appui moral à la cause que je défendais. Je trouvai de la sympathie; l'acte lui plaisait mais il n'avait aucune idée sur l'Affaire et je sentais qu'à cette heure elle ne l'intéressait pas; elle ne l'intéressa que quand le mélodrame fut complet et quand il en vit les personnages. . . La grâce ne frappa [Zola] que

lorsque le drame complet avec Esterhazy le traître, et
Picquart le bon génie et Dreyfus le martyr saisit son
imagination de romancier.[9]

It is a perceptive assessment, amply confirmed by Zola's totally
honest account of the successive stages in his dreyfusard commitment.[10] There was ignorance and indifference in 1896, when
Bernard-Lazare's brochures made no impression; then the Affair
became magnificent *matière littéraire*, especially attractive to the
naturalist always on the look-out for documents supplied by life
itself. 'Quel drame poignant et quels personnages superbes' is the
opening sentence of his first dreyfusard article (*Figaro*, 25 November 1897). The novelist's imagination was stirred. Did Bernard-
Lazare play any part in the growing passion which finally swept
Zola along to *J'accuse*? Probably not as direct a part as Picquart[11]
or the publication of the *acte d'accusation* and, last straw,
Esterhazy's acquittal. And yet Bernard-Lazare's influence over
Zola through later brochures and further visits has perhaps been
more considerable than has hitherto been recognised. I shall come
back to it.

Unsuccessful with Jaurès and Zola, he turned to a former
judge and a scientist: Bérenger and Berthelot. René Bérenger was
the promoter of several humane laws concerned with the resettlement of prisoners in society. Bernard-Lazare had previously paid
tribute to the author of 'la loi Bérenger'. He now called on him,
full of confidence.

Je pensais que le légiste serait révolté par le coup de la
pièce secrète. Il me reçut mal, me déclara même qu'il était
contrarié de me voir. Je lui répondis que je comprenais sa
contrariété, qu'il en était toujours ainsi quand la vérité
venait troubler la quiétude des consciences. On dit, me
répliqua-t-il, que vous êtes l'avocat payé de la famille
Dreyfus. Je protestai.
    L'assertion de l'existence de la pièce secrète le troubla
cependant. Il ne voulait pas y croire. Je lui demandai s'il
voulait voir Demange... Demange alla le voir. Bérenger
ne fit rien.[12]

In Berthelot Bernard-Lazare had defended the very spirit of
science, the search for truth. Moreover this *savant* of international
renown was not an ivory-tower scientist but an intellectual and

humanist with a sense of commitment and public service, a senator, a foreign minister for a brief period (November 1895–March 1896). The sense of commitment among Intellectuals, however, had not yet made itself felt; and when it did it was among scientists and savants (Duclaux, Giry, Grimaux, teachers of the Ecole de Chartes, the Sorbonne and the Collège de France) with no political experience and aspiration, guided solely by the dictates of their conscience and the need for enlightenment. We do not normally follow the fluctuations of political life, Professor Grimaux explained at the Zola trial, but the country's moral life is of concern to us. Referring to the *acte d'accusation* he exclaimed that no scientist would ever have signed such a document. 'Nous autres, hommes de science, nous avons une autre manière de raisonner.'[13] This is the sort of spirit to which Bernard-Lazare had appealed in Berthelot, but it was too early, and Berthelot, having political aspirations, was not the right person. The Foreign Minister Hanotaux, in his relations with the Intellectuals, is an even more striking example of 'politique oblige'. After Zola's trial, no less a figure than Gaston Paris, administrator of the Collège de France, and Gabriel Monod, Hanotaux's former teacher, appealed to the Foreign Minister to help them in their search for truth, begging him to remember that he (Hanotaux) belonged to a milieu of men to whom the search for truth matters and who are accustomed to using their critical faculties.[14] The Minister reacted by breaking off relations with some of his oldest friends. 'Ces intellectuals, qui naguère encore étaient mes amis, me sont devenus odieux. La campagne qu'ils mènent...est abominable'.[15]

Next Bernard-Lazare turned to a republican deputy and a former Minister of Justice: René Goblet. He replied that it was a matter for Dreyfus' lawyer and that he was not interested in the Affair; to which Bernard-Lazare retorted that as deputy he should take an interest in affairs of justice. Between them there would appear to have been a short exchange of letters which the deputy obligingly passed on to the press at the time of General de Pellieux's enquiries into the syndicate's activities. In 1902 Bernard-Lazare and René Goblet found themselves fighting on the same side, against the oppressive anticlerical laws of the Combes régime. Bernard-Lazare reminded the deputy of his past lack of interest in matters of justice and liberty.

On this same occasion in 1902, the former dreyfusard also

found himself in the same camp as the Comte de Mun to whose conscience he had likewise appealed in vain in 1897. M. de Mun preferred not to talk about the Affair.[16]

With editors, journalists and critics, a milieu he knew well, he fared no better at the beginning, though ultimately the warmest tributes were paid to him by fellow journalists.

> Ceux qui ont connu Bernard-Lazare en ces premiers mois terribles de l'âpre et rude combat garderont le souvenir ému de sa merveilleuse opiniâtreté et de son courage. Il n'est pas un ami, pas un camarade du journalisme qu'il ne tentait de convaincre, de gagner à la cause de la vérité. . . On le considérait d'un regard étonné, puis, affligé. On lui con-seillait de renoncer à la réhabilitation chimérique d'un traître. On arrêtait parfois l'entretien d'une parole brève. Et les plus clairvoyants et les plus généreux confiaient que bien des obscurités évidemment subsistaient dans le procès fameux mais qu'ils n'avaient pas l'héroïsme d'en poursuivre la révision. Alors Bernard-Lazare étendait son enquête, recueillant de nouvelles indications, élaborait une argumen-tation plus probante, et revenant à son foyer où étaient toutes ses affections, il y trouvait des lettres d'outrages et des menaces de mort.[17]

Octave Mirbeau and Séverine gave him a sympathetic hearing, but they could not help because they were unable to express themselves freely in the papers for which they were writing (*Le Journal, L'Echo de Paris* among others). Dreyfus was 'indéfend-able' and editorial censorship proved as despotic as any official government might have been. Before becoming one of the leading antidreyfusard intellectuals, Coppée had been persuaded by Zola and Marcel Prévost in November 1897 to write an article in favour of Dreyfus. The director of the *Journal* refused to insert it.

Bernard-Lazare also addressed himself to journalists of suffi-cient reputation and independence to brave editorial censorship or public opinion. Jules Claretie (*Le Temps*) was friendly and even interested, but he had his convictions: the verdict had been unanimous.[18] Bernard-Lazare called on Francisque Sarcey, re-membering perhaps that in 1892 the critic had protested against the antisemitic campaign of *La Libre Parole*. It seems that the avalanche of insulting letters he received had taught Sarcey a lesson. Fear of public opinion is at any rate the reaction Bernard-Lazare noted. 'Je trouvai la brute indifférente et tremblant devant l'opinion publique, fermée à toute générosité, à tout élan.'[19]

With Edmond Lepelletier of the *Echo de Paris*, who at the time of the anarchist trials had clamoured for 'la tête des intellectuels qui défendaient les dynamiteurs', Bernard-Lazare had broken a lance before; but he went to see him all the same and was apparently well received. Lepelletier, however, like the *Echo de Paris*, became progressively more antidreyfusard. Both Zola and Bernard-Lazare accused the paper in 1898 of being in the pay of the War Office. In his biography of Zola (1918), Lepelletier describes Bernard-Lazare's visit and recalls the following interesting details: 'Je dois déclarer que dans cette tentative pour obtenir mon concours...il n'etait nullement question d'une campagne violente à entamer entre l'armée en général, encore moins de faire appel aux anti-militaristes.'[20] This sounds like diplomacy on Bernard-Lazare's part and yet he may well have been quite sincere. He was certainly indefatigable in his efforts to convert anarchist friends, and they were in the main anti-militarist. So was Bernard-Lazare himself. It was part of his nature as well as his philosophy. He had attacked many things military, from the indignity of military discipline and the lack of humanity shown towards the ordinary soldier to the incompetence of military tribunals and the arrogance of the officer corps. No one, not even Zola, could have been more devastating in his criticisms of individual generals and officers concerned in the Affair. But in none of his dreyfusard writings, or his anarchist writings for that matter, does he ever show the violent antimilitarism of an Urban Gohier or indulge in a wholesale condemnation of the army from whose ranks came some brave dreyfusards, starting with *Commandant* Forzinetti. If police records can be trusted, Bernard-Lazare even tried to convert the army by leaving bundles of his brochures in places frequented by the military.[21]

Judet of *Le Petit Journal* had been among the most violent antidreyfusards, but Bernard-Lazare evidently did not see him as a fanatic, at least not in 1897. Somewhat naively he assumed that the presence of a Jew on the editorial board ruled out anti-semitism. The case of *Le Petit Journal* was serious: it had no antisemitic axe to grind, or so he assumed, and it had a wide readership of ordinary people. He called on Judet and he relates the following conversation, which took place some time in 1897.

> Etes-vous absolument convaincu de la culpabilité de
> Dreyfus? – Non, me répondit Judet, tout ce que vous venez
> de me raconter me trouble; je n'écrirais pas aujourd'hui ce
> que j'ai écrit jadis; mais tout ce que vous me montrez ne
> constitue pas, pour moi, des certitudes d'innocence;
> apportez-moi des preuves plus précises, plus positives et je
> verrai. – Je ne devais plus le revoir puisque, sans attendre
> une nouvelle visite, il partit en guerre avec la bonne foi que
> vous savez.[22]

Vaughan's honest *Souvenirs sans regrets*[23] tell us much about
the state of the press, the contemporary state of mind, and
Bernard-Lazare's battle with both. At the beginning of 1897
Vaughan, an experienced, radical newspaperman, wanted to
create an independent, apolitical, libertarian daily paper, with no
political or financial strings attached, with a vast 'programme de
liberté', open to all progressive ideas.[24] The only subject that was
banned was the Dreyfus Affair. When Vaughan ran into financial
difficulties and needed shareholders, Bernard-Lazare, who for his
part was in desperate need of a platform, offered to find some. He
made only one condition: that he should be allowed to continue
the campaign for revision. Vaughan and Clemenceau refused. In
a sense they were of course right to do so, for this was a string;
on the other hand, the *Aurore* was supposed to be open to free
discussion of all matters. Vaughan admits that he was prejudiced
in those days; he believed the Jews capable of the greatest sacrifices in order to save one of theirs, innocent or guilty.[25] What did
Vaughan think of Bernard-Lazare, a man he knew sufficiently
well not to accuse of knowingly defending a guilty man? It is
nicely put, but the gist is still the same: 'Sans mettre en doute
l'incontestable bonne foi de notre ami, nous le supposions guidé
plutot par d'affectueuses sympathies que par des convictions
basées sur des preuves matérielles et mathématiques.'[26] And yet
one would have thought that *Une erreur judiciaire, la vérité sur
l'Affaire Dreyfus*, while not containing any mathematical proofs,
contained sufficient disturbing material to warrant some doubt
on the part of men accustomed to questioning things. The truth
is that a Jewish Voltaire defending a Jewish Calas and challenging the unanimous verdict of seven officers without being able to
produce the real traitor, i.e. the author of the *bordereau*, was all
rather incredible and suspect. All the more suspect since, as

Bernard-Lazare explained in 1898,[27] even the least prejudiced believed that he was not telling the truth for the sake of a good cause. In other words, it looked as if he was defending a traitor, in order to clear a whole people of the charge of treason. But, as Bernard-Lazare goes on to explain, had he believed Captain Dreyfus to be guilty he would not have defended his innocence though he would still have protested against the idea of collective guilt, that all are guilty because one is guilty. The suspicion that he was defending one in order to defend all is the penalty he had to pay for battling at one and the same time for Dreyfus' liberty and against antisemitism.

It seems from Vaughan's account as if Bernard-Lazare dared his way on to the staff of the *Aurore*. 'Vous êtes tellement imbu, sans vous en douter, des préjugés antisémites, que vous ne voudrez pas de ma collaboration à votre journal',[28] he told a protesting Vaughan, who promptly engaged the talented journalist on the understanding that Dreyfus would not be mentioned. Clemenceau likewise insisted on this condition. The young *L'Aurore* was the only paper to accept his articles. Labori, then an outsider, did not fail to notice that the author of *Une erreur judiciaire* dealt with miscarriages of justice, the sad state of the press, legal malpractices.[29] Vaughan himself was not fooled by these transparent allusions, but he was prepared to turn a deaf ear because he admired, in spite of himself, the tenacity of the man who went on trying to make converts, never discouraged by failure.

Many people have commented on the strange mixture of inner fire and outer calm, passion and patience, displayed by Bernard-Lazare throughout the Affair. A young admirer even recalled her disappointment when she first met the paladin of Justice whose very name had made her heart beat faster and who turned out to be a calm, gentle, placid bourgeois. But behind the appearance there raged a passion for justice which consumed him like a fire.[30] Confidence that a just cause cannot be hopeless was at the source of his serenity and it helped him to overcome disillusionment and disappointment, to draw from them not bitterness or cynicism but a sad sort of gentleness and understanding of human weakness – what Péguy in an illuminating passage analyses as 'ces profondeurs de bonté douce incroyable qui ne peuvent être qu'à base de désabusement'.[31] Péguy was so dazzled by this quality, which he eminently lacked, that he regarded it as part and parcel of the prophetic spirit. When the Affair was over, this saintlike patience allowed Bernard-Lazare to face the ingratitude of those he had defended with the same sort of unembittered spirit with which he had previously gone about the task of making converts.

François Coppée was the only other well-known writer whom he approached personally. The gentle poet had written some violent articles against Dreyfus, and Bernard-Lazare decided that Coppée had no right to ignore what was going on. After having read the brochures the Coppées, François and his sister, were very troubled; they did not sleep a wink that night. And yet there was the question of the handwriting; Coppée found that Dreyfus' writing resembled that of the *bordereau*. Bernard-Lazare called again with more documents. This time Coppée seemed convinced and promised his support; he also expressed his admiration for Bernard-Lazare's courage: 'Seul, contre toute l'opinion publique. C'est beau!'[32] Trying to account for Coppée's later position as one of the leading antidreyfusard intellectuals of the *Ligue de la Patrie Française* Bernard-Lazare saw the explanation in Catholic, clerical education, in a mentality fundamentally accustomed to believing and affirming rather than doubting and questioning. Lemaître, too, believed in Dreyfus' guilt because two courts-martial and five ministers of war affirmed it. The country's *élite* rushed to the *Patrie Française* because it needed affirmations and dogma. This, according to Bernard-Lazare, writing in a rare mood of despair, was the difficulty, the blockage the dreyfusards had to face.[33]

The first real success came from a milieu of which Bernard-Lazare was suspicious: politicians. Reinach's contacts and influence were important here. He had learnt that Arthur Ranc, a senator with influence on the staunchly Republican newspaper *Le Radical*, had doubts. Armed with facsimiles, Bernard-Lazare promptly presented himself. Ranc has described the meeting and his state of mind. 'Dès 1894, j'avais conçu des doutes sur la culpabilité du condamné, j'avais pressenti un crime de l'antisémitisme. Mais je doutais seulement. Un jour, Bernard-Lazare, que je n'avais jamais vu, m'apporta les facsimilés du bordereau et de l'écriture de Dreyfus. Nous passâmes la matinée à les examiner mot par mot. . . Dès cet instant ma résolution fut prise. C'est donc à Bernard-Lazare que je dois l'honneur de m'être jeté l'un des premiers dans la bataille pour la justice.'[34]

Other men, all non-Jews, later gave similar reasons for their

early doubts. Few dared to express them publicly. It was the early doubters, men who had been inwardly troubled by the antisemitic campaign, who became Bernard-Lazare's first converts.

Ranc put Bernard-Lazare in touch with one of dreyfusism's most admirable and heroic figures, 'ce courageux vieillard' who intensely moved and not a little exasperated Bernard-Lazare, Scheurer-Kestner, one of the most respected and influential Republican politicians, Vice-President of the Senate and senator for life. Before his first encounter with Bernard-Lazare in March or April 1897, Scheurer-Kestner, troubled ever since 1894, had conducted his own enquiries, talked to highly placed people, had even received Mathieu, a fellow-Alsatian, without being convinced by him and without offering to help him. He had also read and been disturbed by Bernard-Lazare's brochure. For the first time, then, Bernard-Lazare faced someone who was well-informed, who was evidently seeking to be better informed, and perhaps wanted, tormented as he was, to be convinced. He began, relates Bernard-Lazare,[35] by exclaiming that such an abomination was impossible. He then challenged the brochure point by point, raising all the objections expressed by hostile opinion. It was a rigorous test. Bernard-Lazare thought he had passed it but he evidently did not convince his interrogator. Neither did Demange, to whom he took the Senator in June 1897. Bernard-Lazare is probably right in his comment that for Scheurer-Kestner reasoning was not enough to bring about certainty.[36] He needed proofs, all the more so since Bernard-Lazare's reasoning led to a number of suggestions and interpretations – lies, fabrication, forgery, collusion and a possible plot – which must have outraged the good Senator whose faith in the integrity of the Army was complete. Such 'abominations' did not form part of Scheurer-Kestner's thinking, before he knew of Esterhazy and Henry.

On one 'abomination' he had to agree only to him it was not an abomination, and that was the secret communication of evidence. Scheurer-Kestner had learnt of it as early as January 1895[37] without being unduly troubled by it. Reasons of State and possible diplomatic complications were comprehensible arguments to a politician of long experience. To Bernard-Lazare – and to Demange – the secret communication constituted a violation of justice warranting a retrial. It was only later that Scheurer-

Kestner considered this as a possibility and then more for tactical reasons – it was one way of reopening the case – than as a matter of principle.

Scheurer-Kestner's whole approach to Dreyfus' guilt or innocence was different. Like Bernard-Lazare, he had been struck by the absence of any rational motive for the crime; as an Alsatian, he knew something of the patriotism of French-Alsatian Jewry. Unlike Bernard-Lazare, for the sake of the country's honour and his own peace of mind, he was looking for evidence of guilt. And on this point highly placed friends and contacts were ever ready to reassure him, sometimes by supplying him – not necessarily deliberately – with inaccurate information. One such instance concerns the *canaille de D* note. As Scheurer-Kestner knew it the crucial sentence read 'Dreyfus (written out in full) tient la dragée haute.' ('Dreyfus calls the tune' or 'is holding out', i.e. 'for more money'.)[38]

Perhaps most significant of all in this confrontation between a tormented doubter and a passionate believer is a difference in personality. To a patriot with an unshaken trust in his country's institutions, a politician accustomed to the corridors-of-power approach, a conservative afraid of causing a scandal, of anything vaguely resembling revolutionary action, to such a man Bernard-Lazare must have seemed like a dangerous revolutionary firebrand.[39] His anarchist reputation did not help, nor did his public polemics with Drumont. Antisemitism was an unpleasant, embarrassing subject to Scheurer-Kestner. He did not see it or wish to see it as having any connection with the judicial error. It was an affair of justice not a Jewish affair. For that reason the fewer Jews to become involved the better. Mathieu fully appreciated this attitude, regarding it as fair, also as good strategy, that the senator should not wish to work, and especially to be seen to be working with Jews and the Dreyfus family. Not so Bernard-Lazare. He was saddened by this sort of fairness.

The proofs Scheurer-Kestner needed came only a few months later, in July 1897, in the shape of Leblois, the lawyer friend to whom Picquart had told his story in case anything happened to him. Convinced and shattered by what he heard, Scheurer bravely set out on his own campaign and one of the first things he did was to break off relations with Bernard-Lazare: 'En juillet, je reçus une lettre de Scheurer, qui me disait ne plus vouloir me voir dans l'intérêt de la cause. Ce fut l'erreur fatale, celle dont Scheurer

n'est pas responsable, mais qui retombe tout entière sur Leblois et sur laquelle un jour je m'expliquerai.'[40]

The explanation – which Bernard-Lazare never gave – is probably very simple: Picquart. Picquart had sworn Leblois to silence. Unable to bear it, Leblois confided in Scheurer-Kestner, guardian angel of Alsatians (Leblois was also an Alsatian), but insisted that nothing should be done which might expose Picquart and under no circumstances must the Dreyfus family hear of it. Scheurer-Kestner now found himself in the same difficult position which had been Mathieu's all along, that of having impressive evidence but being unable to make full and frank use of it. Nor could he communicate it to Mathieu, even if he had felt inclined to do so. The result was unfortunate. Instead of joining forces in a surprise attack, Scheurer-Kestner was reduced to an ineffectual whispering campaign which ultimately exacerbated would-be converts and played into the enemy's hands. Bernard-Lazare was altogether exasperated by this *urbi et orbi* tactic of letting it be rumoured that there existed conclusive proofs without any of these proofs being produced. It was now his turn to challenge the senator and he did so publicly: what are these proofs and where are they?[41]

In the meantime Mathieu and Bernard-Lazare went ahead with their time-consuming 'International Consultation' which laboriously demonstrated that Dreyfus was not the author of the *bordereau*. And all this time Scheurer-Kestner and Leblois knew who the author was. Scheurer-Kestner, who delayed the publication of the 'International Consultation',[42] regarded as unfortunate the conclusion expressed by some of the experts that the writing of the *bordereau* was not natural but disguised. Unfortunate indeed, in the light of his knowledge. It was all a tremendous waste of time and energy which did the common cause no good and gave the enemy time to mount a counter-offensive, the Picquart diversion being one important part of it. Zola's sarcastic comment on this situation was: 'un drôle de syndicat dont les membres s'ignorent'.[43]

The autumn of 1897, saw, in the words of Maurice Pujo, the future president of Action Française students, 'la sombre aurore de l'Affaire Dreyfus'.[44] Esterhazy's dramatic entry and all it gave rise to obviously raised doubts or at least eyebrows; but it was neither this cloak-and-dagger *roman feuilleton* nor Scheurer-Kestner's whispered rumours which illuminated things for the

Intellectuals. Bernard-Lazare's brochures (the new edition of the first brochure and the publication of the second brochure) were a more effective contribution. We have an interesting account of Bernard-Lazare's growing influence in intellectual circles from the other side, from Maurras, Pujo and Henri Vaugeois. The last two were at that time members of the committee of Paul Desjardins' *Union pour l'action morale* which, we are told, became a moral centre for dreyfusism under Bernard-Lazare's influence.[45] Vaugeois recalls being invited to dine with him at the homes of distinguished scholars and *maîtres* with the sole purpose of listening to him plead the cause of 'his innocent victim'.[46] Vaugeois makes the point that the Intellectuals became 'hooked' on the idea of 'le droit', that the law had been violated and the right of the individual put into jeopardy. Pujo, writing in December 1898, when the anarchists had joined the battle, noted that it was over the question of the rights of man that liberals and anarchists joined forces.[47]

Spontaneous expressions of sympathy and support came at first from a handful of *lettrés* – Monod, Valdagne, Paul Brulat, his old friends Pierre Quillard and Marcel Collière, Salomon Reinach, Lucien Herr among them. They in turn (notably Herr, the librarian at the Ecole Normale and influential in left-wing University circles) made other converts – Charles Andler, Léon Blum, Péguy, even Jaurès, followed Herr. Léon Blum and Péguy do not agree on many things, but they are agreed in their tribute to Bernard-Lazare. 'Bernard-Lazare fut le premier des dreyfusards, celui dont sont issus presque tous les autres... Il y avait en lui un juif de la grande race, de la race prophétique.'[48] In due course the *Revue Blanche*, among whose habitués were some old friends (Fénéon, Octave Mirbeau), also became an active dreyfusard centre. Bernard-Lazare kept the eager team informed.

Scattered in little-known works, memoirs, published and unpublished correspondence, there are many warm tributes to Bernard-Lazare's role as sower of doubts, creator of the moral syndicate, of 'ce bataillon merveilleux qui englobe toutes les belles intelligences du monde, ceux que l'on appelle dédaigneusement les Intellectuels'.[49] The disdain came not only from the military and the politicians, but also from the eminent antidreyfusard Intellectuals of the *Ligue de la Patrie Française* who disputed the right of their dreyfusard colleagues in the *Ligue des droits de l'Homme* to meddle in matters of law and the security of the State.

What does a chemist or a professor of ancient Greek know of such things, asked Brunetière. The scientists and scholars made it their business to find out since it was evident to them that those who should know were misleading the country.[50] It should be noted that 'Intellectual' was at the time usually spelt with a capital 'I', in spite of purists' objections. Both spelling and sense can already be found in the preceding anarchist period, notably in connection with the '*procès des Intellectuels*' (6 August 1894). What was at issue then was the relation between idea and act, whether men whose books had inspired others to throw bombs were also guilty of the crime. In the Dreyfus Affair, the book – Bernard-Lazare's brochure – was the bomb, so to speak, and when the fuse had run its way it caused a rare explosion of idealism, inspiring many acts of courage. And this time the same people were involved in both idea and act.

The dreyfusard movement still awaits its historian. We would like to draw attention to one aspect. The movement is often presented as a movement of rebellious individuals and minority groups feeling oppressed or ostracised for one reason or another: Jews, Protestants, freemasons, anarchists, Alsatians, men such as Clemenceau who had no fixed place in political life. There is obviously a great deal of truth in this view even if Jewry was conspicuous by its absence. Certainly, Bernard-Lazare, Clemenceau, Zola, Ranc were rebellious spirits. And yet one of the most interesting sections of the dreyfusard movement, the hitherto peace-loving, eminently non-rebellious Intellectuals who deserted their studies and laboratories do not fit into this picture. They were not looking for a place in public life; they had found their places and felt secure in their positions. What made them expose this security? Judging by many testimonies, the recognition of the antisemitic peril, and first of all the admission that it existed, was one powerful reason. The 'rumour', as Maurras puts it, 'that Dreyfus was condemned because he was a Jew'[51] was an oppressive thought to men who realised that if this were true Republican idealism and democracy, which they had hitherto taken for granted, were threatened by a force which they had not taken seriously before. Dreyfusism was obviously very much more than a resistance to antisemitism but it was that too simply because in the modern world, with the 'Russian solution' and the 'Armenian solution' making headlines, Dreyfus and Jewry had become a test of French idealism. Gabriel Séailles, at Zola's trial, declared: 'Si

la loi, qui est notre garantie à tous et que nous pouvons avoir à invoquer demain, doit être toujours respectée, ne doit-elle pas l'être surtout quand, dans un individu, ce sont des milliers d'individus qu'on prétend condamner et déshonorer!'[52] Gabriel Monod has left a moving account of the torments and disillusionment he experienced.

> Combien je regrette aujourd'hui de n'avoir pas tout de suite déclaré...ces doutes qui...m'avaient causé de quotidiennes insomnies! Mais je ne pouvais croire que sept officers eussent pu se tromper ou être trompés à ce point, je ne pouvais croire que l'antisémitisme eût corrompu une si grande partie de notre armée et de la France tout entière... Ces anxiétés, ces scrupules, ces tourments ont été ceux de tous les défenseurs de Dreyfus, jusqu'au moment où des torrents d'aveuglante lumière ont fait éclater aux yeux de tous ceux qui ne se refusaient pas volontairement à voir, l'amas des crimes qui avaient été commis pour le faire condamner... A ces tourments, à cette douleur, aux calomnies dont ils furent abreuvés, quelques-uns des défenseurs de Dreyfus n'ont pu résister. Bernard-Lazare, Scheurer-Kestner, Grimaux, Trarieux, Giry, en sont morts à la peine, et bien d'autres en sont restés ébranlés et vieillis.[53]

This brings us back to Zola. I have said that Bernard-Lazare's influence over him was more considerable than has been recognised or was acknowledged by Zola himself. It led one man, Urbain Gohier, to declare that '*J'accuse* fut dicté à Zola par Bernard-Lazare.'[54] Gohier is an untrustworthy source and the idea of dictation seems absurd. Zola was not a man to whom one dictated, and Bernard-Lazare would not have dictated what Zola wrote. But there are certain resemblances, a similarity of viewpoint which is perhaps not entirely due to coincidence or similarity of temperament. It has been little noticed that in the *Figaro* articles preceding *J'accuse* the leitmotif is 'l'imbécile antisémitisme a soufflé cette démence'.[55] Following Bernard-Lazare, Zola makes the Affair into what Scheurer-Kestner tried hard to avoid, 'une affaire juive', or more precisely 'le procès de l'antisémitisme'. Without actually having an antisemitic plot in mind, Zola goes as far as Bernard-Lazare in holding the reign of terror responsible for the error which had been committed. 'Il [l'antisémitisme] est le coupable... Et toute cette lamentable affaire Dreyfus est son oeuvre: c'est lui seul qui a rendu possible l'erreur judiciaire.'[56]

We might add here that Zola must have become conscious of this in retrospect. At the beginning, he either did not know or was not conscious of it; perhaps because he was away in Italy for the crucial initial period, from 30 October to 15 December 1894. When he heard Léon Daudet's description of the mass hysteria at the degradation ceremony, he expressed disapproval of the ferocity shown by the crowds against one man, even if he was guilty.[57] The idea of making this a scene in a future novel also crossed his mind. But the antisemitism of the scene, which so shattered Bernard-Lazare, made little impact on Zola. How little impact it had made can be gathered from 'Pour les Juifs' (May 1896). In it Zola spoke of the campaign waged against the Jews in France without once mentioning the Affair, the most virulent and successful phase of that campaign, as he himself said a year later. In 1896 Zola was optimistic that the good, wise, honest 'petit peuple' could keep its reason in the midst of the most violent incitement. A year later, he saw things very differently: the poison is in the people.[58] Like Bernard-Lazare he blamed the popular press, particularly *Le Petit Journal*, for spreading the poison. It seems likely that Zola was made sensitive to the link between antisemitism and the Affair by the one man who was haunted by that link. And Zola must have realised that he was much better suited to play the role of Voltaire in the new Calas case. In *J'accuse* itself, antisemitism, though rarely mentioned, is never far away. Bernard-Lazare's influence here can be seen in several other respects. For the early history of the Affair (the *canaille de D* note, Du Paty de Clam's behaviour, comments on the first court-martial, the dismissal of the *bordereau* as 'imbécile' and a variety of other details) Zola is evidently indebted to Bernard-Lazare's two brochures, the only available history at the time. Even more significant however is the third brochure *Comment on condamne un innocent*. If anything could have created the impression that Bernard-Lazare had dictated *J'accuse*, it is this angry, provocative, virulent pamphlet published a few days before *J'accuse*.[59] It is like an earlier version of it. It even contains a short 'j'accuse' paragraph: 'j'accuse le commandant Esterhazy de les avoir fabriquées, j'accuse le colonel Du Paty de Clam d'avoir été son complice'.[60] Du Paty de Clam is the main accused.

Professor Thalheimer sees *J'accuse* as a disastrous turning-point because it obscured the clear exposition and line of approach formulated in *Une erreur juidiciaire*.[61] One of two major distortions introduced by Zola, according to Thalheimer, is the elevation of Du Paty de Clam to be prime culprit. It is possible that Bernard-Lazare's highlighting of Du Paty de Clam's role in *Comment on condamne un innocent* is responsible for Zola's mistake. But, and this is a vital difference, whereas Bernard-Lazare accuses Du Paty de Clam of machination and forgery, in confusion to some extent with Henry, Zola elevates him to being 'l'ouvrier diabolique de l'erreur judiciaire' and confuses him with General Mercier. For Bernard-Lazare, responsibility for the original illegality remains with Mercier, at the top and not with the subordinate. In *J'accuse*, on the other hand, Generals Mercier (weakminded), Billot (trying to save a compromised General Staff), Boisdeffre (carried away by religious passion), and Gonse (carried away by Army esprit de corps), are charged merely with being accomplices, under the spell of a half-mad Du Paty de Clam. This is one of several reasons (Zola's concentration on the Esterhazy affair is another) which make it most unlikely that Bernard-Lazare 'dictated' *J'accuse*. But it seems likely that he provided the basic material which Zola's imagination transformed into a superb drama of life-forces in conflict: innocence (Dreyfus) versus treachery (Esterhazy); evil genius (Du Paty de Clam) versus good genius (Picquart).

As an act of moral commitment, *J'accuse* bears the stamp of Zola's combative temperament and generosity of mind. Without in any way wishing to minimise Zola's role, it should be remembered that there was a precedent, albeit an unsuccessful one, to the courageous act of inviting prosecution in the interests of justice. Moreover, even Bernard-Lazare did not invent this revolutionary tactic, though he was the first dreyfusard to use it. It is very reminiscent of anarchist practice. The *enfants terribles* of law and order were masters at standing the legal system on its head and using the courts to expose the truth and get at justice in their own way.

Anarchist participation in the dreyfusard movement is one of the most surprising and unexpected collaborations. Leaving aside the question of Dreyfus' position as a wealthy man and army officer whose conservative and hierarchical mentality was all that the *compagnons* most detested, who would have thought that the sworn enemies of bourgeois law and legality would one day rub shoulders with such men as Trarieux, Reinach, Guyot and other ardent Republicans of the *Ligue des Droits de l'Homme* who had been prepared to deny anarchists their rights and liberties under the *lois scélérates*?

Some *compagnons* indeed, notably Jean Grave, remained suspicious of these new alliances, of the Republican front which ultimately emerged to counter the reactionary peril. Grave, anxious to maintain anarchist purity, never actively participated in the dreyfusard movement and remained critical of the majority which did. There are some cutting comments and insinuations in his memoirs, some more justified than others. He could never forgive Sébastian Faure for having accepted Jewish financial support for *Le Journal du Peuple*, the anarchist dreyfusard daily which ran for a year (February to December 1899) as a successor to *Le Libertaire*. The latter, it should be noted, had gone dreyfusard as early as November 1897 without any Jewish financial assistance though probably under the influence of Bernard-Lazare's brochures.

In his account of anarchist dreyfusism, Jean Maitron has correctly pointed out that not all the *compagnons* immediately rushed to Dreyfus' defence, as is often assumed. Silence, indifference, contempt, hostility were all common initial reactions. Nor was Sébastian Faure's first call for participation, in November 1897, immediately answered by all. There were heated discussions which continued throughout the Affair. However, by February 1898, according to Péguy's testimony,[62] the anarchists were the only people ready to answer Zola's battle-cry. By October 1898 they had formed *un comité de coalition révolutionnaire* which organised counter-demonstrations, defended dreyfusard speakers at meetings up and down the country and acted as bodyguards to witnesses at trials. M. Maitron regards the beginning of 1899 as the date when one can justifiably speak of an active and almost general participation. Give or take a few months, I would not quarrel with this estimate.

I wonder, however, whether in his insistence on the *relative* lateness of anarchist involvement and on the largely self-interested propaganda value which they supposedly tried to derive from it, M. Maitron has not gone to the other extreme and belittled their action. Indeed, he seems almost anxious to minimise 'le rôle prééminent accordé aux compagnons dans le déclenchement et la

conduite de la campagne dreyfusienne',[63] a role mistakenly
attributed to them, we are told, because of Bernard-Lazare's
connections with anarchist milieux. But, Maitron insists, Bernard-
Lazare, though he may have 'professed anarchist opinions' and
courageously defended anarchist militants, cannot be considered
a representative of the libertarian movement. At any rate, as far
as his dreyfusard action is concerned, 'lié d'amitié avec la famille
du condamné', he began his campaign for revision 'en complète
indépendance à l'égard des compagnons'.

The last part of this statement is of course correct, but it does
not follow that the *compagnons* did not appreciate such independent acts or that Bernard-Lazare, whom they held in high esteem,
did not subsequently influence the *compagnons'* commitment.
Even Jean Grave admits that reading the first brochure (1896)
made him think.[64]

There is no evidence that Bernard-Lazare was directly behind
the *Libertaire*'s entry into the battle on 7 November 1897. But it
seems at least likely that his account of the antisemitic terror-
campaign of 1895 had an effect on Sébastian Faure who later
confessed: 'nous avons eu le très grand tort de ne nous élever ni
assez tôt, ni assez vigoureusement contre le courant antisémitique'.[65] One must also add that however timid and full of
reservations this first anarchist intervention may have been, the
Libertaire was nonetheless the first paper, even before *L'Aurore*, to
express sympathy for the dreyfusard cause. It is evident that Faure
and his group on the *Libertaire* played precursors' roles in the
formation of the dreyfusard movement, which did not gather
momentum until then, and it is reasonable to assume that
Bernard-Lazare had something to do with it; if only because the
fight against antisemitism became a major issue in the anarchist
campaign. This pleased at least one young Socialist, Péguy. 'La
rage antisémitique a passé maîtresse dans nos rues et hurlant à la
mort...les anarchistes seuls firent leur devoir;...ils furent les
seuls qui osèrent opposer la violence pour la justice à la violence
pour l'injustice des bandes antisémites.'[66] In addition to Faure
and his group, Charles Malato, Henri Dagan, Zo d'Axa, all
'orthodox' anarchists, fought the antisemitism unleashed by the
Affair. Zo d'Axa did so in his customary vehement way in *La
Feuille* (created in September 1897) which was as hostile to
Drumont as it was to the Jewish barons of finance.

In disagreement, then, with M. Maitron's otherwise excellent history of the anarchist movement, I would conclude that the majority of the anarchists played an important part in the drey-fusard battle, not least because they had the courage to call a spade a spade and saw antisemitism, inseparable from the passions of the times, for what it was, a cancerous growth which one day threatened the rights of one Jew and one minority and the following day might endanger the rights of other individuals and other minorities. Bernard-Lazare's part in all this, I would guess, was considerable: not because he was a 'friend' of the Dreyfus family; not even perhaps because he was a Jew but because he was a perceptive libertarian of great integrity whom the *compagnons* respected. Here is the testimony of one of them, Jacques Prolo, an ardent dreyfusard: '...D'une aménité parfaite, fort goûté des libertaires...Bernard-Lazare, véritable instigateur du mouvement, avait gagné les anarchistes à la défense de Dreyfus et, à son exemple, ils lui restèrent fidèles jusqu'à sa libération'.[67]

On the other hand, one cannot help feeling that Bernard-Lazare had a great deal to do with Joseph Reinach's request in May 1899 to the *Ligue des Droits de l'Homme* to take up the case of five anarchists condemned in 1894 (according to the *lois scélérates*) not for anything they had done but for their opinions.[68] Two of them were released as a result of the intervention. It was a mere drop in the ocean when one thinks of the number of *compagnons* who had been condemned and of whom many died on their devil's islands. But it was a significant gesture on the part of the liberal Republicans of the *Ligue* who had gained a better understanding of the libertarians. At any rate the Dreyfus Affair brought to a close a turbulent era in the conception and administration of justice, and Pierre-Bertrand was perhaps not exaggerating when he paid this tribute to Bernard-Lazare: 'Retrempez-vous dans la joie d'avoir plus que tout autre contribué à la restauration de l'esprit de justice en France. Nulle gloire n'est plus enviable, ni plus haute.'[69]

PART III: AFTER THE DREYFUS AFFAIR

10

ANTISEMITISM RECONSIDERED

Although Bernard-Lazare did not have time to rewrite *Antisemitism, its history and causes* in book-form, it was rewritten many times over, at least the part on modern French antisemitism. The re-assessment began in the dark November days of 1894 with the public admission that he had been mistaken in his previous assessment of antisemitism as a reactionary force confined to a restricted milieu and destined to disappear.

> Nous nous trompions et il a suffi de l'accusation portée contre le capitaine Dreyfus pour nous montrer jusqu'à l'évidence notre erreur. Il est possible qu'il n'existe pas un important parti antisémite, cela est même certain, mais il s'est créé depuis quelques années un état d'esprit antisémite, ce qui est évidemment beaucoup plus grave.[1]

This state of mind, what it is based on, how it is kept alive, by whom and to what end, preoccupied him throughout the Affair and beyond it. And the preoccupation was not merely that of an historian and observer of his age. The fighter joined the observer to expose and denounce the evil.

It must be remembered that his reflections and battles took place against an anti-Jewish hysteria unprecedented in modern France and in Western Europe at that time. By 1898 passions had reached such a pitch that a cool-headed foreign observer with no personal involvement and no personal axe to grind warned his English readers that 'those who shrug their shoulders and ridicule the absurdity of the notion that France, France of the Third Republic, could possibly reproduce the sanguinary horrors of St Bartholomew a century after the French Revolution, will do well not to be too cock-sure.'[2] Clemenceau, Zola, the young Péguy all of whom, for different reasons, had missed the early terror campaign (1895), thought they were living through a medieval nightmare.[3]

And the anti-Jewish riots in metropolitan France, the proposals for anti-Jewish legislation debated in Parliament on and off throughout the Affair, motions which were defeated but at times with such sad statistical tales as 158 votes for and 257 votes against proposals to exclude from public office 'tous les Français qui ne pourraient pas justifier de trois générations d'ancêtres nés en France',[4] such events were as nothing compared with what was going on in Algeria. Bernard-Lazare had gone there in the summer of 1896[5] when the disturbances began. Two years later, it was no longer the Jewish right to vote that was at stake, but the right to live. Russian-style pogroms were not uncommon. 'Cela se passe en territoire français, sous la 3e République', exclaimed Clemenceau.[6] Of the numerous descriptions of the looting and burning so successfully instigated by Drumont's disciples, none is more poignant than the following lines by Bernard-Lazare: '. . .quand les bandes antisémites, à Alger, urinaient sur le ventre des femmes enceintes, saccageaient les quartiers ouvriers israélites et assommaient les habitants à coups de matraque, . . .selon le mot de *la Croix* le Christ régnait à Alger'.[7] Asked for his reaction to Drumont's election to Parliament as deputy for Algiers (there were altogether three successful antisemitic candidates), Bernard-Lazare put on a brave face: 'I am very well satisfied with Drumont's election. There is an end to his anti-Semitism. As a journalist he could attack, agitate, and criticise, as a deputy he will have to establish and reform his ideas in order to make them possible legal enactments.'[8] In private he was far more worried, even discouraged: 'Je crois la République fichue et un coup d'état prochain', he confided to a friend a few months later (February 1899).[9] Drumont for his part declared, in reply to a question of how all this antisemitic agitation would end: 'by a general revolution, which will sweep away our present masters and replace them with some form of one-man power – not necessarily an emperor or a king, but some kind of dictator, a strong, patriotic man who will put an end to Jewish supremacy and clean out our Augean stables of vice and corruption!'[10]

The most extraordinary feature of the crisis was, Drumont observed, 'the blindness of the Jews. . .it is almost pathetic!' On this one point Bernard-Lazare agreed. 'Pauvres esprits et pauvres cervelles, aveugles et sourds, sans intelligence, sans compréhension, sans courage et sans énergie!' he wrote of the Israelites of France[11] who so cowardly received blows without protesting in the hope that the storm would pass. (This is what Péguy later called 'la politique juive'.) He imagined Drumont laughing at the very idea of a Jewish association against antisemitism. But he warned him that it only needed two or three determined fighters to challenge and expose his empty ideas. The energetic and unequivocal declaration of war contained in *Contre l'antisémitisme* was proof that there was at least one determined and fully alert Jew to take on Drumont, his supporters and his backers.[12]

Contre l'antisémitisme, histoire d'une polémique, is the brochure of a four-week public debate (18 May to 14 June 1896) which Drumont conducted from *La Libre Parole* and Bernard-Lazare from the radical paper *Le Voltaire*.[13] As a debate it is more like a 'dialogue des sourds': with one side relentlessly asking what about Christian capitalist exploitation and exploited Jewish workers and the other refusing to believe in the existence of either. In the course of it all, Bernard-Lazare was led to state his own, modified views. Only two years had passed since the conclusions of 1894 but in experience it might have been a life-time.

The major reassessment concerned religious prejudice and clerical politics. The Dreyfus Affair was in this respect a crucial eye-opener, for it had revealed an altogether unexpected, instinctive religious response. This was of course to be expected from Catholic milieux; what was astonishing was its general character. Even anticlericals had recourse to religious symbols to express their convictions of Dreyfus' guilt. 'Il est plus facile d'inventer la machine à vapeur, le télégraphe et la radioscopie que de changer une parcelle de l'atavisme de nos coeurs', commented Clemenceau in 1898.[14] Having just emerged from a study of past religious prejudice, Bernard-Lazare was dumbfounded by the readiness with which late nineteenth-century France viewed and explained Dreyfus in terms of Judas. Rational discussion of such things as motives became largely irrelevant. What price did the traitor, a wealthy man, receive for his crime? The *Echo de Paris*, a broad-minded and liberal paper (to which Bernard-Lazare was a regular contributor at the time) gave the obvious answer: 30 pieces of silver, that is enough.

At first, surprised though he was by the generality of this state of mind so unexpectedly brought to the surface, he derived comfort from the thought that it was *only* religious in character, as if those who felt estranged from and superior to Israel would not endorse the violence of the few Jew-hating and Jew-baiting theoreticians of antisemitism.[15] For one brief moment he tried to console himself with the idea of the previous day, that Christians are concerned with the conversion of Israel and not the oppression of Jewry. However, the part played by the clerical press, *La Croix*, *Le Pèlerin*, *La Vérité* among others, not exactly renowned for their desire to convert the infidel, deprived him of this consolation.

In an altogether different mood he used irony to get even with the Judas-enthusiasts and expounders of a theologically incorrect but very powerful *perfidia Judaeorum*. He had his own version of Judas: 'un des apôtres légendaires, prédestiné de toute éternité et ne pouvant, sous peine de déformer ce fameux plan divin dont on entend encore quelquefois parler, échapper à son destin, [qui] a vendu aux Romains un petit prophète hébreu, socialiste et révolutionnaire, qui troublait la digestion des pharisiens'.[16]

Irony however did not prevent him from drawing the serious conclusion that modern European antisemitism has Christian roots, and that these will subsist as long as there are Jews and Christians – that is, for ever.[17]

Here we come to the question of clerical politics. Antisemitism in late nineteenth-century France, Bernard-Lazare observes, was not created by Drumont; he was merely an echo, perhaps an instrument, certainly a powerful propagandist, but one who might not even be aware of the real forces and aspirations behind the movement. Antisemitism is essentially a clerical movement, he declared. It springs from the clergy which has propagated, maintained and spread it. The history of modern antisemitism in France is a chapter in the history of the clerical party.[18] The long-term aim of the clerical party is the re-establishment of the Christian State. Thus, the fundamental reason for antisemitism in modern France lay in the triumph of the secular State over the Christian State and the Church's desire to reverse this, to take revenge for her defeat in 1789 and to make a comeback. The Jew – at times thought to be the instrument of that Satanic Revolution, object of ancient prejudice easily revived because deeply entrenched in the Christian consciousness – the Jew was the obvious first victim in the bid for a return to power through popular support. But he was *only* the first victim. Freemasons and Protestants were next on the list. For a variety of reasons – dilettant-

ism, coquetry, complacency, cowardice – Republican democracy
looked on without protesting.

It remained to be explained how the antisemitic movement, if it
was clerically inspired and clerical in aims, could have gained
such widespread influence in a country with strong anticlerical
traditions. The presence of unconscious religious prejudice,
powerful element though it was, could not explain the active
support antisemitism was enjoying. Bernard-Lazare looked to the
fears of the middle classes for an answer. The one-time Voltairian
bourgeoisie was too preoccupied with the new threat coming from
the working classes and the red peril to notice the black peril. As
for the lower middle class, threatened by the development of big
capital and industry, it became detached in great part from the
principles of a liberal democracy and attracted by reactionary
forces who promised a return to better economic conditions and
depicted the Jew as the foreigner threatening its heritage.[19] It is
here that the *Krach de l'Union Générale* (1882) came into its own
and took on special significance. What for the future historian,
he writes, would constitute an interesting episode in the struggle
between two forms of capital, was immediately presented as a
struggle between Jewish, i.e. foreign and dishonest, capital against
Catholic, i.e. French and honest, capital. This deliberate mis-
representation did more to foster antisemitism among shopkeepers
than Drumont ever could have done. The successful distortion of
the *Krach* was only the beginning, for antisemitic theoreticians
have claimed ever since that theirs is an economic movement of
liberation, that they are concerned with economic and social ills,
notably with a ruthless capitalist system and financial monopoly.
But, observed Bernard-Lazare, this was the crudest of economic
façades, for behind the Jewish barons of finance the attacks were
directed against *all Jews*.[20] What was at stake was not Jewish
monopoly of the Stock Exchange but the Jew's right as a man
and a citizen. This in itself comprised an inescapable antisemitic
contradiction: the antisemite repeated the old grievance that the
Jew was separatist, alien, unsociable; and what he meant was
that the Jew was too sociable, too dangerous as a competitor.
He cited examples of the constitution of groups in towns all over
France whose motto was: do not buy from Jews or Freemasons.
Recent Catholic congresses in Paris and Rheims had adopted this
as a resolution. 'Pour l'honneur et le salut de la France, dit en
chaire l'évèque de Nancy, n'achetez qu'aux catholiques.'[21] And

what of those who had no money to buy with? Bernard-Lazare confessed here to great naiveté when previously he had quarrelled with antisemitism over the logic and courage of its socialist convictions. Suppression of the Jew, he had said in those innocent days, would not suppress the capitalist régime and the conditions of the working classes would be unchanged. 'Mieux éclairé. . . j'affirme que les antisémites sont les défenseurs du capital chrétien, je veux dire du capital catholique. . . Ils rêvent la réconstitution de l'Etat chrétien.'[22]

Jeannine Verdès-Leroux has recently interpreted the Union Générale scandal in the same light,[23] establishing a similar link between it and the rise of antisemitism in a new economic guise, the real intention being to use it as an instrument of political ideology. Like the conspiracy theory of the Dreyfus Affair, which incidentally acquires an important overture if considered in this light, this interpretation of the *Krach* is difficult to prove in terms of factual evidence though it is immensely attractive as a speculative explanation of things which facts do not explain satisfactorily. When all the *facts* are added up, the seemingly sudden and certainly violent outburst of Jew-hatred in late nineteenth-century France still remains unexplained.

Bernard-Lazare went much further in his historical speculations. He does so in an unpublished study entitled 'La République Catholique'.[24] Antisemitism is hardly mentioned, but it is profoundly the subject, only seen in a very much wider historical and political context, as the first reactionary onslaught on European liberalism which the Church is seeking to destroy in order to re-establish the Christian State. The tactics used to achieve this aim vary from country to country, depending on the position and influence of the Church. Open defiance of such liberalising measures as freedom of worship, civil marriages, Protestant schools, could work in Spain but it was unthinkable in France. There the Church has to rely on persuasion and, in the long-term, on education.

In an original if controversial analysis of clericalism at work in France since the Revolution, the Church is presented as wooing in turn the different republics and the different social and political forces dominating the scene. For this purpose she became Republican, Radical and even Socialist, as the situation required it. The *ralliement*, Leo XIII's *Rerum Novarum* (which could satisfy the most determined capitalist), the present effort to reconcile the principles of the Church with the Declaration of the Rights of Man (after the Revolution had been presented for a hundred years as Satan incarnate), and latterly the appearance of social and even socialist Catholicism, all these are seen as a deliberate tactic on the part of the Church to regain influence and then direct it towards its own ends. In France, where the idea of monarchy was obsolete, this might well take the form of a conservative and Catholic republic which could be the ideal monarchy, with real power in the hands of the Church.

It might well be that Bernard-Lazare, in common with others, was a little obsessed at this stage by 'le cléricalisme, voilà l'ennemi'. There must be other explanations for the *ralliement* and the Pope's efforts to confront social problems, other than infiltration with a view to weakening, and ultimately destroying, Republican democracy. On the other hand, his analysis of the conduct of the bourgeoisie, protecting its interests and ready to form any alliance in its fear of the red peril, is perceptive; almost prophetic in a later context. Led to believe that Europe was in the process of being overrun by revolutionary forces which threatened its fortune, that every strike or popular demonstration was an act of anarchy menacing the established order, the bourgeoisie abandoned its Voltairian ideas without too much scruple and sought refuge in the Church, which was safer than the bank. As for the small capitalist and the shopkeeper, he was already to a large extent disinherited by big capital, traditionally personified in the Rothschilds, and thus ready for anything. On one point, according to the argument, the Church had to exercise great caution: the Declaration of 1789. This had for long been the bourgeoisie's article of faith, its own dogma. The solution was very simple: after having condemned it for many years, the clerical party now stressed the compatibility of the principles of the Church with the sacred civil charter. The workers were next on the list for wooing. It remained to be seen whether making Marxism compatible would prove as easy.

It is strange to compare Bernard-Lazare's subsequent defence (1902)[25] of the right of Catholic schools to educate, if parents wish their children to receive such an education, with the regret expressed in this unpublished text, probably composed at an earlier date, that the Church in France was free to educate. He warns against according her 'le droit d'association' by which she seeks to extend her influence through teaching. In the name of democracy and the Rights of Man, he remarks, the Church in France demands the right to educate, particularly the bourgeoisie whence the ruling class will continue to spring. And when, thanks to the same ruling class formed by her, the Church will be powerful again, she will press for the freedom to educate of others to be abolished should they go against her principles. And finally, 'toute puissante, elle triomphera sur la ruine de la liberté'.

Are these views in contradiction with his later campaign *against* Emile Combes' anticlerical policies, with his libertarian preference for 'la liberté de l'enseignement' to 'l'enseignement de la liberté'? Strictly speaking, the answer must be yes. And yet circumstances had greatly changed between 1898 (it is assumed that 'La République Catholique' was written thereabouts) and 1902. During the Affair, the Church, through 'la bonne presse' and the less violent but unmistakably hostile majority of the faithful, did the persecuting. In 1902, the role was reversed: the religious orders were the persecuted.

Catholic antisemitism and the wider and long-term political aims which he thought lay behind it, had a profound and lasting effect on Bernard-Lazare. It seemed to him a crisis in the history of the Republic, the first signs of which were to be found in the largely clerically inspired anti-Jewish and ipso facto anti-Republican literature of the mid- and late-nineteenth century. In his history of 1894 he had simply noted it, for the record so to speak, half astonished and half amused at the discovery of a weird state of mind among Churchmen lost in dreams of past paradise and explaining its disappearance by imagining Satanic plots. These fantasies had become part of daily life, *a warrant for persecution.* There are several references in the police records to unsuccessful attempts to create an anticlerical counter-propaganda journal. He is said to have helped with the creation of the short-lived *La Mâchoire d'Ane* (directed by A. Mourlon). Later, in November 1898, he apparently planned a review *L'Anticlérical* as a reply to *L'Antijuif*. In March 1897 he is reported to be preparing a brochure entitled *L'Eglise et le Ministère*. It is difficult to assess the accuracy of these reports but judging by the tone and mood of 'La République Catholique' there may be some truth in them. Furthermore, there is an interesting comment in the *Fumier de Job* which might explain why none of these projects, if they existed, ever materialised and why 'La République Catholique' remained unpublished.

> On trouve inconvenant que le Juif parle du catholicisme et
> de l'Eglise romaine ; on lui défend de les attaquer ; ce sont
> là pour lui sujets interdits. C'est contester le droit pour
> l'opprimé de se défendre. Depuis vingt siècles, le Juif est
> pillé, assommé, massacré, brûlé, et on lui conteste le droit
> d'exprimer sa pensée sur l'oppresseur ; cet oppresseur étant
> d'ailleurs aussi l'oppresseur de la pensée humaine, hostile à
> tout progrès.[26]

Could the 'on' refer to Mathieu Dreyfus? He could have provided
the necessary financial backing, but he would have been most
reluctant to have his brother's cause linked with a campaign of
this sort. In general, French Jews were not anticlerical, at least
not overtly; in their own interests perhaps. Bernard-Lazare, being
also an outspoken Jewish anticlerical, had no such inhibitions,
especially as he increasingly came to see the Church as the major
source of antisemitism and the Synagogue as the main obstacle
to Jewish resistance to it. Commenting on the donation of
400,000 francs made by the Jewish community to Catholic works,
to the very 'bonne presse' whence anti-Jewish literature flowed in
such profusion, he wrote:

> Les juifs riches lèchent la main qui les frappe, ils se proster-
> nent devant ceux qui les foulent, ils s'agenouillent devant
> ceux qui les insultent. . . Ce sont les mêmes dont l'influence
> paralyse toute défense, qui arrêtent tout effort ; leur avilisse-
> ment, leur lâcheté est telle qu'elle a provoqué le juste et
> légitime dégoût de leurs ennemis, qu'elle a donné la nausée
> à toute âme juive.[27]

A considerable part of the unpublished papers deals with the
more profound Christian Jew-hatred as expressed in literature,
art, history and theology. It was evidently intended as part of the
re-working of *Antisemitism, its history and causes* which had a
chapter on anti-Jewish literature. Then he had largely contented
himself with describing things. Now he meditates with sadness
and often with bitterness on the countless 'légendes sur les Juifs'
and on 'l'idée que le chrétien se fait du Juif'. The *Fumier de Job*
contains a section on it, though the fragments selected for the
posthumous publication (1928) give little idea of the bitterness and
severity. Saint Jerome, speaking of the Jews weeping over the
ruins of the Temple, sums up Christian sentiments for him: ' "Un

peuple misérable *mais qui ne faisait pas pitié.*" C'est bien le sentiment du chrétien vis-à-vis du Juif. *Il ne fait pas pitié,* car il a méconnu le Dieu qui est venu et a ainsi mérité son sort et tous les malheurs qui fondent sur sa tête sont le châtiment mérité.'[28] Many legends create deformities and defects which are then explained in terms of the eternal punishment. Thomas de Catimpré, for example, gives one of several explanations for the 'Jewish smell': a Jewess called Béatrix had asked the smith who made the nails for the cross to deliver them rusty and especially pointed, so that Jesus would suffer more. 'En châtiment, toutes les femmes juives après 25 ans, ont la bouche pleine de vers, ce qui donne une odeur infecte.'[29] The descendants of all the tribes of Israel were punished with some sort of defect according to the part played by their forefathers in Christ's death. According to St Vincent Ferrer, the tribe of Levy spat on Christ and the descendants are eternally deprived of saliva. Those who had told Pilate to let his blood be on us and on our children lose blood every month. The descendants of the tribe of Reuben, who had taken Christ from the garden, cannot touch a flower without it withering in their hands; they cannot be gardeners and no plant will grow on their graves. As punishment for the crown of thorns, the descendants of the tribe of Gad are made to suffer and bleed by having thorns pressed into their bodies for a whole day every year on 25 March. And so on.

The two legends par excellence, are treason and ritual murder.

> Puisque Judas avait vendu Dieu pour de l'or, pour de l'or Israël devait vendre tout. . . Au moyen âge, Israël tout entier fut Judas, le traître, le meurtre du Christ, et comme Satan au fond du dernier cercle de Dante, broie entre ses dents le corps de Judas, les peuples broyaient Israel. C'est Judas qui incarne la façon dont la race a été calomniée, le mensonge dont elle souffre depuis dix-neuf siècles.[30]

The treason legend was as simple as it was devastating and infinitely adaptable, from the Middle Ages, when Jews were held responsible for the fall of cities and such things as the plague, to leaks in the present-day Intelligence Service.

The ritual murder charge was more puzzling. What was its origin? And how, at the end of the nineteenth century, could men, even educated men, believe in it? Bernard-Lazare had planned a special work on it ever since 1894 and Péguy announced it (*La superstition chrétienne du meurtre rituel*) as a forthcoming publication in February 1902. The matter was indeed urgent. Since the abbé Desportes' pioneering work, *Le Mystère du sang chez les Juifs de tous les temps* (1889), the subject was much written about. In France it remained for the moment theory and rumour in spite of the occasional attempt to bring specific accusations.[31] But in other countries the revival of the legend had already produced results. There had been the Tisza Eszlar case in Hungary in 1882 and in Bernard-Lazare's own days, and much to his sadness and anger, the Hilsener case in Polna.[32] Since he never completed this work, it is difficult to say how he would have explained the origin of the myth. From extant fragments, it seems that he looked for an answer in Christianity's own blood-cult, of which he evidently made a special study. He must have gone round the museums and churches of Europe making notes on the glorification of blood as reflected in Christian art throughout the ages. There are descriptions of paintings from Cologne, London, Florence, Rome, Holland, particularly those depicting the 'pressoir mystique', blood being pressed out of Christ and collected by the faithful.[33] In other fragments he develops the idea, this time with reference to immolations, expiatory sacrifices, visions of blood experienced by saints and martyrs ecstatically offering themselves as victims, of Christ's blood-sacrifice calling for similar sacrifices on the part of those who love him. 'Celui qui a donné son sang se plaît au sang versé pour lui.' Bernard-Lazare adopted a literal, entirely non-mystical attitude to what he called the love of blood in Christianity. Judaism's long-standing freedom from such cults of redemption and sacrifice rank high in his list of its qualities. The tragedy, however, is that Christianity has involved the Jews in its own Molochism, and Christians are ready to believe it. 'Ce christianisme hanté par le sang, qui voit le monde couvert de sang, qui vit dans un rêve ignoble et sanguinaire dont le Juif a horreur, c'est sur le Juif qu'il jette sa lèpre en l'accusant du meurtre rituel.'[34]

In *Le Fumier de Job* he comes to the following conclusion about the Christians' image of the Jew:

> On a toujours fait l'histoire du peuple juif comme une histoire religieuse. On l'a faite au point de vue chrétien, comme si ce peuple n'avait eu qu'un but: faire le Christ et la religion chrétienne. Dès lors, on n'a pas compris qu'il

> osât subsister après avoir fait son oeuvre; de là une cause
> de plus grande haine. On a été inquiet de cette persistance,
> une fois la mission finie. Que faisaient ces gens-là dans les
> nations chrétiennes? Ils étaint un résidu, une pourriture
> d'où venait le mal...[35]

The eternal witness easily becomes the eternal victim and eternal
scapegoat. It is his belief that the catechism of contempt comprised
in the Church's teaching did not originate with the people but
was elaborated at the top and passed down to the people. It was
Church-lore before it became folk-lore, so to speak.

> C'est toujours l'Eglise qui a suscité l'antisémitisme; toujours
> le Juif a vécu en paix avec les populations; celles-ci
> méprisaient le déicide, certes, mais vivaient familièrement
> avec lui. C'est la plainte constante de l'Eglise que la popula-
> tion vive familièrement avec le Juif; c'est toujours l'Eglise
> qui a jeté les peuples sur les Juifs.[36]

Today, after centuries of indoctrination, this familiarity has been
lost to the point that 'le chrétien se trouve devant le Juif comme
devant un monde inconnu',[37] a fascinating, repellent, frightening
mystery. In Breton villages where no Jew has ever set foot people
are ardently antisemitic. And the Church has ultimately been
outdone by the population. For in spite of everything, the Church
preserved an uneasy sort of relationship with Israel.

> La religion juive est pour le chrétien la préfiguratrice. Pape,
> pères, évêques, moines la louent. Le Juif est, lui, l'éternel
> protestataire, celui qui nie indomptablement... De là la
> haine de l'Eglise contre le Juif, haine qui se combine avec la
> nécessité de garder ce témoin qui est la clé de l'édifice et
> doit un jour le couronner par sa conversion.[38]

But for the mass of the faithful, less theologically minded, only
hatred remains.

Bloy and Drumont embody the two Christian dilemmas,
ancient and modern, vis-à-vis the Jew. For the first, Israel is great
and the Jew abject; but this abject creature is a sacred witness.
For the Drumonts only the abject Judas has remained, but for
some reason – by some remnant of Christian charity perhaps –
they cannot quite bring themselves to eradicate the evil, and have
to content themselves with trying to contain it. Whatever indig-

nities Christian Europe may inflict on its Jewish population, Bernard-Lazare once remarked, mass extermination is not something Christians can easily contemplate. On the other hand, the Christian conscience is not too troubled by what happens to Jews.[39]

I imagine that Bernard-Lazare would have been very moved by the penitential prayer composed by Pope John XXIII: 'We now acknowledge that for many, many centuries blindness has covered our eyes. . . We acknowledge that the mark of Cain is upon our brow. For centuries Abel lay low in blood and tears because we forgot thy love. Forgive us the curse that we wrongfully pronounced upon the name of the Jews. Forgive us that we crucified Thee in the flesh for the second time. For we knew not what we did. . .'[40]

Antisemitism, its history and causes was also re-written in several Socialist-inspired studies, of which *Antisémitisme et Révolution* (March 1895) and *La conception sociale du judaisme et le peuple juif* (September 1899) are the most significant.

In the same way as *Contre l'antisémitisme* was at one and the same time an historical re-assessment as well as a polemic and, within that, a re-examination of Bernard-Lazare's personal position as Jew and his relation with the outside world, so here these various elements, historical, polemical and personal, were inextricably linked together. Only things were more difficult here, because he was facing friends whom he wanted to persuade and before whom he felt obliged to justify things which needed no justification when facing Drumont. The right, for example, to remain a Jew. Drumont not only readily conceded this, but thought it impossible that it should be otherwise. In left-wing circles the Jewish socialist's sincerity as a socialist tended to be measured by the degree to which he abandoned Jewishness, recognised in antisemitism a powerful anti-capitalist force to be exploited, complied with the tactic of letting the masses shout 'down with Jewish capital' as a first step, a sort of *entrée en révolution*, to shouting 'down with capital', and generally accepted that the Jewish question was part and parcel of a much wider *social* problem to be resolved in the socialist revolution to come.

At one stage, until his history of the spring of 1894, Bernard-Lazare had more or less subscribed to these arguments; but the time was well past, and it was urgent to awaken the Left. He knew that the Left had its own prejudices and misconceptions, its own antisemitic traditions and *maîtres à penser*, but having himself seen through the social and economic guise adopted by antisemitism, he assumed that an enlightened Left would do likewise, would become the centre of resistance; and he set about enlightening his friends with his usual ardour.

Antisémitisme et Révolution (1895) was the first and only issue[41] of what was intended as a quarterly review, *Les Lettres Prolétariennes*. Bundles of it were apparently left in places frequented by the *compagnons* with the request to distribute it for propaganda.[42] It is a deliberately simple, naively written, directly didactic piece in epistolary form in which Jacques explains to his friend Jean Mouton what Drumont and his backers are all about. 'L'antisémitisme, mon pauvre Jean, c'est bon pour les curés, les réactionnaires et les bourgeois, car ce sont les seuls qui peuvent – ou qui espèrent – en tirer quelque chose.'[43] All the common meeting-points between socialist and antisemite are dealt with: all Jews are capitalists, capitalism is a Jewish creation dating from the emancipation, wherever Jewish movement is unrestricted the host-country has been on the decline, the salaries of French workers are low because of the employment of foreign workers and Jewish exploiters, Jews are parasites and unproductive, living on the work of others, and so on. In 1898, Bernard-Lazare evidently thought that the 'Jean Moutons' needed to have the warning against this sort of 'pseudo-socialism' repeated (as well he might when one thinks how readily a similar pseudo-socialism was accepted some 40 years later) and a second edition of *Antisémitisme et Révolution* was brought out by Stock. It is identical with the earlier version, save in one minor but significant respect concerning Drumont. In 1895 Drumont is attacked, but as 'un vaillant polémiste, un ardent écrivain' who does not really belong to 'les sots qui mangent leur juif quotidien, les bourgeois qui pensent préserver leurs coffres-forts'. Three years later he is presented as the spokesman of these very 'sots' and 'bourgeois'.[44] Behind the deliberate naïvetés of thought and expression one can sense all the urgency and all the fears of a Jewish socialist who is no longer prepared to watch the Jews being devoured while waiting for the age of universal brotherhood, and who sees the *best* men on the Left doing just that. Convinced that the Jewish question was a restricted social problem, to be solved together with all other problems when socialism came to power, they regarded the battle against antisemitism as something of a diversion of socialist energies. More dangerous still were those who flirted with Drumont, either genuinely or for tactical reasons, in order to catch the vote of the *petit bourgeois* whose socialist and revolutionary education could suitably begin with the slogan 'down with *Jewish* capital'.

In December 1898, it was no Jean Mouton but Jean Jaurès who proposed to Drumont a socialism tinged with antisemitism in the correct Marxist tradition.

> Comme Marx, qu'il [Drumont] a cité incorrectement l'autre jour, il aurait pu montrer que la conception sociale des juifs, fondée sur l'idée du trafic, est en parfaite harmonie avec le mécanisme du capital. Et il aurait pu ajouter, sans excès, que les juifs, habitués par des persécutions séculaires à la pratique de la solidarité et façonnés dès longtemps au maniement de la richesse mobilière, exerçaient dans notre société une action démesurée et redoutable. Ce socialisme, nuancé d'anti-sémitisme, n'aurait guère soulevé d'objections chez les esprits libres.[45]

It was not the first antisemitic pronouncement to come from Jaurès.[46] But it was one of the most direct statements of an acceptable 'socialisme nuancé d'antisémitisme' with Marx as justification. Bernard-Lazare was shocked by this strange conception of socialism coming from a distinguished leader of the French Socialist movement, and he replied with a long, erudite study 'La conception sociale du judaisme et le peuple juif'. Although in the first instance a reply to the allegation that the Jewish social conception is mercantile in essence, it goes far beyond the particular occasion and reveals a Bernard-Lazare who has left his book on antisemitism of 1894 far behind. This study contains some of the most drastic of all the diverse and scattered re-writings of his pre-Affair history.

One of the most interesting changes can be seen in his attitude to Marx. Whereas before he had judaised him – probably with a satirical intention – he had now realised the urgency of saying and showing that the man whose assertions had weighed so heavily on the Jewish question was the son of an already converted father, that he was ignorant of all things Jewish – religion, history and social conditions – and that his hastily-composed pamphlet whatever its value as a reply to Bruno Bauer, was no more than a 'vide métaphysique religioso-économique'.[47]

On what did Marx, and Jaurès after him, base the idea that Judaism's social conception is mercantile, that usury, commerce, money affairs are natural to the Jewish 'genius'? If it was on the Talmud, which neither of them evidently knew, then they could not be more wrong. Like the Bible, on which it is a commentary (Bernard-Lazare no longer separated the two), Talmudic law condemns usury. 'A proscrire l'usure sous toutes ses formes, les talmudistes employèrent toutes les ressources de leur casuistique et de leur subtilité.'[48] Manual work is constantly glorified in the Talmud. And what indeed were the Jews when they were a free people in their own land? Predominantly farmers and shepherds at first, and artisans later. The Talmudic ideal is of a nation of workers and scholars, workers who think and scholars who earn their living, as the great rabbis did, by working with their hands. Bernard-Lazare provides a long list of the famous rabbis who were also masons, woodcutters and stonebreakers, in the same way as he provides ample illustration of his main point, namely that the social ethics of pre-diaspora Jewry are as remote from capitalism as could be.

The previous denigration of the Talmud, possibly through ignorance, and its present idealisation, through selection, seem like an eloquent contradiction. And yet it is not so much a matter of contradiction or ignorance: more a matter of having made his peace with Jewish history, of having found a living heritage which he was no longer prepared to throw to the wolves in the vain hope of saving modern Jewry. What is a Jew without his past? Bernard-Lazare had become a little defenceless against the invasion of the past, a past which helped him to live.

> . . .nous sommes plus attachés au passé que nous ne le croyons communément. Sur notre jeune cervelle et sur notre coeur ont été déposées, à notre entrée dans la vie, des croyances que nous ne parvenons pas à tuer par la réflexion. Des fantômes habitent en nous, dont, sans nous en rendre compte, nous entretenons la vie et souvent ils nous guident, nous poussent, nous entraînent: ils sortent de l'inconscient et ils apparaissent à nos yeux étonnés. Nous les regardons d'abord comme des étrangers, des intrus même qui dérangent nos conceptions, mais nous ne tardons pas à les

reconnaître, et nous nous plaisons à nous laisser bercer par eux. . . Ces fantômes font plus encore. Ils sont capables d'engendrer en nous de nouvelles formes; ils se combinent avec nos idées actuelles, ils influent sur nos concepts, ils nous les font voir sous des angles imprévus, sous des aspects étrangers.[49]

On a more conscious level, he had liberated himself from a distorting mirage. It will be remembered that he had always been careful to say that usury was not inherent in Talmudic teaching, but merely that, almost axiomatically, rationalism led to usury. He now appreciated Talmudic rationalism (though not necessarily its more casuistic side); moreover, he had stopped looking at the rabbis through the mirage of eighteenth-century French 'philosophes' and their ideal of individual and material, earthly happiness. He no longer identified French middle-class materialism with the whole of Jewry. On the contrary, he insisted, and most strongly in the article under discussion, that the majority of world Jewry was neither rich, nor engaged in commerce, nor did it exercise the 'action démesurée et redoutable' of which a regrettably ignorant Jaurès spoke.

Bernard-Lazare had made tremendous efforts to steer the Left away from antisemitism.[50] His efforts met with some success, perhaps, in anarchist circles which were much less inclined to flirt with Drumont and which were not guided by the political considerations of their Socialist brothers. The Socialist Left was a disappointment to him. The most 'progressive' party, he later bitterly recalled,[51] looked upon antisemitism as the first stage of the socialist revolution. It is very probable that this disappointment speeded his way towards Zionism, though it was the Dreyfus Affair and his re-assessment of antisemitism in its light as something ultimately ineradicable that played the major part. Zionism presented the only other logical solution to the Jewish Question, or so it seemed. Bernard-Lazare was more than ready for Herzl and his extraordinary vision of a Jewish State.

I I

ZIONISM

Introduction

It is well known that the vision of a Jewish State came to Herzl after he had witnessed the anti-Jewish hysteria of the crowds at Captain Dreyfus' degradation ceremony. He had gone to Paris with no other intention than to report on the events for his Viennese newspaper, and he left with a blueprint for a Jewish homeland. Thus, it can truly be said that the modern State of Israel was conceived in Paris, less than a decade after *La France Juive*. Herzl had encountered antisemitism before. He could not have escaped it in the Vienna of Karl Lueger, the antisemitic mayor to whom, it is said, the young Adolf Hitler used to listen spellbound. But the Dreyfus Affair was a French affair; it came to pass in the country of the Revolution and the Enlightenment. To Herzl it seemed as if the Rights of Man had suddenly been revoked and a century of assimilation had vanished.

The politico-national vision of a Jewish State was new, at least in the detail and along the lines on which Herzl planned it; but behind it lay a long memory, a yearning for Zion which is as old as the Diaspora itself. 'By the rivers of Babylon, there we sat down and wept when we remembered Zion', says the psalm. For centuries Jews have wept at their loss and consoled themselves with the thought of returning. Until the nineteenth century the most concrete form which the return to Zion took was for religious Jews to go to Jerusalem to die. Modern Zionism wanted to go to Jerusalem to live.

This new, revolutionary Zionism had its early, isolated precursors in the mid-nineteenth century, notably in Moses Hess (*Rome and Jerusalem*, 1862), but it only became important as a movement in 1881 after the assassination of Czar Alexander II and the terrible pogroms to which this led. It was then that the *Hibbat*

Zion (love of Zion) movement and its numerous *Choveve Zion* societies (lovers of Zion) came into being and spread rapidly through Russia and Rumania. By the end of 1882, the first settlements in *Erez Israel* (the land of Israel) were being established. The Jews had returned to the land in more senses than one, to be farmers in 'the land of our fathers'.

The *Choveve Zion* groups (not all of which aspired to settlement in Palestine) were by and large *practical* Zionists, thinking in terms of piecemeal colonisation rather than in political terms of a State. One notable exception was Leo Pinsker, who became the leader of the movement. In his proposal (*Auto-emancipation*, 1882) to combat international antisemitism with Jewish nationalism and the creation of a homeland, anywhere in the world, Pinsker comes close to Herzl's point of view (a fact later acknowledged by Herzl who had not known of Pinsker's work). But Pinsker was Russian, and when he appealed to Western Jewry to become involved in the movement the appeal fell on deaf ears. To the assimilated West, in 1882, Pinsker seemed like a desperate man, unnerved by the pogroms. It needed the Dreyfus Affair and a Western Jew to bring East and West together as 'one people'.

There were a handful of pre-Herzlian 'Zionist' groups in the West, even in France. They were largely concerned with resettling the Russian immigrants who poured into European countries or, as Herzl sarcastically put it, with expediting the embarrassing, unemancipated ghetto masses to far-off lands. The I.C.A. (Jewish Colonisation Society) was founded in 1891 by baron Maurice de Hirsch, with the aim of resettling impoverished emigrants in North and South America. The I.C.A. was decidedly not Zionist. The baron left colonisation in Palestine to his rival, baron Edmond de Rothschild who supported, and paternalistically ruled, many of the early Palestinian colonies until the I.C.A. took over their administration in 1899. Emile Meyerson became a leading light in the I.C.A. and through him Bernard-Lazare came to work quite closely with the organisation. Of a very different character was the active Association des Etudiants Israélites Russes, established in the early 1890s, with whom Bernard-Lazare was to have close contacts.

This brief account of modern Zionism before Herzl shows that there was a strong, active, but unorganised and leaderless movement in Russia (also in Rumania) for whom living and working in Erez Israel, even under Turkish rule, signified personal and national emancipation. This Zionism, like that of Herzl, Bernard-Lazare and Nordau, was born out of suffering, disillusion, hurt pride, an outraged sense of human dignity; in short a reaction against antisemitism. But in Eastern Jewry, Zionism also had a strong positive element, because it was bound up with religious and cultural tradition; these Jews lived in close-knit communities and were deeply conscious of being a people. The situation was to be more difficult for assimilated and non-religious Westerners who, before they could see themselves and their aspirations as more than a simple reaction, had to rediscover these traditions and somehow harmonise them with their very different education and outlook. Herzl's role was crucial here, and Bernard-Lazare paid tribute to him:

> Vous avez su remuer les profondeurs d'Israel, vous lui avez apporté votre amour et votre vie, vous l'avez réveillé; aucun Juif digne de ce nom ne devra oublier cela, ni oublier de vous en témoigner sa reconnaissance.[1]

Encounter with Herzl: Zionist dialogues

Herzl's *Judenstaat* appeared in Vienna in February 1896. On 11 March Bernard-Lazare wrote to the author asking whether the 'brochure' was being translated into French and when it would be published. 'Je serais heureux de le savoir et à ce moment-là d'avoir des détails sur vos moyens d'action et sur vos projets pratiques de façon à signaler votre oeuvre ici.'[2]

Bernard-Lazare's reaction to the bold vision of a country for the Jews was swift and typical: he offered to help spread the message. There was much in the message to appeal to his reason as well as to his heart. In fact, Herzl said many things that Bernard-Lazare was thinking and before long was to express in his own way. Herzl's analysis, for example, of antisemitism, assimilation and the current Jewish situation in socio-economic terms, must greatly have appealed to him. *The Jewish State* is probably one of Herzl's most socialist writings, at least in inspiration and general tone, if not consistently in thought. He repeatedly declares that his concern is with the poor, with the most oppressed and wretched, with the 'drifting proletariat. . .driven by poverty and political pressure from place to place, land to land'.[3] In contrast to the pity expressed for the poor and unemancipated Jewry of the East, there is the biting irony towards the assimilated

Jewish bourgeoisie, particularly of France: the 'antisemite of Jewish origin in philanthropist's clothing', anxious to get incoming paupers out as quickly as possible in case they threaten the social position and French identity of their more fortunate brethren. 'They are Israelitic Frenchmen? Splendid! This is a private affair, for Jews alone.'[4] Before long Bernard-Lazare was to have his own say about the Israelitic Frenchmen, and Herzl's irony would seem like pin-pricks in comparison.

Most important of all was Herzl's then quite heretical view of assimilation as something not merely impossible but undesirable, and his proud declaration, in entire agreement with antisemitism, that the Jews are a nation and wish to remain such. Only they need a land, whether in Argentina or Zion, in which to live their lives and be themselves and not what others wish them to be, accuse them of being or have made them into. This was the epoch-making solution proposed to the Jewish question.

There were undoubtedly things in *The Jewish State* to give Bernard-Lazare pause, the seeds of future disagreements. If the vision was bold, the immediate means envisaged – deals with the Sultan, the wooing of the big powers, diplomacy and politics, the European model – all this betokened a mixture of conservative *Realpolitik* and wishful thinking curiously at variance with the revolutionary stand on non-assimilation. The Jew, Herzl seemed to suggest, has a right to be a Jew, but the Jewish State must be like any other European State, made in its image. Bernard-Lazare was altogether more sceptical about the desirability of assimilating and imitating European notions and nations themselves in turmoil and in need of new directions. Then there was Herzl's effort to sell the idea of a land for the Jews to the European powers. If the Jews stayed, given their current state of oppression, they would inevitably be driven into the arms of revolutionary parties. In contrast to the red peril there was the rosy picture of peace and plenty if the Jews departed: governments would be relieved of the troublesome duty of having to protect a minority against an envious majority which would be able to take up the jobs and positions relinquished by the departing Jews. Bernard-Lazare, for his part, wished Jews to participate in all revolutionary movements. As for the second argument, quite apart from anything else, it came close to justifying antisemitism. But these were minor matters, to be settled later, in comparison with the dynamic spirit of the message and its urgency.

Bernard-Lazare tried in vain to find a French publisher for Herzl[5] and finally *L'Etat Juif* appeared, in the country of its conception so to speak, in the *Nouvelle Revue Internationale* in the form of two articles (31 December 1896 and 15 January 1897). A little later it had a *tirage à part*. On 17 July 1896 Herzl and Bernard-Lazare met in Paris and the former noted in his diary: 'Excellent example of a fine, intelligent French Jew.'[6] That same afternoon Bernard-Lazare, 'in full sympathy', brought Emile Meyerson along and he in turn arranged an interview for Herzl with baron Edmond de Rothschild. The baron, it appears, mistook the Zionist crusader for an anarchist and feared for his life. Bernard-Lazare also got Herzl to give a lecture to the association of Russian Jewish students.

It is interesting to note Bernard-Lazare's early contact with this association, the most Zionist group then in existence in France, though not in any specifically political sense. It was there perhaps that Max Nordau and Bernard-Lazare met. As for Meyerson, internationally known for his philosophical works and remembered in Jewish circles for his untiring efforts to resettle the homeless, it is difficult to assess how familiar Bernard-Lazare was at that time with his work in Jewish organisations and as special adviser to baron Rothschild on Zionist matters. Notwithstanding Bernard-Lazare's hostility towards the Rothschilds and his own more nationally-inclined Zionism, he and Meyerson soon became close personal friends as well as collaborators.[7] What their exact relationship was at the time is difficult to say. At any rate by July 1896 Bernard-Lazare must have known him sufficiently well to take him to see Herzl, and the introduction is significant. The intention here was not so much to convert Meyerson as to bring together two branches of Zionism, soon to be known as political and practical, which eyed each other with suspicion and which, Bernard-Lazare felt, could both benefit from cooperation. In *The Jewish State* the policy of *infiltration* in Argentina was dismissed as inadequate and dangerous. The I.C.A., for its part, was proud of its practical colonisation success and suspicious of Herzl's politics of *immigration*. Herzl had an abundance of ideas and he had vision; but he had no capital and no colonising experience. The I.C.A. and similar organisations, Bernard-Lazare later told Herzl, were not Zionist in our sense of the word and they did not look beyond the immediate aim of settling the homeless; but they possessed funds and useful experience, and there was no reason why the two branches of Zionism should not work together. The cooperation, however, did not get off to a good start. Meyerson raised 'all too many objections'. A little later, relations were all but broken off. Bernard-Lazare was at this stage more drawn to Herzl's vision of nationhood as a solution to the Jewish question; he liked Herzl's boldness, his way of addressing himself to the world and not merely to restricted Jewish circles. At the same time, he appreciated the practical work of professional training and resettlement accomplished by such organisations as the I.C.A. As late as January 1899 he urged Herzl to work with or at least side by side with the existing groups.[8] The common action never came to pass, understandably so since there was an unbridgeable gulf between the Zionist with plans to convene a Jewish Parliament and create a State and the compassionate gentlemen of the I.C.A. conscientiously administering a fund designated by its philanthropic founder to solve the immediate problems of the needy and the homeless.

With the exception of 'Le Nationalisme et l'Emancipation Juive', Bernard-Lazare had formulated his Zionist ideas before the First Zionist Congress in August 1897, and two years before his break with Herzl and congress Zionism, as alien to him as congress socialism. He was at first, and to some extent was to remain, under the influence of *The Jewish State*. At the same time however, he took care to clarify his own position. His Zionist writings and lectures should thus be seen on two interconnecting levels: as a statement of his personal views, as well as in some sense as a critique of Herzl's ideas. Before going on to discuss the ideas in greater detail it is useful to clarify the question of dates and publications.

'Le Prolétariat juif devant l'antisémitisme' was a lecture given on 13 February 1897 at the Ligue Fraternelle de Montmartre before an audience of Russian workers, presumably Jewish, who resided in Paris. The text of the lecture was not published until *two* years later, in January 1899, in the first issue of the socialist-Zionist *Flambeau* founded and directed by Jacques Bahar with Bernard-Lazare's support. It was mistakenly interpreted as a manifesto of the left-wing opposition to official Zionism, a mistake all the more understandable since this was in fact what the *Flambeau* became for the rest of its short life. This particular text, however, is a faithful reproduction of the lecture and goes back to early 1897 when there was no thought of conscious opposition in Bernard-Lazare's mind, merely a desire to state his views on a subject of great concern to him. He and Herzl were on the best of terms at the time, as the correspondence testifies.

Considerably more nationalist in inspiration is *Le Nationalisme Juif*. This too was a lecture, given at the Association des étudiants israëlites russes on 6 March 1897 and it was published (by the faithful Stock) the following year as the first – and apparently only – number of the 'Publications du Kadimah'. (The latter should not be confused with the related, bimonthly review *Kadimah* brought out in 1896 by the same student association). 'Nécessité d'être soi-même' (30 April 1897) and 'Solidarité' (31 May 1897) are both articles in *Zion*, a trilingual (French, German, Hebrew) monthly originally created in Berlin in 1895 and of which Bernard-Lazare became the French editor in 1897. In this capacity he exercised considerable influence over his young collaborators impressed by his grasp of things and the 'impeccable logic' of his thought.[9] 'Le Nationalisme et l'Emancipation Juive', the most substantial and the most Zionist of Bernard-Lazare's essays, consists of an amalgamation of two lectures given to this student association, one in June 1898 and the other in the winter of 1899. Extracts from the first were published in *Kadimah* (15 August 1898). The complete study appeared in three successive issues of the *Echo Sioniste* in 1901 (5 April, 20 April, 5 May). By then Bernard-Lazare had more or less withdrawn from official Zionist circles though not from his own, personal brand of Zionism.

Situated in his work as a whole, 'Le Prolétariat juif devant l'antisémitisme' is an interesting transitional text, looking both back and forward. In its preoccupation with and analysis of antisemitism it elaborates and completes ideas expressed earlier. In the solution proposed to counter antisemitism one can feel the liberating national wind released by *The Jewish State*, though Bernard-Lazare's State is for the moment more a state of mind, a return to spiritual roots, entirely identified with revolutionary, socialist roots, rather than roots in the soil. If one compares Bernard-Lazare with Bernard-Lazare, we have a significant move towards Zionism, or nationalism, as he preferred to call it. If one compares his insistence that the Jews are 'une nation sans territoire' with *The Jewish State*, then one can understand Herzl's disappointment.

In his history of antisemitism (1894), Bernard-Lazare had

hopefully predicted that the Jews as a nation would disappear.[10] Jewish spirit, inextricably linked to a moribund Jewish religion, would likewise disappear. It must have cost him dear to pro- nounce this spirit dying since he had devoted a whole stirring chapter to describing its admirable qualities summed up as justice, equality and liberty;[11] but the logic of the thesis required it: antisemitism would perish because the Jews will be absorbed into the majority of the host country.[12] In 'Le Nouveau Ghetto' (November 1894), his first reaction to the Dreyfus Affair, he had *feared* that the revival of antisemitism would in turn revive Jewish national feelings which would otherwise have died a natural death.

All this had radically changed. Assimilation, absorption to the point of disappearance would never again be proposed as solu- tions. From now on his favourite battle-cry will be 'we must judaise the Jew'. Emancipation was a 'bad' word in the Zionist vocabulary. Bernard-Lazare uses it with the meaning of emanci- pating from ghetto Jewishness *and* from assimilation Jewishness, both products of persecution. He recommends a return to the proud spirit of old, to the prophetic traditions. Emancipation was a re-education into Jewishness.

Bernard-Lazare now looked back with pride: 'cette race, combien autrefois, sur le sol des aïeux elle travailla pour la justice';[13] he is saddened by the resigned herd that this once proud nation has become, but looks forward to its rebirth. The Jewish nation he is proud of is the energetic people who lived and worked on the ancestral soil but it is not suggested that the vitality and virtues of old can only be reacquired in the land of the fathers; nor, in fact, that a land is required at all. The recreation of the spiritual and moral nation is his concern. The creation of a physical nation, the question of land, does not for the moment arise; he emphasises throughout that the Jews are a nation without land. Unlike the assimilationists, and at the same time in sharp contrast to Herzl, he advocates a pluralist society in which it is perfectly legitimate for the Jews, as for any other minority, to be a nation within the Nation, and even a state within the State. This is of course a very 'orthodox' anarchist notion expressed in unmistakably anarchist language:

Pourvu qu'ils remplissent leurs devoirs de solidarité humaine, pourquoi leur refusera-t-on le droit de conserver

> leur personnalité? C'est là un vieux préjugé étatiste et
> gouvernemental. . . Le rêve des gouvernements est d'avoir
> pour sujets des êtres aussi semblables que les soldats de
> plomb dont s'amusent les enfants. Toute originalité, toute
> particularité leur est odieuse; au nom d'un certain national-
> isme ils proscrivent toutes les différences et veulent unifier
> militairement les esprits et les consciences.[14]

Far from paying for his Frenchness with his Jewishness, he insists that among the rights of man and the citizen must be inscribed the right of minorities to retain their cultural heritage and historical identity. It is in the fight for this right, as a national group, that he sees the answer, or rather the right attitude to take towards antisemitism.

It is a proud, combative stance which appeals to his temperament. It is also a necessary defence, as he points out in 'Solidarité', for only a nationally conscious and nationally proud people will have the courage and the strength to defend its members and fight for its rights. But it will not eliminate antisemitism. Its persistence may have the tragically positive virtue of reminding Jews of their history and forging bonds of common suffering (this is the well-known paradox of antisemitism keeping alive Jewishness, a paradox illustrated by Bernard-Lazare's personal experience) but it also leads to massacres and to stateless masses driven from the country of their birth. And what will happen if one day these homeless people find immigration laws, often dictated by fear of antisemitism, locking hitherto open doors? These are the terms in which the problem was to be posed in the next essay, and Bernard-Lazare would then move a great deal closer to Herzl.

From a social point of view, however, these two fervent non-assimilationists were and remained as far apart as ever. There was in Bernard-Lazare's non-assimilationist attitude a hostility towards society as at present constituted which came from anarchism, and which made his Zionism a revolutionary, Messianic Zionism reminiscent of Moses Hess. The point is not merely that assimilation has proved impossible both from the Jewish and the non-Jewish points of view, but that the Jew *must* not assimilate to an inequitable bourgeois society morally corrupted by capitalism and intellectually enfeebled by the forces of clericalism. Bernard-Lazare's 'Jewish nation' was in revolt against present society, which it hoped to reform by its example, either by living

as a nation within the Nation or by acting as a nation among
Nations. Herzl shared neither the ideal nor the missionary zeal
and he did not wish to confuse the urgency of creating a Jewish
State with a long-term reform of European society which in any
case he did not see as particularly decadent or demoralised. 'It
would be pure fantasy to believe', he wrote to Bernard-Lazare in
1899, 'that we can transform at one and the same time the
miserable situation of our own people and the general political
and social conditions prevailing in Europe. That is another task,
no less great than ours, perhaps even greater, but at any rate
different from our aspirations.'[15]

Die Welt, Herzl's Zionist organ, while enthusiastic about the
passion and style of 'Le Prolétariat juif devant l'antisémitisme',
was considerably more reserved about the ideas expressed.[16]
Statements such as this would not have been to Herzl's liking: 'Il
nous faut revivre comme peuple, c'est-à-dire comme collectivité
libre, mais à la condition que cette collectivité ne représente pas
l'image des Etats capitalistes et oppresseurs au milieu desquels
nous vivons'.[17] They could even prove to be diplomatically
embarrassing.

How strange to think that seven years before Bernard-Lazare
had proclaimed that what the Czar did with his Jews was no
concern of his. Then he was ashamed of those fearful hordes of
abject immigrants descending on France like locusts. Now he is a
little ashamed of France and weeps with an immigrant whose
new home has been pillaged by a Paris mob. This is the first time
he speaks of the Russian pogroms as meaningful to him. The years
1881 and 1895 are crucial dates in the Zionist calendar, one for
Russian Jewry and the other for Western Jewry, and it is Paris
shouting 'mort aux juifs' that brought the two together.

We have in this respect some telling *transpositions*, curious
re-living in Jewishness of past experiences, scattered throughout
his work. 'L'Ame du philosophe', published as a story in September 1894 in *Le Journal*, describes how the narrator (Bernard-
Lazare) wanders aimlessly through the streets of Amsterdam and
ends, by chance, in the Portuguese Synagogue. Crossing the
courtyard he stumbles upon a crowd of frightful-looking Jewish
refugees from Russia, speaking a barbaric jargon and gesticulating
in a fearful manner; he is glad to get away from these strangers.
In the Synagogue itself he finds very little to attract him, but
before leaving he notices Spinoza's plaque on the wall, and in

that moment the soul of the dead philosopher breathes some life into the place. The immigrants outside in the courtyard remain as unreal to him as before, a piece of present reality unconnected with Spinoza's past and unconnected with Bernard-Lazare's present. In 'Le Nationalisme Juif' Amsterdam is revisited, so to speak, and 'L'Ame du philosophe' becomes 'les voix du passé'. To begin with, he goes in search of the past, to the old ghetto haunted by the spirit of Spinoza, to the same Synagogue where he now remains for a long time, and where he notices, another voice from the past, the wood of the sanctuary which is said to come from Palestine. The crowd of Russian refugees in the courtyard also constitute voices from the past, his past. 'Je me crus reporté aux âges d'autrefois... Tous les siècles de misère, de désespoir, de résignation et d'obstination héroïque revécurent et ce fut l'Ahaséverus (sic) légendaire, l'éternel et misérable vagabond que je crus voir passer. Ce n'est pas l'antisémitisme contemporain qui rayera tout cela de nos mémoires. Et voilà encore un lien vivace entre nous: une histoire commune.'[18]

In 'Le Nationalisme Juif' the nation without a land acquires an unnamed land. The concept of remaining a free nation within the Nation, discussions as to whether antisemitism should or should not gain seats in Western parliaments, all these were academic questions as seen from Russia, Galicia and Rumania, that is to say for over six million Jews. Moreover, was it really possible for spiritual roots to be divorced from physical roots? A national heritage, if it is to be a living heritage and a source of life, needs a land; one must be free to live according to the excellent ethics formulated centuries ago. 'Comment doit-on considérer le nationalisme? Il est pour moi: l'expression de la liberté collective et la condition de la liberté individuelle. J'appele nation, le milieu dans lequel l'individu peut se développer et s'épanouir d'une façon parfaite. C'est dans le développement du nationalisme juif que je vois la solution de la question juive.'[19]

Like the non-religious Herzl, Bernard-Lazare underestimated the love of Zion expressed by practising Eastern Jewry in the ancient words: *next year in Jerusalem*. 'J'imagine que, pour ceux qui gémissent encore dans quelque ghetto, comme pour les aïeux du moyen-âge, ces paroles veulent dire: "L'année prochaine nous serons dans un pays de liberté"...' From this he concludes: 'Le Juif qui aujourd'hui dira: "Je suis un nationaliste", ne dira pas d'une façon spéciale précise et nette, je suis un homme qui veut

point of view, the identification of assimilation with wealth made
the Jewish bourgeoisie an ideal target. And bourgeois assimilation
is given an ancient precedent. The forty thousand men who
returned to Jerusalem from Babylon were the poor, the workers,
the just who wrote the psalms, the prophets with revolutionary
ideas; the rich remained in Babylon. And there, he added, they
must remain. There is, too, an element of self-flagellation: it is
not difficult to recognise Bernard-Lazare's early anti-Jewish
articles in the portrait of the Israelite ashamed of Jews and
congratulating the antisemite on his polemical talent. Bernard-
Lazare was not much given to confession and *'mea culpa'* and
yet he had to exorcise in some way, either by re-living his experiences or by vicarious castigation, a brief period in his life the
memory of which must have caused him much pain. But he had
made good. He has had his 'Amsterdam revisited' and joined the
once-despised refugees with their bundles and their jargon and
their dirty clothes.[28] He despised the assimilated gentlemen for
rejecting in the homeless and unemancipated masses their own
grandfathers and their own past, and all this in the name of an
'étatiste' interpretation of the charter of liberty and in the secret
hope of securing peace for themselves. Whereas before he had
held the *Jew* responsible almost for creating antisemitism, he now
accused the *Israelite*, not of creating it, for that role is filled by
Christian teaching, but certainly of ensuring its success; first, by
not combating it; second, by behaving according to the image
of greed, insensitivity, ostentation, rush for places and honours
that antisemitism wishes to maintain of all Jewry; third, by
insisting that the Jews are nothing more than a religious community when religion is precisely the enemy's main weapon. The
Zionist puts before the Israelitic Frenchmen, Germans and Aus-
trians the following choice: either they fight antisemitism and
exhaust themselves in a personally uplifting but ultimately hopeless struggle; or they continue to acquiesce, in which case they
have to accept antisemitism's solution to the Jewish question.
When all has been said about unfairness and exaggeration, there
are some tragically lucid warnings addressed to intellectuals and
politicians in high office, to free-thinkers or the religious, each
with his own reasons for thinking that antisemitism does not apply
to him. Warnings above all to the patriotic Jewish citizens of
Germany and France who fondly imagine 'les uns qu'ils étaient
autrefois aux côtés d'Arminius dans la forêt de Teutobourg et

promised land to achieve full freedom as a citizen. It was also perhaps a way of answering the reproach that Zionism gave in to antisemitism. Bernard-Lazare proposed to fight it to the last, but he recognised its ultimate inevitability.

The 'Français de confession israëlite' constituted the opposition, the antithesis to what a Jew should be. They represented the 'politics of assimilation' which Bernard-Lazare attacked with vehemence in all his Zionist writings, nowhere more so than in 'Le Nationalisme et L'Emancipation Juive'. They are:

> patriotes, chauvins, valets, sans cervelle, sans énergie, sans volonté, sans fraternité et sans pitié; les détenteurs des biens terrestres et prêts à toutes les abdications, à tous les reniements, à toutes les lâchetés. . .pour conserver le bien-être matériel qui est devenu depuis longtemps leur idéal et leur dieu; . . .il nous faut les extirper de nous, les rejeter comme la pourriture qui nous empoisonne, qui nous souille, qui nous avilit.[27]

He quoted an honourable rabbi as saying that contemporary Israelites find it offensive to have the expression 'the Jewish people' applied to them. Another rabbi is quoted as exhorting the congregation to prove itself worthy of the blessings bestowed on Jewry by the French Revolution. Bernard-Lazare was angered by this kind of servile gratitude and the mentality of liberated slaves which it engendered in Western Jewry. As he saw it, the Jew behaved towards the charter of liberty like a grateful beggar who, after having been given what should never have been taken away from him in the first place, considered himself permanently on probation, anxious to behave 'properly' in case the gift was taken away from him again. And behaving properly in this case meant being French to the exclusion of everything else; at the most one could admit Israelitic descent and toss charity to Jews in other lands. Solidarity, never! The day antisemitism built up this solidarity into a dangerous Jewish International, he observed, the Jewish bourgeoisie protested through the voice of its scholars, its public figures and even its priests. Countless studies, indeed whole volumes, were produced to demonstrate that this solidarity did not exist or at least that it should not exist.

There are many factors involved in these attacks, unfair like any attack *en bloc*. Bernard-Lazare's polemical temperament needed an opponent on whom to sharpen his ideas. From a social took the form of going out to oppressed Jewry. But he went with the intention first and foremost of 'emancipating' them. And here we come to the main idea summed up in the title itself, 'Le Nationalisme et L'Emancipation Juive'; the emphasis falls on 'and'. Emancipation, we have already seen, meant re-education into Jewishness. In the present context it also meant, meant especially, that Jews must fight for their rights in the country of which they are at present citizens. And civil rights and civil liberties are considerably more important than the right to vote. Algeria here was the crucial example: Algerian Jews were ignorant of their civil rights but proud to cast their votes; and now it was their livelihood and their very lives that were in danger, not merely the right to vote which did not protect them. The purpose of the battle for civil rights was to foster self-respect, heighten the sense of human dignity and prevent the slave mentality. It was the old battle against antisemitism, a constant vigilance to prevent antisemitism from encroaching on the civil liberties granted to all citizens or, if Jews were regarded as aliens, to all aliens. All exceptional and discriminatory legislation, restriction in employment and residence, special passes, special taxes, and so on, had to be fought and had to be fought by all Jews for all Jews. This fighting solidarity was one difference between partisans of *emancipation* and those of *assimilation*. The latter, he remarked, offered financial help, if they helped at all, but cared little about the violation of rights to which fellow-Jews were subjected in other countries. The other difference concerned the very nature of emancipation. Bernard-Lazare was emphatic: emancipation does not mean assimilation. We wish the Jews to be emancipated, we do not wish them to become assimilated, he wrote. Here comes the second, Zionist stage. The emancipatory battle which the Jew must wage can never be won, for no law can eradicate prejudice:

> toute émancipation sera vaine, elle sera légale sans doute,
> mais jamais effective, car le préjugé restera. Le jour où les
> Juifs auront compris cela, et nous n'aurons qu'à leur faire
> ouvrir les yeux sur le monde pour qu'ils le comprennent, ce
> jour-là, ils sentiront profondément qu'ils ne trouveront
> jamais la vraie liberté que dans l'autonomie.[26]

Emancipation then was a first stage, a necessary moral struggle which would give the Jew a sense of dignity before he entered the croîtra sa vigne et son figuier. Nous avons assez peiné sur le champ des autres, allons travailler notre propre champ.'[24] The agricultural imagery is not purely literary, since Zionism also meant a return to working the land, to remaking peasants out of pedlars. Where Bernard-Lazare will grow his vine is not explicitly stated. The sky of Judea, the banks of the Jordan, the shores of Lake Galilee and Jerusalem are poetically evoked as the cradle of the Jewish nation, the heroic age when Israel (the term is used to mean Jewish people) fought for its independence; but they are perhaps no more than poetic evocations, though the fact that he has recourse to this imagery is in itself interesting.

The saddest passage, one is almost tempted to say outburst, concerns left-wing antisemitism. 'Pariahhood' is complete now that hitherto unexpressed suspicions and fears have acquired the reality of public admission and the last link with the only solution outside Jewish nationalism to hold any meaning for him has been severed:

> N'espérez-vous pas qu'avec les transformations sociales la haine du Juif disparaîtra. Voyez déjà en Autriche on commence à dire: 'le socialisme sera antisémite ou il ne sera pas'. Chez tous les écrivains réformateurs vous retrouvez quand il s'agit de vous la même injustice. Drumont s'appuie sur Proudhon, sur Fourier, sur Toussenel et il peut invoquer Bakounine qui ne parlait jamais de Marx qu'en l'appelant le Juif allemand. Ne vous obstinez donc pas à vouloir entrer dans une maison où on vous insulte, à vous asseoir à une table dont on vous repousse. Sachez bâtir vous-mêmes votre maison, la maison où vous accueillerez tout le monde.[25]

The sad, decisive step taken by Bernard-Lazare had one liberating effect: he no longer sought the sympathy and approval of others; and this left him free to deal with objections from his own side: the criticism, for example, that the chimera of reconstituting a Jewish nation in some distant future diverted attention and effort from the present intolerable situation of Jews in many lands. This went straight to Bernard-Lazare's heart, especially since the situation was extremely serious, and he gives a list of persecutions and disabilities of one sort or another practised not only in Eastern Europe but also in Algeria, Morocco, and Persia. To some extent Bernard-Lazare himself was to reproach official Zionism for living in the clouds, and eventually his own personal Zionism internationalism. The latter, he argues, far from implying the destruction of nations, presupposes the existence of free and autonomous nations linked by a spirit of fraternity instead of, as at present, by hypocritical diplomacy and an armed peace. As for nationalism, what is odious is protectionism, narrow chauvinism, national egoism and egotism. As against this, as we already know, at certain moments in history, nationalism is an expression of freedom. Moreover, well-informed as he was about national wars of liberation, he reminded his friends that they had all supported, and with good reason, the struggle for autonomy of Cuba, Crete and the Armenians. Had not these been battles for liberty and at the same time for national identity? In what way were the Jews different? Was it because their servitude had lasted longer? Because they had been deprived of their country for longer? Because a sepulchre had taken the place of the Temple?

Essentially, he justifies the creation of a new Nation on the same anarchist principle of a nation within the Nation, only he enlarges it to an international scale: a Nation among Nations. Has revolutionary anarchism not always favoured the concept of fragmentation and federation, an organic structure of small independent cells working together in mutually beneficial association rather than the creation of amorphous, monolithic blocks artificially unified? Unity is desirable and necessary but unification is unnatural and deadly. Like individuals, so groups of individuals draw on a common fund of ideas belonging to mankind at large; but each group has its own way of expressing them, its special way of beholding and creating beauty. Human richness depends on this variety.[22] 'Maintenir une nation c'est contribuer à garder intégrale la beauté universelle dont les facettes sont faites de mille beautés particulières communiant toutes dans le tout.'[23]

It is doubtful whether the Left, including the anarchist Left to whom his appeal was primarily directed, was convinced by his arguments. But one can see how Bernard-Lazare came to reconcile his nationalist aspirations with his anarchist ideas. At the time, anarchism provided the only acceptable and dignified solution to the Jewish question: independence.

'Le Nationalisme et L'Emancipation Juive', written at the height of the Dreyfus Affair, is in all respects the most passionate Zionist declaration in his writings. Nationalism reached its high point in this call to exodus: 'Voilà notre tâche à nous tous: avancer cette heure, l'heure où le pauvre des vieux psaumes, reconstituer un Etat Juif en Palestine et qui rêve de conquérir Jérusalem. Il dira: "Je veux être un homme pleinement libre, je veux jouir du soleil, je veux avoir droit à une dignité d'homme. Je veux échapper à l'oppression, échapper à l'outrage, échapper au mépris qu'on veut faire peser sur moi." A certaines heures de l'histoire, le nationalisme est pour des groupes humains la manifestation de l'esprit de liberté.'[20]

His attitude to the battle against antisemitism has also undergone a shift. The fight is important but as a matter of honour and personal dignity: the individual who suffers indignities without trying to resist them as best he can abdicates his personality and consents to slavery. A permanent state of resistance, however, he now observes, exhausts energies and inhibits free and full development. Was Bernard-Lazare tired of fighting? Was he remembering perhaps his literary ambitions sacrificed to the cause of battling against centuries of prejudice, eternally present and merely rationalised in different ways according to time and place? It is possible. He was above all tired of his people's wanderings: 'les Juifs errent encore sur les chemins du globe; combien de temps encore erreront-ils ainsi? Cependant les temps devraient être révolus où le vagabond pourrait trouver un asile, appuyer sa tête lourde et étendre ses membres las.'[21]

The necessity for the 'nation without land' to have a land having been established, it remained to justify to socialist and anarchist friends his support for nationalism when internationalism was the ideal, the creation of a new nation when frontiers were being abolished, a separation when things were moving towards greater unity. And what about 'workers of the world unite'?

The last of these objections was easily answered: in order to be able to join in the struggle of the Workers' International, Jewish workers needed a minimum of freedom. If they are massacred as Jews they cannot fight as workers. Bernard-Lazare energetically affirmed his faith in the socialist revolution for which he would continue to work. But the golden age was still a long way off. Besides, Bernard-Lazare was not too sure whether, when it came, it would allow Jews to remain Jews.

More difficult to deal with was the objection to the establishment of a new nation in an age seeking to abolish frontiers. Bernard-Lazare has to admit that he is 'orthodoxe en rien': that he can see no objection to nationalism existing side by side with

> leur personnalité? C'est là un vieux préjugé étatiste et
> gouvernemental. . . . Le rêve des gouvernements est d'avoir
> pour sujets des êtres aussi semblables que les soldats de
> plomb dont s'amusent les enfants. Toute originalité, toute
> particularité leur est odieuse; au nom d'un certain national-
> isme ils proscrivent toutes les différences et veulent unifier
> militairement les esprits et les consciences.[14]

Far from paying for his Frenchness with his Jewishness, he insists that among the rights of man and the citizen must be inscribed the right of minorities to retain their cultural heritage and historical identity. It is in the fight for this right, as a national group, that he sees the answer, or rather the right attitude to take towards antisemitism.

It is a proud, combative stance which appeals to his temperament. It is also a necessary defence, as he points out in 'Solidarité', for only a nationally conscious and nationally proud people will have the courage and the strength to defend its members and fight for its rights. But it will not eliminate antisemitism. Its persistence may have the tragically positive virtue of reminding Jews of their history and forging bonds of common suffering (this is the well-known paradox of antisemitism keeping alive Jewishness, a paradox illustrated by Bernard-Lazare's personal experience) but it also leads to massacres and to stateless masses driven from the country of their birth. And what will happen if one day these homeless people find immigration laws, often dictated by fear of antisemitism, locking hitherto open doors? These are the terms in which the problem was to be posed in the next essay, and Bernard-Lazare would then move a great deal closer to Herzl.

From a social point of view, however, these two fervent non-assimilationists were and remained as far apart as ever. There was in Bernard-Lazare's non-assimilationist attitude a hostility towards society as at present constituted which came from anarchism, and which made his Zionism a revolutionary, Messianic Zionism reminiscent of Moses Hess. The point is not merely that assimilation has proved impossible both from the Jewish and the non-Jewish points of view, but that the Jew *must* not assimilate to an inequitable bourgeois society morally corrupted by capitalism and intellectually enfeebled by the forces of clericalism. Bernard-Lazare's 'Jewish nation' was in revolt against present society, which it hoped to reform by its example, either by living hopefully predicted that the Jews as a nation would disappear.[10] Jewish spirit, inextricably linked to a moribund Jewish religion, would likewise disappear. It must have cost him dear to pronounce this spirit dying since he had devoted a whole stirring chapter to describing its admirable qualities summed up as justice, equality and liberty;[11] but the logic of the thesis required it: antisemitism would perish because the Jews will be absorbed into the majority of the host country.[12] In 'Le Nouveau Ghetto' (November 1894), his first reaction to the Dreyfus Affair, he had *feared* that the revival of antisemitism would in turn revive Jewish national feelings which would otherwise have died a natural death.

All this had radically changed. Assimilation, absorption to the point of disappearance would never again be proposed as solutions. From now on his favourite battle-cry will be 'we must judaise the Jew'. Emancipation was a 'bad' word in the Zionist vocabulary. Bernard-Lazare uses it with the meaning of emancipating from ghetto Jewishness *and* from assimilation Jewishness, both products of persecution. He recommends a return to the proud spirit of old, to the prophetic traditions. Emancipation was a re-education into Jewishness.

Bernard-Lazare now looked back with pride: 'cette race, combien autrefois, sur le sol des aïeux elle travailla pour la justice';[13] he is saddened by the resigned herd that this once proud nation has become, but looks forward to its rebirth. The Jewish nation he is proud of is the energetic people who lived and worked on the ancestral soil but it is not suggested that the vitality and virtues of old can only be reacquired in the land of the fathers; nor, in fact, that a land is required at all. The recreation of the spiritual and moral nation is his concern. The creation of a physical nation, the question of land, does not for the moment arise; he emphasises throughout that the Jews are a nation without land. Unlike the assimilationists, and at the same time in sharp contrast to Herzl, he advocates a pluralist society in which it is perfectly legitimate for the Jews, as for any other minority, to be a nation within the Nation, and even a state within the State. This is of course a very 'orthodox' anarchist notion expressed in unmistakably anarchist language:

> Pourvu qu'ils remplissent leurs devoirs de solidarité humaine, pourquoi leur refusera-t-on le droit de conserver

that moment the soul of the dead philosopher breathes some life into the place. The immigrants outside in the courtyard remain as unreal to him as before, a piece of present reality unconnected with Spinoza's past and unconnected with Bernard-Lazare's present. In 'Le Nationalisme Juif' Amsterdam is revisited, so to speak, and 'L'Ame du philosophe' becomes 'les voix du passé'. To begin with, he goes in search of the past, to the old ghetto haunted by the spirit of Spinoza, to the same Synagogue where he now remains for a long time, and where he notices, another voice from the past, the wood of the sanctuary which is said to come from Palestine. The crowd of Russian refugees in the courtyard also constitute voices from the past, his past. 'Je me crus reporté aux âges d'autrefois... Tous les siècles de misère, de désespoir, de résignation et d'obstination héroïque revécurent et ce fut l'Ahaséverus (sic) légendaire, l'éternel et misérable vagabond que je crus voir passer. Ce n'est pas l'antisémitisme contemporain qui rayera tout cela de nos mémoires. Et voilà encore un lien vivace entre nous: une histoire commune.'[18]

In 'Le Nationalisme Juif' the nation without a land acquires an unnamed land. The concept of remaining a free nation within the Nation, discussions as to whether antisemitism should or should not gain seats in Western parliaments, all these were academic questions as seen from Russia, Galicia and Rumania, that is to say for over six million Jews. Moreover, was it really possible for spiritual roots to be divorced from physical roots? A national heritage, if it is to be a living heritage and a source of life, needs a land; one must be free to live according to the excellent ethics formulated centuries ago. 'Comment doit-on considérer le nationalisme? Il est pour moi: l'expression de la liberté collective et la condition de la liberté individuelle. J'appele nation, le milieu dans lequel l'individu peut se développer et s'épanouir d'une façon parfaite. C'est dans le développement du nationalisme juif que je vois la solution de la question juive.'[19]

Like the non-religious Herzl, Bernard-Lazare underestimated the love of Zion expressed by practising Eastern Jewry in the ancient words: *next year in Jerusalem*. 'J'imagine que, pour ceux qui gémissent encore dans quelque ghetto, comme pour les aïeux du moyen-âge, ces paroles veulent dire: "L'année prochaine nous serons dans un pays de liberté"...' From this he concludes: 'le Juif qui aujourd'hui dira: "Je suis un nationaliste", ne dira pas d'une façon spéciale, précise et nette, je suis un homme qui veut

as a nation within the Nation or by acting as a nation among Nations. Herzl shared neither the ideal nor the missionary zeal and he did not wish to confuse the urgency of creating a Jewish State with a long-term reform of European society which in any case he did not see as particularly decadent or demoralised. 'It would be pure fantasy to believe', he wrote to Bernard-Lazare in 1899, 'that we can transform at one and the same time the miserable situation of our own people and the general political and social conditions prevailing in Europe. That is another task, no less great than ours, perhaps even greater, but at any rate different from our aspirations.'[15]

Die Welt, Herzl's Zionist organ, while enthusiastic about the passion and style of 'Le Prolétariat juif devant l'antisémitisme', was considerably more reserved about the ideas expressed.[16] Statements such as this would not have been to Herzl's liking: 'Il nous faut revivre comme peuple, c'est-à-dire comme collectivité libre, mais à la condition que cette collectivité ne représente pas l'image des Etats capitalistes et oppresseurs au milieu desquels nous vivons'.[17] They could even prove to be diplomatically embarrassing.

How strange to think that seven years before Bernard-Lazare had proclaimed that what the Czar did with his Jews was no concern of his. Then he was ashamed of those fearful hordes of abject immigrants descending on France like locusts. Now he is a little ashamed of France and weeps with an immigrant whose new home has been pillaged by a Paris mob. This is the first time he speaks of the Russian pogroms as meaningful to him. The years 1881 and 1895 are crucial dates in the Zionist calendar, one for Russian Jewry and the other for Western Jewry, and it is Paris shouting 'mort aux juifs' that brought the two together.

We have in this respect some telling *transpositions*, curious re-living in Jewishness of past experiences, scattered throughout his work. 'L'Ame du philosophe', published as a story in September 1894 in *Le Journal*, describes how the narrator (Bernard-Lazare) wanders aimlessly through the streets of Amsterdam and ends, by chance, in the Portuguese Synagogue. Crossing the courtyard he stumbles upon a crowd of frightful-looking Jewish refugees from Russia, speaking a barbaric jargon and gesticulating in a fearful manner; he is glad to get away from these strangers. In the Synagogue itself he finds very little to attract him, but before leaving he notices Spinoza's plaque on the wall, and in

les autres près de Vercingétorix à Alésia'[29] and that this ancient
loyalty will save them.

The Second Zionist Congress. Break with Herzl

In May 1898, shortly before he set out for Basle and the second
Zionist Congress, an English journalist interviewed Bernard-
Lazare and asked him for his views on Zionism and Jewish
colonisation. In the reply he then made, Palestine had now
become the country, though it looks as if colonisation rather than
statehood was in his mind.

> I am in favour of colonisation, the establishment of new
> colonies, and the introduction of industries in Palestine. I do
> not hold these views on humanitarian grounds but from the
> political standpoint. There is no Zionism in France, and if I
> am a Zionist it is not because of the hundred thousand Jews
> of France... The question is what shall we do with millions
> of our brethren in Eastern Europe who have been ground
> down by their misery. As I see a future for them in Zion, I
> am a Zionist.

Asked what object Zionism aims to achieve apart from colonisation, he replied: 'We must first form our masses into a Jewish
people. It is therefore our duty besides attending to colonisation
to attend to the education of our people. I will work for that in
Basle.'[30]

Bernard-Lazare was the star of the second congress. Even
before he arrived he was elected to the presidential council and
the action committee by delegates to the vast majority of whom
he was only a name, but a name of dreyfusard fame. Here is a
lively eyewitness account of Bernard-Lazare's entry into the
Casino Hall at Basle, packed with people from gallery to stalls, all
listening with an intense, almost religious silence, to Nordau's
address.

> Tout à coup, par une des portes latérales, un homme entra
> qui, d'un pas tranquille, s'avança jusque vers le milieu de la
> salle, puis s'immobilisa en voyant tous les regards tournés
> vers lui, où se lisait clairement une muette, mais solide
> réprobation... Mais déjà Nordau...avait réparé le
> 'sacrilège' et, d'un geste du bras, l'accueillait, l'imposait
> souverainement. 'Bernard-Lazare, entendit-on, le noble, le
> hardi, le fort!'

> Et soudain, voici toute la salle debout dans un frémisse-
> ment indicible qui éclate en une tempête d'applaudissements
> frénétiques qui semblent ne devoir jamais finir. . . . Juste
> devant moi, Bernard-Lazare se tenait, immobile, interdit,
> semblant ne pas comprendre, et n'osant faire un pas sous
> les milliers de regards qui, avidement, le dévoraient. Un
> moment, je crus qu'il allait s'enfuir. Puis, je vis rosir le
> visage mortellement pâle et, dans les yeux si calmes, quelque
> chose tremblait, . . .quelque chose d'humide et de scin-
> tillant. . . . Sous la chaleur explosive dont l'enveloppait
> l'amour de ses frères inconnus, venus des quatre coins de la
> terre, le masque avait fondu, et nous le vîmes tel que
> devaient le connaître, seuls, ses proches et ses intimes.
>
> L'instant d'après, il s'était ressaisi et, s'étant secoué
> comme au sortir d'un rêve, il reprit lentement sa marche
> vers la tribune, où l'appelait le geste de son grand ami.[31]

Throughout the congress he was acclaimed and honoured. The
association of Zionist journalists (created at the first congress)
gave a banquet in honour of its three most distinguished members,
Herzl, Nordau and Bernard-Lazare. Jacques Bahar recited a poem
composed in his honour and dedicated to Madame Bernard-
Lazare, herself an ardent Zionist. Nordau paid a warm tribute to
the dreyfusard. The greatest excitement came on the closing day,
when news of Colonel Henry's arrest came through.

> . . .From the four corners of the Stadt-Casino came the cry,
> 'Bernard-Lazare, hoch!'. . . Men rushed upon him to devour
> him with embraces, they cheered and they chaired him,
> they sang and laughed, and were almost beside themselves.
> The whole of Basle was moved.[32]

This congress, the first[33] and last he attended, was an unforgettable emotional experience, probably *the* experience of his public
life; and the warmth shown to him by strangers contrasted sharply
with the coolness of prominent dreyfusards at home. But the
Congress was also a disappointment.

To begin with there was the irritating petty preoccupation
with procedural matters. The first Congress, at which all were
welcome, having laid down that in future only delegates representing groups of a hundred people would be admitted, created
problems for would-be French participants who had to look for

electors elsewhere, notably in Galicia and Russia. Thus it was that
Bernard-Lazare represented a group from the small Galician town
of Tuchow whom he had never seen (he went to see them later).
This 'remote' representation evidently worried him, and in a
charming letter to Landau, who helped to secure the mandate, he
asked him to enquire of the people of Tuchow how he could best
represent their interests.[34] The whole question of the election of
delegates was immensely complex: some keen Zionists had no
electors to represent from their own countries; other towns had no
money to send delegates; hence the unsatisfactory arrangement of
one delegate with several mandates. The increasing attention paid
to election and verification of mandates was a bad sign that the
Zionist congress was going the way of all congresses. It was only
one sign, and not the most serious.

Bernard-Lazare's actual interventions were few but pertinent.
He proposed that the proceedings of the congress should be
published in French as well as in German, 'car les juifs du Maroc
et de l'Algérie ont besoin qu'on leur apporte la consolation du
sionisme'.[35] Far more worrying to Herzl was Bernard-Lazare's
opposition to the bank project (the Jewish Colonial Trust, as it
came to be known). He thought it ill-conceived, premature and
not sufficiently discussed by the people in whose name the bank
was being created. Some such body was of course desperately
needed, but in common with other left-wing delegates Bernard-
Lazare was afraid of putting the future of the Jewish people into
the hands of shareholders. Like the socialist Syrkin, he would
have preferred some sort of cooperative institution, or something
on the lines of the National Fund which was later created.
Politically more worrying was the 'democratic' fashion in which
the project was bulldozed through the assembly. The 'government', that is to say Herzl, his advisers and the bank committee,
were keen to have the proposal accepted with a minimum of
discussion. The majority preferred voting to discussion, and
implicitly trusted the leadership, particularly on matters which
it did not understand. There was a vocal, left-wing minority
which wanted full discussion and more precise information. But
the congress agenda was full, time short, and Herzl keen on his
brainchild. An infallible means of quashing discussion *democratically* was to propose a closure vote which was invariably
carried. Thus the bank project before being fully discussed was
put to the vote and carried. Bernard-Lazare expressed his great

disappointment. 'La création de cette banque doit être éminem-
ment démocratique, un peuple ne peut pas voter librement un
projet qu'il ne connaît pas.'[36]

He also strongly supported Saul Landau's proposal for already
existing Zionist *workers'* associations to be represented by their
own delegates on the action committee. The proposal was rejected
and replaced by a resolution calling upon the committee to
examine the question of working-class conditions. This was of
course very different from the original proposal.

One of the Landau 'scenes' is worth recalling, for it illustrates
several elements which contributed to Bernard-Lazare's break
with official Zionism. An ardent socialist with an anarchist temperament, Saul Landau had great difficulty in raising specifically
labour questions, for which the leadership showed no great
enthusiasm. The assembly at large was impatient with his demands for full discussion of the problem. The obstinate Landau
continued to speak in spite of interruptions, a closure vote and
the constant tinkling of a bell calling him to order. His patience
exhausted, a prominent 'leadership' delegate, Dr Mandelstamm,
shouted that socialists should be turned out of the congress. Herzl
did not accept the proposal, but he declared that he would not
allow the congress to be led by one political party. Such scenes
as we have just witnessed, he added, were not uncommon in
parliaments and they had a place in the development of parliaments, but such scenes in a Zionist congress might make a bad
impression. The Congress passed, as after all such 'scenes', a vote
of confidence in the chair.[37]

It was clear that the majority of the 'Jewish Parliament' was
as afraid of its socialist minority as any other bourgeois parliament. It led to such extraordinary statements as that the congress
must not discuss social and political questions, and this à propos
the terrible living conditions of Jewry in Galicia. With diplomacy
no doubt in mind, Herzl even declared that 'the movement has
decided' (who? when?) not to interfere in the social conditions
of Jews in the various countries. As to 'agitation', he admitted its
necessity, but details and methods would not be discussed in open
Congress.[38]

Conceived on the lines of Western parliaments, the young
Jewish parliament was already showing the worst features of
parliamentary democracy and socialist 'congressism': there were
discussions on how to discuss and the minority was rarely allowed

to discuss in peace; the rule of the majority was sacred. In this particular case, the majority had never lived in a democracy, was a politically uneducated and emotionally deeply stirred people, grateful to its leader and ready to ratify decisions it could not understand because it trusted the leadership, educated men of the West who knew best.

If we add to this that at Herzl's initiative the Congress sent a greetings telegram to the Sultan and welcomed the Czar's proposal for a peace conference, then the picture of disappointment, not in the assembly, but in the leadership, is complete.

Basle then was at one and the same time an overwhelming emotional experience and a disappointing political experience. It brought tears to Bernard-Lazare's eyes, which was not something that often happened to him in public. But henceforth he kept a critical eye on the leader and the committee who claimed to speak in the name of the Jewish people.

Before long the storm broke. In January 1899 Bernard-Lazare was asking Herzl to explain his visit to Palestine and audience with the Kaiser.[39] Herzl's autocratic manner of conducting the nation's foreign affairs was not to Bernard-Lazare's liking. The policy itself, the wooing of tyrants, positively alarmed him.

The bank project, though 'democratically' voted at the Congress, remained a source of worry. Bernard-Lazare objected in principle to making 'une banque le pivot d'un mouvement national, surtout quand il s'agit des juifs'.[40] On a practical level, he thought it was destined to failure, for Jewish financiers would be unlikely to support airy-fairy Zionist projects. They had to be obliged to lend their support by being put before accomplished facts. It is difficult to decide who was more realistic or idealistic in this respect, Herzl or Bernard-Lazare. The latter evidently thought that the I.C.A. would not refuse financial help if approached in the right way. He was distressed when David Wolffsohn, Herzl's emissary, broke off relations with the I.C.A. after the latter had rejected the bank project, something for which Bernard-Lazare hardly blamed them. To Herzl, on the other hand, the creation of a bank seemed a regrettable but an indispensable instrument in the realisation of their ideals. 'We cannot at present change the power of money', he wrote to Bernard-Lazare. 'Our cause needs a bank and having no bankers to support us, we must create our own bank. It is a matter of simple logic.'[41] Bernard-Lazare regarded it as capitalist madness to nail the fate of a national movement of liberation to the success or failure of a bank.

Then there was a lengthy argument about a certain Mr Seidener whose services Herzl had enlisted and who, Meyerson had informed Bernard-Lazare, was a financier of doubtful integrity. Such people must have nothing to do with our work, Bernard-Lazare told Herzl, to which the latter replied, and nothing could be more designed to anger Bernard-Lazare, that literary idealists should take care not to become the gullible victims of certain 'rhéteurs de bas étage' determined to blacken the image of the Zionist leadership under the guise of defending the humble.[42] Bernard-Lazare attached great importance to unmasking Seidener in order to teach Herzl a lesson in humility, to make him realise that even the future 'King of Jerusalem'[43] could make mistakes in his choice of advisors.

Finally, there was the protest against the undemocratic way in which Herzl wished to reform the electoral procedure of the Congress (in order to eliminate, as Herzl put it, some 'Lumpen' with irregular mandates) through the action committee without consulting the Congress at large. This offended Bernard-Lazare's anarchist soul.

Herzl's replies to all these objections were unsatisfactory. Moreover, certain of his remarks were in bad taste and this could not have helped matters. The stage was set for the rupture. Herzl tried hard to prevent it. He appealed in a long and moving letter.

> . . .je ne me crois pas du tout l'homme définitif qui établira le nouvel état juif. Je suis un des instruments que l'on laissera après s'en être servi. Est-il déjà le temps de se débarrasser de moi? J'en doute. On a encore besoin de mon travail et peut-être même de mes erreurs qui ne retomberont certes pas sur le peuple, puisqu'il n'en est pas responsable. Je suis le possibiliste dans le sionisme. Voilà pourquoi j'ai réussi jusqu'à ce jour de faire d'un rêve, d'une chimère, un mouvement pris au sérieux par des hommes d'état sérieux.[44]

Bernard-Lazare was unmoved. It is precisely the 'possibiliste' and the 'politique des hommes d'état' that he most feared. In March 1899, he submitted his official resignation from the action committee and the following month he published the vehement text in *Le Flambeau*. Below I quote a passage from the angry letter (4 February 1899) sent to Herzl just before the official announce-

ment of his resignation. It expresses well the ideological differences
which separated two passionate Jews whose Jewish journey had
been very similar. It also expresses Bernard-Lazare's respect for
Herzl and his whole conception of respect and friendship.

Vous êtes des bourgeois de pensée, des bourgeois de
sentiments, des bourgeois d'idées, des bourgeois de conception sociale. Etant tels vous voulez guider un peuple,
notre peuple, qui est un peuple de pauvres, de malheureux,
de prolétaires. Vous ne pouvez le faire qu'autoritairement
en voulant les conduire vers ce que vous croyez être le bien
pour eux. Vous agissez alors en dehors d'eux, au-dessus
d'eux: vous voulez faire marcher un troupeau. Avant de
créer un peuple, vous instituez un gouvernement agissant
financièrement et diplomatiquement et ainsi, comme tous les
gouvernements, vous êtes à la merci de vos échecs financiers
ou diplomatiques. Comme tous les gouvernements vous
voulez farder la vérité, être le gouvernement d'un peuple
qui ait l'air propre et le summum du devoir devient pour
vous de 'ne pas étaler les hontes nationales'. Or, je suis moi
pour qu'on les étale, pour qu'on voie le pauvre Job sur son
fumier, raclant ses ulcères avec un tesson de bouteille. Nous
mourrons de cacher les hontes, de les ensevelir dans des caves
profondes, au lieu de les porter à l'air pur, pour que le
grand soleil les purifie ou les cautérise. Notre peuple est dans
la boue la plus abjecte: il faut retrousser nos manches et
aller le chercher là où il geint, là où il gémit, là où il souffre.
Il faut recréer notre nation, voilà pour moi l'oeuvre solide,
l'oeuvre forte et surtout l'oeuvre première. Il faut l'éduquer,
lui montrer ce qu'il est, le grandir à ses propres yeux, pour
le grandir aux yeux des autres, élever son coeur et son
esprit. . . Votre faute c'est d'avoir voulu faire d'une banque
le moteur de votre oeuvre, une banque n'est jamais, ne sera
jamais un instrument de relèvement national, et quelle ironie
de faire d'une banque le fondateur de la nation juive!. . .
Laissez-moi, mon cher Herzl, vous dire une chose, du plus
profond de mon coeur. Quels que soient les opinions, les
principes, les idées qui nous séparent, rien ne fera que je n'ai
pour vous la plus vive amitié, la plus grande admiration affec-
tueuse. Vous avez su remuer les profondeurs d'Israël, vous
lui avez apporté votre amour et votre vie, vous l'avez réveillé;

> aucun juif digne de ce nom ne devra oublier cela, ni oublier
> de vous en témoigner sa reconnaissance. Mais dit l'adage:
> *Amicus Plato, sed magis amica veritas.* Il n'eût été digne ni
> de vous, ni de moi de laisser subsister dans nos rapports une
> équivoque quelconque. C'est la condition d'amitié comme la
> nôtre de ne se rien céler de leurs dissentiments, idéologiques,
> politiques ou sociaux. Nous aurons encore souvent l'occasion
> de discuter, d'exposer des vues contraires, du moins le
> ferons-nous en fidèles et loyaux amis se serrant cordialement
> le main avant la dispute comme après.[45]

Relations did remain more or less cordial until the violent article, 'Le Congrès sioniste et le Sultan', published in *Pro-Armenia* (January 1902). In it Bernard-Lazare gave vent to all his hitherto suppressed anger against Herzl's diplomacy.

> Le prophète moderne réunit des parlements et fait de la
> diplomatie d'opérette... Hier ils [the Zionist leaders] ont
> mis les Juifs aux pieds de l'Empereur Guillaume; ils les
> agenouillent aujourd'hui devant le Sultan; demain ils les
> coucheront à plat ventre devant le Tzar, et nous aurons le
> grand et beau spectacle d'esclaves léchant le fouet du maître.

Herzl was shocked by this 'vulgar, nasty article'. Apart from a handsome gesture, what interest could he (Bernard-Lazare) have in defending the Armenians, he asked.[46] 'Nasty' it may have been but it was no empty gesture. Bernard-Lazare had not only always defended the Armenians, but the Sultan's solution to the problem of minorities was a veritable nightmare to him: systematic extermination. How Bernard-Lazare, in a Zionist context, would have dealt with the Sultan is not clear. The programme he had intended to put before the Zionist congress of 1900 included reluctant 'negotiations with the Sultan'. Those unspecified negotiations would not have stopped him, we may be sure, from denouncing the crime of genocide which European governments had witnessed without protest in the superior interest of politics and armed peace. He was a prominent member of the Pro-Armenia Congress held in July 1902 in Brussels. Together with Jaurès, de Pressensé and his friend Quillard, the leading light behind the whole movement, he was elected as French delegate to the 'commission d'études' one of whose tasks was to coordinate propaganda and engage the attention of governments.

An independent Zionist

Bernard-Lazare continued to work for Zionism in his own way. For a little while he did so even at congress level, perhaps with the intention of saving the movement from its leaders, as the anarchists had tried to do with Socialist congresses. In 1899 Rennes naturally took precedence but the following year he fully intended to attend the London congress and was only prevented from doing so by the sudden illness of his wife. Lest the delegates should think that the man they had so much acclaimed had deserted them, he explained his position in an open letter to Nordau (*Die Welt*, 31 August 1900). At the same time he asked Nahum Slustsch to present to the congress on his behalf the following proposals:

(1) Attention should be given to the national education of the young.
(2) The creation of workers' associations wherever possible and in all trades.
(3) An invitation to the 'Zionist party' and to the Actions Committee to stop living in the clouds. A useful beginning would be to take the initiative in the important matter of oppressed Rumanian Jewry. If the committee failed to do so, it would be as blameworthy and as useless as the Alliance Israëlite Universelle.[47]

Among his unpublished papers[48] is a comprehensive and radical programme for democratising the constitution and work of the Congress. To Bernard-Lazare it was a matter of some importance, for he considered the Congress to be representative of the Jewish nation as at present constituted. Furthermore, the present *Parliament* in exile could be thought of as preparatory to government when the nation was free in a free country. Hence democratic practices had to be instituted here and now, and to this end he proposed an immediate decentralisation of 'government' by the setting up of seven committees democratically elected by the Congress. The work of these committees, each with its specific tasks, (education, colonisation, finance, economics, propaganda, legal affairs), would be coordinated by a central actions committee having its own members as well as representatives of the other six bodies. This body would be the spokesman in the outside world. A monthly bulletin was to be created in which the work and studies of the various committees would be published in Hebrew, English, German, French, Russian and 'jargon' (i.e. Yiddish) so that the fullest communication was established between different committees and between the latter and the electorate. No one can say that Bernard-Lazare did not take Zionist matters seriously or that the anarchist conception of democracy is totally divorced from reality. A distinction was made between political Zionism and diplomatic Zionism. The latter was rejected. Were it to succeed at that time, he noted, we might have a land but no nation to work it and make it prosper. By political Zionism he understood the right of Jewry to nationhood and the defence of those who were at that time oppressed on the principle of nationality. This, he observed, is something the Alliance Israelite Universelle had never done. Bernard-Lazare did not like the term 'Israelite', though he appreciated the idea of an 'Alliance', and preferred it to 'Congress'. He proposed the creation of an *Alliance juive universelle.*

Such were the suggestions he intended to put before the 1900 congress. As far as can be established he did not attend the following two congresses. Instead, he joined the practical Zionists and participated actively in the work of the Paris Central Committee which had been created in March 1899 with the aim of coordinating the work of the I.C.A., the non-Herzlian Choveve Zion groups and other organisations. Bernard-Lazare attended the first meeting of the Central Committee and together with Emile Meyerson enthusiastically supported the 'Machnayim project' dear to the heart of his friend Saul Landau. This concerned the foundation of an agricultural settlement in Galilee for Galician Jews, run on Socialist lines. He soon became a permanent member of the Central Committee as representative of the English *Choveve Zion* in Paris. In this capacity he attended meetings, notably the Frankfurt meeting of March 1900, where he presented a proposal for the setting up of a commission to investigate education in Palestine. As always, education was dear to his heart. It was essential to educate the colonists who would form the nucleus of the future community. He also proposed the setting up of a fund for the development of industry and colonisation projects.[49] It was probably on behalf of this organisation that he travelled widely in Galicia and Rumania between 1900 and 1902 reporting on the situation of Jewry.

It needed Bernard-Lazare, Salomon Reinach later remarked,[50] to draw the attention of the world to what was happening in Rumania, though documentation on the subject was not lacking and the I.C.A. had in fact already compiled its own report. But, and this is the point, these reports were largely circulated internally within Jewish organisations. The latter, moreover, being in the main concerned with emigration and the settlement of immigrants, had their hands tied by the Rumanian government's latest decision to ban emigration because it drew too much attention to the contravention of successive international treaties guaranteeing the rights of Rumanian Jewry to full citizenship. Bernard-Lazare's approach and aim were entirely different and in the event most successful, at least in drawing the world's attention to a nightmare of legalised oppression. Following a first visit to Rumania in June 1900, three articles appeared in *L'Aurore*: 'Roumains et Juifs' (4 July 1900), 'La Roumanie et les Juifs' (20 July) and 'Emigration Juive de la Roumanie' (9 August). In February 1902 an augmented version in brochure-form complete with bibliography came out in Péguy's *Cahiers de la Quinzaine* (*Les Juifs en Roumanie*). A long extract also appeared in the London *Contemporary Review* (February 1903). It was widely reviewed in the press, translated into German, Rumanian and English and apparently made an immense impact on American public opinion. The Rumanian government unwittingly contributed to the publicity by its reaction to Bernard-Lazare's second and eventful visit in May 1902.

Although Bernard-Lazare had asked rabbi Niemirower of Jassy not to announce his visit lest it should lead to demonstrations and counter-demonstrations, his arrival was celebrated by the Jewish community like that of a saviour. Grateful crowds lined the streets in which he passed, cheering him wherever he went. After five days' of this enthusiastic reception the shouts of 'long live Lazare' reached the ears of the Prime Minister and antisemitic counter-demonstrations followed – patently government-inspired, though the government sought to deny it. The press accused him of being a provocateur and of insulting Rumania; uniformed police distributed anti-Jewish literature in the streets; under the presidency of an official from the Ministry of Education a protest meeting was held at the end of which crowds of students went to demonstrate outside Bernard-Lazare's hotel. In view of all these 'disturbances', the Rumanian government asked the French Ambassador to urge departure on Bernard-Lazare, and when this failed they used blackmail: his visit could lead to 'disturbances' in the Jewish quarters. Bernard-Lazare cut short his visit, afraid that the Jews might suffer. Back in France, however, he used the pages of the *Aurore* to tell the story, and in an open letter called upon the French foreign minister to investigate the treatment afforded by the Rumanian government to a French citizen. One of the most moving testimonies to what Bernard-Lazare had come to mean to Rumanian Jews is an appeal to him following the destruction of 80 houses in the Jewish quarter. The appeal was simply addressed to 'Bernard-Lazare, publiciste, Paris'.[51] It reached him, somebody at the Paris Post Office having sent it on to *L'Aurore*.

Here is a brief summary of his detailed analysis of the legalised oppression practised by the Rumanian government under the eyes of the civilised world.

On gaining her independence in 1878, Rumania, with a long history of antisemitic persecution, undertook by the treaty of Berlin (1878) to give full civil and political rights to all citizens irrespective of religion. However, by declaring all Jews foreigners – irrespective of origin, place of birth, continuous residence, etc. – and by passing discriminatory legislation against foreigners, the government could get round the treaty. And the beauty of it all was that Jews were foreigners but without enjoying the protection of any country. By a series of laws promulgated over the previous twenty years Jews were driven into big urban centres, systematically turned out of all professions: the liberal professions, trading and manufacturing, working in cigarette factories (according to a law of 1879 all employees had to be Rumanian), on the railways and in other public employment. Thus in 1899 all Jewish workmen were dismissed from the railways on the order of the Minister of Public Works. The masses had to fall back on street-hawking. But there was a law passed in 1884 prohibiting itinerant trading in urban districts. Jews were not allowed to go to the rural districts. This made homeless beggars of 20,000 itinerant traders who promptly fell under the law against vagabonds. By another law (1884) Jews were denied, as foreigners, the right of petition; they were liable to expulsion if found to be disturbing the public peace. In 1897 they were forbidden to hold meetings. Thus, concludes Bernard-Lazare, after a factual and poignant exposition of successive legislation and its effects, a community of 269,000 had been driven to despair, reduced to unspeakable misery, by the laws of the land. And the democratic countries of the West tolerated such barbarity.

From a Zionist point of view, the Rumanian journey and report are interesting. In a sense they conform perfectly to the 'emancipation' discussed in 'Le Nationalisme et L'Emancipation Juive'. Indeed Rumania illustrated the urgency of battling for civil rights and liberties. But emancipation was intended only as a first step; 'let us go and work our own land' was the next step. This second stage was not clearly indicated here. Instead it was suggested that the solution to the Rumanian Jewish Question lay with the fanatically antisemitic Rumanian peasants and workers who must be made to see that their oppression would not end even when all the Jews had been driven out. It fell on the Jew to emancipate himself and at the same time to emancipate the Christian proletariat and peasantry from the ruling class which exploited them all. Georges Delahache (one of Péguy's collaborators) recalled two interesting remarks made to him by Bernard-Lazare shortly before his death: 'le Juif est l'homme qui depuis des siècles sait lire'. He thus has a duty. And, à propos the plight of Russian Jewry: 'Il n'y aura sans doute de guérison que dans la guérison générale: les juifs ne seront libres que quand les pays sont libres'.[52]

Had Bernard-Lazare abandoned the Zionist solution to the Jewish Question and returned to earlier ideas? This would seem to be the case.[53] He had drunk deeply at the anarchist cup. According to anarchist philosophy, freedom in isolation is difficult if not impossible. One is not free in a desert, Bakunin had observed many years earlier. And the same master had declared that the liberty of other nations was necessary to his personal freedom, for just as the individual can only develop freely within a free society, so a nation cannot be really free if it is surrounded by tyrannies. Bernard-Lazare never stopped meditating on the anarchist paradox of dependent freedoms, and the very last work he planned, *La Grenade*, was to have dealt with precisely that subject.

As far as Zionism is concerned, what worried his a-nationalist mind was the 'nationalisme qui a pour base le sol'. In *Le Fumier de Job* he had intended to confront in discussion a cosmopolitan Jew with a nationalist Jew.[54] For the first, Zionism is largely a reaction dictated by antisemitism. The Jew is not a peasant, he does not work the land, says the antisemite. We must become peasants, replies the Zionist. To the cosmopolitan Jewish intellectual, this is a step backward to the myth of the soil. To the Zionist it is part and parcel of becoming a normal people again. To the cosmopolitan the whole idea of having 'une patrie' is an answer to the antisemitic objection that the Jew cannot conceive of such a thing. What better reply than to go out into the desert and amid the rocks and sands create a miserable little country which will be 'la patrie'. To which the nationalist replies: 'patrie' for us means freedom and dignity. The cosmopolitan makes up in humanitarian sentiments and attachment to universal values what he lacks in pioneering spirit and national pride. I am a citizen of the world, a son of humanity; love of country, like love of self, is too narrow and inward-turning. My country is justice. And the young nationalist pioneer is proud of his elder and nobler brother but without being deflected from his own task of rebuilding Zion for his people.

The fragmentary state of this uncompleted dialogue does not permit us to draw any definite conclusions. Perhaps there could be no conclusion other than that the young idealist departs and the older idealist stays behind, that each respects the decision of the other, and that each makes his choice in the full knowledge of what is involved. One always regrets leaving Egypt, observes the Zionist, the country where one grew up and suffered pain. 'On pleure le pays de misère avant de conquérir la terre de joie.' Having made justice in the world his land of joy, the cosmopolitan stays in his Egypt fully aware of the tensions to which life in the Diaspora exposes the sensitised Jew, a man, as Péguy said, whose skin bears the wounds and scars of centuries.

What is historically important about this uncompleted dialogue which in one form or another still goes on, is simply that it took place. This in itself marks an epoch in Jewish history and in the personal history of Bernard-Lazare. Who could have predicted seven years earlier that a thoroughly assimilated Jew, proud of his deep French roots, steeped in Western culture, indifferent to his religion, one-time antisemite to boot, who would have thought that a man with such a history would be meditating on the rebirth of an ancient nation in the land of the Bible; that he would send his son – metaphorically speaking – to rebuild Zion? An extraordinary return to roots and one which involved some painful uprooting.

LAST BATTLES AND LAST WORKS

In June 1902, Bernard-Lazare was relating his Rumanian journey in *L'Aurore*. The following month he was at the Pro-Armenia Congress in Brussels. In August, in Péguy's *Cahiers de la Quinzaine*, he fought his last battle (*La loi et les Congrégations*) and it was on behalf of the Church and Catholic schools.

This libertarian act, coming from a man known for his hostile attitude towards the Church, astonished people on both sides. The Catholic Léon Chaîne (one of the rare dreyfusards) was surprised at this most unexpected support from 'un adversaire aussi déterminé que loyal de l'Eglise et des congrégations'.[1] The socialist Gustave Téry ridiculed the new liberals with short memories.[2] No less an authority than Karl Kautsky let it be known that he wished to review the brochure.[3] One can only guess at the reaction of Jaurès, who was severely taken to task for justifying the government's anticlerical policies.

It is possible that in the heat of battle, during the Affair, when many Churchmen did the persecuting, Bernard-Lazare would not have taken the stand he took now. From a purely emotional point of view he could never resist defending the rights of oppressed minorities. And in 1902 the religious teaching orders constituted a persecuted minority. But his response was not merely emotional. He did not care very much for the policy of revenge, especially when not all of the avengers, today so quick to condemn the Church, had exactly distinguished themselves in yesterday's battle for justice. He had not forgotten the reactionary attitude shown by so many prominent Catholics to Republican democracy; but imposing democracy, or reason, by force and through oppression was unacceptable and, in the long term, ineffective. Most important, he saw the anticlerical laws of 1902 as an example of legalised oppression on a par with Rumania's Jewish policy. Whatever the differences between Rumania and France – and there was of course an enormous difference – in *degree* of persecution, the immorality was basically the same, that of legalised oppression committed in the superior interests of the State. In the French context, moreover, the oppressive measures were not even legally and constitutionally arrived at. It was the illegality of the law of 1902, and the dangerous precedent it could set, which most exercised Bernard-Lazare's mind.

Briefly summed up, the legal position, as Bernard-Lazare discusses it, was as follows. According to Waldeck-Rousseau's law of July 1901, the creation of *new* schools by religious teaching orders was prohibited without prior authorisation from the State. Emile Combes, Waldeck-Rousseau's successor, did not think that this law went far enough. But instead of amending it through the proper democratic channels, or presenting to Parliament a new law, Combes *interpreted* the existing law, giving it a retroactive meaning which it patently did not have, and by a simple circular (June 1902) sent to all *Prefets* the Minister's *interpretation* became law. What horrifyingly arbitrary government this could lead to, exclaims Bernard-Lazare, if laws depend on ministerial moods and interpretations. Henceforth, the State, already immensely powerful, will not even have to take the trouble of submitting proposed legislation to parliamentary discussion. It will suffice for one man and his Cabinet to interpret existing laws for a certain group of people to be deprived of their rights from one day to the next. Today it is Catholics. In 1894 it was anarchists, who were hounded as members of 'une association de malfaiteurs'.

It may seem strange that the anarchist should be so concerned with the proper application of the law. Jaurès indeed called those who objected to Combes' manoeuvres 'des légistes ahuris', an expression to which Bernard-Lazare strongly objected. He always welcomed laws protecting the individual against the State. And nothing was more dangerous to individual liberty than arbitrary interpretations of the law by those in power.

He was hardly likely to be in sympathy with the aim behind the Combes *coup* whatever his own feeling towards the Church. Enforced secularisation, State monopoly of education, did not recommend itself to him, any more than Church monopoly of education. In a well-known expression of the time, he preferred 'la liberté de l'enseignement' to 'l'enseignement de la liberté' distributed by the State. 'Nous nous refuserons aussi bien à accepter les dogmes formulés par l'Etat enseignant que les dogmes formulés par l'Eglise. Nous n'avons pas plus confiance en l'Université qu'en la Congrégation.'[4]

What was curious to him was the reversal of roles which 'Combism' produced. Liberal opinion, which yesterday had fought for justice and the rights of the individual, today accepted and generally welcomed a conspicuous case of 'étatism', while those who yesterday shouted 'death to the Jews' were today the most ardent defenders of liberty. Jaurès' attitude in particular distressed Bernard-Lazare, for he went as far as justifying persecution of the Church as a just punishment for the crime against truth and humanity she had committed, particularly in the Affair, 'par sa complicité avec la sottise la plus épaisse et la plus bestiale'. Bernard-Lazare did not care much for this retributive justice. 'Que les crimes politiques, sociaux ou moraux, reçoivent un châtiment, c'est là le dogme judéo-chrétien des récompenses et des peines. Qu'il soit formulé par un des nôtres ou par l'Eglise, sa valeur n'est pas plus grande, et nous ne devons pas davantage l'accepter.'[5] Moreover, he insists on recalling that for a long time the whole of Parliament was antidreyfusard. If punishment were to be meted out, where would the anticlerical radicals stand? With a few notable exceptions they had not played a brilliant role. And what about the Socialists? Were there not some among them who had used antisemitism as 'une entrée en révolution' before becoming dreyfusards at the eleventh hour? Bernard-Lazare is too grateful to Jaurès to remind him that he too was a latecomer. But he makes a point of mentioning Millerand's late adhesion to the dreyfusard cause. Millerand, too, had been a minister in an allegedly dreyfusard government which did irreparable harm to the Affair by stifling it with the disgraceful amnesty. Some of the most bitter comments were addressed to today's defenders of liberty who only a little while ago had applauded the frightful indignities to which Algerian Jewry had been subjected by Drumont's bands. Bernard-Lazare wanted it to be clearly understood that if today he found himself on the same side as these weird lovers of liberty, they were not fighting the same battle. For they were fighting for the privileges of the Church as an institution, and an anti-Republican institution; while he was fighting for the *rights* of the Church, for the rights of those who wish to be part of it and who must be free to do so.

'On ne peut pas embêter les gens parce qu'ils veulent faire leurs prières.'

Léon Chaîne wrote of *La loi et les Congrégations* that it was 'empreinte d'une grande hauteur de vues et écrite avec le souci évident de rester impartial; l'auteur n'a pas fait oeuvre de sympathie; il a cherché à faire oeuvre de justice'.[6] This is correct, but we must add that the 'oeuvre de justice' is all the more admirable since Bernard-Lazare was convinced that antisemitism had Catholic roots and that it was perpetuated through education. It is in this context that Péguy's praise of the work as 'un testament mystique' and of its author as an incomparable libertarian takes on its full meaning. 'Les autorités de tout ordre, politiques, intellectuelles, *mentales* même ne pesaient pas une once. . .devant un mouvement de la conscience propre. Il avait la liberté dans la peau, dans la moëlle, dans les vertèbres.'[7]

Rumanian Jews, Christian Armenians, French Catholics, they were all oppressed minorities on whose behalf he fought his last battles. Few people were to be found on all three battlefields. Péguy was one, and perhaps this is why he and his 'grand ami' came to understand each other so well. No doubt Bernard-Lazare did not exactly expect *La Croix* and Drumont, or even the Comte de Mun, to speak out for Jewish liberties. But he was greatly angered by what happened at the big Pro-Armenian demonstration held at the Château d'Eau in February 1903. The meeting had been called to protest against the Sultan's continued violation of the Berlin Treaty of 1878 which guaranteed the civil and political rights of all citizens. Since Rumania was under a similar obligation according to the same treaty, the president of the meeting, Leroy-Beaulieu, had intended to raise the Rumanian issue but was apparently prevented from doing so by a section of the assembly, among whom were many Catholics, ardent defenders of Christian Armenians against Moslem barbarity, but indifferent, to say the least, to Rumania's treatment of her Jews. Bernard-Lazare, prevented by illness from attending the meeting, wrote an angry open letter of protest.

> La barbarie turque a toujours trouvé en moi un adversaire déterminé, mais je ne voudrais pas qu'elle servît à faire oublier la barbarie chrétienne. . . Si le mouvement phil-arménien doit avoir comme arrière-pensée. . .le triomphe de la Croix – représenté sans doute par le Tsar – sur le

> Croissant, il pourra satisfaire des ambitions, mais non
> l'humanité. Je participe à des mouvements d'humanité et
> non à des croisades.[8]

Not a single speaker at the meeting, the embittered Bernard-Lazare observed, mentioned the fact that Rumania was violating the very rights that the Sultan violated, rights guaranteed by the same treaty. 'La conscience chrétienne est facile quand il ne s'agit que des souffrances juives.'[9]

Péguy never forgot that phrase. One might almost say that he tried to disprove it all his life. Not only were Georges Delahache and Elie Eberlin to continue in the *Cahiers* the work planned by Bernard-Lazare on the oppression of Jewry in Russia;[10] not only did Henri Dagan relate the tragic story of *Les Massacres de Kichinef*[11] (the report appeared two months after Bernard-Lazare's death); but Péguy himself, in *Notre Jeunesse*, brings the Russian 'solution' up-to-date by transcribing stop-press newspaper reports of 1910 on the mass expulsion of Jews from Kiev. What is poignant about these cables is not so much their arid, factual brevity, he comments, but that they go unnoticed nowadays. 'Sous Bernard-Lazare elles ne passaient point inaperçues.' And a little further, commenting on modern French antisemitism, he declares: 'Il ne sera pas dit qu'un chrétien n'aura pas porté témoignage pour eux [les Juifs]. Il ne sera pas dit que je n'aurai pas témoigné pour eux. Comme il ne sera pas dit qu'un chrétien ne témoignera pas pour Bernard-Lazare.'[12]

The aspiration to participate in movements of humanity and his broad vision of humanity brought him into conflict not only with clericals and anticlericals but also with Jews. A correspondent calling himself a Jewish patriot reproached him for devoting his energies to humanity and the world's proletariat when so much remained to be done for the destitute ghetto-masses. Bernard-Lazare took unkindly to this selfish and narrow advice that charity begins at home.

> Croyez-vous que les vieux prophètes ne parlaient que pour
> Juda?... Vous êtes un patriote juif. Rêvez-vous donc
> uniquement pour votre peuple une misérable et égoïste
> vie?... Un peuple ne vit que lorsqu'il travaille pour
> l'humanité. Je ne comprends donc pas vos reproches.[13]

Nothing was more unjust than this reproach, moreover, for

Bernard-Lazare spent much of his time in 1902 on fact-finding missions in these very ghettos. On a postcard sent to his brother Armand from Lemberg (12 May 1902) he lists all the places already visited and those he intends to visit: 'Du matin 7 heures au soir 11 heures, je n'ai pas une minute à moi. . . Je vois beaucoup de choses, beaucoup de gens, je prends beaucoup de notes. Ajoute à cela les chemins de fer et tu comprendras que j'ai peu de temps pour écrire.'[14] Among the places he visited in these sad little towns were the Jewish cemeteries. The story told by the keepers invariably began with the same words: 'In those days there was a persecution of the Jews.' And Bernard-Lazare wept. He had acquired an intense sense of tragedy. Before the Affair, in his symbolist days, his sense of the tragic had been a little literary, a polished gravity. His sympathy for the poor was deeply felt, but he was after all not one of the poor. It was with an all-consuming intensity that he lived through the history of his people, tragically re-enacted, at the close of his life, in the Kishinef massacres of Easter 1903. It would have needed a robust physical constitution to match the intensity of passion.

By the end of 1902, he was exhausted, burnt out. He experienced the first of those incapacitating attacks which were to make the last months of his life an agony of pain. In December 1902 he wrote to Reinach: 'depuis 5 semaines je suis alité, maladie étrange, résultat, dit-on, de surmenage, en tout cas atrocement douloureuse'.[15] A few months previously, in June, he had ordered from a funerary mason a grave for two and a small marble stele.[16] Was this a premonition of death? In the event, Madame Bernard-Lazare, who had been in poor health and whom he had tended between battles and travels, survived her husband by 57 years. She died at the age of 94 in 1960 and was buried in the grave her husband had reserved for both of them eighteen months before his own death in September 1903.

Since no-one knew the cause of his illness, today believed to have been cancer, all sorts of different treatments and dietary regimes were prescribed. Whenever a definite diagnosis was reached, though it in no way lessened the pain, Bernard-Lazare was delighted: once the cause was known, there must surely be a cure for his 'voluminous liver' and his 'fantastic intestines'. Hopefully he went on another diet and dreamt of returning to Paris, to life and to work, whence his physician extraordinary, his brother Armand, had banished him, ordering a strict rest cure

of *chaise longue* and fresh air in the south of France. Restless and
bored, Bernard-Lazare spent some three months, from February
to April 1903, moving from hotel to hotel: from Grasse, where
the *chic* hotel and liveried waiters made life impossible, to a small
hotel in Nice where he vegetated like 'une bête', to Marseilles and
finally home to Nîmes en route for Paris. In his letters to Armand,
to Meyerson and to Péguy he was constantly speaking of coming
back to the capital, describing his worsening physical condition
in almost humorous terms and drawing supreme hope from the
fact that his mental energies were unimpaired, as if a lucid mind
was bound to triumph over a weakening body. 'Rien ne faiblit que
le corps et tout finira par bien aller. Nous avons trop de choses à
faire.'[17] Péguy, probably against doctors' orders, kept him informed of all that was going on, and together they planned their
future campaigns. Once back in Paris he was too ill to lead any
campaigns. Creating a new newspaper, which had been his
dream, and for which purpose he had taken a large apartment
in the Rue de Florence, was out of the question. He lived in this
opulent residence like a pauper, Péguy recalls, worrying about
how to pay the rent. The financial situation was a constant source
of worry, and it is likely that without the support of his family
and that of Zadoc-Kahn, the chief rabbi, he could not have
managed. Having lost long ago any sort of regular income from
his pen, a collection of precious books was his only wealth.

Péguy and Quillard were among the faithful visitors to 7 rue de
Florence, and both have left moving accounts of the extraordinary
serenity of the dying man. He planned his work as if he had a
lifetime before him, comforted the living, took an interest in
everything that was going on, from the opening of the métro
station in 'his district' to the future of Péguy's *Cahiers de la
Quinzaine*, a review after his own heart, for which he tried to
secure support and make propaganda, and where 'le prophète
d'Israel', when he was well enough to go out, had a place of
honour.

It was also, sadly, the time when he had sufficient leisure to
think about his original ambitions as a writer.

Last works: Jesus and Job

Throughout his busy life of public action, Bernard-Lazare the
writer never ceased planning future works: plays, novels, *contes
philosophiques*, historical and philosophical works. He sketched

outlines, did the necessary research, jotted down ideas. At times these mentally conceived or half-written books were hopefully announced as being 'sous presse'. For the *Fumier de Job* Péguy even quoted the proposed booksellers' price of 3 francs 50! Alas, it was not yet completely written. During his illness, Bernard-Lazare had time to write and meditate, but rarely the strength to do so with the necessary concentration and continuity. However, he continued to plan and write: 'Jour par jour, il inscrivait sur des pages éparses, au gré des heures les notes qui trouveraient place dans ses livres déjà conçus.'[18] These *pages éparses* have survived, and amount to a considerable body of unpublished work in various states of completion.[19] The themes are in the main – though not exclusively – Jewish and two stand out: *Jesus* and *Job*.

The figure of Jesus, 'fleur de la conscience juive', haunted his thoughts for many years. Even during the Affair, especially then perhaps, he was meditating on 'his Jesus'. The material for the book on which he started work towards the end of 1898[20] is extensive but very fragmentary and scattered: masses and masses of small *fiches* in no apparent order. Some of these *fiches* carry no more than a sentence, expression of an idea to be developed later, or an instruction to himself to examine this or that aspect. Others contain more substantial notes and reflections. It is difficult in the circumstances to be certain about the form the work would have taken or indeed what exactly his conception was. Some general ideas and intentions, however, emerge quite clearly.[21]

Broadly speaking, one could say that his view of Jesus (he always called him Jesus; Christ is the Christianised Jesus) is not an uncommon Jewish view, at least today. At the time it was unusual for a Jew to be interested in Jesus, still less insist on claiming him for Judaism; almost as unusual as for a Catholic in those days to say without embarrassment that Christ was a Jew. Jesus, he writes, did not consider himself to be the Messiah or the Son of God, but was subsequently transformed into both by the disciples, who had a long tradition and a whole corpus of symbols, parables and figurative language to draw upon to effect the transformation, this being dictated by their own needs and those of the times in which the Gospels were written. He places Jesus firmly in the prophetic tradition, not only from a social point of view but also in the aspiration towards universality and the conception of God as Love, in contrast to an earlier Yahwehism

when the contract between God and man had been one of obedience in return for divine protection against enemies. In his own days of tension, Jesus was one among many rebels, disturbing the peace of the Sadducees and all the more dangerous since the people listened to the rebel and he collected a large following. Jesus was a practising Jew who knew the law well, and in his disputes with the doctors proved himself a reforming and revolutionary Jew, like others. Disputations and different interpretations were not uncommon and existed even within sects (witness the Pharisees whose two leading teachers Hillel and Shammai did not see eye to eye) but these differences in doctrinal interpretation or in attitude towards day-to-day living did not lead to ruptures or schisms.

The diversity of sects within Judaism at the time is important to his argument (as well as appealing to his anarchism). Moreover, he suggests that these sects were not closed groups but more like 'des confrèries religieuses' and that adherents moved with relative freedom from one to the other. This was particularly the case with the Pharisees and the Essenes. As a result, a fair amount of intermingling and crossfertilisation of ideas took place. Jesus may well be an example of this.

He sees Jesus, though not the disciples, primarily as a 'Hilleliste pharisee'. Hillel, the gentle, patient and humble teacher, looms large in Bernard-Lazare's notes. Hillel's teaching, summed up in the golden ethical rule 'do not do unto others that which is hateful unto thee', is considered a key influence behind Jesus' teaching. The Essenes are another sect to which a lot of attention is devoted and to its teaching. From the numerous references it looks as if Bernard-Lazare was familiar or at least intended to acquaint himself with everything that was then known about this community. As for Jesus, he concludes that it is impossible to know whether he was or was not an Essene. This does not greatly matter to him. What he does stress is the presence at the time of diverse influences to which enquiring, rebellious young minds were exposed and on which they could draw. For the Christian, he observes, the question of Christ's connections with the Essenes is of little importance, for what matters to him is what the Gospel-writers, and particularly Paul, have to say about Christ.

The problem was how to disentangle Jesus and his teachings from their presentation in the Gospels, written considerably later when different forces and influences were at work. In an amusing

passage he imagines Jesus' return to earth and his surprise on reading the Gospels.

> Jamais je n'ai dit cela, s'écrie-t-il. Qui est ce Luc, ce Marc, ce Jean? J'ai connu un jour ce Mathieu. Il n'était pas capable d'écrire cela... Quant à Paul, qui est-ce donc ce mauvais juif?... Jésus ne se plaît que parmi les Juifs. Il va à la synagogue. Rencontre un antisémite. Il le prend pour un prophète. Il ne comprend rien à la façon dont on interprète les paroles de l'Evangile.

There have been two major distortions of Jesus, it is suggested. One is due to the Jewish Gospel-writers; the other to Christian interpretation of the Gospels. It seems that he intended to disentangle Jesus and his teachings from their presentation in the Gospels by rediscovering the Jewish sources from which Jesus derived his maxims and parables; 'reconstituer avec les psaumes et les prophètes un agenda du Messie'. The second stage would have been to show that the Gospels (the writings of Saint Paul presented an altogether different problem) do not constitute a New Testament, a new religion, but a transformation into real events of what in Jewish writing had been symbols, parables and figurative speech. It was a concretisation, a need for incarnation so to speak, on the part of Jews writing in a different age and under different influences. With the help of a variety of Jewish sources, from the Old Testament and the psalms to the Midrashim, the Talmudic Haggadah, the Song of Songs and the Apocrypha, Bernard-Lazare intended to demonstrate that there were precedents and parallels for the essential and allegedly new concepts found in the Gospels, from baptism, miracle-workers, the concept of the Son of God, resurrection, to what is traditionally considered to be a very un-Jewish concept, the Immaculate Conception. The Virgin Mary may have had her symbolic predecessors in the Song of Songs and the Apocrypha. The suggestion is, if we have followed his line of thought correctly, that the disciples used a long tradition of symbols, metaphors and parables to transform their beloved master into *the* Messiah, as distinct from the other messianic claimants of whom there were many at this troubled period in Jewish history. 'On a transformé les paraboles en évènements réels.' Symbolism, one might say, at its most creative.

There remained the problem, the immense problem, of Jesus'

trial and crucifixion as they are narrated in the Gospels. It is clear from Bernard-Lazare's notes that he did not think that the different accounts added up to a plausible historical picture or a coherent theology. On the other hand, he was struck by the constant attempt to absolve Rome from all guilt. Were the Gospel writers trying to please Rome at the expense of the Jews? It is an interesting line of speculation; unfortunately there is no indication how he might have pursued it or what conclusion he would have reached.

The unasked question behind the projected work is one that had always intrigued him: when, how and why did the separation come between Jews and the followers of Jesus? Given the diversity of sects, the relative freedom of doctrinal interpretation, the familiarity with claimants to Messiahship, given too Jesus' large following among the people, was the schism inevitable? Saint Paul, whom he sees as the real founder of Christianity, bears a heavy responsibility. He even wonders whether Paul was Jewish. Through him Christianity adopted esoteric, mystical doctrines which, however meaningful to the non-Jewish world, were alien to Judaism and indeed, at the beginning, to Jesus's followers in the Church of Jerusalem. It is not Jesus' teachings, then, but Pauline theology which led to the rupture. Moreover, whereas Bernard-Lazare saw in Jesus a prophetic 'agitator' in the purest Jewish tradition, a 'blasphemer' who would naturally incur the displeasure of the establishment, he regarded Saint Paul's Christ as a retrogressive step in relation to the rational and human values found in both Jewish and pagan, notably Greek, traditions. The following lines, taken from the *Fumier de Job*, best sum up Bernard-Lazare's thoughts on the relation between Jesus and the Jews and the significance of Jesus in Jewish history:

> Le peuple juif n'a pas crucifié Jésus... Il l'accompagna en
> pleurant au pied de la croix... Mais le peuple juif qui avait
> aimé et chéri le vagabond révolutionnaire refusa de recon-
> naître le Dieu qu'Hellènes et Romains voulaient lui
> imposer... Dans Jésus a été incarné le rêve des Psalmistes...
> Jésus est la fleur suprême de l'esprit juif, l'émanation
> la plus pure de la conscience d'Israel. Je parle de Jésus
> évangélique, de celui qui n'est pas chrétien... Tu étais un
> homme admirable; on t'a avili; on a fait de toi un Dieu.[22]

Bernard-Lazare did not hold out much hope at the end of his

life for Jewish–Christian dialogue; but in the improbable event that this happened, both Jews and Christians, he thought, would need to rediscover Jesus.

Le Fumier de Job

Of all the unpublished works, these beautifully written philosophical dialogues on Judaism were nearest to being ready for publication and dearest to Bernard-Lazare's heart. Alas, they never reached the stage of being 'sous presse', as one announcement ran, and what we are left with today are masses of *fiches* and notes (some numbered), together with brief indications of the general structure and the themes to be treated. We must be grateful to the writer's family for having resuscitated from this unwieldy mass of manuscripts a more or less coherent version which, as far as I can see, is faithful to the spirit and intention of the work as conceived by Bernard-Lazare. But it must be pointed out that it is a reduced and, on certain points, severely edited version. The following discussion is based on both published and unpublished material, as well as on notes which develop the same themes as are found in *Le Fumier de Job*.[23]

What is *Le Fumier de Job*? It is impossible to define it in one word, for round the central image of Job, symbol of the Jewish people, depicted 'sur son fumier, raclant ses ulcères, se plaisant dans ses plaies', a variety of forms (autobiography, history, philosophical dialogues, religious meditations, polemic) moods and tones (from the grave, lyrical and sadly meditative to the vehement and mordant) all flow into each other, with the scene rapidly shifting from one place to another and from present to past. Perhaps it can best be described as a tapestry with a diversity of themes and patterns, which derives its unity from the basic conception of a journey through history undertaken by a Jew in search of his identity.

The story begins, like Zangwill's *Chad Gadja*, one passover evening. Shouts outside of 'Death to the Jews' interrupt the traditional reading from the Haggadah, and as past and present become so unexpectedly fused, a shiver passes over the assembled children of the Haggadah. They are a very mixed group by chance brought together by the master of the house: a rationalist philosopher who hates Jews, a sentimental Jew who weeps over Israel's suffering, a cosmopolitan humanist for whom Judaism is a good point of departure, a proud Jew, an old man, a beggar, a worker, a Polish ghetto Jew who remembers having heard it all before. They all have different reactions, tell their different stories, argue and discuss; and through them the reader is meant to catch a glimpse of the different facets of Judaism. This at least was the intention, as revealed by the 'stage directions'. The only story Bernard-Lazare had time to tell, and that incompletely, was his own; that of the philosopher who despised the Jews and who became a proud Jew.

It is the only piece of writing in which Bernard-Lazare examines his early anti-judaism, indirectly through the person of the philosopher, and it is done with great honesty but without apologies. The passover evening is the first stage of a long journey through time and space in order to discover why he is hated by his fellow-men, who he is, and how he can put together his shattered personality.

Within this autobiographical framework, familiar themes are treated afresh, notably that of *Antisemitism, its history and causes* of which *Le Fumier de Job* is a poetic re-writing. The two main areas of responsibility are evoked in the opening epigraph: 'Voyez Job sur son fumier, raclant ses ulcères, se plaisant dans ses plaies. Voyez le peuple comme vous l'avez fait, Chrétiens, et vous, Princes de Juifs.'

The major responsibility lies with Christianity and the prejudices built up throughout the centuries. The section entitled 'anti-Jewish literature' is confronted with 'Jewish history' to stress the difference between legend and reality, between what the Jew became under persecution and how he lived when he was free or allowed to lead a normal life. It is the contrast between 'la cité juive', the free city, and the enforced ghetto. The latter was the inevitable consequence of Jew-hatred and a disaster for Judaism and Jewry.

Here we come upon Jewish responsibility, with which Bernard-Lazare is more concerned, though in an entirely different way from that of his early *Talmudophobia*. Jewish responsibility lies in the fact that instead of remaining the obstinate, proud and rebellious people that the Church feared and therefore belittled and degraded, the Jews ended by being like the hateful image created of them. Christian princes created the ghettos, and the Jews acquired, or created for themselves, a ghetto mentality.

Bernard-Lazare had no nostalgia for the ghetto, as Zangwill had. He looks back to what at one point he calls 'les temps palestiniens' and he finds little of that spirit in the ghetto masses. The children of the ghetto, sad and tearful, were not the descendants of the people whose language, he claims, had twelve verbs to express states of joy. The famous Jewish irony too he regards as a ghetto acquisition, a defence-mechanism against insults. 'On s'étonne de l'amertume de l'ironie, de la précoce désillusion des jeunes juifs: c'est qu'ils sont vieux, c'est qu'ils ont pour peser sur leur esprit deux mille ans d'insultes.'[24] The ironist's opposite number is the *shlemiel*, the submissive, uncomplaining simpleton; he too was born in the ghetto. Even the unique Jewish *shnorrer*, the impertinent beggar reading the rich lessons in social justice, has become a beggar bowing and scraping before the rich. And where is the fearless Talmudic spirit of free enquiry? Where the poor watercarrier who had his own philosophy and his own views of how to solve the problems of the world? 'Le petit Juif appartient à un peuple qui depuis des siècles sait lire et lit.'[25] The ghetto almost killed this, for the rabbi-priest was allowed to read *for* them by a tired, exhausted people.

The greatest vice acquired by persecuted Jewry is the 'sholem', the desire for peace. 'Se taire, disparaître, se faire petit pour avoir le sholem; qu'on ne parle plus d'Israël; que son nom ne soit plus prononcé;...que rien n'appelle sur lui l'attention...désir d'un peuple dont on a parlé trop et qui est frappé.'[26] It sometimes seems as if Bernard-Lazare loves Judaism but despises the Jews, though now in the manner of a prophet and not an antisemite. The assimilated Jewish bourgeoisie comes in for the usual vehement criticism (at least in the unpublished material, for the editors have been as careful in their selections here as with the author's criticism of Christian antisemitism) but so too does the whole of ghetto Jewry, past and present, and this means a lot of Jews and a great deal of Jewish history. The philosopher trying to discover what it means to be a Jew and why the Jew is hated finds himself in an odd position: he has discovered that antisemitism is part of Christianity and he finds that for many centuries now the Jew has conformed to the image created of him; he no longer embodies the 'Jewish spirit' of old.

Many of the *inédits* are variations on the common theme of 'Jewish spirit'. Its essence can best be summed up as love of life, a sense of justice and a rational spirit seeking to understand the universe in human terms and on a human scale. Bernard-Lazare found this essence expressed in literature, history, religious writings and embodied in certain figures, or perhaps one should say he looked to all these sources for confirmation. Negatively he also tried to define Jewish spirit by contrast with Christian spirit. In the hostility he showed towards the latter, two reactions are probably at work. One, very obvious, is against Christian anti-semitism; the second, more intimate, is a reaction against his former self; for what he now most dislikes about the Christian spirit is precisely the mysticism and sad poetry he once most appreciated. Pagan antiquity, which had always fascinated him, Messianic socialism which he had embraced so ardently, a rediscovered Judaism, all now combine to make him look upon Christianity's preoccupation with sin, evil, death, reward and punishment in the next world, resignation to what happens in this life, as contrary to happiness and progress. Bernard-Lazare's Jew is not burdened by a sense of sin; the only sin he knows is infringe-ment of God's law for which a complete pardon is granted upon sincere repentance. The Adam and Eve story, according to him, is an attempt to explain the difference between man and animal: Adam chose knowledge, always more painful, in preference to the bliss of ignorance, a stupefying sort of beatitude which a kind deity presumably advised in order to save man the pain of being a man. The Fall, in his interpretation, is a difficult ascent to the pain and joy of knowledge and the choice was Adam's; his descendants too have a free choice in the matter. Not believing in justice and happiness beyond this life, Bernard-Lazare's Jew does his best to attain both in this life. What prevents him from be-coming a selfish hedonist is a strong sense of collective good and continuity; and what makes him a perpetual fighter is the con-viction that man does not live in the best possible way in the best possible world which the deity probably intended to create. But Bernard-Lazare's love of Judaism is not merely a reaction. In it there is also the genuine joy of having found ancient roots for ideas which had become dear to him and which are thus given stature and unity. Judaism, or at least his interpretation of it, corresponded to his true temperament; it answered his need for a rational religion, a spiritual humanism open to the mysteries of life which enhance the beauty and the joy of living. It gave him a measure of spiritual peace, to the extent at least to which restless souls like his ever find peace.

But what of the Jews? Has this magnificent spirit of past ages left the Jewish soul? Judaism, on this reckoning, would be like

ancient Greece: a memory, a magnificent culture, but dead, with
the torch not passed on. Bernard-Lazare cannot contemplate such
a situation. The truth is that he loved the ghetto masses, Job on
his dungheap, in spite of what they had become, a little perhaps
because of what they had become; they were tragic witnesses to
what Jewish and Christian princes had done, and they justified
his wrath. The most moving passages of the *Fumier de Job* are
the descriptions of the cemeteries and synagogues of Lemberg,
Cracow and Prague. True, the synagogues were sombre and
bleak; the cemeteries so sad that it was difficult to imagine that
the dead had loved life. Aesthetically, they did not speak to
Bernard-Lazare. Spiritually, they did not embody the Judaism
that fired him. He would have wished even the cemeteries somehow to convey the Jewish love of life. Yet these sombre cemeteries
with their ugly tombstones told heroic stories of resistance and in
the gloomy synagogues the flame was kept burning. In their own
strange way the Chassidim, with their 'mysticisme sensuel effréné',
singing joyous songs far into the night without a care for how
they would eat the next day, represented something of the spirit
of Judaism as he loved it. But the modern Job scratching his
boils needed to be emancipated, in Bernard-Lazare's sense of the
word, in order to become the Job of the old story. 'Abandonner
tout ce que la dépression a fait, se développer, redevenir des
hommes libres et non pas des esclaves... Participer à l'oeuvre
humaine en restant soi-même... Etant Juif, tu as moins de peine
à être un homme. C'est pour cela qu'il faut rester tel.'[27] This is
what he finally called 'Jewish nationalism'.

It is offered in the first place as a solution to fellow-Jews, but
humanity in general could benefit from a little judaisation. *La
France Juive* could be a dream! He wrote to Reinach: 'tant qu'on
n'aura pas judaïsé...c'est à dire rationalisé le monde, on ne pourra
pas discuter, ni établir la justice, la liberté et l'égalité'.[28]

This sort of Messianic nationalism not only requires the Jew
to remain Jewish but to remain within nations; Jewish dispersion
is part of the *mission* but it can only work if the Jew remains
himself.

It is evident from the following passage what Bernard-Lazare
himself thought he had accomplished in *Le Fumier de Job*. The
passage comes from a letter to Emile Meyerson, very probably
written in March 1903, at a time when he was already very ill
and 'resting' in Nice.

> L'oeuvre à laquelle je travaille depuis de si longues années déjà *Le Fumier de Job*, qui sera la fleur de mon esprit, ma chair et mon sang, . . .je crois que quand je l'aurai accomplie nul ne pourra parler du Juif, de ce peuple et de cet esprit, sans venir puiser là. Ce n'est qu'à vous que je peux dire cela, d'autres croiraient à de la vanité, alors que ce n'est que la conscience de ce que je fais. Vous verrez, que de légendes détruites, que de vérités relevées et le moment sera beau où j'aurais tracé la dernière ligne de la dernière page.[29]

Le Fumier de Job certainly represents the essence, 'la fleur' of Bernard-Lazare's meditations – frank, passionate and immensely moving – on what one might call 'servitude et grandeur juives'.

Bernard-Lazare's last struggle was with an irresistible anguish at the thought of death, an anguish which threatened the equanimity he wished to preserve as the only fitting and dignified end to his life, and to the Jewish love of life and fearlessness before death which he had extolled. He liked to quote Spinoza, Quillard tells us, who thought that life should be a meditation on life and not on death. The dying man tried hard to put this into practice and before friends he managed to do so. Like the philosopher Marcus, hero of one of his unfinished plays, he wished to be remembered as he had been in life. 'Je ne veux pas que vous emportiez de moi le souvenir d'une agonie et d'un cadavre ni du répugnant appareil de la mort. C'est vivant que je veux vivre en vous et c'est de ma vie que je veux emplir vos mémoires.'

Left alone, as he felt the eternal darkness closing in, his thoughts, confided to paper, were more of death than of life and they were sombre, anguished thoughts.

> Tous sont pourvus, ils ont leurs revues, leur idéal. Ils savent où ils vont et moi seul je l'ignore. Nul flambeau ne luit pour moi, je suis d'une [. . .] finie, épuisée, dont l'énergie s'est dissoute, et qui n'a plus qu'à mourir. Je suis comme la masse raide, molle, sans courage, la masse lâche et [. . .] comme elle je m'enfonce dans la nuit, la nuit d'irrésolution et du doute dont nulle main ne vient m'arracher.

At times he found consolation in the thought that death is another form of life, with the body becoming part of the earth and the scent of flowers, blooming in endless renewal on the grave, pene-trating to the dead body below and awakening the numbed senses with the mysterious and ineffaceable perfume of life. Such poetic moments of peace were rare, however; they were usually broken by haunting questions unceasingly asked by a lucid mind afraid not of death but of the unknown.

Bernard-Lazare died on 1 September 1903, at the age of 38. The funeral was widely announced in the press with the request not to send flowers or wreaths. In accordance with his wishes, the hearse was the 'corbillard des pauvres'. Coming so soon after the incidents at Zola's funeral (which Bernard-Lazare had attended) the previous year, the police kept a watch all along the route from the rue de Florence to the cemetery at Montparnasse. There were no incidents. Péguy speaks of only a handful of mourners. Police estimates vary between 200 and 400. Among the mourners, a very mixed group of people, were such faithful friends as Péguy, Quillard and Stock; the anarchists Félix Fénéon and Charles Malato; a Socialist deputy, Eugène Fournière; a minister and fellow-Nîmois, Gaston Doumergue; family and, the majority, Jewish immigrants. Conspicuous by his absence was Captain Dreyfus, a fact to which some antidreyfusard papers did not fail to draw attention. According to *Le Siècle* (4 September 1903) Mathieu and his brother Léon were present, although this is not confirmed by the police reports or any other account which I have seen.

There were numerous obituaries, in the French as well as in the foreign press.[30] Dreyfusards and antidreyfusards remembered 'l'entrepreneur de la révision', though with different affection and esteem, needless to say. And yet even Bernard-Lazare's enemies expressed their respect and, in Drumont's case, admiration.[31] Drumont's praise led to a brief polemic with Alfred Naquet.[32] *La Libre Parole* could not resist quoting the unforgettable phrase from *Antisemitism, its history and causes*: 'Le Juif est un être insociable'. At the same time it accorded Bernard-Lazare the honour of being a great Jew. This was too much for Naquet who angrily denied both affirmations. One cannot blame him too much, for Drumont's eulogy is indeed perfidious; but there is one sentence in it which is perhaps the greatest tribute of all the warm tributes paid to Bernard-Lazare. It led Péguy, many years later, to make the seemingly outrageous statement that *La Libre Parole* was the only paper to treat Bernard-Lazare according to his real greatness.[33] Drumont was in fact the only person in 1903 to recall his opponent's lofty conception of what it means to be a Jew. 'Nous ne pouvons que souhaiter une chose', wrote the antisemitic leader, 'c'est que les chrétiens se fassent de la grandeur et des devoirs du nom de chrétien l'idée que Bernard-Lazare se faisait de la grandeur et des devoirs du nom de Juif.'

EPILOGUE

BERNARD-LAZARE IN HIS TIMES AND OURS

What Bernard-Lazare signified to his contemporaries and com-
patriots found its most profound and extreme expression in the
hatred and devotion he inspired in Maurras and Péguy respectively. To both men the Dreyfus Affair remained the crucial
experience of their lives, a moral and political crisis in the history
of modern France to be equalled only, in the case of Maurras, by
the cataclysm of 1940 which put an end to 'le triomphe de cette
anarchie juive' which Bernard-Lazare personified.

It is in this context that the extraordinary passions to which the
Action Française was roused by the inauguration of a modest
monument to Bernard-Lazare in Nîmes in October 1908 take on
their full significance. For some time before and after the inauguration ceremony Maurras and Léon Daudet explained what
'la statue infâme' symbolised: disorder, destruction, the ruin of
France, international barbarity, not forgetting the Prussians to
whom the fair-haired, bearded and stockily-built Bernard-Lazare
bore a striking resemblance. Bernard-Lazare's triumph came in
the Dreyfus Affair when he unleashed anarchy over France; and
it was the victory of that Jewish anarchy which the good citizens
of Nîmes were being asked to honour. Maurras felt sure that this
classical city would not suffer such an indignity and for this
purpose the Nîmois, upholders of order and culture, were reminded that 'la science, fille de la tradition et du génie humain,
peut mettre à la disposition des hommes d'ordre des explosifs qui
n'ont pas été réservés de toute éternité à servir les seuls partis de
révolution'.[1]

Maurras' particular kind of *ideogrammatic* antisemitism, rather
different from Drumont's classic Jew-baiting, is perfectly expressed in these calls to arms, addressed in the first instance to

fellow-royalists but also aimed at wider conservative elements. For Barrès and Maurras 'Jew' is an

> ideogram which serves as a shorthand for certain attitudes and doctrines of which they disapprove. . .they decide who is a Jew. Thus for Maurras ideas of liberty and democracy are 'Jewish'; corrupt finance is 'Jewish'; the rights of man are 'Jewish'. . .all that threatens the France of his imagination is 'Jewish'. 'Jewish' means rotten, foreign, democratic, libertarian, anti-clerical, anti-militarist, Marxist. . . Maurras uses the term in the same way that Goebbels used it. When Maurras cried, 'It is Dreyfus' revenge', on being condemned as a collaborator after the end of Hitler's war, he was making a *doctrinal* statement.[2]

Tactically, the kind of organised, violent, provocative confrontation that the Action Française was planning for 'la journée Bernard-Lazare', a confrontation designed to cause panic and chaos among the population, looks forward to the 1930s. 'On organise véritablement une journée de désordre', was the pertinent description by the Paris Sûreté Générale of Maurras' intention.[3] It is regrettable though perfectly understandable in the circumstances that the *Préfet du Gard*, bombarded with alarming information about 30,000 royalist demonstrators – many of them armed – descending on Nîmes, panicked and filled the city with troops (among them six cavalry squadrons), 500 gendarmes, and scores of police whom the chief of the Paris Sûreté Générale came down in person to deploy. The soldiers had arrived by special trains the previous day and spent the night in the Jardin de la Fontaine guarding the statue which was to be unveiled the next morning. On the great day itself the distance separating the Republican gardens from the Royalist Casino, where Henri Vaugeois and Léon Daudet were appealing to their supporters to restore France to the King and to Order, was lined with the forces of law and order trying to keep the rival demonstrators apart. The railway station and the ancient arena also had to be watched, for, to increase the Préfet's headache, the two demonstrations coincided with a bull-fight and big crowds were arriving all morning. An estimated 20,000 people had come to Nîmes for one or other of the three events. If the estimate of 10,000 troops and police is anywhere near correct, then it must be said that the government was taking no chances. However, in spite of the tensions and the siege atmosphere created by the operation, all passed off well and the day turned into a Republican triumph such as Nîmes had not seen for a long time.

The provocations had been such that the normally divided radical and left-wing factions united around the allegorical figure bearing a torch (an appropriate sculpture for the author of *Les Porteurs de Torches*) surmounted by a bust of Bernard-Lazare.[4] The day which Maurras had so enthusiastically planned to be a day of disorder and violence was transformed into an immense *fête républicaine*, 'la démocratie tout entière se dresse frémissante', attended by vast crowds – from the *Préfet* himself, senators, deputies, councillors, the Socialist mayor of Nîmes (Jules Pieyre), friends and family, to ordinary townsfolk and delegations from neighbouring communes. They had been encouraged to come (by invitation card only) to show their 'mépris des bravades nationalistes, pour montrer que nous sommes les dignes fils de 89 et de 93 et les dignes compatriotes de Bernard-Lazare qui donna sa vie à la cause des opprimés et de la Justice'.[5]

Conspicuous by their absence were members of the Dreyfus family.

Like all such occasions of pomp and ceremony, the inauguration had its solemn as well as its comic sides; not all of the many speeches were meaningful or even sincere; it was an unashamed political manifestation and not the commemoration of dreyfusism as a moral force which Pierre Quillard had originally planned. In 1905 he had set up the Bernard-Lazare Monument Committee[6] as a protest against the ingratitude of some dreyfusards and the silence of others, against the glorification of Picquart, and the political harvests reaped by latecomers from the moral ideals which had inspired the man who first re-awakened the conscience of men of conscience. But it was nonetheless an impressive demonstration, notably in expressing the people's rejection of the politics of hatred. This, more than all the forces of law and order, contributed to Maurras' failure on that day in Nîmes.

The story has two sad sequels of destruction, one physical, one moral. On 14 July 1909, 'Bernard-Lazare reçut la nasarde' as one local wit put it. The *Camelots du Roi* badly mutilated the statue, particularly the nose, sign of the Jew, which was broken off. Every year after that, on the 14 July, the Camelots performed the ritual of throwing ink-bottles at 'Lazare dénezard'. According to certain Nîmois who still remember those days, the statue came eventually to be in a deplorable state. In 1940 it was destroyed. Hatred was in power.[7]

More damaging to Bernard-Lazare's memory, because still repeated in certain quarters today, is an outrageous calumny first put out by a certain Georges Bodereau in the *Chronique de Paris* and enthusiastically taken up and embroidered by Rochefort in *L'Intransigeant* (20 August 1906). All prominent dreyfusards were at one stage or other accused of venality. It was the usual smear. Bernard-Lazare suffered relatively little from such campaigns, at least during his lifetime. In 1906, when he was no longer there to defend himself, and when the projected monuments to dead dreyfusards were like thorns in the antidreyfusard flesh because they seemed – and were – victory celebrations (Captain Dreyfus was rehabilitated on 15 July 1906), Bodereau told the story of how Bernard-Lazare got rich during the Affair by taking 25 per cent commission on the syndicate's money which he distributed to journalists for propaganda purposes. Rochefort was delighted.

> Les journalistes et politiciens qu'il a arrosés avec l'argent que le syndicat juif l'avait chargé de distribuer ont décidé de lui témoigner leur reconnaissance en lui élevant un monument... Or, M. Georges Bodereau [...] nous apprend que ce grand initiateur était tout simplement un escroc.

And Rochefort, naturally, goes even further in his interpretation of the slander:

> Il n'a pas du tout entrepris sa campagne révisionniste dans le but d'arriver au triomphe de cette vérité [...] mais enfin de se faire de bonnes rentes en exploitant la cupidité des uns et la crédulité des autres.

One feels sympathy with Quillard and his Monument Committee for having ignored such slurs. Rochefort's remarks are worthy only of silent contempt. They amused even Drumont, who went as far as he could in denying them without appearing to defend a Jew.[8] And yet a challenge to Bodereau's unsubstantiated claim might have rendered a useful service, since future historians of antidreyfusard persuasion might have felt obliged to take note of it, in the interest of historical accuracy. As it is, in the successive editions of his *Précis de l'Affaire Dreyfus*, Henri

Dutrait-Crozon quotes Bodereau's article as if it were true. More recently Patrice Boussel (*L'Affaire Dreyfus et la presse*, Kiosque, 1960) has repeated certain slanders, prefixed with 'on dit' in the case of Forzinetti, and 'selon lui' in the case of Bodereau's story about Bernard-Lazare. Henri Massis, in 1970, repeated the allegation as if it were fact,[9] although his master Maurras had paid no attention to it, not even in the long and denigratory article he had devoted to the 'entrepreneur de la révision' at the time of the monument in 1908.[10]

At the risk of trying the reader's patience, Bodereau's allegation needs to be considered briefly, because it is a serious and unjustified slur on Bernard-Lazare's memory. One of the claims made is probably correct, and we have already mentioned it, namely that Bernard-Lazare acted as intermediary, or at least as one of the intermediaries, between Mathieu's money and propaganda costs. In this sense he may be called the 'syndicate's treasurer'. It could not have been an exhilarating task, but it was a necessary one and there was nothing dishonourable about it. Let us stress once again that in the face of hostility or silence on the part of official circles and the press, informing and appealing to public opinion was an expensive as well as an arduous business. Dreyfus was fortunate to be rich and to have a devoted family prepared to spend the last penny of its considerable wealth on *proving* his innocence in a court of law. That this should have been necessary, that a poor Dreyfus might well have died a victim of injustice, may reflect on the ways of the world but is no moral reflection on Mathieu who provided the funds or on Bernard-Lazare who distributed them. One might also add that those who still speak of the famous 'syndicate', by which is usually meant a Jewish syndicate, pay the generally silent and inactive Jewish community an undeserved tribute while at the same time underestimating the wealth of the Dreyfus family which, as Bernard-Lazare candidly pointed out, needed no financial assistance: 'huit familles ayant de grosses fortunes. . .n'ont eu à faire appel à qui que ce soit pour subvenir aux besoins.'[11]

As for the alleged 25 per cent cut on the funds he distributed, I have found no material proof of this anywhere, and M. Bodereau produced none (though he offered or threatened to do so 'si l'on criait à la calomnie') beyond recalling that in the middle of the Affair, when he could no longer earn his living by his pen, Bernard-Lazare was nonetheless able to move to a bigger and more expensive apartment in the rue Juliette-Lambert. What he does not say, and Drumont does, is that this need not necessarily be an indication of personal enrichment. Ever since the administration of the *Entretiens*, Bernard-Lazare was in the habit of using his home as office and he moved apartments very frequently, both before and during the Affair. He ended in 1899, as I have said, in a spacious apartment in the rue de Florence intended to become the headquarters of a big daily newspaper. When the expected financial backing was not forthcoming and the project fell through, he was forever trying to sublet in order to pay the rent.[12] The truth is that the man who allegedly enriched himself through the Affair was personally impoverished by it, and in the end had to rely on the generosity of family and friends to support him – or find him jobs with some sort of secure income.[13] Mathieu spent liberally when it came to defending his brother; his treatment of the devoted men who helped him seems to have been less than generous. Stock went bankrupt, Forzinetti had to find employment in Monte Carlo, Bernard-Lazare was, according to his own note to Reinach,[14] in material difficulties even during the Affair, when Mathieu presumably supported his 'treasurer' in some way. While we are on the subject, let us mention another mythical claim which a recent historian, Henri Guillemin, could not substantiate when asked to do so,[15] namely that Bernard-Lazare had received the sum of 20,000 francs for writing the first brochure. But Bernard-Lazare publicly declared in 1899, to a journalist who published the interview, 'il est bien entendu que je n'acceptais pas un centime de rétribution'.[16] On that occasion, he also gave the exact figure for the total expense involved in the publication and distribution of the first brochure, popularly imagined to run into millions. It came to 2,300 francs. The bitter irony of these accusations is that Bernard-Lazare died poor,[17] leaving his widow without resources. She had to sell her husband's precious library (to the Alliance Israelite Universelle) and she was supported by Zadoc-Kahn and such faithful friends as Emile Meyerson.[18] It was Meyerson who saw to the personal expenses which she incurred but could ill afford on the visit to Nîmes for the inauguration of her husband's monument.

No one outside the family cherished Bernard-Lazare's memory more passionately than Péguy and no one's life was more filled with that memory than Péguy's. Bernard-Lazare's wish, 'c'est de ma vie que je veux emplir vos mémoires', was superbly realised in Péguy who built a lasting and living monument to his friend in *Notre Jeunesse*. Magnificent as the work is, it is not *the* work which Péguy had originally planned and never completed: 'une de ces oeuvres devant lesquelles on tremble...tant on a peur que l'exécution soit indigne d'un modèle aimé'. He left the task to the maturity of old age, which alas he never reached.[19]

It would be foolhardy even to attempt to evaluate in the space of a few pages a unique and quite extraordinary spiritual friendship, as brief in duration, a bare three years (1901–1903), as it was profound in its impact on Péguy; so profound that he ultimately had to liberate himself from the dazzling image in order to be himself. What I should like to do is to consider, albeit briefly and inadequately, one major aspect and some of its ramifications: the lesson in collective survival which Péguy learnt from Bernard-Lazare.

To Péguy, as to Maurras, Bernard-Lazare embodied 'l'anarchie juive' – only he envisaged it as 'la mystique juive', the prophetic spirit which animates 'la race de l'inquiétude' from whose midst there periodically spring magnificent agitators who save the world by ensuring its long-term spiritual and moral survival, the only survival that ultimately counts. The survival implicit in *politique*, by contrast, is concerned with the short-term, and as such is in constant danger of being short-sighted, arbitrary, geared to the changing interests of the passing moment. The attitude adopted by Barrès during the Affair provides Péguy with an excellent example of 'politique française' which Bernard-Lazare's 'mystique juive' happily overcame, thereby saving 'la mystique française', that is to say, essentially, the Republican ideal of liberty and justice for which so many had fought and died so that future generations could live by it. Saying, as Barrès had done, that one does not sacrifice the peace and unity of a whole city for the sake of one individual, even if he is innocent, may be an act of immediate political wisdom but there is nothing more dangerous in the moral life of nations than such acts of short-term expediency to which there may be no end. Living with a dishonourable peace is dying a little every day. From a Christian point of view, it is an eternal death for the very soul of a nation, and its salvation is put into jeopardy by such short-term acts of wisdom.

The same sort of dangerous, non-heroic, short-sighted and

deadly *sagesse* was to be found in the 'politique juive'. In order
to secure peace from antisemitism and save the community at
large, the silent Jewish majority was ready to sacrifice Dreyfus
and ostracise Bernard-Lazare. In his criticism of the 'politique
juive'[20] (of which the ingratitude of the Dreyfus family towards
Bernard-Lazare and the general hostility he aroused among his
French fellow-Jews are two obvious and immediate facets) Péguy
was continuing his friend's battle for Jewish survival. Nothing
was more dangerous to that survival than the breakdown of
solidarity, for centuries the most important survival factor, as
witnessed in the 'politique juive', the politics of peace, themselves
the result of the 'politics of assimilation'. In order to prove to
philosemites and antisemites alike that they were no longer Jewish,
assimilated Jewry professed or feigned lack of interest in the
sufferings of an innocent Jew.

Péguy understands and writes movingly of the fear of persecution on the part of a people with 'fifty centuries of wounds and
scars'. Moreover, he generalises certain psychological factors at
work in the Jewish persecution-mentality: the readiness to conclude a facile peace rather than fight for a lasting peace, to
sacrifice individuals or principles for the sake of tranquillity, to
cling to what one has, to avoid facing disturbing crises, these are
defence mechanisms common to all conservative majorities. On
the part of Jewry, the fear of trouble and the aspiration to peace
and quiet were understandable reflexes, but matters had reached
a dangerous point. It is not with peace at any price that a people
can survive. It needs to resist the aggressor. Collective resistance
had broken down in the 'politique juive'. 'Ils [the Jews] ne
demandaient qu'à sacrifier Dreyfus pour conjurer l'orage, . . .
pour avoir la paix du ménage politique, . . .la paix des populations
et des princes, la paix des antisémites.'[21]

As Bernard-Lazare's friend, Péguy was particularly well qualified to speak on the subject and he does so with much less severity
than Bernard-Lazare had done. *Chemin faisant*, he also exploded
the latest antidreyfusard myth that the Dreyfus Affair had been
engineered by 'le parti juif' in its own interests, to ensure its
triumph. This strikes Péguy as a tragically ironic misunderstanding of Jewish persecution-mentality. The Affair was indeed 'une
explosion de la mystique juive' on the part of the few, and notably
one man; as such it was of immense benefit to all the other
mystiques which it released; by the same token it went against

all the other *politiques*, notably its own, unintelligent, short-sighted and cowardly *politique juive*.

This is not the place to enter into any long discussion of M. Jacques Petit's recent interpretation of *Péguy face à Israel*.[22] But since he has, in my view, profoundly misunderstood Péguy's criticism of the 'politique juive', among other things, I would like to say this: far from allowing Péguy to vent a conscious or unconscious antisemitism, the condemnation of 'the politics of peace' follows almost textually Bernard-Lazare's condemnation, in *Le Fumier de Job*, of the disastrous Jewish desire for *sholem* (i.e. peace), the result of centuries of persecution and, tragically, also the cause of its continued success. It is surely in this sense that Péguy attacks *la politique juive*, as an understandable defence mechanism but one which is utterly useless as far as antisemitism is concerned and which might prove disastrous to survival.

The survival of the Jewish people was of a quite extraordinary personal importance and a cause of great anguish to Péguy *before* he met Bernard-Lazare. It is not often realised how obsessed the young Péguy had been by the possibility of a Russian solution (pogrom) or the Armenian solution (large-scale massacre) being applied in Republican France. 'Mort aux Juifs' had rung in his ears like a call to genocide. The barbaric modernity of these collective crimes lay in the fact that they were not part and parcel of a terrible war but a matter of deliberate policy, a Weltanschauung, a philosophy of history. Genocide had become a solution to the existence of religious minorities judged to be undesirable or unproductive. It is hard to think of anyone, apart from Bernard-Lazare, who saw antisemitism in such tragic dimensions as Péguy: it was a matter of the life and death of a whole people. He lived in the fear that the Jews might become the Armenians of France, and through her of Europe, and this profoundly offended his very conception and sense of France.[23]

What he could not understand at first were the causes of this terrible 'ravage d'immoralité'. Before long he discovered an unexpected source: the dominating philosophy of progress and its 'mission completed' view of the history of civilisations. According to this view civilisations are born, flourish, decay, die and are succeeded by others in a never-ending cycle of extinction through progressive succession. In such a climate, the disappearance of civilisations and cultural communities is of little importance, as long as they are given, as Renan said, a more or less honourable mention in history-books.

Against this mummification of a living heritage Bernard-Lazare had defended Judaism ('La pensée juive a été une des sources où se sont abreuvés les hommes. Vous voulez la momifier, la descendre dans une hypogée alors qu'elle n'est pas encore morte, en faire un objet de laboratoire et de musée. Pourquoi?')[24] just as Péguy later defended Christianity. Bernard-Lazare may well have been instrumental in bringing Péguy back to the centuries of Christianity which, as a young socialist, he had dismissed in one sweeping gesture as having left no trace in his conscience.[25]

The meeting with Bernard-Lazare, 'un de ces hommes de cinquante siècles', was like a meeting with History, a living monument, a living memory. It was an important spiritual experience for the then uneasy 'atheist' Péguy. Everything about this ancient prophet living in modern times belied the theory of the 'mission completed'; it affirmed, against all the teaching of modern historians and philosophers, the survival of an ancient people and its prophetic mission. He seemed to assure Péguy that the spirit can triumph over the barbarity of the modern age, and through him Jewish survival assumed that significance. Jewry was a living proof, it became an arm to be used against the modern world and the death-sentences it so lightly pronounced in the name of progress. Here is one of several tributes in which Péguy tries to express what he owes to Bernard-Lazare.

> Je dus à cette amitié, à cette élection, de connaître, d'aimer
> je ne dis pas seulement un des plus grands hommes qu'il y
> ait eu. . .mais très particulièrement et très techniquement
> un Prophète. . . A cette amitié je ne dus pas seulement de
> connaître un prophète, comme un îlot, comme un fragment,
> comme un monstre, comme un phénomène isolé. Mais un
> prophète en son lieu, en sa place, en sa race. Un prophète
> de sa race dans la race de son peuple. Un Prophète de la
> race des Prophètes dans la race du peuple d'Israël. . .[26]

Before long Péguy worked out his own theory of historical development, the theory of unique and irreplaceable voices eternally resounding in a universal concert.[27]

In this universal concert, Israel's voice is that of time and justice; its mission is to provoke 'inquiétude' and produce agitators; the supreme lesson it has to teach mankind is a lesson in collective survival. It is evident that Péguy's conception of Israel is at this stage entirely dominated by the figure of Bernard-Lazare. It will also be readily understood why Péguy was an anti-assimilationist: not because he was a zionist, but because he was an anarchist with a respect for diversity as a source of human richness and a respect for the uniqueness of individuals and peoples. The French and the Jews were more unique than most, inimitable and unrepeatable 'réussites'.

Ultimately, however, the *Christian* Péguy could not accommodate the uniqueness and independence of Israel,[28] in spite of his moving efforts. The dazzling image of Bernard-Lazare became theologically oppressive and it had to be broken.

This explains, I think, the strange oblivion of Bernard-Lazare after *Notre Jeunesse* (1910), apart from a few unimportant references. In numerous texts following *Notre Jeunesse*, both in prose and poetry, Péguy meditates on Israel and the Jews, but no mention is made of 'le prophète'. Péguy the Christian had to liberate himself from the memory of Bernard-Lazare in order to feel free as a Christian. *Notre Jeunesse* was a magnificent tribute, a paying of debts, and at the same time an act of spiritual liberation, after which Péguy could develop his Christian theology without feeling guilty or unfaithful.

Contrary to what is sometimes stated, it seems to me that Péguy's view of the relationship between Israel and Christianity does pose the concept of completion and fulfilment. He was perhaps exceptional for the times in his concern with that relationship, in speaking respectfully of the Old Testament, in fully recognising his roots, Jewish and Pagan, even in feeling, some forty years before Pope Pius XI, that 'spirituellement nous sommes des sémites'. But if Péguy fully recognised his roots he also saw their fruition in Christianity. Is there any text in which the Old Testament is not seen in the conventional Christian manner as prefiguring or announcing the New Testament? And is completion not implied in this?

From a Christian point of view, this is perfectly understandable and natural and does not normally pose any problems. It posed problems for Péguy because his relationship with his Jewish friends had been spiritually intense, because he did not separate modern Jews from ancient Israel, and because he realised that a spiritual separation was inevitable, short of christianising his friends or converting them, metaphorically speaking. The trouble was that such very 'Jewish Jews' as Bernard-Lazare did not lend themselves, like Bergson, to christianisation without committing an infidelity. Péguy refused to do this. The nearest he could honestly come to associating his Jewish friends with his own spiritual journey was to dedicate his Christian works to them, as he did in the case of Eddy Marix.[29]

Implicit in *completion* is *dépassement* and this in turn raised the problem of historical development, the 'mission completed' view of things to which Péguy had been so hostile. On a spiritual level, in his attitude to the relationship between Israel and Christianity, Péguy was unable to solve the problem. The spiritual history of mankind told in *Eve* (1913) is Christian in perspective, providential in conception and not pluralist. Israel, symbolised by Eve, has lost its voice. Christ, who has absorbed and surpassed it, is the only speaker. Moreover, in the parallel He draws between the negative and sterile world before His coming and the affirmative and fecund epoch ushered in by Himself, Péguy's Christ verges on the antisemitic. Certainly, Bernard-Lazare would not have recognised his Judaism in this picture of sterility. He might also have been disturbed by some of the reproaches Christ addresses to his mother Eve.

At the risk of disconcerting many Péguy scholars, I would suggest that Péguy not only came fully to accept Judaism's *dépassement* by Christianity – as a Christian he could hardly have done otherwise – but that the *dépassement* is evoked in a manner increasingly denigratory to Israel which is inconsistent with Péguy's previous conception, dominated by Bernard-Lazare. The climax is reached in the curious Jewish–Christian parallel of *La Note Conjointe* (1914) where he goes one step further and destroys the very image of the Jew previously embodied by Bernard-Lazare. From having been the epitome of 'inquiétude' and revolution, the Jew is now presented as an arch-conservative, always happy with what he has and grateful for the smallest mercies. The *politique* mentality (personified here in Julien Benda) now reflects *all* Jewish mentality and the very spirit of Judaism. There is not a trace of *mystique juive*. The once chosen people led by its prophets is demoted to being an exhausted 'race de la non-réussite'.[30]

The antisemitic note in this text is often explained as concealing a polemical and apologetic intention: Péguy deliberately adopts the enemy's antisemitic language and clears Jewry of the charge of being a pernicious, revolutionary agency. It must be said that such a defence *à rebours* would not have been beyond Péguy's polemical talents but the interpretation does not stand up to serious examination. *La Note Conjointe* is indeed a polemical reply, but it is addressed to Bernard-Lazare, and notably to the anti-Christian sentiment expressed in *Le Fumier de Job*.

The Jewish–Christian parallel of *La Note Conjointe* follows quite closely the Jewish–Christian parallel of *Le Fumier de Job*, only everything is reversed. The comparison in Bernard-Lazare is bluntly in the Jew's favour. Péguy incontestably favours the Christian, though his manner is less blunt. Bernard-Lazare's Jew is revolutionary, energetic, in love with life, free from any sense of sin, rational and literary; since he does not believe in an after-life, the earth has to be transformed into paradise. The Christian is the opposite: sad, resigned; he is obsessed with sin and death, and his reasoning is hampered by centuries of dogmatic teaching. Péguy takes up all these points and reverses them. His Jew is exhausted and resigned and his Christian energetic and revolutionary. The Christian sense of sin, in a Pascal, constitutes an opening to 'inquiétude' and so becomes an incomparable revolutionary force. The only Jewish sense of sin is legalistic in comparison, one of disobedience to the law.[31] In *Job* this was presented as an advantage. Péguy's Jew has been unhappy ever since Adam and Eve. Bernard-Lazare's Jew has *chosen* the difficult path of knowledge in preference to an easy, blissful state of ignorance.[32] It is on the question of knowledge and literacy that the most spectacular parallels and differences between the two works occur, for here Péguy almost textually quotes a phrase from *Job* but elaborates it in a contrary sense. Bernard-Lazare wrote: 'il [le petit Juif] appartient à un peuple qui depuis des siècles sait lire et lit'.[33] This, he goes on to say, does not make him any more intelligent, but it saves him from the struggle experienced by the Catholic when confronted by science and knowledge. Whereas Christianity has at times sanctified ignorance, the scholar and the *savant* have always formed the Jewish aristocracy. Péguy uses the phrase: 'Le Juif est d'une race où l'on trouve toujours quelqu'un qui sait lire...le Juif est un homme qui lit depuis toujours'[34] and eventually develops it into a sort of sanctification of *illiteracy* because the letter kills the spirit: 'Littera occidit. Littera necat.'[35] This passage is a good example, incidentally, of Péguy's hesitations and technique. He does not wish to say, and he probably does not even think it, that the long tradition of Jewish literacy has killed the spirit. Jewish reading is a reading of 'le Livre et la Loi'. But all the same, literacy deprives the Jew, as it does the Protestant, of the innocence and simplicity of Péguy's illiterate grandmother. There is a hierarchy implied in the delightful: 'Le Juif est un homme qui lit depuis toujours, le protestant est un homme qui lit depuis Calvin, le Catholique est un homme qui lit depuis Ferry.'[36]

One could show point by point how in *La Note Conjointe* Péguy replies to *Le Fumier de Job* and how, since the memory of Bernard-Lazare does not after all accord with the portrait of the resigned Jew presented here, he is obliged to distort the image of the friend (though the latter is never mentioned by name). At its simplest, it suffices to re-evaluate certain qualities. The previously much praised 'patience', for example, becomes a factor in the resignation. And whereas before Péguy had been dazzled by the coexistence in his friend of 'inquiétude' and 'patience' which produced a saint-like prophet and a splendid revolutionary, 'patience' is now seen to sap 'inquiétude' and lead to a readiness to 'endure' without protest. As an image of Bernard-Lazare this would clearly be a distortion. As part of the mentality of the Jewish *politique* it has its truth.

The ending of this unique spiritual friendship seems sad. On reading certain passages in *L'Argent Suite* (1913) about the Jewish 'fatal entêtement', 'l'effrayante marque et l'effrayante destination spirituelle de cette race. . .et son effrayante destination théologique',[37] one cannot help remembering what Bernard-Lazare said in *Le Fumier de Job* about Israel always being a source of both attraction and exasperation to the Catholic who does not quite know what to do with the obstinate infidel. Péguy's development thus illustrates an important point which Bernard-Lazare had made about Christian attitudes towards Jews, attitudes which ensure the continued existence of antisemitism, conscious or unconscious, for as long as there are Christians and Jews.

However that may be, it is Péguy who understood Bernard-Lazare in marvellous depth and who immortalised his very spirit and soul in *Notre Jeunesse*.[38] One could also say that *La Note Conjointe* shows Bernard-Lazare's influence at its most profound, and it is perhaps the highest spiritual tribute Péguy could have paid his friend: he grafted onto his Christianity the revolutionary spirit he had so admired in the Prophète Juif, though one may feel some regret that the latter had to disappear in the process.

Since the subject of Péguy and Bernard-Lazare inevitably involves Péguy's indestructible love of Jews, it seems appropriate to conclude with this delightful account Péguy is said to have given to Pierre Marcel, one of his Jewish friends, of a dream he once had. He dreamt that they were all dead, feeling immensely happy and free, with many of the questions that had worried them suddenly resolved. At one point, it looked as if his Jewish friends were going to leave him. 'Je vous dis: "Où allez-vous?" Vous avez éclaté de rire et vous avez dit: "Eh bien, nous entrons dans le sein d'Abraham." Je haussai les épaules et je vous dis: "Mais non, venez donc dans le Paradis, on rigole davantage." Et vous vîntes.'[39] At least in a dream the problem of separation between Jews and Christians was solved.

Like all genuine prophets, Bernard-Lazare cried doom and believed that it could be averted. He drew attention to what was wrong and to where it might lead in the unshakeable conviction that moral and political cancers can be arrested if the fundamentally rational but mentally lazy and inattentive majority was alerted to the danger. One could say that in the Dreyfus Affair he played this prophetic role most successfully. On other occasions he shared what is more commonly the fate of prophetic minds: their predictions seem outrageous, like ravings of a feverish brain; their warnings go unheeded. So it is with his vision of what an authoritarian socialist State might be like, where freedom from hunger is achieved at the expense of freedom of thought, where the price of bread as well as truth, beauty and happiness are established for all and enforced by law. He was not alone in this particular prediction of doom; other libertarian socialists shared the nightmare and sounded warnings which went unheeded. In his preoccupation with the causes and consequences of antisemitism he was a more solitary figure. Who in the France of 1895 was prepared to think, let alone say, that the only logical solution to the Jewish question was a massacre? The people who should have been most concerned and who understood him least were his fellow French Jews. As rabbi Liber so succinctly put it, in a reply to Péguy's reproach that 'la politique juive' had buried Bernard-Lazare even before his death: 'La vérité est que les israelites français, la bourgeoisie juive de France ne pouvait pas suivre Bernard-Lazare, qui desservait sa cause en la servant. . .'[40]

Twenty years later, at the significant date of 1933, he was still considered to be dangerous and best forgotten. When a small group of people planned to recall his role and pay tribute to his memory by organising a public commemoration of the 30th anniversary of his death, there was one distinguished Jewish intellectual who objected. In his view such a demonstration was in bad taste at a time when antisemitism was rife and the only allegiance should be to France. Fifty years, the angry patriot wrote, was the traditional anniversary celebration; Bernard-Lazare could well wait until 1953.[41] What a cruel epitaph this would make on the unknown graves of hundreds of Frenchmen, Jewish and non-Jewish, among them members of Bernard-Lazare's own family, who perished in the Nazi death camps. Madame Bernard-Lazare survived the war, and it is to her devotion to her husband's memory that we owe much of the archive material which remains today. Among this material there are one or two documents pertaining to herself which tell a sad tale of racial laws such as France had never known. One likes to think that the lady who in 1941 presented herself to the Vichy authorities as the 'widow of Lazare Bernard' (Bernard was the real family name) derived strength from the name she bore.

One lesson which Bernard-Lazare has to teach us, and it is one which he himself was ready to draw from his own initial mistakes, was not to be deluded by terminologies, comforting distinctions, striking formulae and vital lies, all the formidable apparatus we have at our disposal and wheel out when we do not wish to face the truth. Living on legends and rationalisations may be more comfortable, but the truth is safer in the long run. It is because he had the courage to face the truth, the courage and intelligence to go beyond effects to root-causes, beyond expressed intentions to the potential consequences of the naked idea, that his warnings may strike us as eerily prophetic today.

Today as yesterday, antisemitism raises much wider issues and is ultimately no more and no less than a question of freedom. Bernard-Lazare, a libertarian to the marrow of his bones, fully realised this: 'les Juifs ne seront libres que lorsque les pays seront libres'. He had said this about Russia, and in that context the liberties were very basic. If it was applied to France, if the treatment of minorities is a measure of a country's sense of freedom, how free a country was France?

As far as the Jewish minority is concerned, I imagine that

Bernard-Lazare would have agreed with his coreligionists that for political and civic liberties France was a model. But whereas they asked for no more, whereas they shared with other Republicans a conception of *liberty* which was fundamentally political and middle-class, Bernard-Lazare had a more complex conception of *freedom* and also perhaps a loftier conception of French revolutionary traditions. The right to assimilate, to integrate, to vote, to be considered equal before the law, to enjoy full citizenship, to be like the majority, these were important basic rights which still had to be fought for in Rumania and Russia. But in Western countries, in France, this was past history. There, the emancipated and assimilated minority should also have the right to be different from the majority, if it so desires, to preserve its cultural identity, to have several *patries*. Man has multiple roots, and the more advanced his culture the more multiple they are likely to be. In short, Bernard-Lazare asked French Jewry whose ideal, like those of other Republicans, did not go beyond 'la République une et indivisible' to take a more libertarian attitude to the cultural role they ought to play.

As far as antisemitism is concerned, he saw their refusal to fight it as disastrous in all repects. As one of the freest communities in the world and as citizens of a country where political liberty matters and personal freedom should matter, French Jews should have taken a moral lead. Instead they not only failed the oppressed, and so degraded the very French ideals in whose name they refused to fight; they struck a blow at their own moral dignity. A free man defends himself when he is attacked; only then will he be able to defend the freedom of others. Perhaps this is how Bernard-Lazare came to be, in the words of one of his Jewish admirers, one of 'les plus belles consciences de notre temps'.[42]

NOTES

Chapter 1: Roots, milieu and symbolism

1 The Archives Départmentales de Nîmes proved a fruitful source of information as did the collection of local newspapers and periodicals kept at the Bibliothèque Municipale. Jean Muslak's pioneering – and alas uncompleted – work on Bernard-Lazare (*Revue des Etudes Juives*, Vol. VI, No. 106, 1946, pp. 34–63) also contains some biographical details. The Bibliothèque du Musée Pédagogique in Paris was able to supply general information concerning syllabus, curriculum etc. and a few personal items emerged from the brochures of the 'distribution des prix du lycée de Nîmes' kept at the Bibliothèque Municipale. Unfortunately the lycée's own records do not go back that far. Scattered references to the family history will also be found in the material recently acquired by the Archives Bernard-Lazare (Alliance Israelite Universelle), in particular some details entered by Bernard-Lazare's grandfather on the first page of his Bible (Box 17).

2 Jean Muslak, op. cit. p. 35.

3 Idem.

4 Quoted in A. Hamon: *Psychologie de l'anarchiste-socialiste*, Stock, 1895, p. 28.

5 Phoebus Jouve: 'Sur Bernard-Lazare', *La Chronique Mondaine*, 3 October 1908, Archives de Nîmes.

6 *Figures Contemporaines, Ceux d'Aujourd'hui, Ceux de Demain*, Perrin, 1895, pp. 242–3.

7 For the school-year 1878–9 he is listed as being in the first year of this course (*Distribution Solennelle des Prix*, Nîmes, 1879).

8 J. B. Piobetta: *Le Baccalauréat*, Baillière, 1937, p. 187.

9 *Plan d'Etudes et Programmes de l'Enseignement Secondaire Spécial dans les lycées et collèges*, Delalain, 1882.

10 He came fourth out of 28 candidates.

11 *Evénement*, 4 August, 17 June 1892.

12 *Le Fumier de Job*, Rieder 1928, p. 59.

13 Poster for a lecture given in April 1895 on 'Mysticisme et Révolution' (*L'Oeuvre Sociale*).

14 Phoebus Jouve: 'Sur Bernard-Lazare', art. cit.

15 *Figures Contemporaines,* op. cit. p. vii.

16 *Entretiens Politiques et Littéraires,* 10 January 1893.

17 *Correspondance Inédite d'Ephraïm Mikhaël à Bernard-Lazare,* 1885–1887, *Ecrits Français,* Nos. 3 and 4, 1914.

18 A. Fontainas: *Mes souvenirs de symbolisme,* Nouvelle Revue Critique, 1928, p. 110.

19 Which seems to have been lost. Stuart Merrill: 'Pierre Quillard', *La Phalange,* 20 February 1912.

20 *Figures Contemporaines,* op. cit. pp. 241–50. Gide has left a delightful picture of one of these soirées, this time *chez* Henri de Régnier. '...Chacun en un grand fauteuil, une pipe aux lèvres,...nous avons prolongé le charme des paroles jusqu'à une heure et demie du matin. Nous ne dirons plus de mal de Lazare: vraiment je l'ai trouvé charmant.... Lazare nous a parlé du ternaire, des hérésiarques gnostiques, Paul Adam des envoûtement et de je ne sais quelles magies.' A. Gide–P. Valéry *Correspondance,* Gallimard, 1955, p. 109. The young Gide and Valéry did not have anything good to say about anybody. In the somewhat arrogant contempt they showed for Bernard-Lazare who sang their praise in the press, there was perhaps a serious note. Valéry did not like 'l'Hébreux' and Gide came to be frightened by his conception of committed art.

21 Bernard-Lazare is reported to have told Georges Sorel 'avoir eu en Monseigneur Duchesne un merveilleux maître de scepticisme'. Quillard puts the influence more positively but perhaps it comes to the same in the end. 'Le sagace érudit qui a édité le *Liber Pontificalis* et écrit *Les Origines du culte chrétien,* apprenait supérieurement à ses élèves l'art de confronter les textes et de discerner le vrai du faux dans l'amas des documents et le tumulte des controverses' (*L'Européen,* 12 September 1903).

22 *Le Courrier Français,* October 1892.

23 'Les Quatre Faces', *Entretiens Politiques et Littéraires,* December 1890.

24 *Entretiens,* December 1891.

25 Ibid. April 1892.

26 *Evénement,* 18 December 1894.

27 Quoted in *Chalom* September 1933. (Professor Austin of the University of Cambridge also kindly communicated a copy of this letter to me.)

28 Beginning with this work, his earliest, Lazare Bernard becomes Bernard-Lazare (sometimes spelt without hyphen). Is there any significance in the change of name? Probably not. Georges Michel also changed his to the more unusual Ephraïm Mikhaël.

29 *Le Temps* 6 March 1892.

30 *La Fiancée de Corinthe,* op. cit. p. 53, p. 40.

31 *Le Fumier de Job,* op. cit. p. 59.

32 *Le Miroir des Légendes,* Lemerre, 1892, p. 169.

33 *Le Temps,* 6 March 1892.

34 *La Télépathie et le Néo-spiritualisme, L'Art Indépendant,* 1893, p. 1.

35 *Les Porteurs de Torches,* Colin, 1897, p. 3.

36 Ibid. p. 159.

37 Ibid. p. 161.
38 *L'Aube,* June 1897. See also *L'Homme Libre,* 23–30 July 1899. *Les Temps Nouveaux,* Suppl. Litt. No. 51, 1899, 5–11 September 1903.
39 *L'Ouvrier des Deux Mondes,* 1 April 1897.
40 *Les Porteurs de Torches,* op. cit. p. 196.
41 Ibid. p. 20.

Chapter 2: Journalist with a mission

1 H. Avenel: *Annuaire de la presse française* (1890–1900); *Histoire de la Presse Française depuis 1789 jusqu'à nos jours,* Flammarian, 1900; R. de Livois: *Histoire de la Presse Française,* Vol. II, *De 1881 à nos jours,* Editions Spes, Lausanne, 1965.
2 According to C. Mauclair (*Servitudes et Grandeurs Littéraires,* p. 62) the journalist without a name started at one sou per line. Others could earn 25 francs an article in the bigger dailies.
3 *La Revue Bleue,* 4 December 1897–22 January 1898. (Fouillé's article in the same review 30 October 1897.)
4 *La Nation,* 1 April and 13 May 1891 respectively.
5 'La mort du Mandarin', 4 August 1893.
6 Among the most interesting are: 'La Torture' (27 October 1892); 'La Guerre Future' (6 April 1893); 'Réforme des Supplices' (16 April 1893).
7 From Berthelot, Jules Soury, Gaston Paris, Th. Ribot, G. Tarde among others.
8 See opening issue of *enquête,* 12 January (1895). Also Bernard-Lazare's comments 19 February.
9 Brisson closed the banquet (6 April) by pointing out 'le danger politique que contient l'affirmation que la science a fait banqueroute'. For an interesting review of this enquête signed Agathon, probably Maurras, see *La Revue Encyclopédique,* 15 April 1895, pp. 149–52.
10 Contributions to *Le Voltaire* from 27 March to 12 August 1896. The campaign against Drumont will be discussed in a later chapter.
11 'Progressisme et Socialisme', *Le Paris,* 29 June 1896.
12 Letter to Camille Bloch quoted in Tonnelat: *Charles Andler, sa vie et son oeuvre,* Paris, 1937, p. 110.

Chapter 3: Anarchism

1 Jean Maitron: *Ravachol et les Anarchistes,* Paris, Julliard, Collection Archives, p. 74.
2 Ibid. p. 110.
3 For the reaction of contemporary writers see: *L'Ermitage,* July 1893; *La Plume,* May 1893; *La Revue Anarchiste,* 15–30 September 1893. Some interesting testimonies in A. Hamon: *Psychologie de l'anarchiste-socialiste,* Stock 1895.
4 Bernard-Lazare's dossier (Archives de la Préfecture) is under his real name (Lazare Marcus Manassé *Bernard*) and carries the number Ba/958. It is a fairly substantial dossier, consisting of informants'

reports, inspectors' reports and documents (a few letters, press cuttings, certain of his brochures) and covering the period 1891–1900, with a number of reports on his funeral in 1903, at which demonstrations were expected. Being first considered a respectable young man of good family with political opinions 'acquises au gouvernement actuel', the first few entries are largely formalities. After the seizure in April 1893 of anarchist letters, including one written by Bernard-Lazare, surveillance began and continued throughout the Dreyfus Affair, though it was then more erratic and less thorough than for some months of the preceding anarchist period. On the whole, knowledge of his movements and activities from other sources would suggest that surveillance was not too strict or else that Bernard-Lazare took increasingly more effective precautions. Fascinating and at times instructive as this material is, the accuracy of much of it is open to question, particularly the claims and speculations of eager informants. As for his wife, he married Isabelle Grumbach (1866–1960) in June 1892. My impression that the marriage was a very happy one, with Mme Bernard-Lazare supporting her husband's many battles and hectic public life, has recently been confirmed by M. Cherchevsky (see Preface). See also Bernard-Lazare's letters, to his wife, Archives Bernard-Lazare, Box 15.

5 A. Hamon, *Psychologie de l'anarchiste-socialiste*, op. cit. p. 135.

6 Ibid. p. 168.

7 'Le Justicier', *Entretiens Politiques et Littéraires*, May 1891; La Nouvelle Monarchie', *Entretiens Politiques et Littéraires*, November 1891; 'Nécessité du Socialisme', *L'Endehors*, 1 May 1892; 'Aurea Médiocritas', *L'Endehors*, 25 September 1892; 'Entente possible et impossible', *Revue Anarchiste*, 15–30 August 1893; 'La liberté', *Harmonie*, October–December 1893; 'La Déroute', *Revue Parisienne*, 10 February 1894; 'L'oeuvre nécessaire', *Le Courrier Social Illustré*, November 1894; 'L'Université Nouvelle de Bruxelles', *Magazine International*, December 1894; 'Le Socialisme allemand et ses divisions', *Revue Parisienne*, 10 May 1895; 'Bakounine', *Revue Blanche*, 15 February 1895; 'Izoulet et la Cité Moderne', *Le Devenir Social*, April 1895; 'Fédéralistes et Fédéralisme', *Echo de Paris*, 17 November 1895; 'Fédéralisme Révolutionnaire', 12 December 1895; Articles in *L'Action Sociale* 1–29 February 1896; Articles on 'Le Congrès Socialiste de Londres', *Echo de Paris*, 25 July to 4 August 1896.

8 'La Déroute', art. cit.

9 'L'esprit révolutionnaire dans le judaisme', *Revue Bleue*, May 1893.

10 J. Chastenet: *Histoire de la Troisième République*, Hachette, 1955, Vol. II, p. 257.

11 *Le Paris*, 'La Comédie', 8 July 1896.

12 August 1890.

13 'L'esprit révolutionnaire dans le judaisme', art. cit.

14 *Entretiens Politiques et Littéraires*, April 1892.

15 'Liberté', art. cit.

16 Among others (the date refers to the Supplement of *La Révolte*): 'La Nouvelle Monarchie' (28 Nov.–4 Dec. 1891); 'Nécessité du Socialisme' (15–21 May 1892); 'Le Devoir Présent' (4–10 June 1892): 'Un

Centenaire' (7–13 October 1892); 'Aurea Médiocritas' (15–21 October 1892); 'Libertaire' (24–30 December 1892); 'Barricade' (7–13 January 1893); 'Littérature' (13–19 May 1893); 'Dialogue sur la police, les étudiants et quelques autres personnages (29 July–4 August 1893; 'Anarchie et Littérature' (24 Feb.–3 March 1894). Jean Grave (1854–1939) is probably the most important single figure in French anarchism until the First World War. He is also one of the few theoreticians to be 'peuple' by origin. He came from a poor working-class family (exiled Auvergnards trying to find work in Paris) and himself started work as an apprentice mechanic at the age of eleven, after a few years of schooling. Later he became a skilled cobbler. Politically he started life as a socialist, following in this one respect in the footsteps of his authoritarian father. However, before he was thirty he left behind both cobbling and socialism and turned to printing and anarchism, gaining his first experience in Geneva, then the liveliest anarchist centre, where he took charge of *Le Révolté*, the journal created by Kropotkin in 1879. Henceforth Grave's whole life was devoted to spreading the message of anarchism through writing, mainly through the *Révolté* which in due course transferred to Paris and became, first, *La Révolte* (1886) and then, after its seizure in 1894, *Les Temps Nouveaux*. Printer, editor, director, main contributor, Grave kept the weekly (mostly) journal going for thirty-one years, from 1883 to 1914, with a single-minded devotion which triumphed over all sorts of political and financial difficulties. Nearly all the well-known anarchist thinkers contributed to it, notably Kropotkin and Elisée Reclus; because of its seriousness and the esteem in which Grave was generally held, the journal also enjoyed the support of libertarian and liberal writers, painters and intellectuals. In his spare time, during his periods in prison, Grave wrote several books on anarchism. Among the most influential was *La Société Mourante et l'Anarchie*. Valuable from a historical point of view are his memoirs, *Le Mouvement libertaire sous la Troisième République* (1930) of which the original and complete version has only recently been discovered and published: *Quarante Ans de propagande anarchiste* (1973). Affectionately known as the 'pape de la rue Mouffetard' (the road where he lived and worked), Grave kept a watchful eye on anarchist orthodoxy, showing at times a certain narrowness and puritanism characteristic of the self-taught man, which several friends, including Bernard-Lazare, sometimes found disconcerting.

17 'Entente possible et impossible', art. cit.
18 Police Report of 20 May 1896.
19 'Du Marxisme', *Le Paris*, 21 August 1896.
20 This is one of the major topics in *L'Action Sociale*.
21 See J. Maitron: *Histoire du Mouvement Anarchiste*, op. cit. for anarchist activities and also F. Dubois: *Le Péril Anarchiste*, Flammarion, 1894.
22 *L'Action Sociale*, 1 February 1896.
23 International Institute of Social History, Amsterdam.
24 This was the inaugural lecture of the Collège Libre des sciences sociales

given 16 December 1895. It was subsequently published, under the same title of 'L'histoire des doctrines révolutionnaires' in *Le Devenir Social* (January 1896) and also as a 'tirage à part' (Paris, V. Giard et E. Brière, 1896).

25 *Revue Blanche*, 15 February 1895, art. cit.

26 A substantial part of these records has now been deposited at the Archives of the Université Libre de Bruxelles where they are in the process of classification. See: Andrée Despy-Meyer, *Inventaire des Archives de l'Université Nouvelle* (1894–1919), Brussels, 1973.

27 'Une école de la liberté', *Le Magazine International*, December 1894. The same article appeared in *Liberty* (London), November 1895.

28 A good account of its beginnings in: E. Picard: 'Une Nouvelle Université à Bruxelles', *La Société Nouvelle*, no. 113, 1894 and 'L'Institut des Hautes Etudes à l'Université Nouvelle de Bruxelles', *L'Art Social*, 1897. See also J. Ishill: *Elisée and Elie Reclus. In Memoriam*, Oriel Press, Berkeley Heights, New Jersey, 1927. P. Goffin: *Histoire de l'Institut des Hautes Etudes de Belgique*, Brussels, n.d.

29 H. Varennes: *De Ravachol à Caserio*, Garnier, 1895, p. 134.

30 J. Grave: *Quarante ans de propagande anarchiste*, Flammarion, 1973, p. 315.

31 As far as personal relationships are concerned, the only prominent anarchist from whom he become somewhat estranged was Jean Grave. In a letter (23 January 1896) Bernard-Lazare justified the creation of *L'Action Sociale* on the grounds that divergencies existed between himself and Grave on questions of detail even if there was agreement on broad essentials. Over one sacred essential, abstention from voting in parliamentary elections, Bernard-Lazare and Grave fell out in 1897, with Bernard-Lazare supporting Merlino's decision to stand as independent Socialist in the Italian elections and Grave regarding it as heresy. (See *Les Temps Nouveaux*, 17–23 April 1897). Bernard-Lazare similarly urged the *compagnons* to participate in the 1898 French elections and vote for Socialist and liberal candidates in order to keep the reactionary forces at bay ('Les anarchistes voteront-ils', *L'Oeuvre Sociale*, August 1897). This no doubt earned him the stricture in Grave's otherwise laudatory obituary: 'il eut bien une espèce de recul vers le socialisme parlementaire' (*Les Temps Nouveaux*, 5–11 September 1903). In terms of anarchist doctrine, Grave's intransigent abstentionism was entirely logical and it was supported by normally less inflexible men such as Kropotkin. More will be said about Bernard-Lazare's attitude to voting in a later chapter. Suffice it here to say that he was never enamoured of 'parlementarisme' but he was prepared to 'deviate' from doctrine at a time when the very life of the Republic seemed in danger. He also explained half ironically and half seriously that the parliamentary tribune was a more efficacious platform for propaganda than anarchist periodicals read entirely by the converted. Grave also relates in his Memoirs that when Bernard-Lazare was asked by a mutual friend why he had not kept his promise of contributing to *Les Temps Nouveaux*, the surprising reply was 'il faut que mes articles soient payés' (Grave: *Quarante ans de propagande*

anarchiste, op. cit. p. 346). Grave was astonished by this, as well he might be, and put it down to necessity. Although Bernard-Lazare had to live by his pen, one cannot help wondering whether this was the real reason, if indeed he ever made the statement. However that may be, numerous extracts from *Les Porteurs de Torches* appeared in *Les Temps Nouveaux* throughout 1897, a fact Grave does not mention.

Chapter 4: '*Le Judaisme voilà l'ennemi*'

1 For the extraordinary success story of *La France Juive* and its publication history see Robert F. Byrnes: *Antisemitism in Modern France,* Rutgers University Press, New Brunswick, New Jersey, 1950, pp. 148–55, reprinted, Fertig, New York, 1969. Suffice it here to say that the publishers, though attracted by the prospect of a *succès de scandale,* regarded the venture too much of a financial risk, especially in view of the anticipated libel suits and legal costs. In the end publication was made conditional on Drumont agreeing to meet all litigation expenses as well as the cost of printing the first edition of 2,000 copies. The first edition appeared in 1886, and after the press controversy (started by the *Figaro,* which reviewed the book at Alphonse Daudet's request) was sold out in no time. Some 70,000 copies were sold within the first two months, over 100,000 copies by the end of the year. The delighted publishers could hardly keep up with the demand. There were a number of libel suits and a few duels, notably that between Drumont and Arthur Meyer, the royalist editor of *Le Gaulois,* himself a converted Jew, who had felt insulted. Meyer, for all his airs of a *grand seigneur,* had obviously not mastered the rules of duelling. Drumont made the most of what he called ungentlemanly 'semitic duelling' and the whole burlesque episode fascinated public opinion, thus providing additional publicity for *La France Juive,* (For details see *La France Juive devant l'Opinion,* Marpon and Flammarion, 1886, pp. 205–55.)

As to how Drumont came to write such a book or why he suddenly turned antisemite, after many happy years on the staff of a Saint-Simonian paper (*Liberté*) owned by a well-known Jewish family (the Pereires) who gave him no grounds for complaint, this is not easy to explain. How does one account for irrational hatreds of this magnitude? His ardent Catholicism and his love of a peasant, pre-industrial France of a bygone age, before the advent of the kings of steel and the kings of gold, are probably two basic ingredients. The Jew was anti-Christ and a millionaire tycoon, modern capitalism personified, parasite, exploiter, responsible for the evil and ugliness in Eiffel Tower Paris. On a more psychological level, Drumont's personal sense of failure – until *La France Juive* he had been a frustrated, small-time journalist craving for fame and success – and an accompanying jealousy of his eminently successful employers may likewise have played a part. He also shared with so many of his contemporaries a national defeat complex, the heavy legacy of 1870. Since his nationalism would not allow him to admit the inferiority of the French Army as compared to the Prussian Army, defeat had to be due to some secret treachery. And who more treacherous than Judas, collaborating this time with Bismarck?

2 Quoted by R. F. Byrnes: *Antisemitism in Modern France*, op. cit. p. 164.

3 *L'Autorité*, 18 November 1891.

4 Barrès: *Mes Cahiers*, T. II, p. 247, Plon, 1930.

5 *Le programme de Nancy* (1898) in *Barrès par lui-même*, édit. du Seuil, p. 133.

6 P. Sorlin: *La Croix et les Juifs*, Grasset, 1967.

7 *Entretiens*, 1 March 1890.

8 P. Valéry: *Lettres à quelques-uns*, Gallimard, 1952, p. 13.

9 A. Gide–P. Valéry *Correspondance*, op. cit., p. 94.

10 *Grimaces*, 3 November 1883, p. 778.

11 *La Plume*, 1 March 1893.

12 *Grimaces*, art. cit., p. 780.

13 Ibid., p. 724.

14 *Grimaces*, pp. 252–8.

15 Octave Mirbeau had a complete change of heart later on and it is possible that Bernard-Lazare, who became quite friendly with him, had something to do with it. Mirbeau also became an active dreyfusard.

16 In *L'Antisémitisme, son histoire et ses causes* (1894), to be discussed in the following chapter, Bernard-Lazare criticised Renan's racial theories and in particular his view of semitic inferiority. He added in a foot-note, however, that in later life Renan abandoned his theories of racial inferiority and superiority (p. 122). Drumont, noting a similar change, regretted Renan's later 'conversion to Judaism' (*La France Juive devant l'Opinion*, 1866, p. 166). Needless to say Renan under-went no such conversion; nor did he move from a consistent and all-out antisemitism – in a purely cultural and intellectual sense which did not implicate modern Jewry – to a consistent, all-out philosemitism. But there is a grain of truth in Drumont's comment: in the last decade or so of his life (1880–92), Renan not only repudiated his earlier racial theories, but stressed the positive and permanent contribution made by Judaism to the history of civilisation. Previously, only the prophets and especially Jesus, exceptional Hebrews, had found favour. How Renan, one of the most brilliant and influential scholars of the age, came to transform comparative Semitic philology, on which he was an authority, into a cultural and philosophical antisemitism, deriving in great part from the paradoxical combination of Catholic education and anticlericalism, forms a fascinating chapter in the intellectual history of the time.

Renan's writings on the subject under discussion are numerous. Below we list the most interesting, with the original date of publication given in brackets; the volume reference is to *Oeuvres Complètes*, édition définitive, Calmann-Lévy, 1947–1961:

> *Histoire générale et système comparé des langues sémitiques* (1855), O.C., 8.
>
> *Etudes d'histoire religieuse* (1857), O.C., 7.
>
> *De la part des peuples sémitiques dans la civilisation* (1862), O.C., 2.

Vie de Jésus (1863), *O.C.*, 4.

Histoire du peuple d'Israel (1887–1893), *O.C.*, 6.

Le Judaisme comme race et comme religion (1883), one of several lectures given by Renan to the *Société des Etudes Juives* and published by the Society's review (*Revue des Etudes Juives*) in which other of Renan's later studies also appeared.

17 'La Nationalité et les Juifs', *Figaro*, 27 December 1893.

18 *Archives Israélites*, 4 January 1894; *La Croix*, 3 January 1894.

19 'Juifs et Israélites', *Entretiens*, art. cit.

20 *Le Fumier de Job*, op. cit. pp. 58–9.

21 Ibid. p. 60.

22 'La Divine Espérance', *Revue Parisienne*, 25 December 1893. 'L'attente éternelle', *Magazine International*, April 1895. 'L'attente éternelle', *La Porte d'Ivoire*, 1897.

23 *Le Miroir des Légendes*, op. cit. p. 233.

24 Ibid. p. 243.

25 Ibid. p. 117.

26 *La Libre Parole*, 23 May 1892.

27 See l'Archiviste (Salomon Reinach?): *Drumont et Dreyfus*, Stock 1898, pp. 14–15.

28 *L'Endehors*, 29 May 1892.

29 'Aurea Médiocritas', 25 September 1892.

30 *Evénement*, 28 September 1893.

31 *Evénement*, 23 December 1892.

32 *La Libre Parole*, 22 October 1895.

33 Ibid. 24 October 1895.

34 Together with a report on the competition and a separate study by Emile Rouyer (a member of the jury), Father Jacquet's *mémoire* was published under the title *La République Plébiscitaire* (1897). Also prepared for publication were L. Vial's *Le Juif Roi*, Barruteil-Puig's *Race de Vipères*, A Duval's *L'Esprit de la Révolution*, Marie-Joseph Franck's *Solution de la Question Juive pour la France et tous les pays du monde*.

35 L. Bloy: *Journal*, Vol. 1, Mercure de France, 1956, p. 60.

36 Ibid. p. 59.

37 With characteristic insolence, Bloy replied to the compliment: 'Si les Juifs étaient opprimés injustement, ils m'intéresseraient encore, puisqu'il y aurait un Pharaon à couvrir d'outrages; mais, par bonheur, ils sont opprimés le plus justement du monde, étant eux-mêmes les oppresseurs les plus équitables et les plus abjects qu'on ait jamais vus. Occasion merveilleuse pour moi d'une oecuménique insolence. Je les aime donc pour me l'avoir procuré et, en ce sens, vous avez mille fois raison de m'appeler un philosémite.' In an altogether different vein, Bloy speaks of his conception of God not as omnipotent and magnificent but as 'ce Seigneur qui est infirme de tous ses membres, qui sent très mauvais, qui se râcle sur tous les fumiers de l'Orient ou de l'Occident...' (*Journal*, p. 60). Did this inspire Bernard-Lazare's image of Job: 'Voyez Job sur son fumier râclant ses ulcères'?

38 *Entretiens*, June 1892.

Chapter 5: Antisemitism, its history and causes

1 *L'Antisémitisme, son histoire et ses causes*, Documents et Témoignages, Paris 1969, p. 9. All references will be to the above-mentioned edition which is the most recent French edition. For comment see p. 122.
2 *Antisemitism, its history and causes*, Britons Publishing Company, London 1967.
3 *Entretiens Politiques et Littéraires*, September 1892.
4 Among the studies thus promised: Antijudaism in Moslem countries and Arab–Jewish relations. The history and persistence of the ritual murder libel. An economic history of the Jews. And, most dear to Bernard-Lazare's heart, an assessment of the role played by Jews in the social, moral, intellectual and revolutionary history of mankind.
5 *L'Antisémitisme, son histoire et ses causes*, op. cit p. 19.
6 Idem.
7 Ibid. p. 20.
8 Ibid. p. 14.
9 *Le Fumier de Job*, op. cit. p. 70.
10 'La conception sociale du judaïsme et le peuple juif', *La Grande Revue*, September 1899.
   Marx's *Jewish Question* (1843), written as a reply to Bruno Bauer's study by the same name (1841), was an influential antisemitic source at the turn of the century. Even Drumont occasionally quoted from it. It was not until later, notably in the article mentioned above, that Bernard-Lazare criticised Marx's pamphlet in detail. In the initial stages of *L'Antisémitisme, son histoire et ses causes* he was to some extent influenced by Marx's ideas; by the second part of the book, however, he is clearly reacting against them and seems to be re-writing in his own way *The Jewish Question*.
11 *L'Antisémitisme, son histoire et ses causes*, op. cit. p. 71.
12 Ibid. p. 26.
13 Ibid. pp. 71–2.
14 Ibid. p. 67.
15 Ibid. p. 64.
16 Ibid. p. 170.
17 Ibid. p. 171.
18 Moses Hess, Aaron Libermann, Léon Frankel, Théodore Hertzka among many others. Bernard-Lazare was particularly interested in the Yiddish-speaking circles grouped around *Der Arbeiter Freund* (London), *Die Arbeiter Zeitung* and *Die Freie Arbeiter Stimme* (New York), *Ons' Blad* (Holland) and *Die Wahrheit* (Lemberg). These groups, he argues, do not merely use Yiddish because it is the language in which they can best express themselves, but as an affirmation of Jewishness. In other words, we are not dealing with Socialists who happen to be of Jewish origin but with Socialists who are also conscious Jews and wish to participate as such, as 'Juifs au sens national', in the work of the International (pp. 170–1). Comments of this sort, while contradicting the assimilationist thesis of the work as a whole, look forward to

Bernard-Lazare's subsequently expressed Jewish nationalism of which we have the first hints here.

19 Ibid. pp. 181–2. Among the numerous newspaper and review articles devoted to the Jewish working-classes, following Soloweitshick's work, see the following: *La Petite République*, 3 March 1899; *L'Aurore*, 23 June 1898 and 18 September 1899; *Les Droits de l'homme*, 24 January 1899 and 17 September 1899; *Revue des revues*, March 1899. 1898 saw the formation in Paris of a group of Jewish workers whose public and passionate appeal to French Socialist leaders also did much to draw attention to the plight of a generally unknown Jewish proletariat in France. A copy of this appeal, 'Lettre des ouvriers Juifs de Paris au parti socialiste français', can be seen at the Institut Français d'Histoire Sociale (Fond Picart, 14 AS 213 1). It seems very probable that Bernard-Lazare helped to draft the letter.

20 *La Libre Parole*, 10 January 1895.

21 W. Marr: *La Victoire du Judaïsme sur le Germanisme*, 1879.

22 'Antisémitisme et Antisémites', *Echo de Paris*, 31 December 1894.

23 *La Libre Parole*, 22 May 1896.

24 *Contre l'Antisémitisme*, Stock, 1896, p. 19. For fuller discussion of this brochure see pp. 207–11.

25 *L'Antisémitisme, son histoire et ses causes*, chapter 9, especially pp. 118–22. For a modern account, in some ways less complete than that given by Bernard-Lazare, see R. F. Byrnes: *Antisemitism in Modern France*, New Jersey, 1950.

26 A remark made by Léon Bloy suggested this interpretation. In his *Journal* (Vol 1, Mercure de France, 1956, p. 96) Bloy relates how, after Bernard-Lazare's favourable review of *Le Salut par les Juifs*, he unsuccessfully tried to convince the Grand Rabbin that *Le Salut par les Juifs* was not an antisemitic work: 'Vainement, j'essaie de lui faire sentir l'importance de ma conclusion. Plus vainement encore, j'explique la violence de certaines pages par le dessein *d'épuiser l'objection*, méthode fameuse, recommandée par Saint Thomas d'Aquin. Il tient, absolument, à ne voir que la *lettre* de ces violences et se désintéresse de la conclusion...' While Bernard-Lazare's praise of Bloy's work was probably inspired by more than one reason (see pp. 87–9), it is not impossible that he recognised in it a polemical method, that of 'épuiser l'objection', which he himself was using in his history and this recognition may well have been a further factor in his surprisingly favourable reaction to *Le Salut par les Juifs*. One great difference between the two polemicists is this: whereas Bloy's objections also apply, indeed mainly apply, to present-day Jewry, Bernard-Lazare is concerned with showing the unreasonableness of antisemitic objections when addressed to modern Jewry. Whatever Bloy's secret intention may have been, and whatever the startling unorthodoxy of his ideas, language and imagination, his viewpoint is Christian while that of Bernard-Lazare is social. Let us also note that in *L'Antisémitisme, son histoire et ses causes*, *Le Salut par les Juifs* is listed among modern examples of the old Christian aspiration 'de ramener Israel dans le giron de l'Eglise' and is described as 'un livre singulier' (p. 118).

27 Ibid. p. 199.

28 'Le Nouveau Ghetto', *La Justice*, 17 November 1894; 'Antisémitisme and Antisémites', *Echo de Paris*, 31 December 1894.

29 *Le Nationalisme Juif*, Stock, 1898.

30 Chapter 12, 'L'esprit révolutionnaire dans le judaïsme'. Previously published as an article under the same title in *La Revue Bleue*, May 1893.

31 Gustave Kahn: *La Société Nouvelle*, July–December 1894. Lucien Muhlfeld: *La Revue Blanche*, June 1894. Alfred Naquet: *La Petite République*, 24 September 1903. Théodore Reinach: *Revue des Etudes Juives*, Vol. xxx, 1895. One of the warmest appreciations came from André Fontainas, the symbolist poet and a literary friend, who pertinently wondered whether all readers of *L'Antisémitisme, son histoire et ses causes*, would draw the same salutary lessons as he had done (Archives Bernard-Lazare, Alliance Israëlite Universelle). Forty years later, in 1934, Fontainas was asked by the Bernard family to write the introduction to the re-edition of the work and he did so in a lengthy, well-meaning but disappointing study which greatly simplifies both the personal crisis of identity as well as the wider social and moral issues reflected in the work. A substantial part of this study also appeared in the *Mercure de France* (Vol. 245, 1933, pp. 45–71) under the title 'L'antisémitisme et Bernard-Lazare'. It would have been interesting to know the reaction of such personalities as Kropotkin to whom Bernard-Lazare personally sent copies of the work. It is worth recalling the brief but eloquent dedication in the copy presented to Octave Mirbeau: 'à l'artiste loyal, au révolté, à l'ami' (*L'Avenir Illustré*, February 1934, p. 3).

32 *La Libre Parole*, 10 January 1895. To Drumont the unforgettable phrase which summed up this remarkable work was: '. . .partout, et jusqu'à nos jours, le Juif fut un être insociable'. Bernard-Lazare repeatedly explained that the rest of the book (the phrase occurs in the introductory chapter) demonstrated that the 'jusqu'à nos jours' referred to Jewry in countries where assimilation was rendered impossible but that in the West Jewish unsociability was largely a thing of the past. Drumont, who preferred to ignore much of the second part of the book, remained unconvinced and once again quoted the famous phrase in the strangely moving obituary he devoted to Bernard-Lazare in 1903.

33 *La Libre Parole*, 22 May 1896. It was in reply to Zola's article 'Pour les Juifs' (*Le Figaro*, 16 May 1896) that Drumont praised Bernard-Lazare as an altogether worthier adversary. Straightening things out with Drumont was undoubtedly uppermost in Bernard-Lazare's mind but *Contre l'antisémitisme* is also in some sense a reply to *Pour les Juifs*, for Zola's generosity, courage and good intentions were not matched at the time by any real understanding of the situation. His defence amounted to a defence of the capitalist society in which the Jews, having originally been made into kings of finance through no fault of their own, exercised their gifts, masters of the Stock Exchange where Christian financiers were free to learn from them and beat them

in the healthy struggle of competition. Such a viewpoint, needless
to say, went against everything Bernard-Lazare believed in.

34 *La Société Nouvelle*, July–December 1894, pp. 240–50.

35 'Antisémitisme et Antisémites', art. cit. *Echo de Paris*, 31 December
1894.

36 'Les vraies causes de l'antisémitisme', *Revue Encyclopédique*, January
1895, pp. 31–3. With regard to the identity of 'Agathon', it is most
unlikely to be Henri Massis who was a boy of nine in 1895. Maurras,
on the other hand, then aged 27, was not only a contributor to the
same revue under his proper name but as 'Agathon' he already expressed
in the above mentioned article antisemitic ideas developed later.

37 Extracts from *Antisemitism, its history and causes* appeared in various
reviews for some time after its publication and overlapped with the
Dreyfus affair. The most notable example of the misunderstanding thus
created is afforded by the entry for antisemitism which Bernard-Lazare
contributed in the supplement of Léon Say's *Nouveau Dictionnaire
d'Economie Politique*. By the time the supplement appeared, in 1897,
Bernard-Lazare had moved a long way from the ideas expressed three
years earlier. Yet the dictionary entry, presumably submitted at an
earlier stage, is a summary of *L'Antisémitisme, son histoire et ses
causes*. In this way, the unwary reader could easily be misled, as
indeed were some of Bernard-Lazare's contemporaries, the critic of the
Archives Israelites, for example, (May 1897). It is interesting to note
incidentally that in its original publication (1891–3) Say's Dictionary
carried no entry either for antisemitism or for anarchism. Both figure
in the 1897 Supplement. A sign of the times.

38 Maurras: *Au Signe de Flore*, Grasset, 1933, pp. 51–2, 87–9.

39 *Action Française*, T. xix, 1907, pp. 182 and 184.

40 *Action Française* (the daily paper), 15 September 1908.

41 *Action Française*, T. xix, 1907, p. 177.

42 'Quelques prétentions juives', *L'Indépendance*, 1, 15 May and 1 June
1912.

43 Ibid. 1 June, p. 320.

44 Ibid.

45 'La réaction révolutionnaire', *L'Action Sociale*, 1 and 8 February 1896.

46 *L'Antisémitisme, son histoire et ses causes*, Documents et Témoignages,
1969, p. 7 and back cover.

47 Bernard-Lazare Archives, Alliance Israélite Universelle.

48 *Contre l'Antisémitisme*, op. cit. p. 19.

Chapter 6: Involvement

1 P. V. Stock: *Mémorandum d'un Editeur*, 3° Série, l'Affaire Dreyfus,
Stock, 1938, p. 29.

2 Siegfried Thalheimer: *Macht und Gerechtigkeit*, Munich, 1958. The
author not only appreciates the role played by Bernard-Lazare but
also the significance of his theories concerning the Affair which
Thalheimer has greatly developed, at times with a degree of certainty
not to be found in Bernard-Lazare.

3 Reinach papers, feuillet 214, Manuscripts, Bibliothèque Nationale. Frequent reference will be made to two accounts Bernard-Lazare gave of his activities during the Affair: one to Reinach and the other to Jean-Bernard, a journalist of the *Figaro*. A substantial part of the account to Reinach, henceforth referred to as the 'Reinach Note', has been published by Robert Gauthier in *Dreyfusards* (Julliard, Collection Archives, 1965, pp. 82–95). Page references for quotations from the published part will refer to this book. Quotations from the original manuscript will be indicated as 'Reinach Note F' (feuillet), with the number of the feuillet corresponding to the classification of the Reinach papers at the Bibliothèque Nationale. This account, which takes Bernard-Lazare's activities up to the beginning of 1898, is undated; it was probably written some time in 1899 or 1900. The 'Jean-Bernard interview' took place in September 1899, at the time of the Rennes trial. Although published at the time, Jean-Bernard: *Le Procès de Rennes*, Lemerre, 1900, this interesting testimony is little known.

4 Reinach Note, R. Gauthier, op. cit. p. 84.

5 Jean-Bernard: *Le Procès de Rennes*, op. cit. pp. 329–30. In an article he wrote for an English paper, *The Graphic* (3 December 1898), Bernard-Lazare emphasised the two main points in his early involvement, prior to his meeting with Mathieu: that he had conducted his own enquiries into Captain Dreyfus' life, character, position; and that the negative result of these enquiries helped to confirm his suspicion that France was about to embark on a modern version of the ritual murder trials of old. Two such trials of more recent date were particularly in his mind: the Thomas affair in Damascus 1840 (for this extraordinary incident and its repercussions in French politics, see Léon Poliakov: *Histoire de l'Antisémitisme, de Voltaire à Wagner*, Calmann-Lévy, 1968, pp. 358–63) and the Tisza-Eszlar case in Hungary, 1882. The analogy between these cases and the Dreyfus case struck him even more forcibly when, after having had Mathieu's account, 'I was able to compare the conduct and the attitude of M. du Paty de Clam with those of the Consul Ratti Menton in the Damascus affair and with those of Judge Bari in the Tisza-Eszlar case. In all these cases there was the same system of physical and moral torture, the same perversion and poisoning of public opinion, the same transformation from the very commencement of the accused into a culprit and these ends were effected by all possible means, by injurious reports about the character of the individual, fables about his private life, accounts of false confessions, insinuations of former crimes. The manoeuvres by which the anti-semitic Press made General Mercier compound with his conscience completed my enlightenment...'

6 P. V. Stock: *Mémorandum d'un Editeur*, op. cit. p. 18.

7 'Antisémitisme et Antisémites'; *Echo de Paris*, 31 December 1894.

8 *Une Erreur Judiciaire. L'Affaire Dreyfus. Deuxième Mémoire avec Expertises d'Ecriture*. Stock 1897.

9 Ibid. p. 13.

10 Ibid. p. 15.

11 Ibid. p. 22.

12 Ibid. p. 23.

13 *Macht und Gerechtigkeit*, op. cit. pp. 221ff. and pp. 279–304.

14 E. Duclaux: *Propos d'un solitaire*, Stock, 1898, p. 13.

15 *Le Siècle*, 26 December 1894.

16 *Une Erreur Judiciaire. Deuxième Mémoire*. Op. cit. p. 28.

17 Ibid. p. 9.

18 How Mathieu, and through him Bernard-Lazare, acquired information
gave rise to the wildest speculations and rumours and they constitute
an eloquent testimony of the syndicate complex which bedevilled the
whole Affair. The truth was often much simpler. Thus, no powerful
syndicate was needed for Mathieu to obtain copies of the *bordereau*
and the *acte d'accusation*. Legally he had no right to possess such
copies, and this complicated the use he could make of them, but it
should not have been too difficult to guess their provenance. The
sources for the illegal communication and the *canaille de D* note were
less straightforward: they involved, first of all, a private conversation
between the President of the Republic (Félix Faure) and his friend
Doctor Gibert who, with Faure's permission, told Mathieu. The
second source was provided by casual remarks made by a member of
the court-martial which were overheard by Maître Salles who told
Demange; he in turn verified the existence of the document through
Trarieux and Hanotaux. Chance and personal relations played a great
part in all this but no bribery was involved or needed. The story
illustrates another aspect all too often forgotten by modern historians
who are too ready to charge Mathieu with deviousness and unnecessary
secrecy, all of which, it is claimed, confirmed fears and prejudices. But
Mathieu not infrequently found himself in the dilemma of possessing
vital information and being prevented from using it frankly and
publicly by his informants. Thus, Félix Faure, belatedly realising the
implications, threatened to declare Doctor Gibert insane if the latter
made public their conversation. The generous Gibert, ready to brave
these threats at the Zola trial, was prevented from doing so by Mathieu
who, to the detriment of his own cause, would not let a friend expose
himself to public ridicule and contempt. The remarks made by an indis-
creet officer (who would no doubt have denied them) and confirmed
by highly placed men were equally unusable in any public discussion.
It is perfectly true that Mathieu used secret agents (what else could
he have done in the face of official secrecy, obstacles of all sorts and
constant surveillance?) but it should not be forgotten that his hands
were sometimes tied by cautious or frightened informants and collaborators. Bernard-Lazare found all this very irksome and he tried to
put dreyfusard strategy on a different footing. However, it cannot be
said that the subsequently more open battle fought by more daring
men did much to allay fears of a subversive syndicate being at work.
There comes a point when everything is food for such fears. To what
extent the syndicate myth was a genuine expression of deep-seated
fears and to what extent it was artificially created and deliberately
fanned strikes me as a more pertinent question than Mathieu's contribution to its elaboration and extension.

19 Jean-Bernard: *Le Procès de Rennes*, op. cit. p. 332.
20 For a description of this note see p. 116. The crucial sentence reads: 'Ci-joint douze plans directeurs de Nice que ce *canaille de D* m'a remis pour vous.'
21 Reinach Note, R. Gauthier, op. cit. p. 85.
22 *Une Erreur Judiciaire. L'Affaire Dreyfus. Deuxième Mémoire.* Op. cit. pp. 2–3.
23 Reinach Note, R. Gauthier, op. cit. p. 86.
24 It is unlikely that Bernard-Lazare was involved in the escape story. His absence from Paris at the time tends to confirm this. Creating false rumours, even for the purpose of reviving interest, was not his genre. On the other hand, it is more than likely that he, with his journalistic contacts, put Mathieu in touch with Clifford Millage. Bernard-Lazare was in London in the summer of 1896 and may well have sounded out English press opinion. Later police records speak of his contacts with the *Daily Chronicle*. The paper was ardently dreyfusard as was Millage. In its obituary, the paper paid tribute to Bernard-Lazare's work as primary cause of the revision and the best exposition of the case (3 September 1903).
25 Reinach Note, R. Gauthier, p. 86.
26 The *Eclair* version was altogether distorted. It read: 'Décidément cet animal de Dreyfus devient trop exigeant.'
27 Reinach Note, F 216.
28 Reinach Note, R. Gauthier, p. 87.
29 'Le coût des brochures fut de 186 F; il faut ajouter à cela 1.500 F de mise sous bande, sous enveloppe et affranchissement. Ce fut là la formidable dépense qui fit soupçonner l'existence d'un syndicat!' Reinach Note, R. Gauthier, p. 87.
30 Idem.
31 Ibid. pp. 87–8.
32 'Un défenseur du traître', *L'Intransigeant*, 5 September 1903.
33 Reinach Note, R. Gauthier, p. 88. Bernard-Lazare later learnt that it was Vaughan, the future editor of the dreyfusard *Aurore*, who had influenced Rochefort's initial antidreyfusard stand. On his own confession, Vaughan was not only convinced of Dreyfus' guilt but he also believed that the Jews would use their financial power to set him free. 'Je vivais sur mes préjuges.' For this reason he stopped the publication of an article favourable to Dreyfus which was to have appeared in *Le Jour* of 12 September 1896, following a visit to Forzinetti by one of the paper's journalists, Possien (*L'Aurore*, 5 May 1901). If Vaughan was mistaken in thinking that *Le Jour's* editor, Vervoort, was in the pay of the Jews, he was not altogether wrong to be suspicious for Vervoort had asked the Grand-Rabbin for a large sum of money in return for publishing articles in favour of revision. Zadoc-Kahn declined the offer. According to Robert Gauthier (*Dreyfusards*, op. cit. note p. 86), Possien eventually sold the articles, together with his silence, to the War Office.

Chapter 7: The battle: Une erreur judiciaire

1 Reinach Note, R. Gauthier, p. 85.
2 It is interesting to recall that Forzinetti protested against the exceptional severity of the treatment envisaged which went against regulations, the prisoner not having been proven guilty as yet. The orders were slightly changed. *Enquête de la Cour de Cassation*, Stock, 1899, p. 317.
3 Marguerite-Fernand Labori: *Labori, ses notes manuscrites,* Paris Editions Victor Attinger, 1947, p. 9.
4 One may or may not agree with Bernard-Lazare's interpretation of the *bordereau*. Marcel Thomas disagrees, naturally, given his thesis that the Affair was the result of a guilty Esterhazy and administrative incompetence on the part of essentially honest men. But how justified is he in peremptorily dismissing Bernard-Lazare's discussion of the document's *invraisemblance* as 'contrary to the facts'? (*L'Affaire sans Dreyfus,* Fayard, 1961, p. 351). What are the facts? Bernard-Lazare never denied the *existence* of the *bordereau*; he questioned its authenticity, which is a very different matter, and in the process raised questions which are still open to debate. What one nowadays regards as 'fact' ultimately depends on which of several conflicting testimonies one accepts as true or reasonable.
5 P. Brulat: *Violence et Raison*, Stock, 1898, p. 214.
6 The essential points of Bertillon's strange theories, demonstrated at length in 1894 to a baffled court-martial, were also made public for the first time in Bernard-Lazare's brochure.
7 Speech in the Chamber of Deputies, 18 November 1896, quoted in: P. Marin: *Dreyfus?*, Librairie Illustrée, 1898, p. 290.
8 *Une erreur judiciaire. La Vérité sur l'Affaire Dreyfus*, Stock, 1897, op. cit. p. 83. Marcel Thomas speaks of Bernard-Lazare's 'affirmations péremptoires' and regrets that the 'Etat-Major n'ait pas su faire la part de ce qu'il pourrait y avoir de bluff' (*L'Affaire sans Dreyfus*, op. cit. p. 350). After all, he remarks, Bernard-Lazare only knew three words of the *canaille de D* note. Textually speaking this is probably correct, though he may well have known the gist of the note. At any rate these three words were the important ones. More important still, he knew a fair amount of *background* to the note (date, identity of D, that the clerk had been under surveillance which was eventually abandoned) and it was this which alarmed Gonse who confirmed its accuracy in every detail (*Enquête de la Cour de Cassation*, Stock, 1899, p. 255). Peremptory Bernard-Lazare's affirmations may be at times; the unfortunate result of being unable to disclose Mathieu's sources of information. But they are for the most part factually correct and convincingly woven into the argument as a whole. What mattered to him about the *canaille de D* note is that it was not connected with Dreyfus until *after* the *bordereau*, that it was not used against him until *after* the trial, that the *Eclair* had changed the 'D' to Dreyfus. Where is the 'bluff'?
9 Henry probably composed his *faux* between 31 October and 1 November 1896. The first appearance of Bernard-Lazare's brochure is

occasionally given as the 28 October. If true, it would be an ironic coincidence.

10 *Une Erreur Judiciaire. La Vérité sur l'Affaire Dreyfus*, p. 91.

11 Charles Maurras: *Au Signe de Flore*, op. cit. p. 89.

12 *Une Erreur Judiciaire. La Vérité sur l'Affaire Dreyfus*, pp. 89–92.

13 Archives Bernard-Lazare, Alliance Israelite Universelle.

14 H. Wickham Steed: *Through 30 Years 1892–1922*, London, Heinemann, 1924, Vol. I, p. 61.

15 Zévaès later became a dreyfusard and in his later history of the Affair he explains with some regret initial Socialist hesitations without specifically mentioning his own vitriolic attack on Bernard-Lazare. A propos the latter's standing in Socialist circles at the time of *Une Erreur Judiciaire*, he remarks: 'L'anarchisme de Bernard-Lazare, le bruit de ses relations avec les Rothschild prédisposent peu les socialistes en sa faveur; d'autre part, à l'occasion du tout récent Congrès international de Londres, n'a-t-il pas écrit divers articles contre Jaurès, Jules Guesde et leurs amis?' (*L'Affaire Dreyfus*, Nouvelle Revue Critique, 1931, p. 63). This is probably a fair picture though the *rumoured* relations with the Rothschilds, an unfounded rumour, were presented as fact by Zévaès in 1896. In September 1903 Zévaès wrote a laudatory obituary on Bernard-Lazare (*L'Ami du Peuple*, Grenoble) and in 1933 he enthusiastically supported a projected Bernard-Lazare commemoration ceremony.

16 Fernand Pelloutier's *L'Ouvrier des Deux Mondes* (1 December 1897) was a notable exception: 'Il était bon...qu'une voix socialiste fît entendre la protestation nécessaire contre tout déni de justice.'

17 Jean Grave: *Quarante ans de propagande anarchiste*, Flammarion, 1973, p. 361.

18 Idem.

19 Reinach Note, R. Gauthier, p. 89.

20 It was Teysonnières, one of the 1894 experts, who communicated his copy of the *bordereau* to *Le Matin*. Bernard-Lazare initially thought it was Bertillon, as did Picquart. *Le Matin*'s motives in publishing so important a piece are questionable. Officially they were given as putting a stop to Bernard-Lazare's 'manoeuvres savantes et ténébreuses' and to possible public pity for the traitor Dreyfus (10 November 1896). One cannot blame the War Office for suspecting that the exact opposite was the case, especially since Bernard-Lazare and Mathieu lost no time in making use of what was to them an unexpected piece of good fortune. Perhaps it was the only way for *Le Matin* to express its doubts and help the cause of revision independently of the 'syndicate'.

21 Jean-Bernard: *Le Procès de Rennes*, op. cit. p. 334.

22 Archives Nationales, BB 19 73. Several notes by Gonse and Gribelin express the same alarm.

23 Archives Nationales, BB 19 73.

24 Who was the informant behind the *Eclair* revelations? Bernard-Lazare knew by 1898 that Lissajoux, a journalist from *Le Petit Journal*, was the author of the articles. But this only begged the question. Lissajoux was extraordinarily well-informed. Whence came his information? If

Bernard-Lazare was probably mistaken in attributing 'the leakage' to Mercier, he may well have been right in thinking that it emanated from high. At Rennes, Picquart stated that he recognised Du Paty de Clam's style, though this is not what he told Gonse in 1896. On the other hand, it was Henry who had well-known connections with *Le Petit Journal*. As for the purpose of the articles, Bernard-Lazare ultimately believed that the main aim was to implicate Picquart while at the same time, *chemin faisant*, strengthening public belief in Dreyfus' guilt with information which, it was assumed, would go unchallenged.

25 Archives Nationales, BB 19 73.
26 *Enquête de la Cour de Cassation*, Stock, 1899, p. 256.
27 12 November 1896. Archives Nationales, BB 19 94.
28 Ibid. BB 19 94.
29 *L'Intransigeant*, 23 November 1896.
30 B. Schwertfeger: *The Truth about Dreyfus from the Schwartzkoppen Papers*, Putnam, London and New York, 1931, p. 191.
31 Reinach Note F 220.
32 R. Gauthier: *Dreyfusards*, op. cit. p. 99.
33 Marguerite-Fernand Labori: *Labori*, op. cit. p. 8.
34 Ibid. p. 9.
35 *Le Soir*, 11 November 1896. *Une erreur judiciaire: la vérité sur l'Affaire Dreyfus*, pp. xi–xiii.
36 Letter quoted in *Chalom*, 1933.
37 *Une Erreur Judiciaire, Deuxième Mémoire*, p. 45.
38 Ibid. p. 60.
39 Ibid. p. 63.
40 *Le Procès Zola, devant la Cour d'Assises de la Seine et la Cour de Cassation*, 2 vols. Stock, 1898, Vol. II, p. 189. Eminent authorities working in their own countries for such venerable institutions as law courts, government offices, Scotland Yard, the British Museum, the experts were paid the fees they asked for (some gave their services gratis) and were assured in writing that their findings would be published whether or not they were favourable to the dreyfusard cause (*Une Erreur Judiciaire. Deuxième Mémoire*, p. 53). One of the two French experts was the respected amateur graphologist Crépieux-Jamin, until then known for his antidreyfusard convictions. After publication of his findings (i.e. that the *bordereau* is not in Dreyfus's hand) he became the object of a vicious smear-campaign in the *Libre Parole* which almost ruined him professionally. People did not wish to have their teeth cared for (he was a dentist) by such a man, he remarked with bitter humour (*Le Procès Zola*, Vol. I, pp. 489–95). For the correspondence with the experts and details of fees see Box 19. dossier graphologique, Archives Bernard-Lazare.
41 *L'Aurore*, 23 November 1897. Anatole France liked Bernard-Lazare's brochure for its comment on antisemitism but distrusted all hand-writing expertise. If the judges base their convictions on the latter, that was their affair, he remarked. It was the publication of *l'acte d'accusation* (7 January 1898) which finally convinced A. France.

42 *Le Temps*, 17 November 1897.
43 *Une Erreur Judiciaire. Deuxième Mémoire.* pp. 54–9.
44 Ibid. p. 9.
45 Ibid. p. 10.
46 *L'Aurore*, 30 July 1899.
47 Y. Guyot: *La Révision du procès Dreyfus*, Stock, 1898, p. 145.
48 *Comment on condamne un innocent*, Stock, 1898, p. vi.
49 Police report of 20 January 1898.
50 'Si vous reconnaissez que c'est M. Bernard Lazare, n'en parlons plus.' With these words, establishing that it was Bernard-Lazare who had supplied the expert with samples of Esterhazy's handwriting, the president of the Court dismissed Louis Franck's long and laborious graphological identification of the *bordereau's* writing with that of Esterhazy. Instead of questioning the soundness or relevance of the expert's theories, and some of them were absurd, the authenticity of the documents, in other words Bernard-Lazare's good faith, was being questioned instead. *Le Procès Zola*, Vol. I, p. 534.
51 Ibid. Vol. I, p. 245.
52 Ibid. Vol. II, pp. 130–1.
53 Report dated 24 February 1898. The police believed that Bouton had actually tried to make a deal with the 'syndicate' but that the latter refused to pay the extortionate sum demanded. Hence Bouton's attempted revenge at the Zola trial.
54 *Enquête de la Cour de Cassation*, op. cit. pp. 761–3.
55 *L'Aurore*, 30 July 1899. The Bouton story is not without its interest. Briefly, this is what happened, according to Bernard-Lazare: in the course of collecting material for his history of anarchism, Bernard-Lazare went to see Charavay (whose parents had been involved with a communist group in 1841) who referred him to Victor Bouton, a former agent of the political police and the author of *Profils Révolutionnaires*, which Bernard-Lazare had read. Delighted that Bouton was still alive, Bernard-Lazare called on the octogenarian. During his third and final visit, in December 1896, after the publication of *Une erreur judiciaire: la vérité sur l'Affaire Dreyfus*, Bouton unsolicitedly expressed his conviction that Dreyfus could not be the author of the *bordereau*. Bernard-Lazare was pleased but paid no further attention and here his contact with Bouton ended. 'Je fus stupéfait un jour de le voir à une audience du procès Zola, presque amené à la barre par le général de Pellieux.'
The Charavay visit raises an interesting question. While there is no reason to doubt the motives as related by Bernard-Lazare since we know from other sources, notably the Nettlau correspondence, that he was indeed preparing a history of anarchism at that time, it is nonetheless a strange coincidence that this historical research should take him to a crucial prosecution witness: Charavay was one of the three experts who had attributed authorship of the *bordereau* to Dreyfus (1894). Did Bernard-Lazare perhaps combine two interests dear to his heart? It is also interesting to note that Charavay, although he did not formally retract his early conclusion until 1899, evidently began

to have doubts about the legal use made of his report as early as 1897, perhaps as a result of Bernard-Lazare's brochure. Interviewed by the *Aurore* (23 November 1897) à propos that brochure, Anatole France quoted his friend Charavay as saying: 'Jamais, jamais, je ne voudrais condamner quelqu'un sur un de mes rapports.'

Chapter 8: Behind the front lines

1 Reinach Note, R. Gauthier, p. 95.
2 Quoted in M. Marrus: *The Politics of Assimilation*, Oxford, Clarendon Press, 1971, p. 186, n. 3.
3 'The Dreyfus Case', *The Graphic*, 3 December 1898.
4 He used the foreign press because he could not express himself freely in the French press but he never voiced anti-French sentiments or condoned the francophobia sometimes dressed up as dreyfusism. Like Péguy, he was fully aware that only in France could there have been a Dreyfus Affair and this is what he told an American public ('France at the parting of the ways', *North American Review*, November 1899). In his firm conviction that the outcome of the Affair was of crucial importance to European liberalism, because fundamental ideals of freedom and justice were being challenged in France, he was very French.
5 Report dated 5 May 1898.
6 In the bibliography attached to the English edition of the Schwartz-koppen papers (*The Truth About Dreyfus*, p. 250) Bernard-Lazare is given as the editor of the (three volume) Rennes Proceedings published by Stock in 1900 (*Le Procès Dreyfus devant le conseil de guerre de Rennes*). Though I have not seen this mentioned anywhere else, it is a plausible suggestion. Some of the telling footnotes certainly bear his stamp.
7 *L'Aurore*, 7 September 1898.
8 'Lettre Ouverte à M. Trarieux', *L'Aurore*, 7 June 1899.
9 There were some who were profoundly moved by this gesture, notably Eugène Carrière, the painter. 'Il était bon qu'un Juif parlât et que vous fussiez ce Juif...Israel a encore des héros; nous les mettons avec les nôtres sur les mêmes autels de la fraternité humaine' (Letter quoted in *Chalom*, September 1933, p. 5). Léon Bloy also applauded but not without exploiting Bernard-Lazare's protest in a diatribe against Zola whom he accuses, among other things, of self-glorification, of having forgotten that Bernard-Lazare was a dreyfusard in 1894, 'qui, après la victoire, n'obtient pas même une mention...' (*Je m'accuse*, Edition de la Maison d'Art, 1900, p. 71). While it is true that Zola sometimes tended to forget the battle waged prior to *J'accuse*, it is not at all against him that Bernard-Lazare's protest is directed, as Bloy suggests.
10 *Enquête de la Cour de Cassation*, op. cit. p. 256.
11 It is clear from their confidential notes that they were extremely suspicious of Picquart. However, since suspicion centred on the secret *canaille de D* note, an official investigation – accompanied by possible

leakages – presented certain dangers. The less that was said about the note the better.

12 *L'Aurore*, 13 August 1898.

13 Idem.

14 *L'Aurore*, 12 and 30 August 1899.

15 Reinach Note, R. Gauthier, p. 95.

16 *Labori*, op. cit. p. 287.

17 Salomon Reinach in a letter to Péguy, Archives du Centre Charles Péguy, Orléans.

18 Archives de l'Alliance Israëlite Universelle.

19 *L'Enigme Esterhazy*, Gallimard, Paris, 1962, pp. 110–16.

20 *Echo de Paris*, 30 November 1901.

21 *Le Libertaire*, 1 July 1899.

22 *Procès de Rennes*, op. cit. Vol. i, p. 379.

23 Idem.

24 Ibid. p. 381.

25 Ibid. p. 398.

26 Quoted in R. Gauthier: *Dreyfusards*, op. cit. p. 239.

27 Archives Bernard-Lazare, Alliance Israëlite Universelle. This text, entitled '*Derrière le Mur*', would seem to have been published in *Journal du Soir* (Lyons).

28 Idem.

29 Jean-Bernard: *Le Procès de Rennes*, op. cit. p. 11.

30 Ibid. p. 13.

31 Ibid. p. 14.

32 *L'Aurore*, 8 August 1899.

33 *L'Aurore*, 31 August 1899.

34 *Le Petit Bleu*, 10 September 1899.

35 'France at the parting of the Ways', *North American Review*, November 1899.

36 *Souvenirs*, R. Gauthier: *Dreyfusards*, op. cit. p. 209.

37 'France at the parting of the ways', art. cit.

38 See *Procès de Rennes*, Vol. i, p. 106.

39 Ibid., Vol. i, p. 108; p. 142. Vol. ii, p. 478; p. 576.

40 What follows is a summary of Bernard-Lazare's analysis.

41 Needless to say not all historians share this view. See for example Douglas Johnson's attempt to justify the prosecution's case: *France and the Dreyfus Affair*, London, 1966, pp. 171–9.

42 *L'Aurore*, 31 August 1899.

43 In this coded telegram (intercepted by French Intelligence) the Italian military attaché advised his superior in Rome that if he had had no relations with Dreyfus to issue a *communiqué* to that effect 'in order to avoid press comment'. This was the sense of the second and correct version as decoded by the French Foreign Office. In a first, tentative decoding the last few words were apparently wrongly translated as 'emissary warned'. In the Foreign Office's view neither version was damaging to Dreyfus. The War Office interpreted 'emissary warned' in a different light. Moreover, it would seem as if somebody at some stage – the names of Sandherr and Henry have been suggested

– added the clearly incriminating words of *'precautions taken, emis-sary warned'*.

The telegram, cause of dispute between the Foreign Office and the War Office, has a controversial history into which there is no need to go here. The crucial question remains whether the incorrect, and possibly the embellished, version was shown to the judges in 1894. Alternatively, if Mercier merely withheld the correct version he may not be guilty of presenting distorted evidence, but he is guilty of withholding evidence which, while not amounting to proof of inno-cence, at least showed that Dreyfus had had no relations with Panizzardi (and Italy, as affirmed by Rome); a significant factor when taken in conjunction with the *canaille de D* note in which 'D' evidently was an agent working for both Germany and Italy. One last point: if, as Mercier claimed, no version of the telegram was shown to the judges in 1894, who put the wrong version into the secret dossier?

44 'France at the parting of the ways', art. cit. p. 651.
45 *L'Enigme Esterhazy*, op. cit. pp. 78–92.
46 'France at the parting of the ways', art. cit.
47 Idem.
48 Quoted in *Labori*, op. cit. p. 161.
49 Ibid. pp. 139–40
50 Ibid. p. 162.
51 *Procès de Rennes*, Vol. i, p. 605.
52 *Labori*, op. cit. p. 156.
53 'France at the parting of the ways', art. cit.
54 Archives Meyerson.
55 *Les Temps Nouveaux*, 17–23 April, 1897.
56 'Les Anarchistes voteront-ils?', *L'Oeuvre Sociale*, August 1897.
57 *The Daily Chronicle*, 11 August 1899.
58 Procès de Rennes, Vol. iii, p. 699.
59 Ibid. p. 706.
60 Bloy expressed disappointment in Dreyfus's stiff, military bearing in his own, inimitable way: 'O Hébreux! si tu étais plein de ton père Abraham, si tu pensais à Moïse et aux Prophètes, si tu croyais à la Promesse, tu aurais quelque chose à dire à ces généraux imbéciles autant qu'infâmes, qui saliraient problablement leurs culottes étoilées. . . en t'écoutant' (*Je m'accuse*, op. cit. p. 116).
61 *L'Aurore*, 7 June 1899, art. cit.
62 *Echo de Paris*, 30 November 1901.
63 Police Report dated 23 January 1900.
64 Archives Bernard-Lazare, Alliance Israelite Universelle.
65 S. Thalheimer: *Macht und Gerechtigkeit*, 1958, op. cit.
66 Reinach Note, R. Gauthier, p. 84.

Chapter 9: The Moral syndicate: the dreyfusard movement

1 P. V. Stock: *Mémorandum d'un Editeur*, op. cit. p. 29.
2 *Le Voltaire*, 2 December 1897.
3 Letter, undated (August 1896) quoted in *L'Avenir Illustré*, Casablanca,

February 1934, p. 12. Unlike his brother Théodore, who recommended the silence of contempt as the only dignified response to Drumont, Joseph Reinach was a fighter. Salomon seems to have been somewhere between the two. He was among the first Intellectuals to join the 'moral syndicate' and one has the impression that he was very active behind the dreyfusard scenes. It is generally believed that he is the 'Archiviste' who wrote the well-documented account of the *Libre Parole*'s early involvement in the Dreyfus Affair: *Drumont et Dreyfus, études sur la Libre Parole de 1894 à 1895*, Stock, 1898.

4 Letter dated 28 August 1896. Reinach Papers (Correspondence) MS 24897, Manuscripts, Bibliothèque Nationale.

5 Reinach Note, R. Gauthier, p. 87.

6 Ibid. p. 89.

7 For discussion of initial Socialist attitudes, see:

Ch. Péguy: 'La crise du parti socialiste et l'Affaire Dreyfus', *Revue Blanche*, 15 August 1899; 'L'Affaire Dreyfus et la crise du parti socialiste', *Revue Blanche*, 15 September 1899; A. Zévaès: *L'Affaire Dreyfus*, Nouvelle Revue Critique, 1931.

8 *L'Art Social*, July 1896. Two months earlier, Bernard Lazare had personally written to Zola to express his sympathy and the hope that the next novel, *Paris*, 'serait l'oeuvre sociale qu'il fallait écrire' (Reinach Note, R. Gauthier, p. 92). In a charming reply Zola wrote: '...rien ne pouvait me toucher davantage que cette sympathie inattendue d'un adversaire.... Ah! si la paix pouvait se faire ainsi entre tous les esprits de bonne volonté, sur le terrain de la raison' (11 May 1896, *Chalom*, September 1933, p. 4). All this took place quite independently of the Affair and helps to explain why Bernard Lazare chose to approach the previously much-detested naturalist novelist.

9 Reinach Note, R. Gauthier, p. 92.

10 *Impressions d'audience, L'Affaire Dreyfus*, Garnier-Flammarion, 1969, pp. 241–6.

11 Ibid. p. 242.

12 Reinach Note, R. Gauthier, p. 90.

13 *Procès Zola*, Vol. I, p. 535.

14 Quoted in M. Baumont: *Aux sources de l'Affaire*, les Productions de Paris, 1959, p. 189.

15 Ibid. p. 191.

16 Jean-Bernard, *Le Procès de Rennes*, op. cit. p. 336.

17 Gabriel Bertrand, *La Petite République*, 3 September 1903.

18 Jean-Bernard: *Le Procès de Rennes*, p. 336.

19 Reinach Note, R. Gauthier, p. 91.

20 E. Lepelletier: *Emile Zola*, Mercure de France, 1918, pp. 424–5.

21 Archives Nationales, BB 19 73.

22 Jean-Bernard: *Le Procès de Rennes*, p. 337.

23 They appeared in a series of articles in *L'Aurore* from January to May 1901.

24 Ibid. 14 January.

25 Ibid. 5 May.

26 Ibid. 28 April.

27 *Comment on condamne un innocent*, 1898, op. cit. p. i.

28 *L'Aurore*, 5 May 1901.

29 *Labori*, op. cit. p. 10.

30 *L'Avenir Illustré*, February 1934, rev. cit. p. 4.

31 *Notre Jeunesse* (1910), Gallimard, 1933, p. 85.

32 Jean-Bernard: *Procès de Rennes*, p. 338.

33 'Ce pays est un pays pourri, et meurt lentement de son catholicisme et
dans la bataille que nous livrons, nous devons forcément avoir le
dessous – je ne parle pas du cas particulier Dreyfus, je suis plus que
jamais convaincu de l'heureuse issue pour lui de l'Affaire, je parle
d'une façon générale. Depuis des mois, nous nous efforçons de convaincre nos concitoyens, nous voulons leur expliquer certains faits, nous
tâchons de leur démontrer quelques vérités, nous essayons de les amener
à comprendre. Or, ils sont susceptibles non pas de comprendre, mais
uniquement de croire et nous n'avons pas senti cela. Voyez la masse
énorme qui s'agrège à la Patrie Française. Il ne faut pas se le dis-
simuler, c'est ce qu'on est convenu d'appeler l'élite d'une nation qui
répond à son appel qui se compose de quelques affirmations vagues et
péremptoires. . . Prenez Lemaître, écoutez le raisonneur. Il croit, dit-il,
à une culpabilité parce que deux conseils de guerre et cinq ministres
de la guerre ont affirmé. C'est un mode de raisonnement purement
catholique. . . . Le catholique transporte dans tous les domaines sa
mentalité religieuse. On ne raisonne pas avec les catholiques – j'entends
les catholiques non emancipés. . .' (Letter to Reinach, 14 November
1898 (?), Reinach Papers, MS 24897, Bibliothéque Nationale).

Like its rival, the *Ligue des Droits de l'Homme et du Citoyen*, the
Ligue de la Patrie Française (sad rivalry) was founded in the summer
of 1898. Within the first four days it collected some 10,000 members;
among them 23 members of the Académie Française, 33 members of
the Académie des Sciences, over a hundred doctors, 85 lawyers, distinguished scholars and writers whose names are too well-known to
need to be recalled. In his first lecture Jules Lemaître defined 'intellectual' as 'tous les Français qui réfléchissent sur leur devoir'. One of the
duties was not to question the Affair: '. . .nous n'avons même nullement
le devoir de la [the truth] rechercher pour notre compte' (*Première
Conférence*, 19 January, 1899, Bureaux de la Patrie Française, 1899,
pp. 5 and 25.)

34 *Le Radical*, 4 September 1903.

35 Jean-Bernard: *Le Procès de Rennes*, p. 337.

36 Reinach Note, R. Gauthier, p. 94.

37 Ibid. p. 98. Scheurer-Kestner's *Journal* as well as his correspondence
relevant to the Affair are deposited at the Bibliothèque Nationale in
Paris (Manuscripts). R. Gauthier (*Dreyfusards*) has published a part of
this material.

38 Idem.

39 The 'Gallet incident' did nothing to enhance Bernard-Lazare's standing
with the senator. Having learnt from a journalist (Destès of *La France*)
that *Commandant* Gallet, one of the judges of the 1894 court-martial,
had afterwards been troubled by the verdict, Bernard-Lazare brought

the journalist along. Scheurer, distrusting journalists, consulted with Gallet himself, who promptly denied having expressed such sentiments.

40 Reinach Note, R. Gauthier, p. 94.
41 *Une Erreur Judiciaire. Deuxième Mémoire*, op. cit. p. 45.
42 Reinach Note, R. Gauthier, p. 94.
43 'Le Syndicat', *Figaro*, 1 December 1897.
44 Quoted in Maurras: *Au signe de Flore*, op. cit. p. 87.
45 Idem.
46 Ibid. p. 89.
47 Ibid. p. 90.
48 Léon Blum: *Souvenirs sur 'l'Affaire'* (1935), *L'Oeuvre de Léon Blum 1937–1940*, Albin Michel, 1965, p. 518. Blum's initial reaction was one of amused incredulity when Bernard-Lazare tried to convert the *Revue Blanche* in 1896 (p. 519). The candid picture drawn by Blum of Jewish embarrassment, even hostility to the dreyfusard campaign, is too well-known to be repeated. One needs to remember it in order to understand Bernard-Lazare's wrath against the cowardly conduct of the Jewish bourgeoisie, religious or otherwise.
49 Jean-Bernard: *Le Procès de Rennes*, p. 329.
50 The Intellectuals registered their protest against the prevailing state of affairs in the well-known *Aurore* petitions (January 1898) which Clemenceau called 'la protestation des Intellectuels'. Barrès re-baptised it as 'Bottin de l'élite'. (*Scenes et Doctrines du Nationalisme*, 1902, Plon, 1925, Vol. I, p. 49).
51 *Au Signe de Flore*, op. cit. p. 51.
52 *Procès Zola*, Vol. II, p. 181.
53 G. Monod: Préface, pp. v–vi, F. Puaux: *Vers la Justice*, Fischbacher, 1906.
54 Quoted in H. Dutrait-Crozon: *Précis de l'Affaire Dreyfus*, Nouvelle Librairie Nationale, 1924, p. 126.
55 *Le Figaro*, 25 November 1897.
56 *Le Figaro*, 5 December 1897.
57 Zola, *L'Affaire Dreyfus*, op. cit. p. 29.
58 *Le Figaro*, 5 December 1897.
59 'Je publiai, avant le *J'accuse* de Zola, ma brochure *Comment on condamne un innocent*. J'y accusai Mercier, du Paty, etc.' (Reinach Note, R. Gauthier, p. 95.)
60 *Comment on condamne un innocent*, op. cit. p. v.
61 S. Thalheimer: *Macht und Gerechtigkeit*, op. cit. pp. 294–304.
62 *L'Epreuve*, February 1898. Posthumously published in Marcel Péguy's *Cahiers de la Quinzaine*, xx, 7, Editions Saint-Michel, n.d.
63 J. Maitron: *Histoire du Mouvement Anarchiste en France 1880–1914*, Société Universitaire d'Editions et de Librairie, 2e édition, 1955, p. 312.
64 *Quarante ans de propagande anarchiste*, op. cit. p. 361.
65 S. Faure, *Les anarchistes et l'Affaire Dreyfus*, Au Libertaire, 1898, p. 17.
66 *L'Epreuve*, art. cit. pp. 49 and 54.
67 Jacques Prolo (Jean Pausader): *Les Anarchistes*, Vol. 10, *Histoire des*

partis socialistes en France, M. Rivière, 1912, p. 74. For a tribute to Bernard-Lazare anarchist, dreyfusard and Jew see also André Ibels (formerly editor of the *Revue Anarchiste*): 'A propos du Porteur de Torches', *L'Aube*, June 1897. Pelloutier also supported Bernard-Lazare's campaigns.

68 *Rapport sur le cas de cinq détenus des Iles du Salut*, Stock, 1899.

69 *Les Droits de l'Homme*, 30 October 1898.

Chapter 10: Antisemitism reconsidered

1 'Le Nouveau Ghetto', *Justice*, 17 November 1894.

2 'The threatened St. Bartholomew in France', *Review of Reviews*, February 1898. For a detailed account of the country-wide riots following *J'Accuse* see *The Jewish World* (London) 21 and 28 January 1898. Also A. Zévaès: *L'Affaire Dreyfus*, op. cit. pp. 109–10.

3 Léon Bloy was similarly struck by the 'délire du mensonge, de la sottise furieuse et de la férocité hypocrite' in which he saw the pro-drome of a cataclysm (*Je m'accuse*, op. cit. p. 168).

4 Motion put by a royalist deputy, de Pontbriand, on 17 January 1895. See L'Archiviste: *Drumont et Dreyfus*, Stock, 1898, p. 24.

5 According to a police report.

6 'Mort aux Juifs', *Le Réveil du Quartier*, 14 May 1898. This weekly, left-wing review (which Bernard-Lazare may well have helped to create) carried numerous articles on the antisemitic situation in its May, June and July issues.

7 'La loi et les congrégations', *Cahiers de la Quinzaine*, III, 21 August 1902, p. 216.

8 'Special Interview with Bernard-Lazare', *The Jewish World* (London), 3 June 1898.

9 Letter to Emile Meyerson, Archives Meyerson.

10 'The tocsin and its ringer: an interview with M. Drumont', *Review of Reviews*, February 1898, p. 135.

11 *Contre l'antisémitisme*, Stock, 1896, p. 7.

12 After reading *Contre l'antisémitisme*, Camille Pissarro, the painter, wrote to Bernard-Lazare (13 September 1896): 'Inutile de vous dire combien je partage vos idées sur le mouvement antisémitique et combien je suis heureux de voir un sémite défendre si éloquemment *mes* [ces?] idées; il n'y avait du reste qu'un Juif anarchiste et savant capable d'élever la voix avec autorité! Vous avez été courageux et vous avez fait votre devoir.' (Central Zionist Archives, Jerusalem, K11/77).

13 The brochure comprises the following five articles (1896) accompanied by an important preface, conclusion and notes: 'Contre l'Antisémitisme' (20 May); 'Réponse à M. Drumont' (24 May); 'Ce que veut l'anti-sémitisme' (31 May); 'La quatrieme à M. Drumont' (7 June); 'Les Réponses de M. Drumont' (14 June). Not included in the brochure but dealing with the same subject are: 'Sur l'Antisémitisme' (14 May) and 'L'équivoque antisémite' (28 June). All these articles appeared in *Le Voltaire*.

14 'Mort aux Juifs', *Le Réveil du Quartier*, 14 May 1898.
15 'Le Nouveau Ghetto', art. cit.
16 'Antisémitisme et antisémites', *Echo de Paris*, 31 December 1894.
17 *Contre l'antisémitisme*, op. cit. p. 4.
18 Idem.
19 'Sur l'Antisémitisme', art. cit.
20 *Contre l'antisémitisme*, op. cit. p. 6.
21 Ibid. p. 7.
22 Idem.
23 J. Verdès-Leroux: *Scandale financier et antisémitisme catholique. Le Krach de l'Union Générale*. Centurion, 1969.
24 Archives Bernard-Lazare, Alliance Israëlite Universelle.
25 'La loi et les congrégations', op. cit.
26 *Le Fumier de Job*, op. cit. p. 103.
27 'Abaissement', *Zion*, 31 May 1897, p. 30.
28 *Le Fumier de Job*, op. cit. p. 72.
29 MS Box 3. 'Légendes sur les Juifs'. Most of the relevant unpublished material (indicated as MS) will be found in Box 3 of the Archives Bernard-Lazare, Alliance Israëlite Universelle. When the fragments are numbered, the number will be indicated.
30 MS F500.
31 Even the intellectual review *La Quinzaine* carried an article on 'Les Meurtres Rituels' by Emile de Saint-Auban. The lawyer and former libertarian (he had defended Jean Grave in 1894) 'proved' the charge on the basis of letters allegedly emanating from eminent eighteenth-century rabbis. *La Quinzaine*, November–December 1899, pp. 145–51. On 27 March 1892 Delahaye's paper *Le Journal d'Indre-et-Loire* brought a ritual murder charge and in April 1901 Rochefort in *L'Intransigeant* brought another (see *L'Aurore*, 25 April 1901).
32 *L'Aurore*, 20 May 1901.
33 MS. FS: 634–6, 641–5 among numerous other fragments dealing with the same topic.
34 MS. F320.
35 *Le Fumier de Job*, op. cit. p. 69.
36 MS. F470.
37 *Le Fumier de Job*, p. 70.
38 MS. F470.
39 'Lettre ouverte à Anatole Leroy-Beaullieu', *Cahiers de la Quinzaine*, IV 13, February 1903, p. 83.
40 Quoted in W. Keller: *Diaspora*, Pitman, London 1971.
41 It has recently been republished (n.d.) by the Cercle Bernard-Lazare with a useful introduction by Rabi.
42 Police Report of 29 March 1895. The same report mentions that anarchists have read the brochure with interest and 'Jewish anarchists' (who are they?) with delight.
43 Edition Cercle Bernard-Lazare, p. 11.
44 Cp. 1895 edition p. 14 and 1898 edition p. 15.
45 *La Petite République*, 13 December 1898.
46 Jaurès was no antisemite. No one knew better than he that, in the

well-known expression, 'l'antisémitisme est le socialisme des imbéciles'. But Jaurès could be extraordinarily short-sighted and even prejudiced at times. His discussion of the Jewish question in Algeria, at the time of the ugliest persecution there and riots in France, is breathtaking in its ignorance and insensitiveness (*Journal Officiel*, 19 February 1898). See: E. Silberner: 'French Socialism and the Jews', *Historia Judaica*, xvi, 1954. H. Goldberg: 'Jean Jaurès and the Jewish Question', *Jewish Social Studies*, xx, April 1958. A. Croix: *Jaurès et ses détracteurs*, Editions du Vieux Saint-Ouen, 1967.

47 'La conception sociale du judaisme et le peuple juif', *La Grande Revue*, September 1899, p. 596. (For recent assessments of Marx's pamphlet see Marx: *La Question Juive*, introduction by R. Mandrou, 10/18, 1968. R. Misrahi: *Marx et la question juive*, NRF Idées, 1972).

48 Ibid. p. 606.

49 'La Divine Espérance', *La Revue Parisienne*, 25 December 1893, p. 571.

50 And from the 'réaction révolutionnaire' represented by men like Barrès. This was the purpose of a public lecture Bernard-Lazare gave in February 1896 to a left-wing student audience, lecture interrupted by some 20 antisemitic infiltrators who were finally expelled to shouts of 'Vive la Commune'. Maurras regretted not having heard of the lecture in time: they would have organised themselves. 'Mais patience', he added (*Barrès–Maurras, Correspondance*, Plon 1970, p. 116).

51 'La loi et les Congrégations', 1902, op. cit. p. 225.

Chapter 11: Zionism

1 Letter to Herzl dated 4 February, 1899, Silberner, p. 359. Bernard-Lazare's letters to Herzl are deposited at the Central Zionist Archives Jerusalem (H VIII 479). They have been published, with a commentary in Hebrew, by E. Silberner in *Shivat Zion* II–III Jerusalem, 1953. The Bibliothèque Nationale has a copy under the title *Bernard-Lazare et le sionisme* and all references will be to this edition.

2 Ibid. p. 350. The previous day, he had asked Max Nordau, Herzl's confidant and future collaborator for Herzl's address (10 March 1896, Central Zionist Archives, Jerusalem, H VIII 479). Judging by the formal tone, he did not know Nordau well at this stage. How he came to know him, is uncertain: possibly through the Association des Etudiants Israelites Russes. Two years earlier he had severely criticised Nordau's much discussed *Dégénerescence* (*Revue Parisienne*, 25 March 1894), a psychological analysis of the decline of Western culture as testified, *inter alia*, by French literature and art.

3 Herzl: *The Jewish State* (1896), *The Zionist Idea*, a historical analysis and reader ed. by A. Hertzberg, Atheneum, New York, 1971, p. 212.

4 Idem.

5 Letter to Nordau n.d. Central Archives Jerusalem, H. VIII 479. It appears that Herzl had asked Bernard-Lazare to improve on the French translation (done by somebody else). He agreed, but added:

'Pour la rendre aussi élégante qu'il paraît le désirer, il eut fallu la récrire d'un bout à l'autre' (letter n.d.).

6 *The Diaries of Theodore Herzl* ed. by M. Lowenthal (1956), London 1958, p. 184.

7 Emile Meyerson was a chemist by training, a philosopher by inclination, a generous and compassionate man. The descendant of an East-European family of Talmudic scholars, he was not himself religious but felt the suffering of his people with the same intense passion as Bernard-Lazare. After the latter's death, Meyerson remained Mme Bernard-Lazare's trusted friend. What Bernard-Lazare meant to Meyerson can be gathered from the following letter written to Bernard-Lazare: 'Et vous êtes aussi ma conscience. Je me demande souvent: que dirait Lazare? et, vous l'avouerai-je? cela m'a aidé maintes fois à sortir d'impasses où des scrupules contradictoires m'avaient logé. Comment votre amitié m'est-elle venue à un âge où...la porte de ce temple est fermée depuis longtemps. C'est ce que j'ignore. Mais elle est là, elle est un "fait brutal" – heureusement' (n.d. *Chalom,* op. cit. p. 11). In 1906 Meyerson wrote to Péguy: 'Notre dévotion commune pour Bernard Lazare – c'est le terms qui me parait le plus approprié – émane probablement de sources analogues. Mais vous ne pouvez savoir ce qu'il a été pour moi; il me semble que c'est hier que je l'ai perdu, j'en suis désemparé comme au premier jour.' (Quoted by Jacques Viard, *Revue d'Histoire littéraire de la France,* March–June 1973, p. 358.) Meyerson's best known philosophical works are *Identité et Réalité* (1908) and *Le cheminement de la pensée* (1931). Mme Ardouin, Meyerson's great-niece, has kindly let me consult the correspondence and papers which are in her possession.

8 Silberner, op. cit. p. 355.

9 *L'Echo Sioniste,* 15 November 1903.

10 *L'Antisémitisme, son histoire et ses causes,* op. cit. p. 196.

11 Ibid. p. 158.

12 Ibid. p. 196.

13 'Le prolétariat juif devant l'antisémitisme', *Le Flambeau,* January 1899, p. 13.

14 Ibid. p. 12.

15 Letter (16 February 1899) quoted in S. R. Landau: *Sturm und Drang im Zionismus,* Vienna, 1937, pp. 236–7.

16 *Die Welt,* 3 February 1899.

17 'Le prolétariat juif', op. cit. pp. 13 and 14.

18 *Le Nationalisme Juif,* Publications du Kadimah, Stock, 1898, p. 3.

19 Ibid. p. 10.

20 Ibid. pp. 12 and 15.

21 Ibid. p. 15.

22 Ibid. p. 14. This is also what he told a journalist from the Socialist paper *Avanti* who had asked him how he could reconcile socialism with Jewish nationalism (*Avanti,* 5 September 1898, reproduced in Landau, op. cit. p. 228). He expressed himself even more firmly in a letter of 24 March 1900. 'Les sophismes de l'internationalisme sectaire, tout aussi odieux que le nationalisme chauvin militariste et bourgeois,

ne peuvent rien contre la volonté du peuple juif de travailler à son affranchissement et en même temps à l'affranchissement de la classe ouvrière. Il serait à désirer que nos frères juifs socialistes polonais nous expliquent pourquoi il est nécessaire d'être nationaliste polonais pour être approuvé par les pontifes de la social-démocratie et pourquoi ils ne peuvent être social-démocrates juifs' (Central Zionist Archives Jerusalem, K 11/77).

23 'Nécessité d'être soi-même', *Zion*, art. cit.

24 *L'Echo Sioniste*, 5, 20 April and 5 May 1901, p. 169.

25 Ibid. p. 167.

26 Idem.

27 Ibid. p. 135.

28 In '*Solidarité*' (*Zion*, 31 May 1897, p. 25) he recalls his own journey from Israelite to Jew. 'On se glorifia de ne pas appartenir à la même famille que ceux dont les mains saisissaient encore le bâton du juif éternel. . . . Comment n'en aurait-il pas été ainsi, étant donnée l'education reçue? Je le comprends d'autant mieux que j'ai partagé ces honteux sentiments, j'ai été semblable à Céphas, j'ai dit aussi: "Je ne connais pas ces hommes"; mais je lui ai été semblable jusqu'au bout, car après les avoir un moment reniés, je me suis senti prêt à les accompagner partout dans leur douloureux voyage, et prêt aussi à aider à leur libération, ce qui est aller plus loin que Céphas.'

29 *Le Nationalisme Juif*, op. cit. p. 5. Cp. Blum's reflections in 1935: 'Les Juifs riches, les Juifs de moyenne bourgeoisie, les Juifs fonctionnaires avaient peur de la lutte engagée pour Dreyfus exactement comme ils ont peur aujourd'hui de la lutte engagée contre le fascisme' (*Souvenirs sur l'Affaire*, op. cit. p. 520).

30 *The Jewish World*, 3 June 1898.

31 *L'Avenir Illustré*, February 1934, op. cit. p. 4.

32 *The Jewish World*, 9 September 1898. Bernard-Lazare assured the editor and the readers of the *Gaulois* that contrary to the latest legend Henry's arrest had not been decided by the Zionist congress (7 February 1899, *L'Aurore*).

33 Preoccupation with the Dreyfus Affair prevented him from attending the first Zionist congress in 1897.

34 S. R. Landau: *Sturm und Drang im Zionismus*, op. cit. p. 233.

35 *La Fronde*, 29 (?) August 1898. Box 7 of the Archives Bernard-Lazare. This box contains press cuttings from *La Fronde* which carried an interesting series of articles by Clara Delay on the Zionist Congress. Unfortunately the date has often been cut away and 'internal evidence' has to be used for dating. For Bernard-Lazare's interventions as officially recorded in the Stenographic Report see Silberner, op. cit. pp. 339–41.

36 *La Fronde*, 30 (?) August 1898.

37 For a full account see *The Jewish World*, Supplement 2 September and ordinary issue of 9 September 1898.

38 Summarising the divergencies which, she felt, existed right from the beginning, Clara Delay observed: 'Il y a ceux qui veulent fonder un Etat d'abord et régler les questions sociales après. D'autres craignent

la fondation d'un nouvel Etat bourgeois semblable aux autres; eux, ils veulent que "dans leur république l'égalité ne soit pas un vain mot et que les plaies du prolétariat et du paupérisme ne puissent jamais atteindre le nouveau royaume d'Israel." ' *La Fronde,* 28 August 1898.

39 Silberner, op. cit. p. 354.

40 Ibid. p. 358.

41 Letter dated 16 February 1899 in A. Chouraqui: *Th. Herzl,* Ed. du Seuil, 1960, p. 208.

42 Let. cit. 4 February 1899, Silberner, op. cit. pp. 356–7.

43 Letter to Meyerson of 3 February 1899. Archives Meyerson.

44 Let. cit. A. Chouraqui: *Th. Herzl,* p. 207. This important letter (of which Chouraqui reproduces an extract) was published in full, in the original French, in vol. v of Herzl's *Gesammelte Zionistische Werke* (pp. 480–3) and in a German translation in Landau, op. cit. pp. 235–7.

45 Silberner, op. cit. pp. 358–60.

46 *The Diaries of Theodor Herzl,* ed. by M. Lowenthal, op. cit. p. 464.

47 *Oesterreichische Wochenschrift,* 17 August 1900.

48 Archives Bernard-Lazare, Alliance Israelite Universelle.

49 Central Zionist Archives, Jerusalem dossiers, A2 28, 74, 82. Bernard-Lazare planned to go to Palestine in April 1900, no doubt in connection with the Committee's colonisation work (Letter to Meyerson, 11 March 1900). There is no record of these plans having materialised.

50 *L'Avenir Illustré,* op. cit. pp. 8–9.

51 Archives Bernard-Lazare, Alliance Israëlite Universelle.

52 *L'Avenir Illustré,* op. cit. p. 9.

53 On the other hand he made the following declaration in March 1900, in a letter accepting honorary membership of a student Zionist organisation in Rumania (Central Zionist Archives, Jerusalem, K 11/77): 'J'ai la conviction que le Judaïsme ne peut se libérer de son esclavage qu'en s'émancipant comme nation et non pas en cherchant une vaine émancipation politique dans les pays dans lesquels vivent les juifs.... Le Judaïsme doit s'organiser partout en un parti National prolétarien. Le Peuple Juif doit en conquérant sa liberté affirmer la liberté de son prolétariat et jeter les bases d'une république sociale. Par ces moyens il servira en même temps la cause du prolétariat international... En tant que Juifs, nous sommes un groupement humain et nous avons le droit de vouloir et de rechercher l'autonomie du groupe dont nous faisons partie.'

54 The fragments belonging to this dialogue will be found in Box 4 of the Bernard-Lazare Archives. They do not figure, for the most part, in the posthumously published *Fumier de Job.*

Chapter 12: Last battles and last works

1 L. Chaîne: *Les catholiques français et leurs difficultés actuelles,* Storck, 1903, p. 230.

2 *Petite République,* 13 September 1902.
   Correspondance, Archives du Centre Charles Péguy (Letter E. Buré).

4 *La loi et les Congrégations*, Cahiers de la Quinzaine, III 21, August 1902, p. 228.
5 Ibid. p. 224.
6 L. Chaîne, op. cit. p. 230.
7 Péguy: *Notre Jeunesse* (1910), Gallimard, 1933, pp. 95 and 126.
8 *Cahiers de la Quinzaine*, IV 13, February 1903, pp. 81–2.
9 Ibid. p. 83.
10 Cp. Delahache (Lucien Aaron): *Les Juifs en Russie*; Elie Eberlin: *Le Bund, Cahiers de la Quinzaine*, VI 6, December 1904.
11 Henri Dagan: *Les Massacres de Kichinef, Cahiers de la Quinzaine*, V 1, November 1903.
12 *Notre Jeunesse*, op. cit. p. 177 and p. 183.
13 Quoted by A. Fontainas, 'Preface', *L'Antisémitisme, son histoire et ses causes*, Crès 1934, p. 20.
14 Archives Bernard-Lazare, Alliance Israelite Universelle.
15 Reinach Papers, MS. 24897.
16 I am indebted to the gardien du cimetière Montparnasse, M. Jacques Angevin, for this item of information which is recorded under No 1625 (1903, 8ᵉ arrondissement) in the cemetery records.
17 Letter of 13 April 1903, Archives du Centre Charles Péguy.
18 P. Quillard: *Bernard-Lazare*, an unpublished(?) study, Archives Bernard-Lazare, Alliance Israëlite Universelle. See also Quillard's obituary (*L'Européen*, 12 September 1903) and his address at the inauguration of Bernard-Lazare's monument (*Bernard-Lazare*, Nîmes, 1908).
19 Among them: works on Bar Kochbas and Sabbatai Zevi; a study of Spinoza and his milieu; a philosophical drama, *Hélène*, in which the heroine's self-imposed mission is to liberate mankind from Christian anguish and restore to it a sense of joy and love of life. *La Grenade*, a social drama evidently intended as a sequel to *Les Porteurs de Torches*. There are plans and notes for a number of historical works (some have already been mentioned) and scattered *pensées* on the Bible, the Talmud, ethics and philosophy.
20 Let. cit. 14 November 1898, Reinach papers.
21 Most of the material will be found in Box 9 of the Archives Bernard-Lazare, Alliance Israelite Universelle.
22 *Le Fumier de Job*, op. cit. pp. 142–5.
23 The unpublished fragments will be found mainly in Boxes 3, 4, 5, and 9.
24 *Le Fumier de Job*, op. cit. p. 96.
25 Ibid. p. 115.
26 Ibid. p. 90.
27 Ibid. p. 166.
28 Let. cit. 14 November 1898, Reinach papers.
29 Archives Meyerson.
30 Among them: *L'Aurore, L'Action, Les Droits de l'Homme, La Petite République, Le Radical, Le Gil Blas, La France, Les Temps Nouveaux, Le Temps, La Patrie, L'Intransigeant, La Libre Parole, L'Echo Sioniste, L'Oeuvre Sociale, Pages Libres, La Revue Universelle, Pro*

Armenia, L'Européen; Le Peuple and *Le Petit Bleu* (Brussels); *Avanti* (Italy); *Die Oesterreichische Wochenschrift* (Vienna); *Die Judische Presse* (Berlin); *The Daily Chronicle, The Times, The Jewish Chronicle, The Jewish World* (London).

31 *La Libre Parole,* 5 September 1903.

32 *La Petite République,* 24 September 1903.

33 *Notre Jeunesse,* op. cit. p. 78.

Epilogue: Bernard-Lazare in his times and ours

1 Maurras: 'Bernard-Lazare', *Action Française* 15 September 1908. Other articles and comments in issues of 4–7 October.

2 J. S. McClelland: *The French Right,* J. Cape, London 1970, pp. 30–1.

3 Archives de Nîmes, dossier CA 93 (l'inauguration du monument Bernard-Lazare). We have also consulted the Hubert Rouget Papers (Bibliothèque Municipale) and numerous accounts in the local press. Our grateful thanks are due to the conservateurs and the staff of the Archives and the Library for their help and interest.

4 The sculpture was 7 metres high and was the work of Roger-Bloche and M. H. Lefèbre. It was financed by public subscription, through *L'Aurore,* and with help from the municipal authorities in Nîmes. According to Liber (*Echo Sioniste,* March 1913) a Jewish banker also made a contribution. With donations from various people and organisations, including Meyerson, sufficient funds were raised for a brochure commemorating the occasion.

5 *Le Petit Républican du Midi,* 3 October 1908. According to the Monument brochure 120 communes were officially represented and all Republican and Socialist organisations participated.

6 Members of the Committee: Paul Adam, Jean Ajalbert, Charles Andler, Léonce Bénédite, Jules Bernard, Dr P. Brissaud, F. Buisson, E. Carrière, Marcel Collière, Gaston Doumergue, André Fontainas, Anatole France, E. Gast, Gustave Geffroy, Dr Gley, Edmond Goudchaux, Charles Goudchaux, Gaston Griolet, A. F. Hérold, Lucien Herr, J. Huret, Phoebus Jouve, Narcisse Leven, Stuart Merrill, E. Meyerson, Gabriel Monod, Dr A. Netter, P. Painlevé, G. de Porto-Riche, F. de Pressensé, Pierre Quillard, Ranc, Dr Paul Reclus, Joseph Reinach, Salomon Reinach, Jules Renard, Paul Renouard, Marius Richard, Roll, Victor Simond, E. Vaughan, Em. Vidal-Naquet. Péguy had been invited to join but evidently declined. No doubt the presence of Lucien Herr had something to do with it.

7 In 1966, centenary of his birth, a plaque was erected on the site of the monument under the auspices of the Ligue des Droits de l'Homme. It bears the following inscription: 'Ici était dressée une effigie de Bernard-Lazare qui en des jours difficiles défendit la vérité, la justice et les droits de l'homme, méconnus et foulés aux pieds dans la personne de Dreyfus.'

8 *La Libre Parole,* 19 September 1908.

9 *Correspondance Barrès–Maurras,* ed. by H. Massis, op. cit. p. 117.

10 *Action Française,* 15 September 1908, art. cit.

11 Jean-Bernard: *Le Procès de Rennes,* op. cit. p. 333.

12 Archives Meyerson.

13 Meyerson asked Willy Bambus, a German journalist, to try and secure for Bernard-Lazare a post as Paris correspondent on a German paper. He needs it, Meyerson wrote, 'because the French press remains closed to him' (letter of 6 April 1902 Central Zionist Archives, Jerusalem, A 28/7). In the Meyerson Archives there is a letter by Salomon Reinach recommending that Bernard-Lazare be given a regular salary as a permanent member of the I.C.A.'s staff.

14 R. Gauthier, op. cit. p. 8.

15 The claim was made in the course of a lecture given by Henri Guillemin at the *Centre Universitaire Méditerranéen* on 8 April 1966. When invited, some time afterwards, to substantiate his claim, M. Guillemin was unable to do so. For details see: Jean Guillon: *Bernard Lazare,* Thèse de doctorat, Université de Nice.

16 Jean-Bernard: *Le Procès de Rennes,* p. 333.

17 This fact was mentioned in several obituaries. The following extracts from Bernard-Lazare's will clearly make the point (Archives Bernard-Lazare, Box 12): 'Je ne laisse aucune fortune, je n'ai pas amassé d'argent. Quand mon terme de Juillet et mes contributions auront été payés, il me restera un millier de francs déposés au Crédit Lyonnais. Je n'ai à moi que mon mobilier, ma bibliothèque et la propriété de mes livres. Je prie qu'on mette ma bibliothèque en vente, le montant permettra de payer ce que je puis devoir. Je lègue tout ce que je possède à ma femme bien aimée, celle qui a illuminé, rejoui, embelli et charmé ma vie... En terminant, il me reste à recommander à mes amis celle que je laisse sans ressources et sans soutien, sans fortune, mais sans doute avec l'orgueil de mon nom.'

18 Meyerson Archives.

19 Envisaged on a grand scale as the history of a conscience, the Bernard-Lazare portrait was begun in September 1903 but abandoned after some sixty pages of 'Introduction'. After several promises to his readers that the portrait would be completed, Péguy returned to the task in 1907 but this time too he felt unable to do justice to that 'homme extraordinaire' and the second 'sketch' was likewise abandoned. They were published posthumously in *Par ce demi-clair matin* (Gallimard, 1952) and *Un poète l'a dit* (Gallimard, 1953) respectively. Had it not been for the pressure of certain events which made it imperative for Péguy to declare his position, the only completed version of the portrait as it appears in *Notre Jeunesse* (1910) might never have been written. Apart from these three major texts and Bernard-Lazare's two contributions to the *Cahiers* (*Les Juifs en Roumanie* and *La loi et les Congrégations*), there are a number of allusions to him scattered in several of Péguy's works. Those familiar with Bernard-Lazare's ideas will be conscious of his presence in many more, in the same way as one feels Bergson's presence. They will more readily appreciate why the man whom Péguy had only known for two or three years was honoured as 'l'ami intérieur' and 'le patron des Cahiers'.

20 *Notre Jeunesse,* Gallimard edition 1933, pp. 68–79.

21 Ibid. p. 68.
22 Jacques Petit: *Bernanos, Bloy, Claudel, Péguy: Quatre écrivains catholiques face à Israel*, Calmann-Lévy, 1972.
23 See his articles in the *Revue Blanche*, 1899, notably 'Le Ravage et la Réparation', 15 November 1899.
24 'Nécessité d'être soi-même', *Zion*, 30 April 1897.
25 Péguy's spiritual evolution was in some ways similar to that of Bernard-Lazare: Same initial rejection and revolt; same return to roots, via a personal sense of solidarity with the persecuted religion, but on their own revolutionary terms.
26 *Un poète l'a dit*, op. cit. pp. 157–9.
27 Notably in *Bar Cochebas* (sic), *Cahiers de la Quinzaine*, VIII 11 February 1907, which is dedicated to Bernard-Lazare; also in *Un poète l'a dit*, where Bernard-Lazare serves as a supreme illustration of that theory.
28 Some of M. Petit's observations are very pertinent in this respect (*Bernanos, Bloy*, etc., op. cit.).
29 *Le Porche du Mystère de la Deuxième Vertu* was dedicated to Eddy Marix. I wonder whether in his recent study 'Prophètes d'Israel et Annonciateur Chrétien' (*Revue d'Histoire Littéraire de la France*, Mars–Juin 1973) Jacques Viard has not somewhat underestimated the growing complexity of Péguy's attitude, not to his Jewish friends, to whom he remained attached, but to Judaism in its relation to Christianity. Bernard-Lazare and Eddy Marix were as hostile to Renan's 'métaphysique du progrès' as was Péguy; neither Judaism nor Christianity had a place in it. But it does not follow that they would have approved of the place ultimately given to Judaism by the Christian Péguy, something which they did not live to see. Marix enthusiastically approved of 'l'immortalité des grands systèmes' defended by Péguy in *Bar Cochebas*. Would he have been as enthusiastic about *Le Mystère des Saints Innocents* in which, as Jacques Petit rightly observes, 'l'Ancien Testament n'est plus qu'une "figure", une "image" du Nouveau et semble perdre son sens, sa valeur propres' (op. cit. p. 152)? Marix also told Péguy that he was 'en faveur de la tradition juive pure – contre le christianisme' (J. Viard, art. cit. p. 359). It was not easy for Péguy to establish Judeo–Christian ties on the basis of such sentiments. Bergson was an entirely different story.
30 *Note Conjointe sur M. Descartes et la philosophie cartésienne* (1914), Pléiade, *Oeuvres en Prose 1909–14*, p. 1367.
31 Ibid. p. 1372.
32 *Le Fumier de Job*, op. cit. p. 113.
33 Ibid. p. 117.
34 *La Note Conjointe*, p. 1375.
35 Ibid. p. 1383.
36 Ibid. p. 1375.
37 *L'Argent Suite* (1913), Pléiade, *Oeuvres en Prose 1909–14*, p. 1220.
38 'S'il vous est doux de savoir que nul ne l'a apprécié et connu comme vous; que nul autre que vous a su voir en lui l'âme éternelle d'un peuple, et le génie harmonieux de toutes les époques de beauté...'

Letter (8 August 1911) from Mme Bernard-Lazare to Péguy. Archives du Centre Charles Péguy.

39 Quoted in *Signes du Temps*, September 1964.

40 *Echo Sioniste*, 10 March 1913.

41 Personal Archives of W. Rabi (who was one of the organisers of the commemoration ceremony which did not finally take place).

42 Letter (16 June 1933) by Albert Crémieux. Rabi Archives.

Notes to plates

1 Drumont's scurrilous paper enjoyed a wide circulation during the Dreyfus Affair. On this page Drumont's favourable reaction, shared by half the country's press, to the Rennes verdict. Top right-hand corner, the paper's motto: 'La France aux Français!'

2 It was this second Paris edition of Bernard-Lazare's work which made the real impact. It was also the first of the numerous dreyfusard publications to flow from Stock's presses. (Reproduced from the copy of *Une erreur judiciaire: la vérité sur l'Affaire Dreyfus* in the London Library.)

3 This antisemitic cartoon from *La Libre Parole* expresses a not un-common reaction to Bernard-Lazare's *Une erreur judiciaire* – a powerful Jewish syndicate defending Judas-Dreyfus by means of bribes. (Reproduced by kind permission of Armand Colin from J. Lethève, *La caricature et la presse sous la IIIᵉ République*, Armand Colin, Paris, 1961.)

4 Dreyfus before the court at Rennes. One notices the ill-fitting uniform. Dreyfus had lost a great deal of weight during his four and a half years on Devil's Island. Several drawings depicted him as a skeleton. In spite of obvious physical weakness, extending at times even to his powers of speech, his bearing throughout the long trial is said to have been irreproachably military. Seated behind him is maître Demange, his counsel. (From the *Graphic*, 2 September 1899.)

5 A dreyfusard view of General Mercier and Dreyfus. (The drawing originally appeared in *Le Siècle* and is here reproduced by kind permission of the publisher from P. Boussel, *L'Affaire Dreyfus et la presse*, Armand Colin, Paris, 1960.)

6 The figure seated on the extreme left of the main platform is very likely Bernard-Lazare. At the centre, standing, is Herzl addressing the delegates who had come from the four corners of the earth. (With kind permission of the Zionist Archives, Jerusalem, who supplied the photograph.)

BIBLIOGRAPHY

I WORKS BY BERNARD-LAZARE

Books, brochures and major studies

Arranged according to *main* theme and in chronological order of publication within each theme section. Unless otherwise stated the place of publication is Paris.

Literary and Critical

La Fiancée de Corinthe, Dalon, 1888 (in collaboration with Ephraïm Mikhaël).

'Les Quatre Faces', (*Entretiens Politiques et Littéraires*) December 1890.

'De la nécessité de l'intolérance', (*Entretiens Politiques et Littéraires*), December 1891.

'Des critiques et de la critique', (*Entretiens Politiques et Littéraires*), April 1892.

'Les Initiés', *La Wallonie* (Liège), November 1891 and September 1892.

Le miroir des Légendes, Lemerre, 1892.

La Télépathie et le Néo-spiritualisme, *L'Art Indépendant*, 1893.

'Napoléonisme et Goethisme', *Revue Parisienne*, 25 February 1894.

Figures Contemporaines Ceux d'aujourd'hui, ceux de demain, Perrin, 1895.

'Enquête sur la *Banqueroute de la science*', Echo de Paris, 12 January– 6 April 1895.

L'Ecrivain et l'art social, Bibliothèque de l'art social, 1896.

La Porte d'Ivoire, Colin, 1897.

Les Porteurs de Torches, Colin, 1897.

Political and social

'La réglementation de la guerre', *Entretiens Politiques et Littéraires*, November 1890.

'Le Justicier', *Entretiens Politiques et Littéraires*, May 1891.

'La Nouvelle Monarchie', *Entretiens Politiques et Littéraires*, November 1891.

'Nécessité du Socialisme', *L'Endehors*, 1 May 1892.

'Aurea Médiocritas', *L'Endehors*, 25 September 1892.

'Entente possible et impossible', *Revue Anarchiste*, 15–30 August 1893.

'La liberté', *L'Harmonie* (Marseilles), October–December 1893.

'La Déroute', *Revue Parisienne*, 10 February 1894.

'L'oeuvre nécessaire', *Le Courrier Social Illustré*, November 1894.

'L'Université Nouvelle de Bruxelles', *Magazine International*, December 1894.

'Bakounine', *Revue Blanche*, 15 February 1895.

'Le Socialisme allemand et ses divisions', *Revue Parisienne*, 10 May 1895.

Articles on the opening of the Kiel Canal and its political significance, *Echo de Paris*, June–July 1895.

'Izoulet et la Cité Moderne', *Le Devenir Social*, April 1895.

'Le Socialisme en Angleterre', *Echo de Paris*, 27 July 1895.

Articles on the strike at Carmaux, *Echo de Paris*, August–September 1895.

'Fédéralistes et Fédéralisme', *Echo de Paris*, 17 November 1895; 'Fédéralisme Révolutionnaire', 12 December 1895.

Articles on the Socialist Congress in London, *Echo de Paris*, 25 July to 4 August 1896.

Histoire des doctrines révolutionnaires, V. Giard and E. Brière, 1896. (Inaugural lecture given 16 December 1895 at the Collège Libre des sciences sociales. Also appeared in the review *Le Devenir Social*, January 1896).

Major articles which appeared in *L'Action Sociale* (weekly paper founded by Bernard-Lazare in February 1896).

    'La réaction révolutionnaire'; 'Grève des Journalistes'; 1 February.

    'Toujours la Presse', 8 February.

    'Fédéralisme et Révolution', 22 and 29 February.

    'Les Dupes', 22 February.

    'Analogies', 29 February.

'Tribunes Politiques' in *Paris*:

    'La réaction', 23 March 1896.

    'Le parti de l'étranger', 9 April 1896.

    'Le Parti Radical', 20 April 1896.

    'L'agonie d'un parti', 30 April 1896.

    'Socialisme et radicalisme', 12 May 1896.

    'Principes Radicaux', 21 May 1896.

    'Définitions', 8 June 1896.

    'Progressisme et Socialisme', 29 June 1896.

    'La comédie', 8 July 1896.

    'Le Congrès de Londres', 22 July and 5 August 1896.

    'Du Marxisme', 21 August 1896.

    'Fétichisme', 2 October 1896.

'Justice Militaire et Justice Sociale', *Le Voltaire*, 4 April 1896.

'Emancipation des Femmes', *Le Voltaire*, 17 April 1896.

'Nos Moeurs', *L'Aurore*, 21 October 1897.

'L'Opinion Publique', *L'Aurore*, 25 October 1897.

'Les Malades', *L'Aurore*, 29 October 1897.

La loi et les Congrégations. (*Cahiers de la Quinzaine*, III 21, August 1902.)

Dreyfus Affair

'Le Nouveau Ghetto', *La Justice*, 17 November 1894.

Une Erreur Judiciaire. La vérité sur l'Affaire Dreyfus, Brussels, 1896.

2nd edition (augmented), Stock, 1896 and 1897.
3rd edition, Stock, 1898.
Une Erreur Judiciaire. L'Affaire Dreyfus, (Deuxième Mémoire avec des Expertises d'Ecritures), Stock, 1897.
Comment on condamne un innocent, (l'acte d'accusation contre le capitaine Dreyfus), Stock, 1898.
'France at the parting of the ways', *North-American Review* (Boston and New York), Vol. CLXIX, November 1899. Important study of the Rennes trial).
'Lettre ouverte', *L'Intransigeant*, 23 November 1896.
Interview avec Bernard-Lazare, *Die Jüdische Presse* (Berlin), 25 May 1898.
'L'instruction contre le colonel Picquart', *L'Aurore*, 13 August 1898.
'Expertise Militaire', *L'Aurore*, 26 August 1898.
'Henry', *L'Aurore*, 7 September 1898.
'The Dreyfus Case', *The Graphic* (London), 3 December 1898.
'Lettre au Président Mazeau', *L'Aurore*, 16 April 1899.
'Lettre ouverte à M. Trarieux', *L'Aurore*, 7 June 1899.
'Autour du Procès': interview with Bernard-Lazare, *L'Aurore*, 8 August 1899.
'Le faux de *l'Eclair*', *L'Aurore*, 12 August 1899.
'Un entretien avec Bernard-Lazare', *L'Aurore*, 31 August 1899.
'Derrière le Mur', *Journal du Soir* (Lyon), 6 July(?) 1899.
Dispute Labori–Bernard-Lazare: *Echo de Paris*, 28–30 November, 1, 6 and 7 December 1901. *Le Journal*, 4–6 December 1901.
Unpublished notes written by Bernard-Lazare for Joseph Reinach giving details of his activities during the Dreyfus Affair. Reinach papers, Bibliothèque Nationale, Manuscrits, M.S.24897, n.a.fr. Extracts have been published in R. Gauthier: *Dreyfusards*, Collection Archives, Julliard, 1965, pp. 82–95.
Jean-Bernard: *Le Procès de Rennes*, Lemerre 1900 (Contains an important account given by Bernard-Lazare of his activities during the Affair).
Archives of the Préfecture de Police: *Dossier Lazare Marcus Manassé Bernard*, Ba/958.
Dossiers on the Dreyfus Affair, in particular: No. 1042 (press reactions to Bernard-Lazare's first brochure); No. 1043 (Esterhazy's trial, Rennes trial); No. 1044 (Esterhazy affair).
Archives Nationales. *Dossiers on the Dreyfus Affair. Of special interest:*
BB 19 73 (comprises four reports on Bernard-Lazare);
BB 19 94 (comprises reports and notes on Bernard-Lazare's first brochure and on suspected relations with Castelin, Bernard-Lazare's letter to the Minister of War asking to be brought to trial);
BB 19 88 (Castelin, de Pellieux and handwriting expertise).

Jewish and Zionist

'Juifs et Israelites', *Entretiens Politiques et Littéraires*, September 1890.
'La solidarité juive', *Entretiens Politiques et Littéraires*, October 1890.
'Antisémitisme', *L'Endehors*, 29 May 1892.
Review of Edmond Picard's *La Synthèse de l'Antisémitisme* in *Entretiens Politiques et Littéraires*, June 1892.

'L'antisémitisme et ses causes générales', *Entretiens Politiques et Littéraires*, September 1892.

'Un philosémite: Léon Bloy', *Evénement*, 16 October 1892.

'Juifs et Antisémites', *Evénement*, 23 December 1892.

'L'esprit révolutionnaire dans le judaisme', *Revue Bleue*, May 1893.

'Cornélius Herz', *Evénement*, 28 September 1893.

'La Nationalité et les Juifs Français', *Figaro*, 27 December 1893.

'L'antisémitisme au Moyen Age', *Revue Blanche*, April 1894.

L'Antisémitisme, son Histoire et ses Causes, Léon Chailley, 1894.
  Second edition (Introduction by André Fontainas), Crès 1934.
  Recent reprints: La Librairie Française, Documents et Témoignages, 1969: *Antisemitism, its history and causes*, Britons Publishing Company, London 1967.

'Antisémitisme', in Léon Say (ed.): *Supplément au Nouveau Dictionnaire d'économie politique*, 1897.

'Antisémitisme et Antisémites', *Echo de Paris*, 31 December 1894.

'Antisémitisme et Révolution', *Les Lettres Prolétariennes*, No. 1, 1895.
  Reprinted recently by the Cercle Bernard-Lazare (n.d.) with an introduction by Rabi.

'Antisémitisme', *Almanach de la Question Sociale*, VI, 1896 (extract from 'Antisémitisme et Révolution').

Le Concours de *La Libre Parole*, *Libre Parole*, 24 October 1895.

Contre l'Antisémitisme. Histoire d'une Polémique, Stock, 1896. (Reprint of articles, accompanied by a preface and notes, which had appeared in *Le Voltaire* 20, 24, 31 May and 7 and 14 June 1896 in reply to the antisemitic campaign waged by Drumont in *La Libre Parole*.

'Sur l'antisémitisme', *Le Voltaire*, 14 May 1896.

'L'Equivoque antisémite', *Le Voltaire*, 28 June 1896.

'Le prolétariat juif devant l'antisémitisme', *Le Flambeau*, No. 1, January 1899. (Lecture given 13 February 1897).

Le nationalisme juif, Publications du Kadimah, No. 1, Stock, 1898.
  (Lecture given to the Association des étudiants israélites russes, 6 March 1897).

'Nécessité d'être soi-même', *Zion* (Berlin), 30 April 1897.

'Solidarité', *Zion* (Berlin), 31 May 1897.

'Le Nationalisme et l'Emancipation Juive', *L'Echo Sioniste*, 5, 20 April, 5–20 May 1901. (Lectures given in 1898 and in 1899).

'Special interview with Bernard-Lazare', *The Jewish World* (London), 3 June 1898.

'Le Berger Moïse', *Der Jüdische Arbeiter*, (Vienna), No. 3, 1 November and No. 5, 1 December 1898. (This journal, created by Saul R. Landau in August 1898, was the first Zionist paper devoted to the interests of the Jewish working-classes. Bernard-Lazare warmly welcomed it: No. 2, 1 September 1898. 'Organ der Wiener Poale-Zionisten' was the paper's subsequent title.)

Letter of resignation from the Action Committee of the Zionist Congress, *Le Flambeau*, No. 4, April 1899.

'La conception sociale du judaisme et le peuple juif', *La Grande Revue*, September 1899.

Letter (24 March 1900) to the Cercle des Etudiants Sionistes de Bucarest',
(Central Zionist Archives, Jerusalem).

Letter to Max Nordau, *Die Welt* (Vienna), No. 35, August 1900.

Letter to Nahum Slustsch, *Oesterreichische Wochenschrift* (Vienna), No. 35, August 1900.

'Capitalisme Juif et Démocratie', *L'Aurore*, 20 May 1901.

'Le Congrès Sioniste et le Sultan', *Pro Armenia*, No. 4, January 1902.

Articles on Rumania's Jewish policy which appeared in *L'Aurore*:
    'Roumains et Juifs', 4 July 1900;
    'La Roumanie et les Juifs', 20 July 1900;
    'L'émigration juive de la Roumanie', 9 August 1900;
    'Lettre à M. Delcassé', 23 May 1902;
    'Lettre à M. Delcassé', 28 May 1902;
    'Politique Roumaine', 24 June 1902.

Les Juifs en Roumanie. (*Cahiers de la Quinzaine*, III 8, February 1902.)

'The Jews in Roumania', *Contemporary Review* (London), vol. LXXXIII, February 1903.

Lettre ouverte à Anatole Leroy-Beaulieu. (*Cahiers de la Quinzaine*, IV 13, February 1903.)

Le Fumier de Job, Editions Rieder, 1928. (Posthumously published fragments selected and edited by Bernard-Lazare's family. A considerable body of unpublished material which was evidently intended for *Le Fumier de Job* will be found in the Bernard-Lazare Archives at the Alliance Israelite Universelle.)

Job's Dungheap; Essays on Jewish nationalism and social revolution, Schocken Library, 10, New York, 1948. (An English translation of selected Jewish writings, including extracts from the Rieder edition of *Le Fumier de Job*, with a preface by Hannah Arendt.)

II JOURNALISM

The main newspaper articles and review studies have been discussed in the course of the book and are listed in the first section of the bibliography according to major theme treated. Below we give a brief chronological survey of Bernard-Lazare's considerable and widely ranging journalistic work from 1889–1896, that is to say until his involvement in the Dreyfus Affair which brought to an end his career as a journalist.

(1) *Big daily newspapers*

La Nation

Weekly review 'Les Livres'; 27 January to 9 November 1891. Total of 34 articles.

L'Evénement

Weekly column (except for the first two months): 'Mouvement Littéraire', and from 14 November 1892, 'Chronique d'Aujourd'hui'; 3 May 1892 to 28 September 1893. 59 articles.

Le Journal

Short stories and social comments, more or less twice a month; 19 September 1892 to 24 December 1894. 29 contributions.

Le Figaro (*Supplement Littéraire*)

'Figures contemporaines, ceux d'aujourd'hui, ceux de demain', more or less weekly, from 10 February 1894. 20 'portraits' (published in book form under the same title in 1895).

L'Echo de Paris
Social and political articles, special reports, literary work. Irregular intervals from 13 November 1894 to 15 February 1896 and from 25 July to 8 August 1896. About 50 pieces.

Paris
'Tribune politique', 23 March to 2 October 1896. 13 articles.

L'Aurore
About 15 articles, October 1897 to June 1902.

(2) *Reviews, periodicals, etc.*

Literary reviews, 1889–1892. Contributions consisted mainly of symbolist short stories most of which were subsequently collected together in *Le Miroir des Légendes*:

   La Wallonie (Liège) (April 1889; September 1890; January, November
      1891; September 1892).
   La Revue Indépendante (September 1890).
   La Jeune Belgique (Brussels) (November, December 1890; January 1891).
   L'Ermitage (May, July, December 1890; May 1891).
   Mercure de France (January 1892).

Entretiens Politiques et Littéraires (July 1890 to May 1893; diverse contributions. He directed/edited the review from August 1891).

Anarchist, libertarian, socialist reviews, 1892–1896:

   L'Endehors (17 January, 1 May, 29 May, 25 September 1892).
   La Revue Anarchiste (15–31 August 1893).
   L'Harmonie (Marseilles) (December 1893).
   La Revue Parisienne (25 November, 25 December 1893; 10 and 25
      February, 25 March, 10 May 1894).
   Le Courrier Social Illustré (November 1894).
   Le Magazine International (December 1894; April 1895).
   La Revue Blanche (April 1894; February 1895).
   L'Oeuvre sociale (February, March, April 1895).
   La Manifestation du 1er mai (1 May 1895).
   Liberty (London) (30 November 1895).
   Le Devenir Social (April 1895; January 1896).
   L'Aube (April 1896).
   L'Art Social (July 1896).
   Almanach de la Question Sociale (VI, 1896).

Les lettres Prolétariennes, March 1895 ⎫ Weeklies founded by Bernard-
L'Action Sociale, 1–29 February 1896 ⎬ Lazare. For details see first
⎭ section of the bibliography.

Le Voltaire (more or less weekly column, 27 March to 28 June 1896).
Between 1891 and 1894 Jean Grave's anarchist paper *La Révolte* reproduced several of Bernard-Lazare's articles and studies.
In 1897 *les Temps Nouveaux* (replacing *La Révolte* in May 1895) published numerous extracts from *Les Porteurs de Torches*.

III PRINCIPAL CORRESPONDENCE
(PUBLISHED AND UNPUBLISHED)

'Correspondance inédite d'Ephraïm Mikhaël à Bernard-Lazare, 1885–7', *Ecrits Français*, Nos. 3 and 4, 1914.

Letters (unpublished) from Bernard-Lazare to Jean Grave, 1891–6, Institut Français d'Histoire Sociale.

Letters (unpublished) from Bernard-Lazare to Max Nettlau, 1894–5, International Institute of Social History, Amsterdam.

Letters (unpublished) from Stock to Max Nettlau, 1894–5, International Institute of Social History, Amsterdam.

Letters (unpublished) from Bernard-Lazare to Joseph Reinach, 1896–1902, Bibliothèque Nationale, Manuscrits, MS. n.a.fr. 24897.

Letters (unpublished) from Bernard-Lazare to Max Nordau, 1896–7, Central Zionist Archives, Jerusalem.

Letters from Bernard-Lazare to Herzl, 1896–1900, Central Zionist Archives, Jerusalem. This correspondence (11 letters) has been published by E. Silberner: *Bernard-Lazare et le sionisme, Shivat Zion*, Jerusalem, 1953 (Brochure Bibliothèque Nationale).

Letters from Herzl to Bernard-Lazare.

See: E. Silberner: op. cit.

 Archives Bernard-Lazare, Alliance Israëlite Universelle.

 Saul Raphael Landau: *Sturm und Drang im Zionismus*, Vienna 1937.

 Herzl: *Gesammelte zionistische Werke*, Berlin, Jüdischer Verlag 1934, Vol. 5.

 Herzl: *Tagebücher*, Berlin, Jüdischer Verlag 1922, Vols. 1 and 2.

Letters from Bernard-Lazare to Saul Raphael Landau, 1898–1902, in *Sturm und Drang im Zionismus*, op. cit.

Letters (unpublished) from Bernard-Lazare to Emile Meyerson, 1896–1903; also from Mme Isabelle Bernard-Lazare to Emile Meyerson, Archives Meyerson, private possession of Mme Ardouin, Paris.

Letters (unpublished) from Emile Meyerson to various leading figures in Jewish and Zionist circles. (For this interesting correspondence, at present unclassified, see particularly Willy Bambus: A28/7, and the Choveve Zion files, notably A2/73, Central Zionist Archives, Jerusalem.)

Correspondence Péguy–Bernard-Lazare/Bernard-Lazare–Péguy. 1902–1903. Centre Charles Péguy, Orléans; Feuillet No. 24, December 1951, Amitié Charles Péguy.

Bernard-Lazare et son temps, d'après une correspondance inédite, presented and prefaced by A. Cherchevsky, *Chalom*, September 1933.

Letters (unpublished) connected with the projected commemoration ceremony of Bernard-Lazare's death in 1933, Archives, W. Rabi.

Archives de l'Alliance Israelite Universelle (letters and notes).

IV WORKS, ARTICLES ON OR CONCERNING BERNARD-LAZARE

Although there is no comprehensive single study of Bernard-Lazare's llfe and work, a fair number of articles have appeared over the years, especially immediately after his death. References to him are also found in various memoirs and diaries. Below are listed (1) the essential biographical sources; (2) the most interesting critical appreciations by Bernard-Lazare's contemporaries; (3) recent studies. In general, material dealing with specific activities already described in the book, (e.g. the Dreyfus Affair) is not listed again.

(1) *Biographical Sources*

Archives of l'Alliance Israëlite Universelle
Archives departementales du Gard
Archives of the Préfecture de Police (Paris)
L'Avenir Illustré, Casablanca, February 1934, special number devoted to Bernard-Lazare.
Bernard-Lazare, Discours prononcés à l'inauguration du monument, 4 October 1908, brochure, Nîmes.
Gabriel Bertrand, 'Bernard-Lazare', *La Petite République*, 3 September 1903.
Baruch Hagani, *Bernard-Lazare*, les Forgerons, 1919.
Augustin Hamon, *Enquête sur la psychologie de l'anarchiste-socialiste*, 1895.
Hirsch Hildesheimer, 'Bernard-Lazare', *Die Jüdische Presse* (Berlin) 10 September 1903.
The Jewish World (London), 'Bernard-Lazare', 4 September 1903.
Phoebus Jouve, 'Sur Bernard-Lazare', *La Chronique Mondaine*, Nîmes, 3 October 1908. *Les lettres et la société*, Petites Etudes, Nîmes, 1906.
Stuart Merrill, 'Pierre Quillard', *La Phalange*, 20 February 1912.
Jean-Maurice Muslak, 'Bernard-Lazare', *Revue des Etudes Juives*, vol. VI, No. 106, 1946.
Note (unpublished) by Max Nettlau on Bernard-Lazare the anarchist. International Institute of Social History, Amsterdam.
M. Nettlau, *Elisée Reclus: Anarchist und Gelehrter*, Berlin 1928.
Pierre Quillard: 'Bernard-Lazare', *L'Européen*, 12 September 1903. See also, *Discours prononcé à l'inauguration du monument 1908*, listed above.

(2) *Contemporary appreciations*

Jean Ajalbert: *Mémoires en vrac, au temps du symbolisme*, A. Michel, 1938.
'Bernard-Lazare, *Le Flambeau*, April 1899.
'Bernard-Lazare', *Le Réveil du quartier latin*, 19 November 1898.
Léon Bloy: *Journal*, vol. 1, Mercure de France, 1956.
Je m'accuse, 1899.
Léon Blum: *Souvenirs sur l'Affaire*, Oeuvres, vol. IV 2, Albin Michel, 1965.
Pierre Bertrand, 'Lettre Ouverte à Bernard-Lazare', *Les Droits de l'Homme*, 30 October 1898.
Léon Daudet, 'La Statue Infâme', *Action Française*, 4 October 1908. *Au temps de Judas*, Nouvelle Librairie Nationale, 1920.
'Hymne à la Justice', *L'Effort (Toulouse)*, 1 October 1899.
A. Fontainas, 'La Mort de Bernard-Lazare', *Mercure de France*, T.48, October 1903. *Mes souvenirs de symbolisme*, Nouvelle Revue Critique, 1928. 'Préface', *L'Antisémitisme, son histoire et ses causes*, Crès 1934.
André Gide, *Journal (1939–1949)*, La Pléiade, 1954.

André Gide–Paul Valéry, *Correspondance*, 1890–1942, Gallimard, 1955.

Jean Grave, *Quarante ans de propagande anarchiste*, Flammarion, 1973.

André Ibels, 'A propos du Porteur de Torches, Bernard-Lazare', *L'Aube*, June 1897.

Joseph Ishill, *Elisée et Elie Reclus. In Memoriam*, Berkely Heights, New Jersey, Oriel Press, 1927.

Gustave Kahn: 'L'oeuvre littéraire de Bernard-Lazare', *L'Aurore*, 9 September 1903. 'Trente ans de symbolisme', *Nouvelles Littéraires*, 12 October 1929.

Saul R. Landau, *Sturm und Drang im Zionismus*, Vienna 1937.

Jean Longuet, 'Bernard-Lazare', *Le Combat Social* (Nîmes) 3 October 1908; reprinted *L'Humanité*, 5 October 1908.

Charles Maurras (Agathon), 'Les vraies causes de l'antisémitisme', *Revue Encyclopédique*, January 1895. 'Bernard-Lazare', *Action Française*, 15 September 1908. *Au Signe de Flore. La fondation de l'Action Française*, 1898–1900, Grasset, 1933.

Charles Péguy, *Bernard-Lazare* (1903), included in *Par ce demi-clair matin*, Gallimard, 1952; *Un Poète l'a dit* (1907), Gallimard, 1953 (pp. 145–65); *Notre Jeunesse*, Cahiers de la Quinzaine, 1910.

P. V. Stock, *Mémorandum d'un Editeur*, 3rd Series, Stock, 1938.

Louis Vauxelles, 'Quelques syndiqués: Bernard-Lazare', *Les Droits de l'Homme*, 24 May 1898.

(3) *Recent studies*

Hannah Arendt, 'The Jew as a pariah', *Jewish Social Studies*, New York, 1944, Vol. 6 No. 2.

Jean Guillon, *Bernard-Lazare*, Thèse de doctorat, Université de Nice, 1967.

Michael R. Marrus, *The Politics of Assimilation*, Oxford University Press, 1971.

Edmund Silberner, *Bernard-Lazare et le sionisme. Shivat Zion*, 1953, Jerusalem. (Brochure Bibliothèque Nationale).

Nelly Jussem-Wilson, *Controverses et Polémiques dans l'oeuvre de Bernard-Lazare*, Thèse de doctorat, Université de Paris, 1958. 'Bernard-Lazare's Jewish Journey', *Jewish Social Studies*, July 1964. 'Bernard-Lazare: ennemi des lois et passionné de justice', *Esprit Républicain*, Klincksieck, 1972. 'Le vrai visage de Bernard-Lazare', *Les Nouveaux Cahiers*, No. 35, Winter 1973–4.

V GENERAL WORKS

(1) *The Dreyfus Affair*

The basic sources remain:

the published documents (trial proceedings, official records and documents);

the newspapers of the period (interesting collection of press cuttings is to be found in the archives of the Préfecture de Police, Paris);

personal papers (Mathieu Dreyfus, Scheurer-Kestner, Joseph Reinach, Zola) Bibliothèque Nationale, Manuscripts;

dossiers at the Archives Nationales.

The 'collection Ochs' (Bibliothèque Historique de la Ville de Paris) has some interesting pieces on the antisemitic literature of the period.

From the voluminous literature to which the Dreyfus Affair gave rise at the time, I have selected the following publications – often neglected by modern historians – as being of special interest:

L'Archiviste (Salomon Reinach?), *Drumont et Dreyfus, études sur la Libre Parole, 1894–1895*, Stock, 1898.

Maurice Barrès, *Scènes et Doctrines du Nationalisme*, F. Juven, 1902.

Paul Brulat, *Violence et Raison*, Stock, 1899.

Cagniard, 'Les Intellectuels et l'Affaire Dreyfus', *Revue Socialiste*, vol. 29, April 1899.

Léon Chaîne, *Les catholiques français et leurs difficultés actuelles*, Storck, 1903.

Edouard Drumont, *Les Juifs contre la France*, Librairie Antisémite, 1899.

Sébastien Faure, *Les Anarchistes et l'Affaire Dreyfus*, Au bureau du Libertaire, 1898.

Anatole France, *30 ans de Vie Sociale*, T. 1, *1897–1904*, Emile-Paul, 1949.

Jean Jaurès, *Les preuves*, La petite République, 1898.

Raymond Lacan, *Histoire des Juifs, leurs trahisons de Judas à Dreyfus*, A. Pierret, 1899.

Marguerite-Fernand Labori, *Labori, ses notes manuscrites*, Editions Victor Attinger, 1947.

Jules Lemaître, *La Patrie Française. L'oeuvre de la Patrie Française*, Bureau de la Patrie Française, 1899. *Opinions à répandre*, Société française d'imprimerie, 1901.

Capitaine Paul Marin, *Dreyfus?* Librairie Illustrée, 1898 (Well documented account of the initial campaign for revision. The other ten variously entitled volumes which the same author devoted to the Affair also provide an excellent documentation on public reactions, the press, etc.)

Roger Martin du Gard: *Jean Barois*, Gallimard, 1913. (In this novel Martin du Gard not only gives Bernard-Lazare his proper historical role but he also used Péguy's portrait of Bernard-Lazare in *Notre Jeunesse* as a basis for creating Woldsmuth, one of the characters of the novel.)

Charles Péguy, 'La crise du parti socialiste et l'Affaire Dreyfus', *Revue Blanche,* 15 August 1899. 'L'Affaire Dreyfus et la crise du parti socialiste', *Revue Blanche*, 15 September 1899. 'Le Ravage et la Réparation', *Revue Blanche*, 15 November 1899.

Abbé L. Pichot, *La conscience chrétienne et l'Affaire Dreyfus*, Société d'Editions Littéraires, 1899.

Francis de Pressensé, *L'idée de patrie*, Ligue Française des droits de l'homme, 1902.

Pierre Quillard, *Le Monument Henry*, Stock, 1899.

Joseph Reinach, *Histoire de l'Affaire Dreyfus*. 7 volumes, 1901–8. (Vol. 1, Editions de la Revue Blanche, II–VII Fasquelle. Vol. VII contains an index and corrections.)

Henri de Saint-Poli (abbé J. Brugerette), *L'Affaire Dreyfus et la mentalité catholique en France*, Storck 1904.

Jules Soury, *Une Campagne Nationaliste 1899–1901*, Imprimerie de la Cour d'Appel, 1902.

H. Wickham-Steed, *Through 30 Years 1892–1922*, London, Heinemann, 1924.

Henry Varennes and L. Henry May, *Les étapes de la vérité*, Stock, 1898.

E. Villane, *L'Opinion publique et l'Affaire Dreyfus*, Stock, 1898.

Alexandre Zévaès, *Une génération*. M. Rivière, 1922. *L'Affaire Dreyfus*, Nouvelle Revue Critique, 1931.

Emile Zola, *L'Affaire Dreyfus*, Garnier–Flammarion, 1969 (The first complete collection of Zola's dreyfusard articles. They are preceded by the article 'Pour les Juifs', *Figaro*, 16 May 1896, and followed by Zola's notes 'Impressions d'audience', published for the first time in *La Nef* in February 1948. Zola's novel *La Vérité*, 1902, is a romanced version of the Affair.

Some recent works:

Maurice Baumont, *Aux sources de l'Affaire*, Les Productions de Paris, 1959.

Patrice Boussel, *L'Affaire Dreyfus et la presse*, Colin (Kiosque) 1960.

Guy Chapman, *The Dreyfus Case*, Rupert Hart-Davis, London, 1955.

Cécile Délhorbe, *L'Affaire Dreyfus et les Ecrivains Français*, Attinger, 1933.

Robert Gauthier, *Dreyfusards*, Julliard (Archives) 1965.

Henri Guillemin, *L'Enigme Esterhazy*, Gallimard, 1962.

N. Halasz, *Captain Dreyfus: The story of a Mass Hysteria*, New York, Simon and Schuster, 1955.

William Herzog, *From Dreyfus to Pétain: The struggle of a Republic*, New York, Creative Age, 1947.

Douglas Johnson, *France and the Dreyfus Affair*, London, Blandford Press, 1966.

Pierre Miquel, *Une énigme? L'Affaire Dreyfus*, Presses Universitaires de France, (Clio) 1972 (a grave error as far as Bernard-Lazare is concerned: he was certainly not the author of the *Eclair* articles of September 1896.)

Les Carnets de Schwartzkoppen, edited by B. Schwertfeger, Rieder, 1930.

B. Schwertfeger, *The Truth About Dreyfus from the Schwartzkoppen Papers*, London and New York, Putnam, 1931.

Siegfried Thalheimer, *Macht und Gerechtigkeit*, Munich, C. Beck, 1958. (Contains extracts from Bernard-Lazare's brochures).

Marcel Thomas, *L'Affaire sans Dreyfus*, Fayard, 1961.

(2) *The Anarchist Movement*

Excellent bibliographies will be found in: Max Nettlau: *Bibliographie de l'anarchie*, Stock, 1897; Jean Maitron: *Histoire du mouvement anarchiste en France, 1880–1914*, Société Universitaire d'éditions et de librairie, 1951. Below are listed works concerned with Bernard-Lazare or with particular issues which were of concern to him as well as some recent publications.

Michel Bakounin, 'La Commune de Paris', *Entretiens Politiques et Littéraires*, August and October 1892. *Lettres à Herzen et à Ogareff*, Perrin 1896. *Oeuvres*, Stock, 1895; introduction by Max Nettlau (reprinted editions Stock, 1972).

A. Bataille, *Causes criminelles et mondaines de 1894*, E. Dentu, 1895.

Félix Dubois, *Le Péril Anarchiste*, Flammarion, 1894.

Jean Grave, *La Société Mourante et l'anarchie*, Stock, 1893. *La Société Future*, Stock, 1895. *L'Anarchie, son but, ses moyens*, Stock, 1899. *Le*

Mouvement libertaire sous la 3e République, Crès, 1930. *Quarante ans de propagande anarchiste*, ed. Mireille Delfau, Flammarion, 1973.

Augustin Hamon, *Les hommes et les théories de l'Anarchie*, La Révolte, 1893. *Psychologie de l'anarchiste-socialiste*, Stock, 1895. *Le Socialisme et le Congrès de Londres*, Stock, 1897. *Socialisme et anarchisme*, Sansot, 1905.

Pierre Kropotkine, *Paroles d'un révolté*, Flammarion, 1885. *La morale anarchiste*, La Révolte, 1891. *La Conquête du pain*, Stock, 1892. *L'anarchie, sa philosophie, son idéal*, Stock 1896. *Un siècle d'attente, 1789–1889*, La Révolte, 1893.

Charles Malato, *De la Commune à l'Anarchie*, Stock, 1894. *Philosophie de l'Anarchie* (1889), Stock,1897. *Prison fin-de-siècle*, Charpentier-Fasquelle, 1891.

F. Merlino, *Nécessité et bases d'une entente*, Brussels, 1892. *Formes et essences du socialisme*, Stock, 1898.

Domela Nieuwenhuis, *Le Socialisme en danger*, Stock, 1897.

Jacques Prolo (Jean Pausader), *Les Anarchistes*, T.X of *L'Histoire des Partis Socialistes en France*, Rivière, 1912.

Henri Varennes, *De Ravachol à Caserio*, Garnier, 1895.

Jean Bancal, *Proudhon, pluralisme et autogestion*, 2 vols., Aubier-Montaigne, 1970.

Gian Mario Bravo, *Les socialistes avant Marx*, Petite collection Maspero, 3 vols., 1970.

Daniel Guérin, *L'Anarchisme*, NRF Idées, 1965.

Eugenia W. Herbert, *The Artist and Social Reform, France and Belgium, 1885–1898*, New Haven, Conn., Yale University Press, 1961.

Patrick Kessel, *Les gauchistes de 89*, 10/18, 1969.

Ni Dieu, ni Maître, anthologie historique du mouvement anarchiste, ed. D. Guérin, Lausanne, n.d. (1970?).

Bertrand Russell, *Roads to Freedom, socialism, anarchism and syndicalism* (1918) Unwin Books, London, 1970.

George Woodcock, *Anarchism*, Harmondsworth, Penguin Books, 1963.

(3) *Antisemitism*

For the period under consideration, useful bibliographies will be found in:

Robert F. Byrnes, *Antisemitism in Modern France*, New Brunswick, New Jersey, Rutgers University Press, 1950.

Léon Poliakov, *Histoire de l'antisémitisme, de Voltaire à Wagner*, Calmann-Lévy, 1968.

Hannah Arendt, *Sur l'Antisémitisme*, Calmann-Lévy, 1973.

The Origins of Totalitarianism, New York, Harcourt Brace, 1951, 3rd ed 1968. (The above book, *Sur l'Antisémitisme*, comprises Part I of this work.)

The following contemporary and recent works are of special interest to the aspects treated in this book:

Maurice Bloch, 'La Femme Juive au théâtre et dans le roman', *Revue des Etudes Juives*, Vol. XXIII, 1892.

François Bournand, *Les Juifs et nos contemporains*, Pierret, 1898.

Henri Dagan, *Enquête sur l'antisémitisme*, Stock, 1899.

Paul Démann, *La catéchèse chrétienne et le peuple de la Bible*, Cahiers Sioniens, Nos. 3 and 4, 1952.

Edouard Drumont ou l'anticapitalisme national présenté par E. Beau de Loménie, Pauvert, 1968.

E.S.R.I. (Etudiants Socialistes Révolutionnaires Internationalistes), *Antisémitisme et Sionisme*, Edition de l'Humanité Nouvelle, 1900.

Augustin Hamon, *L'Agonie d'une Société*, Savine, 1889.

Arthur Hertzberg, *The French Enlightenment and the Jews*, New York, Columbia University Press, 1968.

Jules Isaac, *Jésus et Israel*, Albin Michel, 1948. *L'antisémitisme a-t-il des racines chrétiennes?* Fasquelle, 1960. *L'Enseignement du mépris*, Fasquelle, 1962.

Werner Keller, *Diaspora*, Pitman, London 1971.

Pinchas Lapide, *The last three Popes and the Jews*, Souvenir Press, London 1967.

Joseph Lémann, *L'entrée des Israelites dans la société française*, Lecoffre, 1886.

Robert Misrahi, *Marx et la question juive*, NRF Idées, 1972.

A. Mossé, *Histoire des Juifs d'Avignon et du Comtat Venaissin*, Librairie Lipschutz, 1934.

Edmond Picard, *Synthèse de l'antisémitisme*, Brussels, Larcier, 1892. *Aryano-Sémitisme*, Brussels, 1899.

Pierre Pierrard, *Juifs et Catholiques Français 1886–1945*, Fayard, 1970.

Edmund Silberner, *Sozialisten zur Judenfrage*, Berlin, Colloquium Verlag, 1962. 'French Socialism and the Jews', Historia Judaica, XVI, 1954.

Pierre Sorlin, *La Croix et les Juifs*, Grasset, 1967.

A. Tabarant, *Socialisme et antisémitisme*, Kugelmann, 1898.

E. Tcherikower (ed.), *Yidn in Frankreich*, 2 vols., New York, Yiddish Scientific Institute 1942 (in Yiddish).

Jeannine Verdès-Leroux, *Scandale financier et antisémitisme catholique. Le Krach de l'Union Générale*, Ed. du Centurion, 1969.

Sam Waagenaar, *The Pope's Jews*, Alcove Press, London, 1974.

Eugène Weber, *Satan Franc-Maçon*, Julliard (Archives), 1964.

(4) *Zionism*

Rich documentation at the Central Zionist Archives, Jerusalem, notably on the work of the Choveve Zion groups and the I.C.A. (Jewish Colonisation Association) with which Bernard-Lazare was connected.

Alexander Bein, *Theodore Herzl*, London, East and West Library, 1957.

H. Bodenheimer, *Im Anfang der zionistischen Bewegung*, Frankfurt, Europaïsche Verlag–Anstalt, 1965.

Ber Borochow, *Sozialismus und Zionismus*, selected writings edited by M. Singer, Vienna, privately published, 1932.

Isaac Gruenbaum, *The history of Zionism*, Part I: *The pre-Herzlian period*, Tel Aviv, Haaretz, 1946.

Arthur Hertzberg, *The Zionist Idea*, New York, Atheneum, 1971.

Theodor Herzl: The Jewish State (1896) London, Pordes, 1972. *Tagebücher*, Berlin, Jüdischer Verlag, 1922. *The Diaries of Theodor Herzl*. London, V. Gollancz, 1958, ed. by Marvin Lowenthal.

Max Nordau, *Discours prononcé au 2e Congrès sioniste*, Stock, 1899.
Ecrits sionistes, Librairie Lipschutz, 1936.
Nahum Sokolow, *History of Zionism*, London, Longmans, 1908 (rather inaccurate on Bernard-Lazare).
Zionism, Jerusalem, Keter Publishing House, 1973 (has a good bibliography of more recent works).

(5) *Miscellaneous*

A. G. Lehmann: *The Symbolist aesthetic in France, 1885–1895*, Oxford, Blackwell, 1968. For the symbolist movement see the memoirs of: Fontainas, Kahn, Mauclair, Mazel, Retté and many others.
H. Avenel, *Annuaire de la presse française* (1890–1900). *Histoire de la Presse Française depuis 1789 jusqu'à nos jours*, Flammarion, 1900.
Daniel Ligou, *Frédéric Desmons et la Franc-Maçonnerie sous la 3e République*, Gedalge, 1966.
René de Livois, *Histoire de la Presse Française*, Vol. ii, *de 1881 à nos jours*. Lausanne, Editions Spes, 1965.
L. Soloweitschick, *Un prolétariat méconnu: la situation sociale et économique des ouvriers juifs*, 1898.

INDEX

Dreyfus Affair (*cont.*)
trial, 164, 166–77, 178; Zola's
J'Accuse, 151, 153, 155, 182, 186,
197–9, 309 n.9, 314 n.59; Zola
trial, 155–6; *see also under* press
and names of protagonists;
Bernard-Lazare: early doubts, 121–
3, 302 n.5; disturbed by press
campaign, 123–8, 179; meeting
with Mathieu Dreyfus, 121, 128–
9; prepares first brochure, 129–30;
publication delayed, 130–1; first
Brussels edition (1896), *Une erreur
judiciare: la vérité sur l'Affaire
Dreyfus*, 132–4; subsequent
editions, 134; as history, and
J'Accuse, 130–42; press reaction,
142–5; Picquart's report on, 146;
War Office reactions, 145–7, 160–
3, 305 n.8; Government and public
reactions, 140, 147–8; B.-L. invites
prosecution, 147; doubts of 'silent
minority' confirmed, 148–9; reactions of prominent men B.-L.
approached personally, 181–94;
second brochure, *Une erreur
juciciare: l'Affaire Dreyfus.
Deuxième Mémoire avec Expertises d'Ecritures* (1897), 149–52,
156, 194, 307 n.40, n.41, 308
n.50; B.-L. and 1897 poster campaign for revision, 152–3; third
brochure, *Comment on condamne
un innocent* (1898), 154–5, 198–9;
Bouton incident, 156–7, 308 n.55;
B.-L. withdraws from forefront of
battle, 158, 163; his work behind
the scenes, 158–9, 162, 175–6,
309 n.4, n.6; open letter to
Trarieux (president of *Ligue des
Droits de l'Homme*), 159–60;
suspected of collusion with
Picquart, 160–3; relations with
Picquart, 163–6, 194; at Rennes
trial, 166–77; 'France at the
Parting of the Ways' (B.-L.'s study
of the Rennes trial), 168–73;
attitude to pardon and amnesty,
177–9; dispute with Labori, 178–
9; 'persuasion-visits' and role in
growth of dreyfusard movement,
181–202; impact of Affair on
B.-L., 177–8, 205–21 *passim*; for
B.-L.'s monument and antidreyfusards, *see* Bernard-Lazare,

monument; for relations with
individual protagonists in Affair,
see also their names
Dreyfus, Alfred, arrested, 113;
character assassination, 117; dictation by Du Paty de Clam, 137;
notes on events, 129; not at
Bernard-Lazare's funeral, 270;
pardoned and rehabilitated, 179;
at Rennes, 166–7; Plate 4, Plate 5
Dreyfus family, 113, 132, 147, 178,
274, 276, 279
Dreyfus, Madame Lucie, 139
Dreyfus, Mathieu, difficulty of
publicly using information he had,
130, 136, 303 n.18; early campaign, 118–41 *passim*; later campaign, 153–69 *passim*; embarrassed
by Bernard-Lazare, 151, 158, 160,
163, 193; escape story, 131; favours
retrial, 168–9; and Labori at
Rennes, 173–5; and Picquart, 165;
sources of information and disclosure, 162, 303 n.18
Drumont, Edouard, and Algerian
antisemitism, 206; on antisemitic
revolution, 206; attacks Jewish
Army Officers, 82, 83; background, 295 n.1; debate with
Bernard-Lazare, 207, 315 n.13;
duel with Bernard-Lazare, 86; *La
France Juive* and its success, 66–
70, 295 n.1; *Libre Parole's*
competition for 'best solution to
the Jewish question', 86–7, 297
n.34; obituary of Bernard-Lazare,
270–1, 275; involved in press
campaign against Dreyfus, 123–7;
response to Bernard-Lazare's
Antisemitism..., 105, 300 n.32
Duchesne, Abbé (later Monseigneur),
15, 290 n.21
Duclaux, Emile, 126, 186
Dühring, Eugen, 99, 100
Du Paty de Clam, *Commandant*,
accused by Bernard-Lazare, 139–
40, 154; defended by Castelin in
Parliament, 140; dictation to
Dreyfus, 137; initial investigation,
117, 136; main accused in Zola's
J'Accuse, 198–9
Dupuy, Charles-Alexandre, 125
Dutrait-Crozon, Henri, 275–6, 314
n.54

Mun, Comte Albert de, 187
Muslak, Jean, 289 n.1

Naquet, Alfred, 105, 270
Natanson (Brothers), 70
Nettlau, Max, 56, 60, 61
Nordau, Max, 226, 239–40, 247,
317 n.2

Ohnet, Georges, 69
d'Ormescheville, *Commandant*, 116–
17, 134, 144

Panizzardi, Colonel, 116; telegram,
310–11 n.43
Paris, Gaston, 39, 186, 291 n.7
Péguy, Charles, vii, 201, 206, 259–
60, 270, 322 n.6; response and
tributes to Bernard-Lazare, 190–1,
195, 256, 257, 277–86, 323 n.19;
criticises Jewish community's conduct ('politique juive'), 278–80;
on Jewish–Christian relations,
282–6; letter from Mme Bernard-
Lazare, 324–5 n.38; letter from
Meyerson, 318 n.7; *La Note
Conjointe* as a reply to *Le Fumier
de Job*, 283–5
de Pellieux, General, 118, 156, 186
Pelloutier, Fernand, 45, 57, 306 n.16,
315 n.67
Périvier, Antoine, 19, 133
Petit, Jacques, 280, 324 n.29
Picard, Edmond, 62, 88, 100, 105–6
Picquart, Lieutenant-Colonel, 118–
19, 146, 159; accused at Zola
trial, 154–7; mutual antipathy
between him and Bernard-Lazare,
163–5; suspected of collusion with
Bernard-Lazare, 146–7, 160–6;
at Rennes, 174
Pinsker, Leo, 223
Pisarro, Camille, 315 n.12
Poliakov, Léon, 302 n.5
Pouget, Emile, 45, 64
Press, and anarchism, 36, 63; and
antisemitism, 68–9; crisis, 31, 41;
development, 30, 35; and the
Dreyfus Affair, 124–7, 133, 187–
90, 304 n.33; reactions to *Une
erreur judiciare*, 133–4, 142–5
de Pressensé, Francis, 246, 322 n.6
Prévost, Marcel, 187
Prolo, Jacques (Jean Pausader), 202,
314 n.67

Proudhon, Pierre-Joseph, 9, 36, 45–6,
50, 60, 99, 235
Proust, Marcel, 16
Pujo, Maurice, 194–5

Quillard, Pierre, and Armenians,
246; dreyfusard, 159, 195; friendship with Bernard-Lazare, 259;
initiator of Bernard-Lazare monument, 159, 274, 322 n.6; in
symbolist circles, 14–17 *passim*;
writings on Bernard-Lazare, 321
n.18

Rabi, Wladimir, ix, 316 n.41,
325 n.42
Ranc, Arthur, 42, 191–2, 322 n.6
Ravachol, 43–4, 47
Ravary, *Commandant*, 154, 161, 162
Reclus, Elisée, 45, 47, 61, 64
Reclus, Paul, 64, 322 n.6
de Régnier, Henri, 14–15, 20, 290
n.20
de Reinach, baron Jacques, 83
Reinach, Joseph, relationship with
Bernard-Lazare, 120, 144, 181–2,
258, 313 n.33, 322 n.6; dreyfusard,
174, 183, 311–12 n.3; Reinach
Note, 302 n.3
Reinach, Salomon, 195, 248–9,
312 n.3, 322 n.6, 323 n.13
Reinach, Théodore, 74, 105
Renan, Ernest, 76, 296–7 n.16
Rochefort, Henri, 125, 126, 133–4,
275, 304 n.33, 316 n.31
de Rodays, Fernand, 133
Roger-Bloche, 322 n.4
Roget, General, 164–5, 170, 177
Rohling, Father, 68, 99, 100
de Rothschild, *baron* Edmond, 223,
226
Rothschilds, the, 69, 72, 82–5 *passim*,
157, 183, 306 n.15
Rouanet, Gustave, 183
de Rougemont, Albert, 150
Roux, Jacques, 60
Rouyer, Emile, 297 n.34
Rumania, Rumanian Jews, Bernard-
Lazare and, 249–51, 253, 256–7

de Saint-Auban, Emile, 316 n.31
Salles, Maître, 303 n.18
Sandherr, Colonel, 114, 118–20, 146,
183, 310 n.43
Sarcey, Francisque, 187